FROM AMERICA TO NORWAY
Norwegian-American Immigrant Letters, 1838-1914

FROM AMERICA TO NORWAY

NORWEGIAN-AMERICAN
IMMIGRANT LETTERS
1838-1914

VOLUME ONE: 1838–1870

EDITED AND TRANSLATED BY
Orm Øverland

Norwegian-American Historical Association
Distributed by the University of Minnesota Press
NORTHFIELD, MINNESOTA, 2012

THE NORWEGIAN-AMERICAN HISTORICAL ASSOCIATION

OFFICERS

Brian D. Rude, *President*
Karen Annexstad Humphrey, *Vice President*
Karen F. Davidson, *Treasurer*
Liv Hustvedt, *Secretary*

COUNCIL OF EDITORIAL ADVISERS

Todd W. Nichol, *Editor*
Betty A. Bergland
Ann M. Legreid
Terje I. Leiren
B. Lindsay Lowell
Deborah L. Miller
Orm Øverland
Janet E. Rasmussen
Clarence Burton Sheffield, Jr.

Copyright 2012
Norwegian-American Historical Association
Northfield, Minn. 55057
www.naha.stolaf.edu

Distributed by the University of Minnesota Press
111 Third Avenue South, Suite 290
Minneapolis, Minn. 55401
www.upress.umn.edu

A Cataloging-in-Publication record for this book
is available from the Library of Congress.
ISBN 978-0-8166-8517-2

CONTENTS

Foreword	15
Preface	17
Reader's Guide	22
Introduction	25
Letters	45
References	469

	1838	
1:1	FROM: Svein Knudsen Lothe, *Chicago, Illinois, 10 July 1838* TO: Sjur Knudsen Aga, *Ullensvang, Hordaland*	47
	1841	
1:2	FROM: Brynjulv Lekve, *Wyota, Wisconsin, 8 December 1841* TO: Arne Brynjulvsen Lekve, *Ulvik, Hordaland*	49
	1842	
1:3	FROM: Hans E. Møller, *Porsgrunn, Telemark, 29 March 1842* TO: Halvor Bjørnsen Tonga, *Heddal, Notodden, Telemark*	56
1:4	FROM: From Ellev Bjørnsen, *Larvik, Vestfold, 29 May 1842* TO: Tora Hansdatter Gjestrud, *Heddal, Notodden, Telemark*	57
	1843	
1:5	FROM: An unknown immigrant, *Koshkonong, Wisconsin probably 1843* TO: Knud Ellingsen Liane, *Holt, Tvedestrand, Aust-Agder*	58
	1845	
1:6	FROM: Gaute Ingebretsen Gunleiksrud, *Dunkirk, Wisconsin 9 May 1845* TO: Ingebret Torsteinsen and Birgit Gunleiksrud, *Tinn, Telemark*	61
1:7	FROM: Ole Eriksen Sando, Nils Tollefsen Roe and others *Rock Prairie, Wisconsin, 26 August 1845* TO: Ole Olsen Skrinde, *Aal, Buskerud*	63
1:8	FROM: Ole Herbrandsen Osland, *Kendall, New York 2 September 1845* TO: Ole Andersen Narverud, *Kongsberg, Buskerud*	66

1846

1:9   FROM: Ellev Bjørnsen, *Pine Lake, Lebanon, Wisconsin*   68
          17 January 1846
          TO: Anlaug Christophersdatter Tunga, *Heddal, Notodden, Telemark*

1:10   FROM: Gjermund Gjermundsen Barboe, *Muskegon, Michigan*   70
          and Chicago, Illinois, 3 November 1846
          TO: A friend, in *Aust-Agder*

1:11   FROM: Ellev and Ole Bjørnsen, *Ashippun, Wisconsin*   76
          7 December 1846
          TO: Anlaug Christophersdatter Tunga, *Heddal, Notodden, Telemark*

1847

1:12   FROM: From Gulbrand Engebretsen Thulien, *Oswego, Illinois*   79
          7 February 1847
          TO: Engebret Gulbrandsen Thulien, *Ringebu, Oppland*

1:13   FROM: From Ole Stensen Karlsrud, *Muskego, Wisconsin*   80
          18 February 1847
          TO: Sten Olsen and Gro Anfinnsdatter Karlsrud, *Tinn, Telemark*

1:14   FROM: Ole and Halvor Lauransson, *Christiana, Wisconsin*   82
          2 April 1847
          TO: Lavrants Knutsen and Knut and Tov Lavrantsen Hogndalen
          Seljord, Telemark

1:15   FROM: From Gullik and Ole Gulliksen Dorsett, *Indian Creek,*   85
          Illinois, 22 December 1847
          TO: Gullik Evensen Daaset, *Flesberg, Buskerud*

1848

1:16   FROM: From Elise Tvede, *Nacogdoches, Texas, 5 January 1848*   86
          TO: Taale Andreas Gjestvang, *Løten, Hedmark*

1:17   FROM: Ellev Bjørnsen, *Ashippun, Wisconsin, 14 May 1848*   94
          TO: Anlaug Christophersdatter, Halvor Bjørnsen, and Helge
          Bjørnsdatter Tonga, *Heddal, Notodden, Telemark*

1:18   FROM: Jakob Abrahamsen and others, *Muskego, Wisconsin*   96
          27 August 1848
          TO: Abraham Jakobsen and others, *Tinn, Telemark*

1:19   FROM: From Ole and Gullik Gulliksen Dorsett, *Indian Creek,*   99
          Illinois, 20 October 1848
          TO: Gullik Evensen Daaset, *Flesberg, Buskerud*

1849

1:20   FROM: Ellev and Torgon Bjørnsen, *Ashippun, Wisconsin*   100
          17 May 1849
          TO: Anlaug Christophersdatter, Halvor Bjørnsen, and Helge
          Bjørnsdatter Tonga, *Heddal, Notodden, Telemark*

1850

1:21 FROM: Ole Johansen Holtseteren, *Oconomowoc, Wisconsin* 103
4 November 1850
TO: Ingeborg Olsdatter and Peder Johansen Holtseteren
Gausdal, Oppland

1:22 FROM: Herbrand Paulsen Osland and Ole Herbrandsen Osland 106
Kendall, New York, 27 November 1850
TO: Hellik Paalsen Aasland, *Flesberg, Buskerud*

1:23 FROM: Elise Wærenskjold, *Four Mile Prairie, Texas* 109
16 December 1850
TO: Taale Andreas Gjestvang, *Løten, Hedmark*

1:24 FROM: Torgon Bjørnsdatter, *Ashippun, Wisconsin* 113
28 November–15 December 1850
TO: Anlaug Christophersdatter, Halvor Bjørnsen, and Helge
Bjørnsdatter Tonga, *Heddal, Notodden, Telemark*

1851

1:25 FROM: Gullik Gulliksen Dorsett, *Indian Creek, Leland, Illinois* 115
4 February 1851
TO: Gullik Evensen Daaset, *Flesberg, Buskerud*

1:26 FROM: Elise Wærenskjold, *Four Mile Prairie, Texas* 116
20 February 1851
TO: Taale Andreas Gjestvang, *Løten, Hedmark*

1:27 FROM: Nella Bjørnsen, *Ashippun, Wisconsin, 18 September 1851* 118
TO: Anlaug Christophersdatter Tonga, *Heddal, Notodden, Telemark*

1:28 FROM: Jacob Olsen Østern, *Paint Creek, Lansing, Iowa* 119
3 November 1851
TO: His family, *Bærum, Akershus*

1852

1:29 FROM: Gaute Ingebretsen Gunleiksrud, *Dunkirk, Wisconsin* 123
7 January 1852
TO: Ingebret Torstensen and Birgit Gautesdatter Gunleiksrud
Tinn, Telemark

1:30 FROM: Onon Bjørnsen Dahle and Knud Halvorsen Dahle 125
Yreka, California, 12 June 1852
TO: Ansteen Johnsen Næss, *Nissedal, Telemark*

1:31 FROM: Svend Larsen Houg, *New York, New York, 16 July 1852* 140
TO: Ole Larsen Haug, *Aal, Buskerud*

1:32 FROM: Elise Wærenskjold, *Four Mile Prairie, Texas* 144
26 September 1852
TO: Taale Andreas Gjestvang, *Løten, Hedmark*

1:33	FROM: Elise Wærenskjold, *Four Mile Prairie, Texas* 21 November, 1852 TO: Taale Andreas Gjestvang, *Løten, Hedmark*	147
1:34	FROM: Mari and Ingrid Helgesdatter Skare, *Spring Valley, Wisconsin* 28 December 1852 TO: Helge Gundersen and Eli Andersdatter Skare *Eggedal, Sigdal, Buskerud*	151
1:35	FROM: Svend Larsen Houg, *Elgin, Iowa, 28 December 1852* TO: Ole Larsen Haug, *Aal, Buskerud*	153
1:36	FROM: Jacob Olsen Østern, *Paint Creek, Lansing, Iowa* 29 December 1852 TO: His family, *Bærum, Akershus*	159

1853

1:37	FROM: Jacob Olsen Østern, *Paint Creek, Lansing, Iowa* 9 February 1853 TO: His family, *Bærum, Akershus*	162
1:38	FROM: Reinert and Sigbjørn Aslakson, *Coon Prairie, Wisconsin* 24 October 1853 TO: Osmund Atlaksen Ovedal, *Sirdal, Vest-Agder*	165
1:39	FROM: Ole Johansen Holtseteren, *Oconomowoc, Wisconsin* 20 November 1853 TO: Ingebor Olsdatter and Peder Johansen Holtseteren *Gausdal, Oppland*	167
1:40	FROM: Svend Larsen Houg, *Elgin, Iowa, 21 December 1853* TO: Ole and Knud Larsen and Mari Larsdatter Haug *Aal, Buskerud*	168
1:41	FROM: Magrete Nilsdatter and Ole Olsen Heve *Cambridge, Wisconsin, 19 December 1853* TO: Martha Haldorsdatter Nesheim, *Granvin, Hordaland*	172

1854

1:42	FROM: Tosten Levorsen Hvashovd and Hellik Olson Lehovd *Christiana, Wisconsin, 14 January 1854* TO: Ole Nirisen Vangestad and Ole Helgesen Lehovd *Flesberg, Buskerud*	177
1:43	FROM: Gullik Olsen Østern, *Paint Creek, Lansing, Iowa* 14 February 1854 TO: Engebret Olsen Steen, *Skedsmo, Akershus*	180
1:44	FROM: Herbrand Paulsen Osland, *Christiana, Wisconsin* 11 March 1854 TO: Hellik Paalsen Aasland, *Flesland, Buskerud*	182
1:45	FROM: Nils Ludvigsen Elvetun, *Madison, Wisconsin, 12 July 1854* TO: Ludvig Kristiansen Elvetun, *Solvorn, Luster, Sogn og Fjordane*	183

1:46	FROM: Johanne Svenningsdatter Songe, *Howard, Illinois* *16 July 1854* To: Her family, *Songe, Holt, Tvedestrand, Aust-Agder*	186
1:47	FROM: Christopher Jacobson, *Batavia, Illinois, 18 July 1854* To: Hans Jakobsen Hilton, *Kløfta, Ullensaker, Akershus*	188
1:48	FROM: Elias Hansen Narjord, *Dorchester, Iowa* *4 September 1854* To: Hans Pedersen Narjord, *Os, Hedmark*	190
1:49	FROM: Hellik Olsen Lehovd, *Christiana, Wisconsin* *12 November 1854* To: Ole Helgesen and Joran Paulsdatter Lehovd *Flesberg, Buskerud*	193
1:50	FROM: Jacob Olsen Østern, *Paint Creek, Lansing, Iowa* *9 August–26 November 1854* To: Engebret Olsen Steen, *Skedsmo, Akershus*	195
1:51	FROM: Svend Larsen Houg, *Elgin, Iowa, 13 December 1854* To: Ole and Knut Larsen and Mari Larsdatter Haug *Aal, Buskerud*	198
1:52	FROM: Juul and Ole Gulliksen and Susana Halvorsdatter Dorsett *Earlville, Illinois, 20 December 1854* To: Gullik Evensen and Tostein Gulliksen Daaset *Flesberg, Buskerud*	201

1855

1:53	FROM: Anders Helgesen Skare, *Decorah, Iowa, 7 February 1855* To: Helge Gundersen and Eli Andersdatter Skare *Eggedal, Sigdal, Buskerud*	203
1:54	FROM: Elias Hansen Narjord, *Dorchester, Iowa, 30 March 1855* To: Hans Pedersen Narjord, *Os, Hedmark*	204
1:55	FROM: Hellik Olson Lehovd, *Christiana, Wisconsin, 14 April 1855* To: Ole Helgesen Lehovd, *Flesberg, Buskerud*	207
1:56	FROM: Johanne Svenningsdatter Songe, *Howard, Illinois* *28 May 1855* To: Her family, *Songe, Holt, Tvedestrand, Aust-Agder*	208
1:57	FROM: Sigbjørn Aslakson, *Coon Prairie, Wisconsin, 12 July 1855* To: Osmund Atlaksen Ovedal, *Sirdal, Vest-Agder*	210
1:58	FROM: Johanne Svenningsdatter Songe, *Howard, Illinois* *7 October 1855* To: Her family, *Songe, Tvedestrand, Aust-Agder*	211
1:59	FROM: Hellik Olson Lehovd, *Christiana, Wisconsin* *12 December 1855* To: Ole Helgesen and Joran Paulsdatter Lehovd *Flesberg, Buskerud*	213

1:60 FROM: Holger Petterson Helle, *Leland, Illinois*   215
           28 December 1855
      To: Hans Ormsen Øverland, *Nedstrand, Tysvær, Rogaland*

1856

1:61 FROM: Gaute Ingebretsen and Kari Sigurdsdatter Gunleiksrud   217
           Dunkirk, Wisconsin, 28 January 1856
      To: Ingebret Torstensen and Birgit Gautesdatter Gunleiksrud
           Tinn, Telemark

1:62 FROM: Lars Nilsen Nesheim, *Chicago, Illinois, 28 March 1856*   219
      To: Martha Haldorsdatter Nesheim, *Granvin, Hordaland*

1:63 FROM: Elias Hansen and Ane Kristine Tørrisdatter Narjord   220
           Dorchester, Iowa, 26 December 1856
      To: Hans Pedersen Narjord, *Os, Hedmark*

1857

1:64 FROM: Hellik Olson Lehovd, *Christiana, Wisconsin*   223
           24 January 1857
      To: Ole Helgesen and Joran Paulsdatter Lehovd
           Flesberg, Buskerud

1:65 FROM: Anders Helgesen and Ingeborg Helgesdatter Skare   225
           Nerstrand, Minnesota, 4 February 1857
      To: Helge Gundersen Skare, *Eggedal, Sigdal, Buskerud*

1:66 FROM: Hellik Olson Lehovd, *Christiana, Wisconsin*   226
           10 April 1857
      To: Ole Helgesen and Joran Paulsdatter Lehovd
           Flesberg, Buskerud

1:67 FROM: Torgrim Olsen Lee, *Black Earth, Dane County,*   228
           Wisconsin, 24 July 1857
      To: Anders Olsen Lie, *Hedalen, Sør Aurdal, Oppland*

1:68 FROM: Ole Hansen Rustand, *St. Ansgar, Iowa*   231
           28 September 1857
      To: Elling Olsen Elsrud, *Aadalen, Ringerike, Buskerud*

1:69 FROM: Hellik Olson Lehovd, *Christiana, Wisconsin*   234
           25 November 1857
      To: Ole Helgesen Lehovd, *Flesberg, Buskerud*

1:70 FROM: Elias Hansen and Ane Kristine Tørrisdatter Narjord   236
           Dorchester, Iowa, 7 December 1857
      To: Hans Pedersen Narjord, *Os, Hedmark*

1858

1:71 FROM: Magrete Nilsdatter and Ole Olson Heve   240
           Cambridge, Wisconsin, 4 January 1858
      To: Martha Haldorsdatter Nesheim, *Granvin, Hordaland*

1:72	FROM: Gullik Gulliksen Dorsett, *Leland Station, Illinois* 21 January 1858 TO: Torsten Gulliksen Daaset, *Flesberg, Buskerud*	242
1:73	FROM: Gaute Ingebretsen and Kari Sigurdsdatter Gunleiksrud *Dunkirk, Wisconsin, 15 March 1858* TO: Ingebret Torstensen and Birgit Gautesdatter Gunleiksrud *Tinn, Telemark*	244
1:74	FROM: Elise Wærenskjold, *Four Mile Prairie, Texas* 16 October 1858 TO: Thomine Dannevig, *Lillesand, Aust-Agder*	245
1:75	FROM: Hellik Olson Lehovd, *Christiana, Wisconsin* 28 October 1858 TO: Ole Helgesen Lehovd, *Flesberg, Buskerud*	249

1859

1:76	FROM: Svend Larsen Houg, *Elgin, Iowa, 18 January 1859* TO: Ole Larsen Haug, *Aal, Buskerud*	251
1:77	FROM: Gullik Olsen Østern, *Paint Creek, Iowa* 18 January 1859 TO: Engebret Olsen Steen, *Skedsmo, Akershus*	256
1:78	FROM: Ole Hansen Rustand, *St. Ansgar, Iowa, 24 January 1859* TO: Torgrim Olsen Haugerud, *Aadalen, Ringerike, Buskerud*	259
1:79	FROM: Juul and Ole Gulliksen Dorsett, *Earlville, Illinois* 22 February 1859 TO: Gullik Evensen and Torstein Gulliksen Daaset *Flesberg, Buskerud*	260
1:80	FROM: Christopher Jacobson, *Ogalla, Wisconsin, 13 March 1859* TO: Hans Jakobsen Hilton, *Kløfta, Ullensaker, Akershus*	262
1:81	FROM: Gaute Ingebretsen Gunleiksrud, *Stoughton, Wisconsin* 25 August 1859 TO: Ingebret Torstensen and Birgit Gautesdatter Gunleiksrud *Tinn, Telemark*	264
1:82	FROM: Ole Olsen Haugerud the Younger, *Yale, British Columbia, Canada, 3 November 1859* TO: Guri Rustand, *Aadalen, Ringerike, Buskerud*	265
1:83	FROM: Hellik Olson Lehovd, *Mantorville, Minnesota* 30 November 1859 TO: Ole Helgesen Lehovd, *Flesberg, Buskerud*	267

1860

1:84	FROM: Erik Theodor Schjøth, *Sturgeon Bay, Wisconsin* February 1860 TO: Christian Fredrik Wyller Schjøth, *Oslo*	271

1:85	From: Elise Wærenskjold, *Four Mile Prairie, Texas* 25 March 1860 To: Thomine Dannevig, *Lillesand, Aust-Agder*	272
1:86	From: Erik Theodor Schjøth, *Sturgeon Bay, Wisconsin* 2 June 1860 To: Gulov Gulovsen, *Oslo*	273
1:87	From: Hellik Olson Lehovd, *Christiana, Wisconsin* 4 November 1860 To: Ole Helgesen Lehovd, *Flesberg, Buskerud*	276
1:88	From: Ole Olsen Haugerud the Younger, *Albert Lea, Minnesota, 12 December 1860* To: Guri T. Rustand and Torgrim Olsen Haugerud *Aadalen, Ringerike, Buskerud*	278

1861

1:89	From: Hellik Olson Lehovd, *Christiana, Wisconsin* 18 January 1861 To: Ole Olsen Lehovd, *Flesberg, Buskerud*	281
1:90	From: Svend Larsen Houg, *Elgin, Iowa, 27 February 1861* To: Ole Larsen Haug, *Aal, Buskerud*	283
1:91	From: Ole Johansen Holtseteren, *Watertown, Wisconsin* 11 November 1861 To: Peder Johansen Holtseteren, *Gausdal, Oppland*	287
1:92	From: Ole Olsen Haugerud the Younger, *Albert Lea Minnesota, 23 December 1861* To: Guri T. Rustand, *Aadalen, Ringerike, Buskerud*	288
1:93	From: Ole Aslesen and Ingrid Helgesdatter Myran, Elling Ellingsen and Mari Helgesdatter Wold and Ingeborg Helgesdatter Skare, *Decorah, Iowa, 27 December 1861* To: Helge Gundersen Skare, *Eggedal, Sigdal, Buskerud*	290

1862

1:94	From: Juul Gulliksen Dorsett, *Newburg, Minnesota* 23 January 1862 To: Torstein Gulliksen Daaset, *Flesberg, Buskerud*	293
1:95	From: Ole Jesperson Taksdal, *St. Louis, Missouri, 2 March 1862* To: Tobias Tørresen Kvia, *Nærbø, Haa, Rogaland*	295
1:96	From: Knud Ivarson Vike, *Fifteenth Wisconsin Regiment near Island No. 10, Missouri, 29 March 1862* To: Dordei Knutsdatter Vike, *Spring Prairie, Wisconsin*	298
1:97	From: Jacob Olsen Østern, *Paint Creek, Lansing, Iowa later than 15 March 1862* To: Engebret Olsen Steen, *Skedsmo, Akershus*	300

1:98	FROM:	Anders Helgesen Skare, *Minnesota, 8 April 1862*	303
	To:	Helge Gundersen Skare, *Eggedal, Sigdal, Buskerud*	
1:99	FROM:	Hellik and Ole Olson Lehovd, *Christiana, Wisconsin 10 June 1862*	306
	To:	Ole Helgesen and Joran Paulsdatter Lehovd *Flesberg, Buskerud*	
1:100	FROM:	Guttorm Olsen Lee, *Blue Mounds, Wisconsin 25 July 1862*	308
	To:	Anders Olsen Lie, *Hedalen, Sør Aurdal, Oppland*	
1:101	FROM:	Gunder Helgesen Skare, Ole Aslesen Myran, Elling Ellingsen Wold and Ingeborg Helgesdatter Skare *Decorah, Iowa, 13 August 1862*	310
	To:	Helge Gundersen and Eli Helgesdatter Skare *Eggedal, Sigdal, Buskerud*	
1:102	FROM:	Knud Ivarson Vike, *Fifteenth Wisconsin Regiment Nashville, Tennessee, 20 December 1862*	311
	To:	Dordei Knutsdatter Vike, *Spring Prairie, Wisconsin*	

1863

1:103	FROM:	Erik Theodor Schjøth, *Sturgeon Bay, Wisconsin 14 January 1863*	312
	To:	Jens Rudolph and Christian Schjøth, *Oslo*	
1:104	FROM:	Elling Ellingsen Wold, Ole Aslesen Myran and Ingeborg Helgesdatter and Gunder Helgesen Skare *Decorah, Iowa, 19 January 1863*	314
	To:	Helge Gundersen, *Eggedal, Sigdal, Buskerud*	
1:105	FROM:	Barbro Tollefsdatter Sando, *Estherville, Iowa 10 September 1863*	316
	To:	A sister, *Aal, Buskerud*	
1:106	FROM:	Anders Helgesen Skare, *Norway Lake, Minnesota 27 September 1863*	318
	To:	Helge Gundersen Skare, *Eggedal, Sigdal, Buskerud*	
1:107	FROM:	Ole Olson Lehovd, *Christiana, Wisconsin 28 December 1863*	319
	To:	Ole Helgesen and Joran Paulsdatter Lehovd *Flesberg, Buskerud*	

1864

1:108	FROM:	Juul Gulliksen Dorsett, *Newburg, Minnesota 5 September 1864*	323
	To:	Torstein Gulliksen Daaset, *Flesberg, Buskerud*	

1:109	FROM: Sigbjørn Aslakson, *Coon Prairie, Wisconsin* 10 October 1864 To: Osmund Atlaksen Ovedal, *Sirdal, Vest-Agder*	324
1:110	FROM: Hellik Olson Lehovd, *Salem, Minnesota* 26 December 1864 To: Ole Helgesen and Joran Paulsdatter Lehovd *Flesberg, Buskerud*	326
1:111	FROM: Ole Olson Lehovd, *Madison, Wisconsin* 29 December 1864 To: Ole Helgesen and Joran Paulsdatter Lehovd *Flesberg, Buskerud*	330

1865

1:112	FROM: Svend Larsen Houg, *Elgin, Iowa, 17 April 1865* To: Ole Larsen Haug, *Aal, Buskerud*	335
1:113	FROM: Hellik and Ole Olson Lehovd, *Salem, Minnesota* 8 June 1865 To: Ole Helgesen and Joran Paulsdatter Lehovd *Flesberg, Buskerud*	338
1:114	FROM: Rakel Tonette Aslakson, *Coon Prairie, Wisconsin* 22 June 1865 To: Osmund Atlaksen Ovedal, *Sirdal, Vest-Agder*	341
1:115	FROM: Elise Wærenskjold, *Four Mile Prairie, Texas* spring or summer of 1865 To: Thomine Dannevig, *Lillesand, Norway*	343
1:116	FROM: Siri and Rakel Tonette Aslakson, *Coon Prairie, Wisconsin, 20 December 1865* To: Osmund and Berent Atlaksen and Sara Atlaksdatter Ovedal, *Bakke, Sirdal, Vest-Agder*	346

1866

1:117	FROM: Barbro Tollefsdatter Sando, *Estherville, Iowa* 14 January 1866 To: Guri Tollefsdatter Bøygard and Randi Tollefsdatter Opheim, *Aal, Buskerud*	349
1:118	FROM: Hans Nielsen Gamkinn, *Spring Grove, Minnesota* 6–10 June 1866 To: Niels Jensen Gamkinn, *Gran, Hadeland, Oppland*	350
1:119	FROM: Elise Wærenskjold, *Four Mile Prairie, Texas* 22–27 June 1866 To: Thomine Dannevig, *Lillesand, Aust-Agder*	352

1:120	FROM: Hans Nielsen Gamkinn, *Spring Grove, Minnesota* 23 September 1866 To: Niels Jensen Gamkinn, *Gran, Hadeland, Oppland*	358
1:121	FROM: Ole Tollefsen Opsata, *St. Ansgar, Iowa* 25 September 1866 To: Haagen Tollefsen Opsata, *Aal, Buskerud*	360
1:122	FROM: Paul and Ole Olson Lehovd, *Kasson, Minnesota* 28 October–18 November 1866 To: Ole Helgesen and Joran Paulsdatter Lehovd *Flesberg, Buskerud*	363

1867

1:123	FROM: Jul Gulliksen Dorsett, *Bratsberg, Minnesota* 15 December 1866 To: Gullik Evensen and Even Gulliksen Daaset *Flesberg, Buskerud*	367
1:124	FROM: Hans Nielsen Gamkinn, *Argyle, Wisconsin* 13 January 1867 To: Niels Jensen Gamkinn, *Gran, Hadeland, Oppland*	368
1:125	FROM: Erik Theodor Schjøth, *Sturgeon Bay, Wisconsin* 15 March 1867 To: Christian Fredrik Wyller Schjøth, *Oslo*	370
1:126	FROM: Hans Nielsen Gamkinn, *Argyle, Wisconsin* 7 April 1867 To: Niels Jensen Gamkinn, *Gran, Hadeland, Oppland*	373
1:127	FROM: Elise Wærenskjold, *Four Mile Prairie, Texas* 15–30 April 1867 To: Thorvald Dannevig, *Lillesand, Aust-Agder*	374
1:128	FROM: Guttorm and Ole Olsen Lee, *Primrose, Wisconsin* 29 May 1867 To: Anders Olsen Lie, *Hedalen, Sør Aurdal, Oppland*	377
1:129	FROM: Berger Tollevsen Rogstad, *Norman Hill, Texas* 1 June 1867 To: Peder Eriksen Furuset, *Romedal, Stange, Hedmark*	379
1:130	FROM: Hellek G. Branson, *Eureka, Kansas,* 22 July 1867 To: Ole Gulbrandsen and Anne Andersdatter Lande *Flesberg, Buskerud*	381
1:131	FROM: Hans Nielsen Gamkinn, *Wiota, Wisconsin* 26 July 1867 To: Niels Jensen Gamkinn, *Gran, Hadeland, Oppland*	383

1:132	From:	Hellik Olson Lehovd, *Salem, Minnesota* *5 November 1867*	384
	To:	Ole Helgesen and Joran Paulsdatter Lehovd *Flesberg, Buskerud*	
1:133	From:	Hellek G. Branson, *Eureka, Kansas, 8 November 1867*	387
	To:	Ole Gulbrandsen and Anne Andersdatter Lande *Flesberg, Buskerud*	
1:134	From:	Magrete Nilsdatter and Ole Olsen Hove, *Vernon,* *Minnesota, 31 December 1867*	390
	To:	Martha Haldorsdatter Næsheim, *Granvin, Hordaland*	

1868

1:135	From:	Rakel Tonette Aslakson, *Coon Prairie, Wisconsin* *14 January 1868*	392
	To:	Osmund and Beren Andreas Atlaksen, and Sara Atlaksdatter Ovedal, *Bakke, Sirdal, Vest-Agder*	
1:136	From:	Ole Olson and Jøran Halvorsdatter Lehovd *Kasson, Minnesota, 13 March 1868*	394
	To:	Ole Helgesen Lehovd, *Flesberg, Buskerud*	
1:137	From:	Christopher Jacobson, *Idaho City, Idaho* *22 March 1868*	399
	To:	Hans Jakobsen Hilton, *Kløfta, Ullensaker, Akershus*	
1:138	From:	Hendrik Olsen Dahl, *Norman Hill, Texas* *30 May 1868*	402
	To:	Peder Eriksen and Siri Kristiansdatter Furuset *Romedal, Stange, Hedmark*	
1:139	From:	Tor Torstensen Vigenstad, *South Bend, Minnesota* *and Spring Prairie, Wisconsin, June 1868*	403
	To:	Ole Torstensen Vigenstad, *Dovre, Oppland*	
1:140	From:	Sara and Rakel Tonette Aslakson, *Coon Prairie,* *Wisconsin, 27 July 1868*	405
	To:	Osmund and Beren Andreas Atlaksen Ovedal *Bakke, Sirdal, Vest-Agder*	
1:141	From:	Gunder Helgesen Skare, *Minneapolis, Minnesota* *5 September 1868*	407
	To:	Helge Gundersen Nerdrum (Skare), *Eggedal,* *Sigdal, Buskerud*	
1:142	From:	Elise Wærenskjold, *Prairieville, Texas* *29–30 September 1868*	409
	To:	Karen Poppe, *Lillesand, Aust-Agder*	
1:143	From:	Ole Johanson Holtseteren, *Watertown, Wisconsin* *27 November 1868*	412
	To:	Peder Johansen Holtseteren, *Gausdal, Oppland*	

1869

1:144	FROM:	Rakel Tonette Allikson, *Medo, Minnesota* 14 January 1869	414
	TO:	Osmund and Berent Atlaksen Ovedal, *Sirdal, Vest-Agder*	
1:145	FROM:	Thor Torstensen Vigenstad, *Spring Prairie, Wisconsin,* 1 February 1869	415
	TO:	Ole Torstensen Vigenstad, *Dovre, Oppland*	
1:146	FROM:	Elling Ellingsen Wold, *Decorah, Iowa,* 1 March 1869	418
	TO:	Helge Gundersen Skare, *Eggedal, Sigdal, Buskerud*	
1:147	FROM:	Svend Larsen and Halsten and Lars Svendsen Houg *Elgin, Iowa,* 4 March 1869	420
	TO:	Ole Larsen Haug, *Aal, Buskerud*	
1:148	FROM:	Iver Ellingsen Elsrud, *Rock Creek, Iowa* 18 May 1869	424
	TO:	Elling Olsen and Olea Olsdatter Elsrud *Aadalen, Ringerike, Buskerud*	
1:149	FROM:	Hendrik Olsen Dahl, *Norman Hill, Texas* 27 June 1869	426
	TO:	Dahl Peder Eriksen and Siri Kristiansdatter Furuset *Romedal, Stange, Hedmark*	
1:150	FROM:	Gaute Ingebretsen Gunleiksrud, *Stoughton, Wisconsin,* 31 July 1869	428
	TO:	Ingebret Torsteinsen and Birgit Gautesdatter Gunleiksrud *Tinn, Telemark*	
1:151	FROM:	Ole Aslesen and Ingrid Helgesdatter Myran *Decorah, Iowa,* 18 August 1869	429
	TO:	Helge Gundersen Skare, *Eggedal, Sigdal, Buskerud*	
1:152	FROM:	Christopher Jakobson, *Hot Creek, Nevada* 27 September 1869	431
	TO:	Hans Jakobsen Hilton, *Kløfta, Ullensaker, Akershus*	
1:153	FROM:	Iver Ellingsen Elsrud, *Rock Creek, Iowa* 27 November 1869	434
	TO:	Elling Olsen and Olea Olsdatter Elsrud *Aadalen, Ringerike, Buskerud*	
1:154	FROM:	Hellik Olson Lehovd, *Salem, Minnesota* 27 December 1869	436
	TO:	Ole Helgesen and Joran Paulsdatter Lehovd *Flesberg, Buskerud*	
1:155	FROM:	Guttorm Olsen Lee, *Primrose, Wisconsin* 31 December 1869	438
	TO:	Anders Olsen Lie, *Hedalen, Sør-Aurdal, Oppland*	

1870

1:156   FROM: Ole Olsen Haugerud the Younger, *Rock Creek,*   441
                 Iowa, 9 January 1870
        TO: Guri Torgrimsdatter Rustand, *Aadalen, Ringerike, Buskerud*

1:157   FROM: Eli Helgesdatter and Gunder Johnsen Moen   443
                 Decorah, Iowa, 10 January 1870
        TO: Helge Gundersen Skare, *Eggedal, Sigdal, Buskerud*

1:158   FROM: Ingeborg Helgesdatter and Ole Evensen   444
                 Norway Lake, Minnesota, 15 February 1870
        TO: Helge Gundersen Skare, *Eggedal, Sigdal, Buskerud*

1:159   FROM: Svend Larsen Houg, *Elgin, Iowa, 11 April 1870*   446
        TO: Ole Larsen Haug, *Aal, Buskerud*

1:160   FROM: Elise Wærenskjold, *Prairieville, Texas*   449
                 19 May 1870
        TO: Thorvald and Thomine Dannevig, *Lillesand, Aust-Agder*

1:161   FROM: Ole Tellefsen Opsata, *Estherville, Iowa*   451
                 4 July 1870
        TO: Guri Tollefsdatter Bøygard, *Aal, Buskerud*

1:162   FROM: Hendrik Olsen Dahl, *Clifton, Texas*   454
                 10 July 1870
        TO: Peder Eriksen and Siri Kristiansdatter Furuset
                 Romedal, Stange, Hedmark

1:163   FROM: Christopher Jacobson, *Hot Creek, Nevada*   455
                 6 September 1870
        TO: Hans Jakobsen Hilton, *Kløfta, Ullensaker, Akershus*

1:164   FROM: Ole Olsen Lee, *Primrose, Wisconsin*   458
                 29 September 1870
        TO: Anders Olsen Lie, *Hedalen, Oppland*

1:165   FROM: Jul Gulliksen Dorsett, *Bratsberg, Minnesota*   461
                 15 October 1870
        TO: Torstein Gulliksen Daaset, *Flesberg, Buskerud*

1:166   FROM: Paul Torstensen, *Leeds, Wisconsin*   462
                 26 October 1870
        TO: Ole Torstensen Vigenstad, *Dovre, Oppland*

1:167   FROM: Iver Ellingsen Elsrud, *Rock Creek, Iowa*   466
                 22 December 1870
        TO: Elling Olsen and Olea Olsdatter Elsrud
                 Aadalen, Ringerike, Buskerud

FOREWORD

Historians spend their time trying to make a story out of past realities. They look for beginning and endings, for paragraphs and chapters, for themes and even meanings. When the work is well done, it is instructive but it remains only constructive, something made up out of all data the historian is able to or cares to use. It never quite captures the life of the past. Reality, one accomplished historian used to like to remind his students, was not made for scholarship's sake.

Letters, like histories, are also constructed. They have writers and recipients, all situated variously. Letters have beginnings and endings. They have purposes. Some things are included and some are left out. They are more or less candid and truthful as the case may be. Letters nevertheless are often qualitatively different from most of the other sources historians use in constructing their narratives and presenting interpretations. They are different from most of these sources because they give us the voice of the ordinary individual. Especially from about 1870 forward, most letters are private and confidential, usually from one writer to one or just a few recipients. Letters thus give entry and, in many instances, a clear sense of the lives of individuals. They provide, among other things, evidence for consideration of individual agency. Emigration and immigration, from this perspective, can be thought of as the movements of thousands of individuals and families undertaken for a variety of reasons with a multitude of purposes, rather than as a mass movement to be explained by mighty, even irresistible forces. The opportunity to hear the voice of the individual is an important reason to read letters like those gathered here. These letters enrich scholarship not so much with new findings or generalizations but with nuance and qualification.

There are other reasons to read letters like these. Various readers will find a wealth of information on kinfolk, places, agriculture, church life, politics, clothing, food, language, and more. And there is at least one more reason for many to read this correspondence. These letters are quite simply interesting and engaging. You can pick them up and put them down, read them in small pieces or take a large slice at once. They are good reading.

The gathering, editing, translating, and publishing of letters has been a high priority for the Norwegian-American Historical Association since its founding. The present volume and the two volumes and cumulative indices projected to follow it continue a long tradition. While together they will become a landmark in the history of the association, we may hope that they are not the final volumes of correspondence to be published. Much more remains to be done with the correspondence of individuals in various situations.

It is a privilege to thank many colleagues for their assistance in bringing this work to print. First thanks go to Orm Øverland. Professor Øverland is a model of what the English call a person of parts. He is one of the editors of the several volumes of the Norwegian edition on which the present version is based. Splendidly accomplished in English as well as in his native Norwegian, Øverland is also both the editor and the translator of the American edition. The selection, the translation, the introduction, and the notes are entirely the work of this single, versatile scholar. Amy Boxrud has provided able and ready assistance in producing this volume. Holmes Design created the graphic design and typography. Jackie Henry, administrative director of the Norwegian-American Historical Association, has provided superb counsel and patient, effective support for the effort. I thank all these individuals as well as the entire membership of the Norwegian-American Historical Association for assistance in publishing this volume.

Todd W. Nichol, Editor
Northfield, Minn.

PREFACE

COLLECTING AND SELECTING IMMIGRANT LETTERS

The three-volume *From America to Norway: Norwegian-American Immigrant Letters, 1838–1914* is based on a Norwegian edition in seven volumes, *Fra Amerika til Norge* (1992–2011, referred to throughout as Nor. ed.). The Norwegian edition in turn is based on the collection of immigrant letters in the Norwegian National Archives (*Riksarkivet*), sponsor of the Norwegian edition. It is fitting that the Norwegian-American Historical Association (NAHA) is the initiator and copublisher of these volumes. The collection of immigrant letters in *Riksarkivet* had its beginning in the mid-1920s, when few European historians had demonstrated any interest in studying the mass movement of people from their continent to the United States in the preceding century.[1] The initiative was taken by members of the group of Norwegian Americans who created NAHA in 1925, the year that marked the centenary of Norwegian emigration to the United States. They feared that the sources for the history of the exodus of their ethnic group would be lost, and the primary aim of NAHA was to collect, preserve, and publish such sources. The first person to make a systematic search for sources for a history of Norwegian emigration was a young graduate of Luther College, Gunnar Malmin, who, advised by Theodore C. Blegen, then at the Minnesota Historical Society in St. Paul, went to Norway in 1923. The wealth of material Malmin found in public archives and private collections encouraged Blegen in his plans to write a large history of the migration. Perhaps the most important conclusion drawn by Malmin after his visit was the historical value of the letters written by immigrants and sent to family and friends in the country they had left. Some letters had been printed in contemporary newspapers and a few had by chance found a home in public archives, but the vast majority of the letters that had survived were in the homes to which they had been sent, mainly farms.

Blegen was convinced of the value of these letters. Indeed, as early as 1920 he had published a brief article titled "The America Letters" in the

---

1. See Orm Øverland, "Recovering Memories of the Migration: NAHA and the Making of a Collection of Immigrant Letters in the Norwegian National Archives, 1923–1929." Øyvind T. Gulliksen, ed., *Norwegian-American Essays 2008*, 189–214 (Oslo: NAHA-Norway, 2008).

Norwegian-American magazine *The North Star*, probably the first published use of this term by an American historian.[2] After attempts by several of the founders of NAHA to organize the collecting of letters in Norway, Blegen had the opportunity to visit Norway: he received an invitation from the American Historical Association to be one of the American representatives at the International Congress of Historians held in Oslo in August 1928. A scholarship made it possible for him to spend ten months in Norway with his family and gave him access to Norwegian historians as a respected colleague. His most valuable contact was Professor Oluf Kolsrud, who sponsored the publication of the paper Blegen gave on immigrant letters at the International Congress by the Norwegian Academy of Science and Letters,[3] and who opened the way for making the Norwegian National Archives the home of a growing collection of immigrant letters, a collection that now numbers between four and five thousand items. In addition to these there are the many letters in regional public archives. These three volumes present only a small selection of the preserved letters.

In its first decades NAHA focused on finding and locating source material for the early history of Norwegian immigration, a policy that also reflected the main research interest of Theodore Blegen, who served as editor of NAHA from 1925 to 1960. Most of the immigrant letters in his pioneering edition, *Land of Their Choice* (1955) are from the pre-Civil War period and the letters published in the many volumes of *Norwegian-American Studies* edited by Blegen are also mainly from the early decades. These published translations have not been republished in the present edition, where letters from before the Civil War make up about half of the first volume.

The decision not to include letters written later than 1914 may appear arbitrary even if this is the year of the beginning of the First World War, an event that had a significant impact on immigration from Europe. When work on the Norwegian edition began in 1987 it was natural to reflect on the ethics of publishing private family letters. By having 1914 as a cut-off year we wished to ensure that neither the writers nor the recipients of the published letters would be among the living. Moreover, all letters had been given to archives by the descendants of recipients who knew that they were thus making the letters available to the public.

---

2. (February 1920), 43-45.

3. Theodore C. Blegen, "*The America Letters*," Avhandlinger utgitt av Det Norske Videnskaps-Akademi i Oslo. II. Hist.-Filos. Klasse. 1928. No.5. The pamphlet concluded with an appeal to those who had such letters to send them to Professor Kolsrud at the Norwegian National Archives.

It has been an important aim to make a representative selection reflecting the demographics of Norwegian immigration in this period. Consequently there are few letters from or to cities. As Odd Lovoll has reminded us, "By the criterions set in the federal census, Norwegians were statistically the most rural of all major nineteenth century immigrant groups."[4] The majority of the letters in *Riksarkivet* have been sent to rural addresses in Norway. This may be not only because a significant majority of the immigrants came from rural areas but also because letters had a better chance of surviving in a family where generation followed generation on the same farm than in an urban working-class family with frequent changes of address.

Many of the decisions made in the process of selecting letters for *From America to Norway* have been arbitrary in the sense that all letters have potential interest and all letters reflect some aspect of immigrants' experiences. Some letters—such as a long 1852 letter about a journey to California at the time of the gold rush—may be unique in that they are different from most other letters, but letters that largely speak of the same kinds of experience as do many others are valuable precisely because they confirm the shared nature of such experiences. One guiding principle has been to give series of letters priority over single letters. A series of letters by one writer or by related writers may give special insight into periods in immigrant lives. The longest series of letters in *From America to Norway* is by Elise Wærenskjold and begins in January 1848, some months after her arrival in Texas, and concludes with a friend's report of her death in 1895. In 1852, Sven Houg, a young farmer's son from the valley of Hallingdal began writing home about his departure, and his last letter in this edition was written in 1896, ten years before his death at the age of 102. Another series by Sigri Svendsen (1891–1898) may be of special interest to some readers because the writer is both niece and daughter-in-law of Gro Svendsen, whose letters were published in 1950.[5] Giving priority to series of letters does not mean that single letters have been excluded.

Translating Immigrant Letters

These letters are translations, and translation is always a challenge. One of the special challenges of translating immigrant letters is that their writ-

---

4. *Norwegians on the Prairie: Ethnicity and the Development of the Country Town* (St. Paul: Minnesota Historical Society Press, 2006), 4.

5. Pauline Farseth and Theodore C. Blegen, eds. *Frontier Mother: The Letters of Gro Svendsen* (Northfield: NAHA, 1950).

ers were often uneducated and unused to expressing themselves in writing. Indeed, they were at times semiliterate in the sense that they did not master syntax, punctuation, or spelling. Interpreting the handwriting of some of the early letters is also difficult. To such difficulties may be added the interpretation of English words (often place names) written by people who had only heard them spoken by other Norwegian immigrants. For instance, only context makes it possible to read *Fordats* as Fort Dodge or *Cowru* as Gowrie, both in Iowa. Reading strange words aloud makes it possible to read *Jova* as Iowa and *yunaitisstet* as United States and, with more inspiration, *Bethslers* and *Beth Storse Cabyn* as bachelors and bachelor's cabin.⁶ Such strange-looking spellings often reflect the spoken language of immigrants. In their new lives they met with much that they had no words for in the language of their former lives and they would often simply incorporate English words in the language they used among themselves. Linguists call such interference of one language in another code switching. The way English words (often spelled phonetically) are used in letters written to people who knew no English suggests that the writers did not think of such words as foreign. In 1888 (2:218) Anne Bjorli wrote about *kalko*, meaning calico, and *grønri*, meaning granary. Neither these words nor her explanation of the latter, *grønhus* (green house), would have made sense to her readers, but these were evidently words she used when speaking Norwegian in what is now North Dakota. Indeed, variations of *grønri* throughout these letters suggest that this was a common word in the language of Norwegian immigrants. Spellings such as *preire* and *prærie* for a landscape they had not encountered before immigration are also common.

Difficult handwriting, phonetic spellings, and code switching are merely technical problems and different translators may solve them in different ways. The greatest challenge for a translator of these letters is to translate these nineteenth-century texts by untrained and uneducated writers into English texts for educated twenty-first century readers. This should be regarded as an ethical issue more than a technical one. All too easily we may tend to equate poor mastery of language, written as well as spoken, with poor intelligence. The writers of these letters, however, were intelligent, resourceful, and enterprising people who had involved themselves and their families in more radical and demanding adventures than most of us present-day readers can imagine. My guiding principle has been that these writers'

---

6. Information on the spelling of these and other English words is often included in the note following the letter.

deficient education must not be understood as a deficient intelligence and that they deserve to be presented in a grammatically correct and readable English translation. It is an ethical imperative that both reader and translator approach these texts with respect.

Acknowledgments

From America to Norway is indebted to the late Steinar Kjærheim, for many years the head of *Kjeldeskriftavdelingen* (The Department of Written Sources), since 1991 a division of the Norwegian National Archives, and co-editor of the three first volumes of *Fra Norge til Amerika*. Knut Sprauten, Tor Ulset, Halvor Kjellberg, and Jo Rune Ugulen, all at the Norwegian National Archives, were of special help in preparing the Norwegian volumes. Todd W. Nichol, King Olav V Professor of Scandinavian-American Studies at St. Olaf College, first suggested the making of an American edition and has been an encouragement in moments of despair. Amy Boxrud has been of invaluable assistance in preparing these volumes for publication. My main support is Inger, my wife of more than half a century.

Orm Øverland
Aukra, Norway

READER'S GUIDE

In this collection each letter is assigned a number, found in its heading, which indicates its volume and number in this edition. For instance, 1:110 indicates Volume One, the 110th letter. This is followed by the name of the letter writer, a place name (for instance, a township or a post office) that indicates the writer's address, the name of the (present) state, and a date. The name of the recipient in Norway is followed by the name of his or her township (*kommune*) and county (*fylke*), both according to the present administrative borders. As the borders and/or name of a township may have changed, the name of the township is at times preceded by the name of the specific area to which the letter was sent. Most letters have notes. Full bibliographical information for references in these notes are given in a separate listing at the end of this volume titled References.

In the period covered by these three volumes most Norwegians did not have family names but a patronymic. A daughter Inger and a son Helge of a man named Ole would be Inger Olsdatter (Ole's daughter) and Helge Olsen (Ole's son). In addition they would also be known by the name of the farm they lived on (whether it was their farm or not) and if they moved to another farm they would be known by the name of the new one. By the end of the nineteenth century it became increasingly common for families to take such names as family names, that is, it would be their name regardless of where they lived. At the same time, patronymics also became family names, particularly in towns and among people who did not live on farms. Then Lars, son of Helge Olsen, would be Lars Olsen rather than Lars Helgesen. While a family name was not made mandatory by law in Norway until 1923, immigrants to the United States entered a society where a family name was required. Their farm names were often difficult to pronounce and this was met either by changing the spelling of a farm name, for instance from Lie to Lee, or by adopting a patronymic as a family name. In the latter case, Inger Olsdatter would become Inger Olsen/Olson. The Americanization of a Norwegian name often evolved over several years. American versions of family names have been used when these are known, but with changing names, consistency may be difficult.

The spellings of first names, family names and place names were not standardized and the letters may give such names in ways that are not easily traced in census reports. An added problem is that the spellings of names of farms and people in older census reports may not coincide with the spelling by which these farms or people are known today. Thus the father of Ole Stensen who wrote to Karlsrud in Telemark in 1847 (1:13) will not be found in the 1801 census if one does not use the spelling Carlsrud. Indeed, the township where this farm is located, Tinn, may not be found if one does not look for the spelling Tind. The notes will give some information on names and headings. The notes and forthcoming index will use standardized versions of names that may have a variety of spellings in the letters.

The pronunciation of Norwegian names will be unfamiliar to many readers. Those who would like to acquire a sense of how names were pronounced by those who wrote and read these letters may consult the "Table of Norwegian Phonemes and their Approximate English Equivalents" in the inside cover of Einar Haugen's *Norwegian English Dictionary*. The extra vowels that conclude the Norwegian alphabet—æ, ø, and å—may cause the greatest problems for readers. The English equivalents given below are as in Haugen's table:

Æ, æ is pronounced as in l*ai*rd or l*ai*r. (A common way of writing prairie in the letters is *prærie*.)

Ø, ø is pronounced as in tr*u*st or b*i*rd.

Å, å was written Aa, aa during most of the period these letters were written, and this is the form used in this edition. It is pronounced as in g*o*t or c*au*ght.

Some further technical information may be useful:

Translations of words that are underlined in a letter are underlined.

Words spelled as in the original are in italics.

Added text is placed in square brackets: [ ].

Illegible text in the original or lost text is indicated [...].

The previous and next letter in a series of letters are found at the end of the notes and are indicated by << and >>.

The volume and number of the letter in the Norwegian edition (Nor. ed.) are listed at the end of each note and preceded by NE.

Measurements, weights, and currencies can be problematic. When giving a distance the letter writers often specify "English mile" (*engelsk mil*), that is the standard U.S. mile, or 1.6 kilometers. This may be the intended mile when it is unspecified, but it may be the Norwegian mile that traditionally was 11.3 kilometers, and after the introduction of the metric system it became 10 kilometers. When the mile is either specified as "English" or unspecified, the translation is simply "mile."

Acreage is usually indicated in acres (with a variety of spellings) even though most recipients may not have known what this meant. A quarter-section (160 acres), often written *kvart*, was the standard homesteading unit. A fourth of a quarter is also often mentioned in the letters as *en førti* and whether the writer intended "a fourth" or "a forty," the meaning would be the same: forty acres.

When writing about their harvest, writers usually used the measure of their market: bushel, even though this unit may not have been meaningful for the recipients. At times they used the traditional Norwegian measure for volume, *tønde* (now spelled *tønne*, literally: barrel), or explained that four bushels equaled one *tønde*.

The Norwegian *speciedaler* (or simply *daler*) was worth slightly more than one U.S. dollar. The translation uses "dollar" except in cases where the exchange rate is an issue. The shilling (worth twelve and a half cents, also called a bit) used in the United States should not be confused with the Norwegian *skilling*, of which there were 120 in one *speciedaler*.

At times there is simply no commonly understood English equivalent for words in the letters. One example may be *vadmel,* for which there is an older English word *wadmol*, which has been explained as "a coarse rough woolen fabric formerly used in the British Isles and Scandinavia" or as "fulled woolen cloth." Rather than use an unfamiliar word or give a long explanation, the translated text simply reads "homespun." Similar solutions are used throughout. Some translation issues are explained in the notes.

INTRODUCTION

Listening to the Voices in Immigrant Letters

Reading is a difficult exercise—as suggested by the many books and articles offering different and often contrasting interpretations of well-known literary texts. While most realize that readings of literary works may change over time and vary from reader to reader, many may not have thought of the simple letters by uneducated immigrants as texts that require the attention we give to the work of great writers. Just as optimal readings of good writers, however, require informed readers, immigrant letters also make their demands on readers. The only way to become an informed reader of immigrant letters is to read many of such letters. Respect for the writers, however untrained and uneducated they may be, is a prerequisite.

A READING

I will illustrate this with a reading of a letter from 1875, written by a young woman who admits that this is her first attempt at writing. The writer is Anne Andresen or Ane Andresdatter as she was known in Rennesøy in Rogaland before her emigration. In the 1865 census she is listed as eight years of age at the croft Nordhusle. Her father, Anders Pedersen, was a brother of Morten Pedersen, the farmer at Nordhus and father of Peder (who was twelve in 1865), to whom the letter is addressed. Her letter is dated 8 October 1875. At the time of writing she was eighteen and a servant in a home in or near Marengo, Iowa.

> Dear cousin, Peder Mortensen,
>
> This evening I am so lonely and think only of you and I remember all the happy and entertaining times we had together in the days of our childhood. Pardon me that I take the liberty to write these lines to you now that I am so far away from you. You spoke of getting to know what America was like when I came there. You will get to know this now. I think that for me and all boys and girls it is twice and yet again twice as good as in Norway. A boy may earn a hundred dollars faster than he can make twenty in Norway and isn't that pretty well done?
>
> Dear friend, you mustn't forget me. Remember me. Come and let me

see you again if you should once come to America. You never leave my thoughts. I think I have had a very good time since I came to America. Well, you would also have thought so if you had been here. Time passes quickly for me this evening and soon it is time for me to go to bed and get some rest. I have had much to do today and tomorrow it is Saturday. Then too I will have a lot of work but then it is Sunday and then I have nothing to do except to visit friends.

   I must stop for now. I will do better another time. Do not forget to write back to me. Please remember this. You must tell me all the news you know there at home. Send me your portrait. Dear cousin, I don't know what news to tell you from here except that it looks very nice. It is as before with Bertel and Dorthe Iversen. Please give my greetings to my parents and siblings and to Uncle and all of Gonel and Serene's cousins. But first and last you are lovingly greeted from me, your cousin

ANNE ANDRESEN

My address is *Anne Andressen Nordhus, Marengo PO Iowa Co. Iowa North America.* You mustn't be puzzled by this letter. It is only for fun and once it will have to be the first time I think.

At first glance Anne's letter may seem of little interest. Indeed, it is so poorly written that parts of the original are difficult to interpret. As she reveals in her postscript, this is the first time she tries to express herself in writing; at school writing had been only a mechanical exercise. Even though she makes light of her effort in her postscript, claiming that "It is only for fun," this letter documents an important moment in this young woman's life: the night she becomes a writer. For the first time she creates sentences of her own that she can contemplate and share with someone else. In a few weeks they will be read by a cousin she used to talk with but now can only write to. So momentous is this act that it demands notice: "Pardon me that I take the liberty to write these lines to you now that I am so far away from you." There is a sense of daring here and also a need to explain this extraordinary communication. Not only does the new distance between them demand writing but, she reminds him, he had asked her to report on "what America was like when I came there." Her style is stiltedly formal and very different from the dialect she would have used if speaking with her cousin.

   Her conditions are not ideal for this important undertaking. It is night; she has had a long day of work and will have to get up early the next morning for another long day. The time used for writing is at the expense of much needed sleep. No one else may be awake in the house. This does not necessarily mean that she is alone. She has no room of her own. I assume she is either surrounded by the sounds of sleeping people or sitting in a kitchen.

No wonder that her first sentence speaks of loneliness and nostalgia for the carefree days of childhood. It is as if she is overwhelmed by longing as soon as she sits down to write to her cousin in a distant land. But I do not think this means that Anne was usually longing for Norway. Indeed, it is wrong to read expressions of nostalgia in immigrant letters as indications of a general longing among those who wrote them. It is natural that an immigrant who may not have given much thought to her former home in her daily life is filled with a sudden nostalgia when sitting down to write to mother, family, or friends. This is something I have called situational nostalgia and I think it is quite evident that Anne's initial nostalgia was created by her writing situation.

It is as if Anne herself became aware of the possible misconstruction of her opening sentence as soon as she saw what she had written. For her message is that it is far better in the United States than in Norway: "I think that for me and all boys and girls it is twice and yet again twice as good as in Norway. A boy may earn a hundred dollars quicker than he can make twenty in Norway and," she adds, "isn't that pretty well done?"

But she is not done with her awakened sense of having left her home and friends behind, and she writes: "Dear friend, you mustn't forget me. Remember me. Come and let me see you again if you should once come to America. You never leave my thoughts." Again it is as if she sees that she must make sure that she is not misunderstood: of course she does not imagine returning to Norway. It is only if her cousin comes to America that she would like to see him again. And there is good reason for him to come, she explains: "I think I have had a very good time since I came to America. Well, you would also have thought so if you had been here." And now she has written enough. Time has passed quickly, she writes, but I also think that she has labored to get these few words down on paper. She writes of all the work she has to do, but also that she is free to do as she wants on Sundays. "[T]hen I have nothing to do except to visit friends." And her sense of loneliness with which she opened her letter is gone with the thought of the friends she will be visiting on Sunday.

She must end her letter and get to bed. She thinks that she will be able to write a better letter the next time, so her first attempt has given her confidence. Reviewing her letter, we realize that she has said very little about her life in Iowa beyond the phrase "it looks very nice." There is no description of the landscape, no details about her work or the people she is among. Indeed, the letter does not even make clear whether she is on a farm or in a small town.¹ She may simply not have been able to describe her life and her situation. She may, however, have thought that her life here was so different and so strange compared to what they knew in the old country, that they would not understand an attempt to describe it. So she writes, as did so many, that she does not "know what news to tell you." But she does want to have news from home and admonishes her cousin to let her know everything about family and former neighbors and to send her his photograph. Read with respect as well as attention, such a brief (and very poorly written) letter may give an image and perhaps even a sketch of the life situation of a young immigrant in or near a small town in Iowa in 1875.

In a brief introduction it is impossible to discuss the many factors that may enter into an informed reading of immigrant letters. In the following I will focus on these issues: changes in distance and postage, genre, canon, the ethics of reading immigrant letters, method, and the value of immigrant letters as historical sources.

CHANGES IN DISTANCE AND POSTAGE

Pre-Civil War immigrants from Norway traveled long distances from their old homes to their new. More than ten weeks was a typical sailing time between a Norwegian port and Quebec or New York. Rail gradually provided faster travel than the canal from New York to Lake Erie and boats on the lakes. By 1860 steamships via Hull and Liverpool were competing with sailing ships for the immigrant trade. In Norway agents for British steamship lines sold complete packages for both sea and land travel via Hull and Liverpool to Montreal or New York and on to destinations in the Upper Midwest. Although sailing ships were slower and uncomfortable they offered a cheaper voyage, and their use was prolonged because Norwegian ships in the lumber trade between Canada and Britain could offer cheap passage.² Immigrants continued to travel by sail via Canada long after steamships had come to dominate trans-Atlantic passenger traffic, but by 1870 immigrants from Norway came by steamship.³

---

1. She may not have been able to have meaningful conversations with her employers. An 1880 "Marengo Business Directory" does not list anyone with a Scandinavian name. Martin Ulvestad does not mention Marengo in his 1901 town-by-town listing of Norwegian male immigrants.

2. See the Introduction to Orm Øverland, *Johan Schrøder's Travels in Canada, 1864* (Montreal and Kingston: McGill-Queen's University Press, 1989).

3. For 1871 the Norway Heritage website lists twenty-two sailing ships of various kinds going from Norwegian ports to Quebec with emigrants and twenty-one steamships that carried emigrants to European or British ports or direct to New York. For 1874 only two sailing ships are listed bound for Quebec with emigrants, and from 1875 none are listed.

In the 1840s steamships began to carry mail between North America and England, and by the 1860s most mail to European ports went this way.[4] The awareness that a letter could be read three weeks after it was sent rather than in as many months surely had an effect on the writers of letters. The radical change in mail delivery was facilitated by changes in the organization of international mail in the 1860s. The first step was an American initiative, a Postal Conference in Paris in 1863 with delegates from fifteen countries followed by a number of bilateral postal treaties. Before a postal convention between the United States, Sweden, and Norway took effect in 1873, setting the price of a prepaid fifteen-gram letter to Norway at six cents, other bilateral agreements had had an effect on the cost of correspondence between Norwegian immigrants and their former homeland.[5] When the General Postal Union was established in 1875, the cost of letters between the United States and Norway had already been drastically reduced. American postage stamps—that would soon cost only a fraction of earlier prices for mail to Europe—had become valid all the way from a town in Iowa to a farm in a Norwegian valley. Before the radical reorganization of international postal service, the price for a letter was so high that it was difficult for most people in Norway to send and receive letters from the United States. It was not quite as difficult for the immigrants, who were living in a cash economy. Ole Reistad wrote from Wisconsin to his parents in 1863 and urged them to send their letters unpaid. He explained: "... when I work for one day I can pay for two or three letters, and then you will understand that I am happy to receive all the letters we can get."[6] A day's work to pay for a couple of letters may not strike us as cheap, but they were so valuable that they seemed well worth it.

Postage from Wisconsin to Oslo (Christiania) in 1860 was about fifty cents. A woman's wages were from fifty cents to two dollars a week. A hired man earned one dollar a day during summer, but next to nothing during winter. And most immigrants were saving as much as they could to invest in a farm and a home. Naturally, much of the early correspondence was about money, including the cost of letters. But the situation had become different in 1868 when a writer commented on the new postal rates: "I assume you

---

4. George E. Hargest, *History of Letter Post Communication between the United States and Europe, 1845–1875* (Washington, D.C.: Smithsonian Institution Press, 1971), 109–146.

5. Hargest, *History*, 150–151, 158–159. Examples are an 1862 letter from San Francisco to Norway prepaid ninety-two cents and an 1870 letter from Wisconsin via the North German Union prepaid fifteen cents.

6. The letter is not included in this collection. See Nor. ed. II:106.

have news about us from Hellik but I will nevertheless send you a letter as the postage now is cheaper according to the law, so a letter to Norway via Hamburg or Bremen is now twenty-five cents and from Norway twenty-eight cents" (I:136). Even though he admitted that his letter was not "necessary" since his brother had already written, he and his wife wrote many pages. Some years earlier such a long and "unnecessary" letter would not have been sent. From this point on correspondence across the Atlantic was determined more by desire than by economic constraints. So marked was the change in the writing of letters after the international postal treaties and after steamships had shortened the distance between the new and old homelands that an awareness of these factors must enter into our reading of immigrant letters.

The Genre of Immigrant Letters

Is the immigrant letter a textual genre? Can it be characterized or defined? In Norway, letters from immigrants in the United States became known as *Amerikabrev*, that is America letters. The Americans who began the collection of *Amerikabrev* in Norway in the 1920s did not have difficulties in recognizing letters that belonged in such a collection.[7] Indeed, it is always easier to point to examples of a genre than to define it. Those who initiated the collection of America letters in Norway did not speculate on definitions. They simply looked for letters written by Norwegian immigrants.

The pioneering edition of immigrant letters is *Land of Their Choice* by Theodore Blegen in 1955.[8] Many others have followed. The practical definition on which all collections have been based is: *American immigrant letters are letters written (in some cases dictated) by immigrants (and to some extent by their descendants) in the United States and sent to addressees in the country from which the immigrants came.* One thing that distinguishes such letters is the radical transformations in the lives of those who wrote them. The transformations have varied with nationality, time, gender, age, and class, and from individual to individual, but in a shared experience of departure, of migration, and of hopes and fears, there is so much that these writers have in common that it is meaningful to consider the immigrant let-

---

7. See my article "Recovering Memories of the Migration: NAHA and the Making of a Collection of Immigrant Letters in the Norwegian National Archives, 1923–1929." Øyvind T. Gulliksen, ed., *Norwegian-American Essays 2008*, 189–214 (Oslo: NAHA-Norway, 2008).

8. Theodore C. Blegen, *Land of Their Choice: The Immigrants Write Home* (Minneapolis: University of Minnesota Press, 1955). Blegen organized the letters thematically and many are presented in fragments or are heavily edited.

ter as a genre. While a definition of immigrant letters must be brief in order to include all letters we wish to read as immigrant letters, it may nevertheless be useful to look at some characteristics.

BEFORE 1870: LETTERS AS PUBLIC TEXTS

The international postal conventions in the late 1860s had such an effect on letters between the United States and Norway that we may make a distinction between letters before and after 1870. In addition to the high cost of postage there are additional factors to consider.

By the first half of the nineteenth century most Norwegians could read but had little training in writing. Some letters in *From America to Norway* were dictated. For most writers, their first immigrant letter was the first text they had composed. In school they had learned to write but not to express themselves in writing. Their letters are characterized by poor orthography, syntax, and punctuation, but also by the writers' lack of training in description, narrative, and the expression of emotions. Another factor in the frequent awkwardness of immigrant writing is the significant gap between the Norwegian dialect they spoke and the written language they had been taught at school. Indeed, the written language of Norway was then Danish, a legacy of the several centuries' long union between the two countries that came to an end in 1814. It is important that we appreciate that these weaknesses were not individual and that they do not reflect intellectual deficiencies in the writers. We must also appreciate that these letters were not private letters but public texts. They were read aloud, sent around to other farms and copied so that others could read them. Some were also passed on to newspapers and the published text available to us may be edited. Indeed, at a time when newspapers did not have foreign correspondents, immigrant letters were an important source of information about the United States.

While there are a variety of reasons that the early letters may seem both awkward and impersonal, there was one area of life where many immigrants could express themselves quite fluently in writing: their Christian faith. Bibles and religious books were in most homes, and in church they heard their pastor preach in the same formal language they were used to from their reading in school and at home. They had a written language for their faith that they lacked for other areas of life, including their emotions. This does not mean that their pious phrases were superficial clichés, but rather that here the letter writer had a familiar written language.

Since the writers were aware that their letters would be read by people outside the close family circle, they were naturally cautious about what they wrote. One way of getting around this was to write about private matters on an enclosed slip of paper and in such cases the preserved letters may not give a full picture of what was communicated. Another factor that may make a letter seem impersonal is that private matters could be omitted when a letter was copied.

Most letter writers in this period were of the peasant class. Their letters are quite different from the few letters we have by immigrants of a higher social class, such as Olaus Duus, Frithjof Meidell and Elise Wærenskjold.[9] It is not merely in grammar and punctuation that letters by these three are essentially different from most early letters. While the audience of most writers had a personal interest in emigration, Duus, Meidell, and Wærenskjold wrote to people who had no notion of leaving their comfortable home. Moreover, they could describe events and places in an entertaining manner. They could be humorous and give expression to personal emotions. Their letters were both personal and private. Most early letters are not only characterized by poor writing skills but by a cultural reluctance to talk about matters that Duus, Meidell, and Wærenskjold expressed in so natural a manner. It is not only that the early letters were public texts but that they so often seem impersonal: there is as little there about the emotions as about the beauty of a landscape.

THE PROPAGANDA MYTH

It is a myth that immigrant letters, particularly the early ones, gave an overly positive account of life in the New World in order to entice more to follow. Both negative and positive propaganda letters have been preserved, but these are limited to a few written during the first two decades of Norwegian immigration. Copies of these letters were widely distributed, either by hand or published in newspapers, and became quite well known at the time.

The best-known negative letter was sent from Missouri in 1838 by Sjur Haaeim to the Bergen Bishop Jacob Neumann, well known for his opposition to emigration, who had it published in newspapers.[10] Most pro-immigration letters were reactions to the anti-emigration movement in Norway. An example is a letter sent from Chicago in 1838 (1:1) that argues against

---

9. *Frontier Parsonage: The Letters of Olaus Fredrik Duus, Norwegian Pastor in Wisconsin, 1855–1858.* Translated by the Verdandi Study Club of Minneapolis and edited by Theodore C. Blegen (Northfield: NAHA, 1947); *The Lady with the Pen: Elise Wærenskjold in Texas.* Edited by C. A. Clausen (Northfield: NAHA, 1961). Letters by Meidell are in *Fra Amerika til Norge*, as are more letters by Wærenskjold.

10. Haaeim's letter is included in Blegen 1955.

the recently published anti-emigration pamphlet by Neumann.[11] The most influential propaganda letters were written by Gjert Hovland in 1835. When Hovland emigrated in 1831, he knew from circulating letters that he would find a Norwegian settlement on the shores of Lake Erie. A few years later, however, most of the settlers realized that they should move to an area with more available land in order to achieve a concentration of Norwegian settlers sufficiently large to have their own institutions such as church and school. Their scout Cleng Peerson went west to find new land and he returned advising them to go to an area near Fox River in the present La Salle County in Illinois. A majority decided to move and Hovland was given the task of writing letters so that new immigrants would know where to find them. Two letters he wrote in April of 1835 are in Blegen's *Land of Their Choice*.[12] The lay preacher Elling Eielsen was so impressed by a Hovland letter he read while on Karmøy that he made a copy and read it to people on his way home to Voss. Thus Hovland's letter became known over a large area and had a significant impact on emigration. While Sjur Haaeim's letter was welcomed by people in high places and was published in newspapers, Hovland's letters depended on popular support and were spread from hand to eye and from mouth to ear.

Even though Hovland had been asked to write so that more would follow, he is quite sober in his account of his life in the United States and refrains from urging others to come: "I do not advise any to emigrate or not to emigrate, but if any wish to come here then sell all you have and turn it into cash, except for your everyday clothes and bed clothes and bring food that will keep on the voyage." Hovland was happy with his own choice but would not take responsibility for the decisions of others. He may have met an unhappy immigrant who had complained about positive reports about the New World. The knowledge that an immigrant might turn up next spring with a copy of a letter in hand was one reason why writers were so careful about encouraging others, but they also wrote with a sense of responsibility. For several decades Hovland's phrase about not wanting to

---

11. For a reading and discussion of this letter see my article "Religion and Church in Early Immigrant Letters: A Preliminary Investigation" in Todd W. Nichol, ed., *Crossings: Norwegian-American Lutheranism as a Transatlantic Tradition* (Northfield: NAHA, 2003), 35–38.

12. Blegen 1955, 14–20. One of these letters is discussed in Øverland, *The Western Home: A Literary History of Norwegian America* (Northfield: NAHA, 1996), 20–23. Hovland's letters were taken to Norway by Knut Slogvig, who was given the task of recruiting emigrants. He returned in the summer of 1836 with 110 emigrants on the brig *Norden*. The smaller brig *Den norske klippe* followed with fifty-seven. In addition there was a group that went via Gothenburg.

advise any to emigrate or not to emigrate was repeated in America letters, often in such a way that it is evident that the writer is conscious of writing in a tradition. Most writers of immigrant letters had been readers of such letters. A good illustration of a writer's awareness of writing in a genre is in a letter from a young woman in 1854: "It is not easy to tell you about American conditions and be correct. So I will have to sing the old song and not advise anyone to come or not to come." (Nor. ed. I:97)

AFTER 1870: PRIVATE LETTERS

With the radical increase in the rate of emigration after the Civil War it was no longer natural for writers to regard themselves as members of a vanguard with the responsibility of giving information to those who planned to follow. Moreover, there were two other sources of information about the United States: visiting Norwegian Americans and Norwegian-American newspapers, which were quite widely distributed in Norway. After the international postal conventions, letters from immigrants in the United States became more and more like private letters sent to friends and family. Even more than before, they focused on a close circle of family and friends in the New World. In a recent article I considered why so few letters mention Native Americans, but I also observe that there is little mention of other people than those already known to the recipients.[13] It is quite common that writers after 1870 explain that they have no news of interest. Earlier writers may have had economic reasons for not writing at length but they rarely said they did not have anything of interest to write about. When this becomes common it is probably because the writers assumed that their readers would not be interested in people and events they knew nothing about.

THE LETTER SERIES: A SPECIAL GENRE

In some cases we have letters written by one writer or related writers over several years. The three prolific letter writers mentioned earlier have become known to historians through publication by the Norwegian-American Historical Association: Olaus Duus, Gro Svendsen and Elise Wærenskjold.[14] *From America to Norway* has several such series. There are good reasons

---

13. Orm Øverland, "Intruders on Native Ground: Memories of the Land-Taking in Norwegian Immigrant Letters." Udo Hebel, ed., *Transnational American Memories* (Berlin and New York: DeGruyter, 2009).

14. *Frontier Parsonage* (Olaus Duus), *The Lady with the Pen* (Wærenskjold), and *Frontier Mother: The Letters of Gro Svendsen*. Translated and edited by Pauline Farseth and Theodore C. Blegen (Northfield: NAHA, 1950).

to regard letters in series as a special genre, a genre related both to diaries and autobiographies. A series may offer chapters of an immigrant life from the voyage and to an advanced age. Examples in this edition are letters by Elise Wærenskjold from 1846 to 1894, by Svend Houg from 1852 to 1896 and from Hellik Lehovd from 1854 to 1894. There are many others. An example of a series over two generations is by immigrants from Søre Li, a farm in Hedalen in Valdres. It begins with Torgrim Olsen Lee's account of his voyage and his arrival in Wisconsin in 1857 (1:67) and continues with more letters by him and his brother Ole, and then letters by three nephews. These are series that bridge all three volumes. Another example is the letters sent to the farm Gudmundsrud in Aal in Hallingdal, a series begun by Gro Svendsen and continued by two of her immigrant brothers and by two sons and a niece. The historian David A. Gerber has paid particular attention to the Gro Svendsen letters and to letters in series in an important article on immigrant letters.[15] With reference to Gro Svendsen, the American Studies scholar Øyvind Gulliksen has explained why such series may fascinate readers. "Her collected letters function as a chronicle, composed over a few years, composed in moments of writing in which the writer does not know what will happen to her in the future, nor can she edit what she has earlier recorded and set in the past."[16] This is an important genre difference between the immigrant letter series and the diary and the autobiography. A letter series may give a different reading experience as well as more insight into the life of an immigrant than a single letter.

A Canon of Immigrant Letters

There are good reasons to use the terms canon and canonization processes about immigrant letters.[17] The letters that have been preserved and are publicly available in publications or in archives are in effect a canon. The process that has given us this selection may be compared with the process of literary canonization. One important difference between the two is that forgotten literary texts have been public and therefore have a history; they

---

15. David A. Gerber, "The Immigrant Letter between Positivism and Populism: The Uses of Immigrant Personal Correspondence in Twentieth-Century American Scholarship." *Journal of American Ethnic History* 16:4 (1997), 3–34.

16. Øyvind Gulliksen, "Interdisciplinary Approaches in American Immigration Studies: Possibilities and Pitfalls," Todd W. Nichol, ed., *Interpreting the Promise of America: Essays in Honor of Odd Sverre Lovoll* (Northfield: NAHA, 2002), 45.

17. The first to do this was Stephen Fender in his *Sea Changes: British Emigration and American Literature* (Cambridge: Cambridge University Press, 1992), 17–20.

may be rediscovered in libraries and their place in a canon may be reconsidered. Our canon of America letters, however, consists of the letters that have been preserved. The odds against such preservation are of course great even though unknown letters continue to come to light.

The first step in the process of selection that has given us a canon of immigrant letters was the decision to write. An awareness that many, indeed, probably most immigrants did not write letters is central to any use of immigrant letters as a source in immigration history. In 1836, the first year we can speak of a beginning mass emigration, 200 Norwegians went to the United States, either on two brigs from Stavanger or via Gothenburg. If all of them had written two or three letters, this group alone would have produced 600 to 800 letters. The first letter in *From America to Norway* is by Svein Lothe, one of the 200 who emigrated in 1836. I am not aware of any other letter by a member of this group in a public archival collection. Even though it is likely that some letters have been lost, I think it safe to assume that a majority of these 200 and of the many thousands who followed did not write letters. One factor may be that the early period is characterized by family migration and that it was one family member, usually a man, who wrote. But most families were probably not heard from. In the period with high postage rates the availability of post offices would also be a factor limiting the number of letters. The letters themselves are evidence of how difficult it could be for many to set words to paper. Other limiting factors were the often primitive living conditions in the early years, the lack of a private space, hard physical labor as long as there was daylight, and a scarcity of writing material. Some kinds of immigrants were more likely writers than others: successful immigrants, for instance, compared with unsuccessful ones. We may assume that law-abiding immigrants were more likely writers than criminals. And, particularly from the early period, we have more letters by men than by women. When we read immigrant letters we must keep in mind that the writers may not be representative of all immigrants but that they were probably among the most resourceful and successful ones. There is also good reason to assume that those who wrote letters under difficult conditions were strongly motivated to do so.

Even if most did not write, far more letters were written than those that have been preserved. Again, the one letter we have by an 1836 emigrant may serve as an example. The physical letter that Lothe sent from Chicago to Hardanger in 1838 no longer exists. The preserved text is a copy that a law officer in Aga had a clerk make so that he could send it to Bishop Neumann in Bergen because of its subversive polemics with the bishop. This copy eventually found a home in the university library in Bergen. Had not Lothe's letter attracted the attention of an officer of the law it would not have been preserved, even though the letter demonstrates that Lothe was well-informed and had polemical skills. We may say the same of some of the letter writers who were published in newspapers. Such publication may sometimes have been pure chance, but it was more often due to resourceful recipients. A good example may be the published letters by Ellev Bjørnsen from Telemark. His brother, who received these letters, became a prominent local politician and it was on his initiative that some of his brother's letters were published in newspapers.[18] The letters published in newspapers comprise a special sub-genre and since newspapers are often preserved in archives and libraries these were the letters that first caught the attention of historians.

Some early writers became widely known in their own time. Two instances are Cleng Peerson and Gjert Hovland, and some of their letters have been preserved for much the same reason that books by well-known writers tend to be remembered. But what we may call a family culture is a more important reason why some letters have been selected for preservation and thus canonization. Writing seems to have been second nature for Ellev Bjørnsen and he fully mastered the Danish that was then the written language of Norway. He wrote his first preserved letter before the brig *Washington* left Larvik in 1842 (I:4), and he continued to write from Wisconsin. Those of his siblings who emigrated did not write as well as he did, but their letters were also taken care of by their family in Telemark. Some of these letters are now in archives while others are still in the possession of descendants. When Svend Houg emigrated from Aal in 1852 he too began writing before his ship had left Drammen. His last letter to his brother was written in 1896 and he is represented in all three volumes. Such behavior suggests a strong sense of family and his letters were taken care of by later generations. Immigrants from some families felt an obligation to write while the notion of writing was unknown to others. A family culture could be the reason for both writing and preservation.

A family culture is more likely passed on if the family remains in one place for many generations, as on a farm. This would also facilitate preservation. Even though there might not have been a great interest in the letters in every generation, they could be preserved simply because they were at the bottom of a chest. Urban working class families were often on the move and this may

---

18. See *"Det smærter mig meget at nedskrive disse Linjer til Eder." En utvandrerhistorie i brev* (Notodden: Notodden Historielag/Telemark Historielag, 1995), 16–17.

be a reason why we have relatively few letters sent to urban working class recipients. The 1896 letters found hidden in a wall in Grimstad would not have been preserved if they had not been stolen by two unfaithful mail carriers, tempted by the money often enclosed in immigrant letters. Another factor that may have worked against preservation is also suggested by the Grimstad letters: many of them were from people who moved back and forth between Norway and the United States or were sent to people who were about to become immigrants themselves.[19]

Many immigrants returned to their former homelands. Statistics are inconclusive, but the historian Mark Wyman has estimated that 15.4 percent of the immigrants from Denmark, Norway and Sweden returned.[20] Few letters by returned immigrants have been preserved and one reason may be that the letters no longer held interest after the writer had come home. The "failed immigrant" is also underrepresented in our canon.[21] So there is a conglomerate of reasons for the process that has given us a canon of America letters. More letters will surely come to light and be placed in public archives, but our canon will not undergo radical change in the way a literary canon may be changed because of changing aesthetic or political attitudes.

The Ethics of Reading Immigrant Letters

One does not read other people's mail. Letters are private. Even though many may read about the private lives of others in magazines that thrive on scandals, few would argue that such publications have high ethical standards. But other people's mail is published in *From America to Norway*, so we must consider both how and when a private letter may become a publicly available text. Early in the editing process for the Norwegian edition such issues were considered. One reason for setting 1914 as the cut-off date was that the ethics of publishing letters about personal matters would be problematic with more recent letters. We decided that important ethical concerns were adequately addressed by not publishing letters less than a century old. Moreover, as mentioned in the Preface, it is descendants of the

---

19. A selection is included in the third volume.

20. Mark Wyman, "'No Longer Freedom's Land:' Scandinavians Return from America, 1900–1930." Knut Djupedal et alia eds., *Norwegian-American Essays* (Oslo: NAHA-Norway, 1993), 80.

21. One exception is the collection of letters by Hans Andreas Øverland to his father 1887–1893: Before he could return he had to ask his father for money for his ticket. His letters are translated in Solveig Zempel, ed., *In Their Own Words: Letters from Norwegian Immigrants* (Minneapolis: University of Minnesota Press, 1991).

recipients themselves who have placed the letters in public archives and thus made them publicly available.

But such concerns may be legal rather than ethical. Even though there is little risk of being sued for having published these letters, I am still faced with the ethics of reading other people's mail. Authors, politicians, and other public people know that their letters may be read by scholars and published. Except for those early letters that were deliberately written for a wide range of readers, most writers in these three volumes had no notion of becoming published. Letters that were written in late hours in a cold room after a day of heavy work may now be exposed to critical readings. Letters packed with orthographical and grammatical errors will now be evaluated by readers who are used to regarding poor writing as a sign of poor intelligence. It is essential that immigrant letters are read with respect based on the understanding that the authors were exceptional people with the initiative, intelligence and character necessary for their brave and daring venture into the unknown. If we read immigrant letters with respect for those who wrote them I do not believe that we will violate ethical norms.

A METHOD OF READING

To read with respect is to read with understanding. It has been said that "Letters give history a voice."[22] But in order to do so letters must be read so that we hear this voice. It is naive to believe that the letters speak for themselves. They must be read, and to read is to interpret. So when we speak of immigrant letters we speak of our interpretation of these letters. It is the reader who recreates the voice of the writer. A discussion of genre is a discussion of ways of reading, so in a sense much of this introduction is about how we may read immigrant letters: notions of genre govern our reading. Readers must also be conscious of their purpose in reading the letters: what we see in a text is also governed by what we are looking for and how we look; the answers we get are governed by the questions we pose.

In his book on the literature of early British emigration, David Fender insists that immigrant letters are American literature: "...there seems no justification in logic for not reading these documents in the same way as we would the canonical texts."[23] I read the letters both as a historian and as a literary scholar, the two major fields I have been trained in. In a sense I

---

22. Lisa Grunwald and Stephen J. Adler, "Introduction," *Letters of the Century: America 1900–1999* (New York: The Dial Press, 1999), 1.

23. *Sea Changes*, 20.

may ask a historian's questions of the letters and interpret them as a literary scholar. But in practice my two research identities are so integrated that I cannot separate them. Sociologists have developed systematic methods of content analysis of large bodies of texts.[24] My readings, however, are concerned with individual texts as the personal expression of specific writers in as specific a historical context as possible. But in order to achieve a good reading of a single text it is necessary to be familiar with the immigrant letter as a genre. Only by reading many letters may we learn how to read a single letter.

The analysis of an 1875 letter by the young Anne Andresen at the beginning of this introduction illustrates how a reading of a single letter may give insight into the life of an immigrant. At first glance the letter may simply seem naive and awkward, but if this impression dominates our reading, it will be a barrier to further understanding.

All knowledge of the context of a letter contributes to the quality of a reading, but we may often not have any information. In my reading of the letter by Anne Andresen an imagined description of her situation is part of my interpretation. It may be objectionable that my interpretation makes the letter interesting, but I would insist that the aim of all readings must be to express the intentions, emotions, and thoughts the writer strove to express or that she might not even have dared to express. Blegen has claimed that immigrant letters are part of the folk literature of America, a literature of the unlearned.[25] But if this folk literature is to have any significance it must, as all other literature, have a tradition of interpretation and criticism and it must have its "literary history" and its "literary theory." Without creative criticism the letters cannot give history a voice.

Immigrant letters represent one half of a correspondence. In the 1920s the realization among a few Americans that letters were important sources for immigration history gave the impetus to a systematic collection of letters in Norway. Even though we may not have both parts of the correspondence, however, our reading must attempt to create an image of the recipient and of the conversation between the sender and the recipient. Another important element that has not been included in readings of America letters is the pho-

---

24. The earliest scholars to make a systematic use of immigrant letters were the sociologists William I. Thomas and Florian Znaniecki in the five-volume *The Polish Peasant in Europe and America* (1918–1920), and their work was important for the development of content analysis as a scholarly method. See David A. Gerber, "The Immigrant Letter between Positivism and Populism."

25. Theodore C. Blegen, "The Literature of the Unlettered," *Grass Roots History* (Minneapolis: University of Minnesota Press, 1947), 26–27.

tographs that were so often enclosed after 1870. Very many letters refer to photographs and without them our reading misses an important dimension of what was communicated. In her excellent book on Norwegian-American photographers and their images, Sigrid Lien has helped us see and understand this understudied aspect of America letters.[26]

The Limited Value of Immigrant Letters as Historical Sources

The Norwegian-American Historical Association was a product of the increased interest among some Norwegian Americans in their history at the time of the 1925 centennial. Its primary task was to collect and preserve sources for this history and it was NAHA that took the initiative to collect America letters in Norway.[27] It did not take long for Theodore Blegen to recognize their inherent value. In his 1947 introduction to the letters of Olaus Duus he writes, "The chief interest of the Duus letters...is to be found in their vivid pictures of life in his own home—of Norwegian-American domestic life, particularly child life, on the midwestern frontier."[28] He did not merely recommend these letters as sources for a historian, but as texts with their own value for readers. Blegen's view of America letters is more fully expressed three years later in his introduction to Gro Svendsen's letters. After a brief outline of her life he adds, "Such, in outline, is the story that comes out of the letters of Gro Svendsen, but its spirit and meaning must be sought by the reader in the letters themselves, with all their detail and unconscious revelation of character."[29] Both Duus and Svendsen wrote letters that stand on their own literary merit, making them different from many of the writers in *From America to Norway*. But the letters by Olaus Duus and Gro Svendsen as well as the short and rather naive letter by Anne Andresen demand a good reader, whether the intention of the reader may be to use them as historical sources or to read them for their own value. Indeed, if the letters are not first read for their own sake and for all they are worth and with all the skills at our disposal, they will not be of optimal use as historical sources.

---

26. Sigrid Lien, *Lengselens bilder: Fotografiet i norsk utvandringshistorie* (Oslo: Spartacus forlag, 2009).

27. See Øverland "Recovering Memories of the Migration."

28. *Frontier Parsonage*, vi.

29. *Frontier Mother*, xiv.

What value, then, may immigrant letters have as historical sources? I think their value is somewhat limited. There may be no better source for an individual's immigration experience than her letters, and in a history that focuses on the individual experience, letters may indeed be the best sources. For the historian letters may perhaps give some information that is not available in other sources, but for the most part the limited role of letters may be to give life and color to an account heavy with facts and figures. I have already quoted a statement by the editors of *Letters of the Century*, "Letters give history a voice," and they explain their statement with the observation that the difference between having factual knowledge of an historical event and reading a letter by someone who experienced the event is "like the difference between knowing the words of a song and hearing it sung."[30] In an article where I used the letters of two generations of immigrants from the farm Søre Li in Hedalen in Sør-Aurdal for a discussion of chain migration I concluded:

> From one point of view, then, these letters are of a somewhat limited use to the historian. There is so much that they cannot tell us and that can only be known through the use of quite different methods and quite different sources. That only one in each of the two generations followed in this article stayed in Hedalen is one of the more obvious pieces of information revealed by these letters, but that information is available from other sources and, moreover, says nothing about the effect of mass migration on the parish as a whole. At the other end of the chain, in Dane County, the letters alone are not a reliable source for the lives of immigrants in the second half of the nineteenth century. Census reports, records of land ownership, of births and deaths and of taxes, church records, churchyards, local newspapers—all and more must be studied for anything approximating a full picture. If the letters are left out, however, something essential will be missing from the story of the immigration. What will be left out is all that was most important for the people involved: the way in which they themselves experienced the momentous act of migration.[31]

So when I claim that immigrant letters have a limited value as historical sources, this is to make clear that they, like other sources, cannot stand

---

30. Grunwald and Adler, 1.

31. Orm Øverland, "Letters as Links in the Chain of Migration from Hedalen, Norway to Dane County, Wisconsin, 1857-1890," Todd W. Nichol, ed., *Interpreting the Promise of America: Essays in Honor of Odd Sverre Lovoll* (Northfield, Minnesota: Norwegian-American Historical Association, 2002), 98.

alone. If used critically, immigrant letters are indeed invaluable for a historian who wishes to understand how the immigrants themselves experienced their migration.

In this introduction I have focused more on reading letters than on using them. For all texts, for poetry, or for immigrant letters, questions of reading must come before questions of use. The better we develop our ability to read letters, the better we will be able to use them. After many years in a close relationship with immigrant letters, I still have a lot to learn. Few letters have received so much attention as the letters Gro Svendsen sent to her family in Aal. David Gerber concludes his valuable article on immigrant letters with reflection on Gro Svendsen and how her letters still demand new readings: "Her letters remain to be analyzed to understand the changes in her that made her successful in such pioneering ventures in negotiating the modern world."[32] As literary texts yield new insights with new readings, immigrant letters are texts that readers with varying interests and from different scholarly traditions may read with new insights and new interpretations. In his introduction to *Saa nær hverandre,* a book that presents what may be described as a family chronicle in letters, Øyvind Gulliksen has characterized his relationship to America letters in a way that deserves to be repeated in translation:

> America letters are primarily historical documents, but they offer us a wisdom born of experience that we may still benefit from. The more I study such letters, the more I realize the enormous consequences of our choices—for our own lives and for those who surround us. The letters also make me reflect on the frailty of life, on how rarely it proceeds according to plan and how much it depends on accidental circumstance. To read these letters is to pause for some minutes to take in words from the dead. And even though they may have experienced life as full of vicissitudes, they nevertheless also experienced a familiar and appreciated structure in their lives based on Bible and hymnbook, the shared texts of many generations.[33]

May his wise words serve as a fitting conclusion to my introduction.

---

32. Gerber, 27.

33. Gulliksen, *Saa nær hverandre,* 19.

LETTERS

1838 — LETTER 1:1

FROM: Svein Knudsen Lothe, *Chicago, Illinois, 10 July 1838*
TO: Sjur Knudsen Aga, *Ullensvang, Hordaland*

Dear brother, Sjur Knudsen Aga,

Time permits that I report to you on my situation. I'm now in good health, but just after my last letter I got sick and was in bed for several weeks and a doctor came every day for three weeks. The doctor said that it would be the death of me, but I recovered. My wife couldn't get out of bed for six weeks after her fever. It wasn't so good for us according to the ways of this world but I hope and believe that it will be to our best. Praise and thanks to God who has upheld me so long that I could learn to thank Him for it. I have a great desire to visit you but an even greater desire to see you here in my home in Chicago. I hope to see you and your wife and children here. All land is fertile on the prairies of Illinois. But all places are not equally good. In some places there is too much water. The land is free for anyone to take and then pay one dollar an acre when it comes on the market. This won't be until three to ten years after you have taken the land. There is also government land that you may pay for in cash. And there are wealthy buyers who buy much land and then sell it to others for five, ten and fifteen dollars an acre. Come to me my brother! Your children will thank you for it.

My friendly regards to all my siblings! Tell Ole Samsonsen Bleie and Willich Olsen Bleie that I would like to see them; special greetings to Johannes Hovland, Knud Olsen Børven, and his brother Ole Olsen Espe. You must give our regards to my wife's brother Anders, her sister Gunnild and her mother Durta. Tell her that my wife is in good health and would be glad to have Anders with us. You must believe we live well. I've heard that there is a rumor that it isn't good here. That is true; I don't believe it is good here on earth: could I not look forward to death, then it wouldn't be good. I thank our God and father who gave me the desire to come here. You can live well here and make a good living.

I've already read Neumann's thoughtful little book. But it is a book that many praise, few read, and no one understands. He wrote: where is your pastor? But I ask: where is his [illegible]? I believe he speaks of that which he is ignorant. Here are good schools where you don't pay a cent, and his school where you have to pay money is not better. But I know his position; he represents Christ and should speak well and tend to people's souls. I also believe he is a clever bishop—for the fishing of money I believe he has an eye on each finger. Should his peasant slaves leave him, then he would himself acquire a peasant's hands and back in order to make money. Here in America all men work. I worked for a pastor whose name was Uchalemo and he worked just as hard as I did. I know him and he knows me; he loves me and I love him, and that is our duty.

Every day I live as well as a wealthy man does in Norway. I would compare the bishop's intelligence to that of a flea. The flea will bite according to its understanding; and he speaks according to his understanding; so they are alike. That is all I have to say on this matter. He who lay in the manger in the stall did not work for money. He traveled from one place to the other to find those who desired to be made pure. But He didn't take on the authority of the beast in Revelation 13. You speak of the three cold valleys in North Norway, but that is far too little compared to the twenty-four United States of the good North America; all Norway is too small compared to any place in America.

Neumann has written that Troy sank. That is a lie. I've passed this city and seen it. The bishop has never seen so beautiful a city in all his days, nor do I believe he has ever seen it with his own eyes. He does right in warning his brothers, because the one road is long and dangerous. But some who don't go further than to the church die, and some die at home; but I believe it is the same how I die if I die with trust in God, whether I die at home and am buried in the churchyard with ringing bells or die at sea. Take on the shield of faith and the helmet of salvation, which is the word of God; it is the armor of God that leads forward to life.

I'll conclude with loving regards to all who inquire about me. I have much to tell but don't have the time. Farewell! Beware of blind guides; woe to you who whitewash for the eye. Friendly regards from your friend and brother,

SVEND KNUDSEN

. —— .

> SKL and Sjur Jørgensen Haaeim were among the eleven who emigrated from Ullensvang in 1836, influenced by a letter by Gjert Hovland (Blegen 1955). This letter was copied by the local sheriff, who evi-

dently found it subversive, and sent it to Bishop Neumann in Bergen. The letter responds to a series of rhetorical questions in Neumann's anti-emigration pamphlet (Neumann 1837), one of which warns that emigrants are depriving themselves of pastoral care. Neumann recommended settlement in Alta in the far North as an alternative to emigration, and asked his readers to reflect on how it would be to die in a strange country: "... when you are far away from all that has been dear to you, who shall close your eyes in the last hour of life? A stranger's hand! And who shall weep at your grave? Perhaps—no one!" (Neumann, 108–109). When Lothe writes that land is free, he is referring to the Preemption Act of 1830 that gave squatters on public land the right to purchase up to 160 acres at $1.25 an acre when the land was put on the market. Some phrases at the end of the letter are from Ephesians 6:10–16 and Matthew 23:25–26. NE 1:1

1841 — LETTER 1:2

FROM: Brynjulv Lekve, *Wyota, Wisconsin, 8 December 1841*
TO: Arne Brynjulvsen Lekve, *Ulvik, Hordaland*

Beloved unforgettable parents, siblings, friends and relatives!

For two months I've been waiting for letters from you. Immigrants have arrived, but since they were from East Norway I could hardly expect them to have letters for us, especially as they told us that emigrants would be leaving Bergen in the company of a Swede. We hoped they would bring letters, but no letter has arrived. We hope you have the letter we sent you last January, but as I cannot be sure I'll repeat some of the information. Your letter of March 1840 came to us January 20 and there we learned that many things have changed. Many families have been diminished: however, those that concern us were growing, so what has happened later can only be imagined. As for us, we've enjoyed good health and been content except that Anders, Johannes, and I had the bilious fever in the fall of 1839. The man we've worked for is the owner of a blast furnace and a lead mine. Since March, after we had completed our work on 830 cords of wood for seventy-five cents a cord, we have had twenty dollars a month and board.

I see that such unpredictable turncoats as Sjur Jørgensen have made you anxious. You have no reason to worry; your concern should be for yourselves and your children. I haven't heard of anyone but Sjur who wants to return to Norway. This was his purpose when he left Chicago last spring and as far as I know there were few who sent letters with him because they feared they wouldn't be delivered as they all spoke against him. Even his wife disagreed with his unwise decision. The reason for his dissatisfaction with America was probably all the illness; he lived in a very unhealthy place. There are no infectious diseases here but the climate has an effect on people who live near swampy places, stagnant water and slow flowing rivers as in Illinois, where the land is flat and swampy. Here in Wisconsin the land is high and dry and there is running water everywhere and diseases are rare. It would of course be different if you settled near slow rivers or sloughs. Even Americans get ill. So you have to be careful. If you break down your constitution you can ruin your health in the world's healthiest climate. Many have suffered this fate in Wisconsin.

I wouldn't discourage anyone from coming to America, but rather encourage them—in particular young people who don't have a steady income in Norway, but not those who are used to sitting by the stove. Those who are willing to work and have enough saved up to pay the travel costs should come as soon as possible. In a short time you can make enough money to buy a piece of land that will provide for anyone who will work. Good craftsmen can earn money. Servant girls are particularly wanted; when Norwegians land in Chicago or Milwaukee, people ask for *"Norwegian Girls,"* pronounced *Norvigjen Gørls*. Norwegians are generally respected. For old people it is less suited; in particular it is difficult for them to learn the language, and many never do, and they are reluctant to give up their old ways and traditions, so I think it is better for them to stay home. Of course, if a father and mother bring their entire family, then it may work, but they should not come to seek their future happiness in America.

On this piece of paper I'll briefly give as precise information as possible since I don't have the space to explain everything.
1. There is little reason to fear the voyage across the Atlantic if you have a good ship and a reliable captain. Some will be seasick but this is not to be feared; it isn't fatal.

2. Concerning the character and division of the country: a) county b) township that is six square miles c) section one mile; there are thirty-six sections in a township. A section is 640 acres and is divided in this manner. [*Here, between letters indicating west and east, is inserted a small sketch with two rows of four squares.*] All divisions are according to the compass. The situation here is not as in Illinois, Indiana, and Missouri, where the land has been claimed. Many of the Americans who first settled here claimed the best land, in particular forest land. The newcomers were fools to buy their rights; when the land came on the market they still had to pay the government price, 125 cents per acre. But people are now better informed and not so easily fooled and they prefer to come to this more northern state that is quite similar to our cold Norway, but more fertile. All land here has been on the market. If you select a piece of land that hasn't been bought and you know the number of the township and section and the quarter-, eighth- and sixteenth-section, which is the smallest you can buy from the government, you can go to a land office and buy it at the set price. In the western part of the state there are lead mines almost everywhere and also copper. Land where minerals have been found may not yet be bought, but if minerals are discovered after you have bought it, the rights are yours.

3. Wages differ: for a blacksmith from twenty to forty dollars, a carpenter about the same, for farm labor ten to twenty dollars a month. Those who mine for lead have thirty to forty a month. For seamen, captains, who don't need to know navigation, from thirty to fifty dollars; a common deck hand sixteen to twenty. Servant girls earn from four to twelve dollars a month. The situation for women is better than in Norway; they enjoy more respect and they only work indoors, never in the fields. Clothes are cheaper here compared to income; you can buy a set of clothes of good cloth for thirty dollars.

4. The main inconvenience for the immigrant is ignorance of the language and of customs and manners, but such stumbling blocks are fewer now that Norwegians have settled almost everywhere in this state and can give advice to their countrymen.

5. What should be brought from home: provisions according to Rønning's advice—bedding, feather, and down pillows, new blankets and sheets, not so many bedcovers since these are generally too small, but rather homespun cloth. Men's clothing according to town fashion of short coats and jackets, as used here. You mustn't bring women's clothes as used back home, but thin woolen cloth is useful; thick clothes of homespun are too warm and heavy for the summer and may also make employment difficult. No American will hire a woman in such clothes. Moreover, thin and light

clothes cost less than your thick and heavy clothes and are according to the fashion here. Don't interpret this to mean that we bachelors want to entice Norwegian girls to come to us. No! But this is because several of my friends have asked me to inform them about everything, something I'm not quite up to. But what is written here is true.

Here is a page from *Bergens Stiftstidende* from 1840 with a letter from Sjur Jørgensen Haaeim, placed there by Bishop Neumann. He complains about the poor situation of the Norwegians here in America. I had heard these rumors before seeing Sjur's letter and I must repudiate some of his points.

The author says: "When we came to what should be called their homestead we saw some structures that looked like rough log cabins." This is, of course, true but one cannot see heaven and earth between the walls when they are completed; but the settlers cannot build great homes at first. I think it is more practical to live in a simple cabin with a surplus of food than in fully furnished homes with empty cupboards.

"Then we became aware of something else: a hoard of half-naked children and parents in torn rags." I have not yet seen such a sight: all are well fed and clothed.

"Then there was a disease among the Norwegian people so that it was a pitiful sight." This is true. Diseases ravaged in 1838 and '39, but not only among the Norwegians; the Americans were also afflicted. This was mainly along the canal and in swampy areas in Illinois, Indiana, Michigan, and Missouri, where the land is lower and disease is more common.

"Some emigrated from Norway on account of their hatred of the clergy and others in authority, others on account of hatred of their neighbors, and others because of unvirtuous behavior, and when all of this comes together in one neighborhood you can easily imagine what goes on in these American forests." A beautiful characterization! I do not believe it was because of hatred or misdeeds, but in order to achieve greater freedom and less servitude. Here there is no more respect for people in authority than for any honest man; both servant and master may seek their future happiness and welfare here.

The author continues: "There is no church within a hundred miles." Nor is this true; the small towns are not far apart and they have churches. Moreover there are good schools for those who wish to attend; there are two or three school houses in each township and these also serve as meeting houses where church services or devotions are held almost every Sunday. Of course, not all can understand much of what is said, but they learn little by little.

He begs the Bishop to "teach his brothers in Christ not to think of making the journey here." And the Bishop would have done many a better service had he kept his pastoral letter to himself. Mr. Neumann says there are families here who have written asking their friends and acquaintances to come but that this was only for their own benefit in order to acquire servants at a lower price than are available here. Some rose to the bait and whole shiploads from East and West Norway made the journey across the Atlantic and filled the holes made by the yellow fever and other diseases among the Norwegians on the American prairies. This gives us good reason to believe that the bishop is ignorant or that it is in his own interest to scare people with a yellow fever that doesn't exist in these northern states. Such a man should have better knowledge of geography.

Last summer we were visited by a Swede from Stockholm named Johan Gustav Smidt. He said he'd been a pastor at the Royal Court and he has offered to be a teacher among us. He says he left his position because he disagreed with some of the church practices, but we don't know whether he is an honest man or a cheat. I have, however, found him learned. I would like you to investigate whether he is the man he claims to be or not. If you write to *Morgenbladet* and give them his name and his story, they could provide information. He speaks a good Norwegian. I've heard him preach twice and I rather liked his sermon. We haven't committed ourselves because some from East Norway have applied to Peter Valeur, a theological candidate, who has decided to come but hasn't yet arrived. Nor has he written. We wish to have a teacher who can maintain and spread the word of God, so we have appointed the above mentioned for this year awaiting further information. We would prefer Valeur, but if he doesn't come nothing will be decided until we have reliable information about Smidt. I hope you'll be able to find out more about him and send this information to me.

I'm glad to learn about progress in my homeland. I see in your letter that the herring fisheries, one of the country's main products, continue. Recent immigrants have told me that the silver mine gives a good profit and there is no lack of silver. This shows that the government is in good shape. Nevertheless, I have no wish to be a citizen of Norway. I see that you wish for my return and it is possible I may make a brief visit so I may once more see you and my loved ones if we live to 1843. I hope these lines will lighten your sorrowful hearts in your concern for your beloved son. Father! Be satisfied in your calling. Should you feel confronted by adversities, remember that our Savior's life was full of adversities that we his sinful followers don't have the strength to bear. God give you strength in your old age so you can continue in your calling. And God help me to live according to your teaching and example so we may hope for our reward on the other side if we have wandered in accordance with God's words and commandments.

There is much more to write about that would be of interest, but I don't have space and must limit myself to what is necessary. In a letter of August 25, Ingeborg Bitøen asks me to give her regards to relatives and friends and say that she and her children are happy and in good health. Lars Torblaa is at Fox River in Illinois and is doing well. All our countrymen are, to my knowledge, also well. Anders and Johannes have left their work here; Johannes is with a shoemaker in Galena, a small town thirty-five miles from here and Anders has steady work near here. When I said I was leaving my employer gave me a raise of five dollars a month so I now earn twenty-five dollars. I work as a carpenter and will stay here this winter. Then I'll make wagons. A master smith, Knud Knudsen from Drammen, works for the same man for forty dollars and has his own board. Food is cheap. Flour is one dollar and twenty-five cents a bushel. Pork is one and a half to two cents a pound, butter twelve to eighteen, and other provisions accordingly. I will conclude my insufficient and poorly organized letter with brotherly and friendly regards to parents, siblings and friends from your faithful

B. LEQVE

P.S. It won't be necessary to make inquiries concerning the claimed pastor; I've thought about it and we may get better information from the Swedish and Norwegian Consul or you could try to do it quietly without advertising in the newspapers. Ask Miss C. Kølle whether she knows of a Major Smith who used to be at the Royal Palace.

I've forgotten to give information to craftsmen about tools. It isn't useful to bring tools since much better tools may be had here almost as cheaply as at home. American products are superior to those of all other nations except for copper pots; medium-sized ones are useful for farmers. Don't bring heavy chests, but light and simple ones, since transportation will cost more than they are worth. But bring books by good authors on religion and history in English and Norwegian and an English grammar, and, if possible, I would like C. Bastholm's book of homilies.

Since there is no space for my address I will write it here on a separate piece of paper as follows: *Brynnild Laque, Wyota, Iowa County Territory of Wisconcin in North Amerikan*. This is my address in English and I have been ensured that it will reach me if it is given to a post office in Norway. Write to me about all things. I'm not concerned about the price of postage even if you should write two sheets. If convenient, ask Ole Ljone to write; also Paal Torblaa. Greetings to the Misses Kølle; Sjur and Herborg Lekve; mother's sister and her husband; father's brother; father's sister and her husband; Peder and Ole Romestvedt; Jens Holmen; other friends; and those who speak of me. Finally, greetings to all at Wiig from us three,

B. LEQVE, ANDERS, AND JOHANNES OMMUNDSEN VIK

Those who plan to come shouldn't bring old coins, but *speciedaler*; there are additional charges for other currencies. Norwegian silver is as good as Spanish or English.

· ——— ·

> The January letter that BL refers to is in Blegen (1955). This one refutes the negative views on immigration by Sjur Jørgensen Haaeim, who after trying life in Missouri sent a letter from Illinois on April 22, 1839, to Bishop Jacob Neumann. The bishop published Haaeim's letter in *Bergens Stiftstidende* [*Bergen Diocese Times*], *Tiden* [*The Times*, Drammen], and other Norwegian newspapers (Blegen 1955, 48–55). Lars Torblaa was from Ulvik. He later moved to Winneshiek County, Iowa, and in 1857 was among the first settlers in Clay County, S. Dak. (Ulvestad 1913, 972). BL refers to Ole Rynning's book of advice to emigrants (Rynning 1838). The canal is the Illinois and Michigan Canal that connected Lake Michigan and the Chicago River with the Illinois River just below Ottawa and was completed in 1848. There was reason to doubt the credentials of Johan Gustaf Smidt. He worked for a while in Koshkonong, Wisc., where he was exposed by Pastor J. W. C. Dietrichson in 1844. He then went on to Chicago, where he pretended to be both a clergyman and a physician (Holand 1908, 102–105). *Morgenbladet* [The Morning Paper] was a conservative newspaper in the capital. On Peter Valeur see Blegen (1931, 120–122). Knud Knudsen's account of his journey to the United States was published in Drammen in 1840. Catharine Hermine Kølle (1788–1859) was the daughter of a vicar in Ulvik in Hardanger who traveled on foot over much of Europe painting landscapes in a primitive style. Christian Bastholm (1740–1819) was the author of a popular book of devotion (1783). The farm name Wiig is now written Vik. NE I:2

· ——— ·

1842 — LETTER 1:3

FROM: Hans E. Møller, *Porsgrunn, Telemark, 29 March 1842*
TO: Halvor Bjørnsen Tonga, *Heddal, Notodden, Telemark*

To Halvor Bjørnsen Tunga, Hitterdal

   As promised, I am writing you these lines to inform you that I am willing to receive some passengers to New York on my brig *Washington* that is expected to be ready to sail from Larvik in May. I expect there will be room for forty or perhaps even more passengers. As soon as the ship has come home and I have had an opportunity to speak with the captain I will send you more complete information. I will, however, repeat what I have said earlier, that I in no way seek and even less urge anyone to emigrate, and I will advise all to consider such an important step very carefully before making a final decision. Having considered the issue more carefully, I have decided that it would not be right to refuse taking passengers, in part because I have no right to oppose the free will of reasonable people, and in part because I have no way of knowing whether emigrants may become more satisfied in America than here. But I will advise all to consider the issue very carefully and I will add that emigrants without some cash or with only their empty hands would surely meet with many difficulties. Sincerely,

HANS E. MØLLER

   Although this is not an immigrant letter, it illustrates the complications of trans-Atlantic travel before emigration became common and ships advertised passage on a regular basis. The brig *Washington* left Porsgrunn on June 3 and arrived in New York on August 1 with sixty-two passengers, among them Ellev Bjørnsen, age twenty-seven, and his sister Anlaug, age twenty-three. »1:4 NE 1:3

1842 — LETTER 1:4

FROM: Ellev Bjørnsen, *Larvik, Vestfold, 29 May 1842*
TO: Tora Hansdatter Gjestrud, *Heddal, Notodden, Telemark*

To Thora Hansdatter Gjestrud,

As I have some time I must write you some lines and thank you so much for your well-considered letter. As the old adage goes: the one gives the other a hand! So I hope that you will accept a small but well-intentioned gift! As for my new situation, you will understand that I cannot say anything certain about the outcome, but I am happy in the hope that it will be an improvement. I will have to leave all in the hands of the Almighty.

When I arrive at my destination with the help of God I will give you a precise account, and if you should see it in your interest to come after me I will do all I can to make this possible. I send greetings from Anlaug. She has courage and until now all has gone well. I suppose I could have more to say but as there is little time I will conclude with a heartfelt farewell to family and friends. If my mother should grieve for us I must ask you to give her comfort every time you speak with her. In haste,

ELLEV BJØRNSEN TANGEN

Although the departure was planned the day he wrote, the ship was delayed a few days. «1:3 »1:9 NE I:4

1843 — LETTER 1:5

FROM: An unknown immigrant, *Koshkonong, Wisconsin, probably 1843*
To: Knud Ellingsen Liane, *Holt, Tvedestrand, Aust-Agder*

My dear friend Knud Ellingsen Liane,

At the time we took our farewell it was said I should write, but there was no mention of postage. People here write and their letters are paid on arrival, so I don't know whether it is possible to pay for it here. This letter is not written for you alone but for all who wish to see it, so I think all who wish to read the letter should share in its cost. Jørgen Anderson offered to pay me half a *speciedaler* if I would promise him or his brothers information by letter as soon as possible. I refused his money and I don't remember the cost of the letter. Hans Liane and the tailor Huus in Arendal have also asked for information. Where I have been there seems to be a lack of craftsmen; but America is so large that if you have money to go where there is employment, living here is not expensive. For those who are young and who are used to all kinds of work, conditions are excellent.

The Monday after I arrived there was a Norwegian who wanted me for haying. He came to America four years ago and had one hundred dollars that he used to buy land; he was married and his wife came with him. They both went to Chicago in Illinois for two years in order to make money to buy cattle. He has nine cows. He can sell half his wheat as well as corn and potatoes. He has cultivated fourteen acres; each acre costs ten shillings and is measured with a rod that is 16½ feet: 20 times 8 rods. You cannot buy less than forty acres from the government. But it is possible to claim land for one year without money. When I heard he had been in Chicago I asked whether he knew someone called Sjur Jørgensen. When he came from Norway he brought a letter and […] was forced to lie. In the fall, before he returned to Norway, he sold his land and moved to Chicago where he stayed the whole winter and would not do any work so it was impossible for him to support himself. There is hardly a merchant here who does not work.

The man I now work for came here one year ago with hardly any money.

He bought land for one hundred dollars four years ago. One year later he married a Norwegian widow with two children and he now has 180 acres; seventeen are cultivated. He can sell half his wheat. They have four children and a farmhand. Fertilizer is not used in Wisconsin. A man here came from Norway four years ago. He didn't have money to go further than to a city named Rochester with his wife and five children. He was paid one dollar a day and his oldest child six shillings in the summer—less in the winter. When he had been there one year he had 200 dollars. Then they got sick and had to pay fifty dollars to get to Chicago where he bought land with the 100 dollars he had left, and then they worked some more to get money for cattle and food. This year he sold what he had in Chicago for 425 dollars and bought 200 acres and in two years I am sure he can have double the harvest of the man he bought it from for less labor. In Chicago the forest is so large and dense that it is not possible to have fields without clearing the forest. But there are places three to four miles away with scarcely a tree.

I consider these prairies to be as difficult as Norway. There is a disease they call the ague. It makes you shiver and is contagious and deadly if it doesn't change to a different fever. In Chicago many have been sick and some have died; here too there has been some illness; one woman and a child have died, but the others in this settlement are well. There are not such dangerous animals as they said in Norway and probably not as many kinds as in Norway. In Ole Rynning's account you may read more about this […] as they have been here.

A day laborer earns half a dollar but a bachelor here earned one dollar for haying last summer; you may contract for one and a half dollars. A bushel of wheat costs half a dollar. A barrel of salt about the size of a mackerel barrel is from twelve to sixteen shillings, potatoes from one to three shillings a bushel, corn from two shillings to half a dollar for the same, turnips from eight to ten cents, meat from two to four cents a pound, pork from two to six cents a pound, tallow one shilling a pound, butter from eight cents to one shilling when I arrived, and now from fifteen cents to twelve shillings. The prices vary because there are so many recent arrivals in some places. After all the people and misery I witnessed in Milwaukee it is now a puzzle where they have all gone and how they have been fed. There is little hunger to be heard of. A horse from fifty to one hundred dollars, a couple of oxen forty to fifty-five, a cow from eight to fifteen, sheep from one and a half to two dollars, pigs from one and a half to eight dollars; some wares bought by the bushel are sometimes expensive, sometimes cheap, so they may be considered about as in Norway.

I will not advise for or against coming here, but should any decide to come I would first of all warn you against being cheated by scandalous Norwegian skippers or ship owners. I would advise against going by Havre if you have more money than for the passage. I heard from those who had gone that way that people are ready to cheat you there too, and then it is much worse. A man left home with 900 *speciedaler*. When he came to Milwaukee he had only fifty that his wife had hidden from him. I suppose the man was a drinker as well as overly generous, but there are many like him. [...] I would advise those without family and who plan to buy land on arrival to take work along the canal. I would also advise all not to bring more heavy things than are necessary. Norwegian knives and scythes are not used here.

Should anyone wish to write, then write to Koshkonong, Wisconsin, North America. Regards to all. I am so well off that if I had been the owner of the best farm in Norway and could sell it at its value, I would not have stayed in Norway. Please spread this letter well. Should anyone bring a copy here I will prove every word in it. One man in our company cursed every letter he had seen from America when he was in Norway. [*The rest of the letter, including the signature, has been lost.*]

. —— .

> The Norwegian text of this letter is according to a contemporary copy. The convoluted syntax and poor punctuation at times make the text difficult to understand. This may be in part because the copyist had problems interpreting the letter. The letter illustrates the high cost of postage and the way news about Norwegian settlements was spread in Norway. Along with this copy is a brief fragment that explains the value of American money, that there are eight shillings in a dollar etc. NE 1:5

. —— .

1845 — LETTER 1:6

FROM: Gaute Ingebretsen Gunleiksrud, *Dunkirk, Wisconsin, 9 May 1845*
To: Ingebret Torsteinsen and Birgit Gunleiksrud, *Tinn, Telemark*

Dear Father,

On this occasion I must write you a few lines to let you know our situation in America. When we came to Havre de Gras in France we negotiated with an American captain for our ocean voyage and paid nine and a half dollars per person. We left on June 24 and crossed the large ocean in thirty-one days. Our voyage was very fortunate since we had no illness. As soon as we came to New York my wife became ill and then we experienced what we had been protected from. From New York we had to pay seven and a half dollars per person and seven dollars for our baggage. My wife's illness soon changed to a common fever called bilious fever. We struggled to get to our destination, Muskego, where we were received by Helge Grimsrud. But that place was too disease-ridden and poor and unsuitable as a permanent home. I was told about another place called Koshkonong Prairie in Dane County, about sixty miles further west, where some Norwegians had settled. I went there to look around and bought 160 acres. When I returned to my wife I too became ill. Soon Helge and his entire family were sick, and we were eight people, all sick, in the same house so not one could help the others. Our neighbors were also sick so no one was able to help us. On December 6 we moved from this house of illness to Gunder Gautesen Midtbøen and stayed there till the end of March, when we began to get better. And then we moved to the land I had bought. There I built a simple house and I've fenced thirty acres and plowed eight. I've bought six cows and a couple of oxen for forty dollars, a wagon for twenty-three dollars, and a plow for fifteen. While the first year was difficult and full of adversity, things have gone well later. At present we are satisfied, but some are not.

The land is fertile and has a pleasant appearance. The only bad thing about America is all the sects and parties that are created daily. There is much more opportunity for reading than in Norway, so he who wishes to hold on to the Christian faith of his childhood will have to confront both outer and inner enemies. Several have been re-baptized and some have refused to baptize their children. There are also terrible errors concerning Holy Communion. This has been accepted by lay people and some believe that there is no purpose in denouncing this practice. But we now have a pastor from our dear homeland, and it seems that most of us will be taken care of in spiritual matters. This pastor has worked tirelessly for the true welfare of man. He has had two churches built and furnished so we now have church services as in Norway.

Our friendly regards go first to our parents and siblings, and we beg you to write us as soon as possible and let us know whether there have been any changes and also whether there are some who have thought of coming here. We cannot give you any advice on such a decision until we have heard from you. Should a war break out in Norway, I would advise my brothers to leave for America immediately. Helge Sigurdsen Grimsrud lives next to us here on the prairie and has had much adversity but is now more satisfied. He'll soon write you about his situation. In March he had a son named Ole. He and his family are healthy, have built a house and fenced fifteen acres. We had a baby boy April 22. He hasn't yet been baptized, but we'll name him Ingebret. We don't have more to report now. All relatives, my parents, sisters and brother, grandfather, my wife's father, and my uncles and aunts are included in my friendliest regards. I wish all of them the best. Since we have little hope of seeing each other again in this world, it is all the more important for us to live in such a way that we all in joy may be embraced by God. And may God our father in heaven give us his merciful blessing for the sake of Jesus.

GAUTE INGEBRETSEN

Half of the last page is missing. GIG and his wife Kari Sigurdsdatter were in a group of emigrants from Tinn in 1843. The letter was probably penned by another member of their group, Jon Ingebretsen Hvalen, a former teacher. Koshkonong, Wisc., was one of the main areas of early Norwegian settlement. Gunleiksrud's account of the first years in Koshkonong is in Clausen (1982, 126–127). Muskego, southwest of Milwaukee, was one of the first Norwegian settlements in Wisconsin, founded by the group of immigrants from Telemark led by John Nilsen Luraas in 1839. It soon got the reputation of being an unhealthy place because of several malaria epidemics. The pastor at Koshkonong was J. W. C. Dietrichson. »1:29 NE III:TI

1845 — LETTER 1:7

FROM: Ole Eriksen Sando, Nils Tollefsen Roe and others
Rock Prairie, Wisconsin, 26 August 1845
To: Ole Olsen Skrinde, *Aal, Buskerud*

Our dear parents, siblings, relatives, and friends,

As we know that you're anxious to learn whether we have come to our destination, I'll tell you about our journey to America and up to Wisconsin. As I wrote in a letter dated May 18, we went from Drammen at six in the evening and sailed with a pleasant wind into the North Sea. In the evening of the twenty-first, we bid farewell to our fatherland Norway and sailed northwest. Then almost all the passengers got seasick with constant vomiting and a headache. Barbro and Kari were quite sick, but not for long. On the twenty-fifth we entered the English Channel and enjoyed looking at the land. On the twenty-eighth we entered the Atlantic and the wind was very favorable but it later became variable and on June 1 we had head wind. On the fifth there was a terrible storm, but it didn't last long. On the twelfth there was another storm, but not as powerful as the first. We were surrounded by the enormous frightful ocean and a terrible wind. On the twenty-second there was another storm, but Our Lord helped us. On the twenty-fourth we came to the Newfoundland Bank where we saw large icebergs. On the morning of July 1 we again had a storm and the rain was so powerful that I haven't seen anything like it my whole life, but it didn't last long. For the most part we had calm weather and a head wind. On July 11 a pilot came onboard, on the fifteenth we saw our new land, and at midnight we anchored one mile from New York. In the morning we were boarded by a doctor and all were found healthy and our captain went into the city, and at three a steamboat brought us to the wharf. We were like mad people unable to understand anyone. Then we were approached by our countrymen who flattered us and offered to arrange for our journey up through the country. Our captain negotiated on our behalf and told us to pay eight dollars for adults, two children under twelve as for one, and suckling babes free to Milwaukee.

We continued on a steamboat that towed fourteen large freight barges. We came to Albany on the twenty-sixth, boarded a canal boat, and were pulled into the canal. We had to pay four dollars for all. Two horses pulled the boat and there were 130 people onboard with all their baggage. I believe there were a hundred locks that were so intricately made that I cannot describe them. We came to Buffalo on the morning of the thirty-first. Then something happened that was the fault of Søren Christensen from Drammen, and we had to pay an additional dollar and a half in order to avoid waiting there for a week. We're quite sure that the person mentioned was responsible for this fraud. We then went on a steamboat with many people, some of them German, bad people who were not at all nice to us. We sailed into Lake Erie and a small child from Hemsedal died there. The child was carefully placed in a coffin and brought ashore for burial. We sailed past many small towns and came to Milwaukee August 6. We had then traveled 1,849 miles from New York.

We met some Norwegians who offered to take us up through the country and we agreed to pay twelve dollars for each cartload pulled by two oxen with the baggage and the children of two families to Jefferson Prairie, which was seventy-six miles. Here Levor Myli met us with two ox teams and two wagons and took all our baggage and the children. We came to his home August 12 and we now live with him, along with Ole and Halvor Hersgaard and their families. Levor has land here in Rock Prairie and lives well. We've also visited Endre Tryhus and other Norwegians. We all bought two cows and six sheep each. We've begun haying and we plan to stay here for the winter. Then we and some others in our company will go further west to a country called Iowa that has recently been purchased from the Indians and taken into the union as a state, as you may see in more detail in a book by J. R. Reiersen called *Pathfinder for Norwegian Emigrants*. In Wisconsin and Illinois all arable land, in particular forest land, has been bought by speculators so it's much more expensive than free land. Moreover, we're told that in Iowa the water is healthier and there is a better balance of forest and prairie. The land around here is considered very fertile but Muskego was a very unhealthy place. The land there is low with large swampy areas. Most Norwegians there want to sell their land and move further west. Hermod Tufte and his brother-in-law, who has made himself a pastor, live there.

The land in Illinois is much better than in Wisconsin. They've already harvested the wheat and the corn is now at its best. The houses are poor, built with logs of hardwood stripped of their bark with some clay in between. A few have set up better houses, but there are few barns and stables. Grain and hay are stacked in the field and threshing is mostly done with a machine. Some thresh with oxen by placing all the ears of grain on a field and letting the oxen trample it. I've seen this. We must now conclude with loving regards to our dear parents and siblings from all who have placed our names here.

NILS TOLLEFSEN AND KARI TOLLEFSDATTER ROE
OLE ERIKSEN AND BARBRO TOLLEFSDATTER SANDO
INGEBORG TOLLEFSDATTER BLAKKESTAD AND
OLE AND LARS TORSEN BLAKKESTAD

Should any of our relatives or friends have plans to follow us, I won't recommend it. You must realize there are many difficulties from the moment you go ashore. Many who are poor in our company come daily begging for help. You must realize that the best public land has been bought. Moreover, you must consider the cold winters and life among strangers. Therefore you should put such plans aside until next year when I'll send you better information.

NILS ROE AND OLE SANDO

All who receive this letter are asked to share in its cost. The letter costs 104 *skilling*. Please write about your situation to *Levor Hærbrandsen Myli i Rock Prerie i Viskonsin Teritori, Nord Amerika*.

· ——— ·

> This is a collective letter by members of a group that left Aal in Hallingdal in the spring of 1845. They shared the cost of the letter and hoped that those who received it would share the cost at the other end. Members of this group were Erik Kittilsen Barskrind (b. 1825); Ole Syversen Leikvold (1823–1898); Ole Svensen Halvorsgard (b. 1824); Aslak Olsen Høstteigen (b. 1826); Ole Eriksen (1817–1882) and Barbro Tolleivsdatter (1818–1903) Sando and their son Erik (1839–1879); Erik Eriksen (b. 1798) and Guri Olsdatter Sataslaatta (b. 1802) and their five children; Nils Tollefsen (from Opsata, 1813–1861) and Kari Tollefsdatter (from Blakkestad, 1812–1891); Ingeborg Tollefsdatter Blakkestad (b. 1814); and the twins Lars and Ole Torsen Blakkestad (b. 1826). Nils Tollefsen took the name Roe from a farm in neighboring Gol where he had lived before emigrating. Blakkestad is

in Gol. Hermod Nilsen Tufte and his sister Sigrid emigrated with their parents Nils and Kari Tufte and came to Muskego, Wisc., in 1834. Sigrid married Elling Eielsen in 1843. In New York immigrants were approached by agents for hotels and transportation companies, as well as by conmen of their own nationality. Levor Herbrandsen Myli was from Nes. Endre Tomassen Tryhus emigrated from Gol in Hallingdal in 1844. »1:105 NE II:T7

1845 — LETTER 1:8

FROM: Ole Herbrandsen Osland, *Kendall, New York, 2 September 1845*
TO: Ole Andersen Narverud, *Kongsberg, Buskerud*

My respected and beloved friend, Ole Andersen Narverud!

Bjørn Haslestad from Stavanger is going to Norway and expects to return next year. So I must make use of this opportunity to write to you even though I wrote a letter that Mathis Mathiassen Krosshus took with him to my dear parents-in-law at Ramberg as well as to you and others on August 19. But he is a drunk and I've been told he is still wandering around in Rochester, so I fear he won't do as he promised and may forget to go to Norway. I have had much bother with him and can prove that I've lent him fifty-seven dollars and thirty-six cents. He has promised to give me the money next winter but I don't believe it. This is why I ask you, my good friend, to do me the great favor of inquiring about his situation in Norway and report back to me at your first opportunity. Is it true that his family is coming to America next year? Mathis has said so, and he also claims to be good for more than 4,000 dollars in Norway. So if he doesn't pay me I'll have to send you his receipt so you may claim it on my behalf, as well as my additional expenses as specified on the receipt.

Should my first letter not have arrived I must also tell you that my oldest daughter Anne has died. This was a great loss for me and her mother. She died 30 October 1844, after a very short illness. I assume you've heard that my son Halsten died in Rochester 3 January 1839. But God has blessed us with two boys in this country. The first is five and is called Hellik and the second, Knut, was born last spring on May 27. Both have been baptized and brought up in the Christian faith so I've all reason to say with Job that the Lord gave and the Lord has taken away and blessed be the name of the Lord. I have the same number of children as when I emigrated. As for other news, we are all in good health, for which we must thank God, and we live well, and I hope to hear the same from you. We live in a very pleasant and healthy place and we can harvest 200–300 bushels of wheat on my farm as well as peas, corn, potatoes, and more. We also have many barrels of apples. I've threshed my wheat and although it hasn't yet been to the mill, I think we have about 300 bushels. We plant about one and a half bushels per acre and the yield is from twenty to thirty bushels and more. There are many good farms for sale here but the price is from twenty to thirty dollars an acre, all buildings included at no extra cost. I would like to make this known in case any of my friends would like to come here, but only if they have the necessary money. Those who have little money should go further west. In conclusion, my loving regards to you and yours as well as to my dear parents-in-law at Ramberg and my other family and friends from yours truly,

OLE HERBRANDSEN OSLAND

. ——— .

OHO (1795–1864) emigrated from Flesberg near the town of Kongsberg in 1838 as the leader of a group of about twenty emigrants. He paid some of their travel expenses and after a short stay in Kendall, N.Y., he bought a large area of land in Indiana that he planned to divide among the members of his group. But the land was not good for agriculture and he lost most of his invested capital. He then returned to Kendall where he took up farming (Anderson, 264–266). The first group of Norwegian immigrants settled in Kendall in 1825. Most of them moved on to Illinois a few years later but a few remained there and in Rochester. OHO wrote to Ole Narverud August 17, 1846 (Nor. ed. I:11) and November 8, 1847 (Nor. ed. I:24). Narverud had to pay 1 *speciedaler* and 27 *skilling* ($1.20) for this letter at the post office in Kongsberg. »1:22 NE I:7

. ——— .

1846 — LETTER 1:9

FROM: Ellev Bjørnsen, *Pine Lake, Lebanon, Wisconsin, 17 January 1846*
TO: Anlaug Christophersdatter Tunga, *Heddal, Notodden, Telemark*

Dear Mother!

From my heart I wish these lines will find you in as happy and healthy a situation as I'm in myself. My only regret is that you, my loving mother, so often have fond thoughts of seeing and hearing how your children are doing in so distant a land. Yes mother, we would indeed have been happy to see you, and how happy wouldn't you have been to see us again! But as we don't wish to live in Norway, this would be too great a sacrifice; nature has set up too wide a separation between us. We'll therefore have to content ourselves with occasional reports from each other as we consider that although we have chosen this separation ourselves, it has been created by God, and if we live Christian lives we won't be forgotten by him, wherever we may be on earth. Let this be our comfort, mother, when you are troubled in your thoughts. Be happy in knowing that you've done your duty as a mother. Yes, we thank you from our hearts for having so lovingly taught us the way of virtue, that both I and my sister faithfully promise to follow, something that will ever bind us to you who so carefully planted virtue in us from our childhood.

Yes mother, you may have waited a long time to hear from us, but because N. Gasmann was expected to return to America in the spring, I decided to wait as I thought my brother would be coming with him. Thus, in order to save on postage, you could have news from him in the same letter. N. Gasmann finally came in July and brought a letter from Ole saying he wasn't coming, and then, after a few days, I had yet another letter from him that he was determined to come this year. So I waited, but in vain, and I now realize there is no more reason to wait. I really don't know what to say about Ole's wavering about going to America; if he doesn't become more strongly motivated than he now seems to be I'm very much in doubt. There is so much inconvenience related to the difficult journey and ignorance of the language that one must be armed with as much fortitude and determination as possible. But no more of this!

You may not know that I sold my canal claim at Pine Lake in the summer of 1844 and bought eighty acres seven miles further north, that I was engaged to Miss Nella Gasmann that fall, and that we were married on May 25 last year. Since you don't know my dear wife, I'll permit myself to note that she's a very nice and pleasant person; her loving, friendly and good-natured company makes my life sweeter than I'm capable of describing. In my letter to Ole Semb last year you saw that I adopted the little orphaned Ingeborg Halvorsdatter Aasildrud. Please tell her relatives that she is a good and obedient child and is healthy and happy. I've received a letter from her grandmother with some clothes for her. Please tell them they shouldn't grieve for her. She no longer seems to miss her natural parents. My sister is in good health and is doing well. When she doesn't want to work for others she is here with me and she doesn't long for her homeland. Finally, should Ole or some other emigrant come next year, please ask him to buy and bring two of Guldberg's hymnbooks and two pairs of good quality carding combs. I will pay what they may cost. In conclusion I'll advise anyone who comes to America to go to a doctor as soon as he feels sick. Here the old farmer's adage—that doctors and medicine are not needed because nature helps itself—doesn't work. I have, praise God, not tried this myself but I've seen examples of many who have followed this presumptuous advice and have had to pay with their lives. I'll conclude with loving regards to all my friends, first and foremost my mother and siblings. I would like to have a letter from Halvor next summer. Yours faithfully,

ELLEV BJØRNSEN

> EB played a short but important role in the pioneer community at Pine Lake with his better-known father-in-law Hans Gasmann (a former member of the Norwegian parliament) and the Swedish Gustaf Unonius. He was better educated than most early immigrants. Some of his letters were published in newspapers and thus entered the public debate on emigration. Two such letters dated 6 January 1843, and 14 January 1844, are in Blegen (1955). Øverland (1995) presents EB's correspondence in a narrative context. His brother, Halvor Bjørnsen, bought the larger farm, Holta, and became a leading figure in his community. In his letter of 6 January 1843, EB reports that he has taken land where a canal had been planned and where "two to three families

of Swedish gentlemen" had already settled. But disputes about rights delayed the canal and it was probably Hans Gasmann who advised him to sell his claim and buy a quarter section near the small town of Ashippun, in northwestern Dodge County. First published in 1778, Ove Høegh-Guldberg's *Psalme-Bog* [hymnbook] was also printed in the United States. «1:4 »1:11 NE 1:10

. ——— .

1846 — LETTER 1:10

FROM: Gjermund Gjermundsen Barboe, *Muskegon, Michigan and Chicago, Illinois, 3 November 1846*

To: A friend in *Aust-Agder*

⇢≡◉≡⇠

My friend!

This time *you* will have to pay the cost of my letter. I could have sent it to my brother but I don't think he is home. Thanks to you as well as my parents and my brother for your letter that I received 14 December 1845. It was good to see something about my dear family and friends. And then I must let you know that I am at present in good health and doing well—thank God! But this has not been so all the time since I last wrote to Norway. In late July in 1845 I had an attack of the cold fever and this kept me from work for six months and I didn't make as much as two cents. Then I only had occasional wages for three months. I had a great loss because of this illness. Not only did I have thirty dollars in expenses, but I also was without income.

In my last letter I promised that I would tell you about America some other time, but you may understand that I cannot say much more now than I could before, as I haven't had much opportunity to gather information and experience about such things that you would have pleasure in learning. I've been where I now am almost all the time since I left my travel companions, except for the time I was ill when I lived with Berruld Øina. This is a rather isolated place and the main business is not farming but lumber. Nor do I believe that the soil here is of the best for farming. But this is not true of all of the state of Michigan. Still, little as I know, I will now tell you a little and I don't care whether it agrees with the accounts of others or not, as I know that what I say is quite true.

The climate may be somewhat different from that of Norway, as there is more malaria here than there. But I will say as before that I don't think this is something each and every one will suffer from. (I may change my mind about this later.) Nor is it only for newcomers; no, natives enjoy the same privilege. Nor have I seen that it distinguishes between those who are frail and those who are in good health. But it seems that once you have had it, it won't be so tough if it returns. It may also be interrupted by good medicines.

I hear they say that government land is available is various places, in Wisconsin Territory as well as in the states of Michigan and Illinois, but there is more of it further west, as well as to the south and in Texas. The price for government land is ten shillings an acre. One shilling is twelve and a half cents. I would say that a cent is about the same as a Norwegian *skilling*. A dollar is eight shillings or one hundred cents. Land for one hundred dollars, or eighty acres, is, I believe, sufficient for a man with an average family, but I think it should be possible to do fairly well on forty acres. Forty acres is one-quarter English mile on each side and they say that an English mile is 5,280 Norwegian feet. The most difficult thing one has to do is to decide on a piece of land since all land of course is not of good quality and I at least would choose forest land rather than prairie land. (Prairie land is land without forest but all the more grass, but there are different kinds of such land as well.) Where would I otherwise get lumber? I have heard that it costs from two and a half to four dollars an acre to have prairie land plowed but for forest land it costs much more before it can be planted. Houses are not so expensive so one can get along the first years, because when a settler wants to build his first house he lets his neighbors know and they will come to help him. I don't believe that it's ever difficult to sell one's produce. It is only a question of having something to sell.

Prices for food mainly depend on time and place so there is no such thing as an average price. Nevertheless I will select a few items and give approximately lowest and highest prices. One *tønde* wheat flour costs from three to six dollars; one *tønde* rye is usually one dollar less. One pound of pork is from five to eight cents; a pound of butter from ten to fifteen cents; a bushel of potatoes from twenty to thirty-seven and a half cents; a pound of coffee eight to twelve and a half cents; a pound of tobacco from eighteen to fifty cents and up to a dollar. Here you will see the prices for some items and for many other things the prices are as in Norway or less. But you will of course also find things that cost more than in Norway.

But enough of this; I will turn to something else. We have summer and winter as in Norway so I don't think I have felt the cold much more than in Norway, but it doesn't last long. You may take this for what it's worth, but I know that it is possible to hurt both hands and feet from the cold. In the two winters I have been in America I haven't seen the snow deeper than about two feet. I don't know what to say about the difference between summers here and in Norway. It is true that there is many a hot day but I seem to remember that this could happen in Norway as well, and I haven't had reason to complain of sunburn on my hands and other such things as a certain writer of letters has done. You may be asking: are there no other difficulties or afflictions? Yes, in summer, in particular evenings and mornings, mosquitoes are unpleasant guests, in particular if you are working in the woods. I hate them; they are bloodsuckers, but on the good side I must admit that they are not always so bad. We have no dangerous animals or snakes. One of the worst kinds of snakes here is the rattlesnake and it is said to be rather poisonous, but you can beat or trample it to death. Nor do I believe that there are many of them since I have yet to see one. It happens that harvests may be damaged by too much or too little rain or by frost; nor is potato rot unknown.

I have earlier written that it costs about forty *speciedaler* for each adult to come here including meals; this is what it cost me. I do not know the precise distance between Norway and America but I assume it is about 3,200 miles, but from New York to Milwaukee it is about 1,400 miles and eighty to one hundred miles more to Chicago. You can go from New York to Milwaukee or Chicago in eight or nine days and not have to handle your luggage more than two or three times. One of the questions I was asked when still in Norway was what may be so expensive that it is worth bringing here. Bring money, not paper money but gold and silver coins; all else is only more trouble and more expenses. But let me nevertheless try to give an answer. Good woolen clothes—both for wearing and bedclothes—are about the best things you can bring and certainly better than selling them at a low price before leaving. But I would warn against bringing any tools of iron or wood and no more pots and pans than needed on the journey, because all you need can be bought in towns here for less than the cost of hauling them here. Moreover, such things are more practical here.

My friend! I believe that you and all intelligent people may ask: who does wisely and who does wrong in moving to America? Well, I am in a way without a clear answer as it is impossible for me to give a satisfactory answer to this question. Nevertheless I will say something. Working people—of both sexes—generally enjoy a better pay for their work than in Norway and they may consequently hope to have a living. This is also true for him who has a sufficient amount of money to realize his plans. To this you may answer, hm! Both these kinds of people may live in Norway as well. To this I too will answer yes, but I have a reservation: with a difference! An example: a man buys eighty acres government land for one hundred dollars. To this may be added 150 to 200 dollars for things that are necessary to farm this land. I will not include expenses for food, as this will naturally depend on the size and needs of the family, but any intelligent person will work out that quite a lot will be needed for one and a half to two years. If such a man will work industriously on his land I believe that, according to my experience, his land will produce what he needs and perhaps a little surplus in the course of a couple of years. Obviously, the greatest problem has now been solved. After this, with continued hard work, they may year by year expect a larger surplus. So here you have my view about this kind of people. But I am also convinced that people who have a nice home and a good income and have reason to believe that they will keep this should stay home. And cowardly and frail people who lose their courage when confronted with any little discouragement and who whine or growl at anything they don't like and who are strangers to worries and difficulties would do well in thinking all this over carefully before they set out on such a journey. So now you have my views on who should and shouldn't come, but I will not in any way advise anyone for or against moving to America because even though I am satisfied with my emigration I would not assume that all others would be so. No, I have met people who have told me that they wished to move back to Norway.

    I love both America and Norway in different ways. If I could live with as good prospects as here, then I would choose my fatherland, which I will always remember with love and respect as the years of my childhood and youth were spent *there* so that I often turn in my thoughts to where I know my fatherland lies. And I am no stranger to the hope that I will once again be able to see my dear fatherland, but time will show whether this will ever happen. But if I think of America as it relates to my income, then it has a great advantage: I can make three times as much here as in Norway and this is true of the large majority. Seamen may also make a good living here, as there is a great traffic on the lakes. Anyone who will and who can work in almost any occupation may, I believe, make more here than in Norway.

I am of course thinking of members of the working class; those who live by speculating are beyond my imagination.

You may know more than I do about my companions on my journey from Norway since you may have read their own accounts. But I will tell you briefly what I know. As far as I know none of them regrets his emigration. In the fall of last year Beruld Øina and his family, with the exception of Christen, had malaria. All the others were in good health when I last saw them in May. I haven't heard about them since then, as I am more than one hundred miles from them. Beruld and his family have settled near a small town called Port Washington, about twenty-eight miles north of Milwaukee. Here he has bought eighty acres and he has worked so much that last fall—the first year he had a harvest—he got not only all the potatoes he needs but also sold quite a few bushels. He also harvested several bushels of corn as well as some vegetables. Salve Tallaksen and Beruld Baardsen jointly bought forty acres nearer town so that they can work there and go home every evening. They have also worked a good deal on their land. I plan to visit them next spring but do not know where I then will go. I have been living here in Muskegon and will perhaps stay here this winter. Now that I have learned a little of the language and consequently acquainted myself with things here I have no lack of work. One of the greatest difficulties one should be prepared for is not to know the English language because then you are often left both confused and embarrassed. I can without difficulty accept all other differences but the language is something else for me.

So there, my friend! Now I have spoken about a few things, some rather briefly, but there is so much I wanted to tell you that might be of interest. Try to understand it as well as possible and please forgive me if I have not expressed myself clearly or misunderstood anything. I must now conclude my letter to my distant fatherland, but first I will ask you to take the trouble to give my regards to my parents and siblings and let them know that their distant son and brother is in good health and doing well and that I wish them and my other relatives and friends the same. You will all understand that I would appreciate some words from you. I think you would have the same wish were you in my place. I know very well that this is no small expense for you but for me it doesn't cost more than ten to twelve cents.

Friendly and loving regards from me, your former and now distant friend. You may appreciate that I sometimes wish that I had my parents and siblings as well as some of my good friends here with me. Indeed I do! Had they been here I would have helped them and given them advice as well as I could, but such a wish must be laid aside as worthless and I accept that

I must wander about on my own. Farewell my good friend! Farewell all my family and friends! Farewell all who live in my dear fatherland—a farewell from me who lives in the distant West but who not so rarely turns his eye on the East! Farewell from your devoted

GJERMUND GJERMUNDSEN BARBOE

PS: After I had written this letter I decided to go to Port Washington and on my way there to mail my letter at the post office in Milwaukee. But rather than going to port in Racine, a city further south, a windstorm brought us to Chicago, a city at the end of Lake Michigan. For this reason I dated my letter here even though it was written in the state of Michigan. Since I had not at all planned to come here I think I will cross the lake again and go back to where I was. Should anyone write to me they should do this as soon as possible so I will find it in Port Washington when I get there next spring.

I must also add that there has been much illness this last year and in Chicago I have talked with quite a few people who have been ill for some time and who for this reason are in straight circumstances. For many reasons I cannot sufficiently warn anyone who is set on going to America that he should not make himself too great expectations and ideas of America, but consider it all very carefully before taking such an important step.

· ——— ·

> GGB (1812–1883) immigrated from Froland, Aust-Agder in 1844, and settled in Saukville, Wisc., in 1850 (Bjerke 1994). Beruld Baardsen was from the farm Øen (Øina) near Grimstad and came to Port Washington, Wisc., in 1844. He moved to Evansville in Douglas County, Minn., in 1868 (Ulvestad 1913, 530). The traditional Norwegian *tønde* was about four bushels. The Norwegian text is according to a contemporary copy. GGB's reference to information given by other letter writers is also a reminder of the public nature of the early letters. If he only paid twelve cents to send this letter from Chicago, the recipients in Aust-Agder would have had to pay a far more substantial sum at their local post office. NE I:13

· ——— ·

1846 — LETTER 1:11

FROM: Ellev and Ole Bjørnsen, *Ashippun, Wisconsin, 7 December 1846*
To: Anlaug Christophersdatter Tunga, *Heddal, Notodden, Telemark*

Dear distant mother!

Time is uncertain; this is an old and experienced truth. Who could have known that my good and loving sister Anlaug would end her earthly life so soon? You may already have seen this in Halvor Akerhaugen's letter. I know this causes grief, dear mother, but you must not forget how natural a road this is for us all. You should be glad for her transfigured state. She was a model for us all and was always virtuous and good-natured. Yes, peacefulness, patience, and religion were her guides, so I can say with good reason that she was too good for a long life in the chaos of the world. She was always in good health after she came to America. She was optimistic and was never homesick, but often spoke of mother and Torgon and always wished that her sister would come here. She was granted this pleasure but for a very short time; she got ill a couple of days before Ole and Torgon arrived in Milwaukee. There seemed to be no danger and the doctor said she would soon be well. She told the other Norwegian girls she would be back to work in a couple of days. But this was not to be. The next day the doctor said her illness had taken such a turn that she couldn't be helped: she had an inflammation of the heart. Torgon and Ole came to Tremont House in Milwaukee on August 24, and on the twenty-fifth she fell quietly and peacefully into her long sleep to salvation. You should note that when she became dangerously ill her employer sent me a letter, but since the distance is about twenty-five miles and the letter was delayed a day more than necessary, I didn't get the sad news until the afternoon of the twenty-seventh. I left immediately but when I came to Milwaukee the next morning she was already buried because of the intense heat at this time of year.

I was dismayed; this was the hardest blow I had ever experienced. Just think that one month earlier she had been in our home for three weeks and was healthy, merry, and happy—and now I'll never see her again. She had decided to stay with us for some time because my wife wasn't well. But she had promised her employer she would return to Milwaukee in about three weeks and he came with horse and wagon to fetch her since another girl at the hotel was ill. She asked me what she should do and I said it was up to her, and she said that they were good people and she was reluctant to disappoint them. So she went with him. Strangely, on her departure Anlaug and my wife wept and she ensured us that she would be back within a month. I have regretted and will ever more regret that I didn't advise her not to go. She would have done as I said and then I would at least have had the comfort of taking farewell with her in my arms. But we humans are shortsighted.

When I came to Milwaukee I was told that Ole and Torgon had left town with their baggage just a couple of hours earlier and were on their way to me. Since I had to set off immediately to guide them, I asked the owner of Tremont House to take good care of Anlaug's clothes and other belongings, and he ensured me he would do this. Three Norwegian girls who had served with her said that her clothes were being laundered and that everything would be packed with care so nothing would be lost. He also presented a bill for the doctor, coffin, burial, etc., a total of twenty-five dollars, and said he was still owed ten dollars and asked whether I would pay. Since I couldn't imagine that this wasn't as it should be, I promised to take care of it. He said he would accept half the sum but I didn't have the heart to talk any more about it and went off to find my brother. When I came home it was time to plant wheat. This kept me busy for two to three weeks and no sooner was I finished than I for the first time experienced the dreadful ague and this has since kept me at home. With the doctor's help and a lot of medicine I was soon able to leave my bed but after an hour in the yard doing the most necessary work, I had to take to bed again for several days and had further expenses for medicine. And this has been five times now and I fear it will happen again. But there is no reason to despair! With God's help I hope I will be as healthy as ever before winter is over.

You'll appreciate that I was unable to go to Milwaukee to look more carefully at my sister's bills and take care of her belongings, so I sent Ole to talk with the innkeeper at Tremont House with the help of an interpreter. But he was no longer there and a new man had taken his position and he wouldn't let any of my sister's belongings leave the house until the ten dollars had been paid. So my brother asked to see her things and it seemed that more than two thirds had disappeared and that what was left was hardly worth the money. So my sister lost twenty dollars because of the bankruptcy of Mr. Vahl. She was always too good and trusting and had lost money other places too, so her capital at her death is negligible. If any of you wish to see a specified account I will send it to you.

Because of my limited space I'll write no more about this sad event and in a few last sentences turn to a brighter one, namely that my dear wife on July 27 gave me a handsome and healthy son. We have named him for my father-in-law and father except that we have followed the conventions of this country and changed my father's name to Berenhard. So Hans Berenhard is his name and he sends greetings to his grandmother. I will add that he is an unusually large and beautiful child. Greetings from me and my dear Nella,

ELLEV BJØRNSEN

I will now briefly tell my dear mother and siblings that I and Torgon have been in good health and that I've bought forty-four acres from Halvor Akerhaugen and Nils Løiningen for fifty-five dollars. My land borders on unsettled land that won't be sold because it is unsuitable for settling but good for pasture. I've planted wheat on one acre and will work more on my land so I can plant more in the spring. I've also worked for others. I've mostly lived with Ellev. Last winter I lived at Halvor Akerhaugen's. I'm quite satisfied with my journey. I was asked to give my friends advice about emigration but I dare not say anything about it. The land is fertile and wages are good. There has been much illness this fall, but few have died. The land near here has been bought. I haven't heard of any lack of work for an able man. Dear mother and siblings, farewell in God.

Tell Thor and Ole Svenagsen that I don't dare give them any advice. I've heard that many who are sick have wished to return but when they have regained their health they have been satisfied. The worst thing is that there is no more good land for many miles around here. Probably no one will be satisfied their first year because the language and everything else is difficult to begin with. But those who have been here for awhile are always more content than they were in Norway. We were nine weeks at sea and the weather was always good. I was very seasick, but not Torgon. She has been with Ellev all the time and likes it there as his wife is such a good person and easy to be with. Greetings from us both! Space doesn't permit me to send greetings to other friends.

OLE BJØRNSEN

Dear mother and siblings. Torgon sends her best wishes and says she is in good health and very satisfied. She lives with me but plans to get employment with Americans soon so she can learn the language.

E. BJØRNSEN

Some sentences in this letter are illegible. Ole clearly does not have as good an education as his older brother as is demonstrated in his spelling, syntax, and punctuation. «1:9 »1:17 NE I:15

1847 — LETTER 1:12

FROM: Gulbrand Engebretsen Thulien, *Oswego, Illinois, 7 February 1847*
TO: Engebret Gulbrandsen Thulien, *Ringebu, Oppland*

In my long absence I must write to my beloved parents, brothers, and sisters about my health since I left my fatherland Norway. As soon as I came to America I became ill, as I told you in my first letter, if it arrived, but since then I have been in good health. In January I moved from Wisconsin to Illinois, 130 miles further south. I am happy here and not a single day have I wished I were back in Norway. When my purse was empty I was glad I was well and could begin to work. At first I had thirteen dollars a month and later, in summer, I had more and could earn a dollar a day and I have now made 200 dollars. I plan to buy a piece of land with this money. Then I will have a larger farm than my father has at home. And I have now learned the language so well that I can speak with anyone I wish as well as in my land of birth, Norway.

If it were so well that some of my brothers and sisters or friends will come here, I will help them with all I can in all ways, and if some should come I suppose they will wish to find me; I am not yet married if there is someone who wishes to find me. I will not advise anyone to marry before they come here and then they may do as they wish, either take a Norwegian or an American. Because here there are nice girls for any sincere and honest bachelor and the same is true for maidens. And a girl may earn from four to six dollars a month. I will not advise anyone to come or not to come. They will have to decide for themselves. I can say for myself that I do not wish to see Norway again, because here I live better every day than one did on Christmas Day in Norway. And I will implore my friends to beware drunkenness and other misconduct. No more for now except that I wish to know how my parents and my brothers and sisters have lived till now.

G. E. THULIEN

· —— ·

>Gulbrand later became Gilbert and he married Marit Sjursdatter. The spelling in this letter is so idiosyncratic that interpretation is at times difficult. It is dated "Ossabel Craad i Illinois Stet," and my reading of this rather cryptic name is Oswego Road. Thulien's first letter, dated 5 December 1845, is published in *Nordmands-forbundet* 27 (January 1934, 14–16). There he writes about the voyage on the *Præsiosa* and the inland journey to Wisconsin. NE 1:20

· —— ·

1847 — LETTER 1:13

FROM: Ole Stensen Karlsrud, *Muskego, Wisconsin, 18 February 1847*
TO: Sten Olsen and Gro Anfinnsdatter Karlsrud, *Tinn, Telemark*

⇢≡⇠

Dear parents and siblings,

As I have received your letters of October and 17 May 1846, with a glad hand and heart, I as well as others here will send you both good and bad news and fates, some of which may be for your encouragement and edification and some will give you both disgust and fear and may be a mirror so that we may turn from the old Adam and the world's raging fantasy. I see that my father Sten and my mother Gro, my dearly and of my heart beloved dear parents, are living in good health, as are my brothers and sister Anfinn, Hans, and Søren—and Sigrid. And I must congratulate Søren on being a soldier and Sigrid on her marriage with Knud Husevold. I have as far as possible given your greetings to those relatives and friends mentioned in your letters.

Now I will tell you about my life and situation since I last wrote to you January 11 of last year. I am living with Halvor Østensen Luraas and will stay here this winter. I have been ill several times, of bilious fever, the dumb ague, and the common ague, or climate sickness, that I have now had for six months. I am better now but still weak. During my illness I have been depressed but tried to be as patient as possible even though I know that I am as nothing in my reckoning with God. But praise God who gives us a daily burden. We have a God who also daily supports us and a Lord—dear Lord!—who saves us from death.

I have had money and bought medicine that seems to have helped and I now hope soon to see an end to this illness even though it has ravaged this year with roots in last year's exceptionally cold and hot weather, so it has crowned itself as king and governor, with branches all over Wisconsin, and its fruit has driven many from their work and in to bed for many weeks and, eventually, many, in particular the little ones, to the dark and narrow bed of the grave. But as it got colder last fall the illness diminished and it now seems to be over. Except for this I suppose some would imagine "being his own master." Others would think, "Here is the land of Canaan." Yet others would think and say, "Here is Tabor; here I will build and live." For my part I cannot find reason to praise or to criticize because of all my illness. At present I have enough for my daily bread. It is true that the soil here is bountiful and day laborers are paid well but there are expenses for clothes, bread, medicine, and other things that are necessary so it is not quite as wonderful as some have written, even though I have not pointed to anything but my lack of health, and this is of great value.

As there are others who wish to enclose letters to their relatives in my letter I will now conclude with a request that you will continue to honor me with letters about your situation. My warmest and heartfelt greetings go first and last to my father and mother and then to my brothers and my sister and her husband, as well as to my uncles and aunts and other relatives and friends, in particular to my good friend and uncle Hans Olsen and his wife who I thank for the letter I received last fall. I wish that you will all wander so that [we meet again in heaven] even though we now will not be able to greet each other except with our pen. May we all work while it is day and while the sun of grace shines upon us so that we may stand ready when the groom knocks and that we then may come in to Him and that we then may be found worthy because of the grace of Jesus and become the bride of Jesus and there celebrate the wedding of eternity so that we may then greet each other with firm hands and in one heart praise God for the troubles here in time and the immeasurable happiness there in the eternal. Yes, may all this come to be; this is the wish of your sincere friend

OLE STENSEN

The Norwegian text of this letter is as in the newspaper *Rjukan Dagblad* 19 June 1937. The words in brackets have been added by the present editor. In 1765 Sten and Gro, then eighty and seventy-eight, were still living at Karlsrud (Carlsrud) in Tinn. OSK's brother Søren emigrated in 1851 and wrote to his parents on 11 September from Racine, Wisc., about his arrival (Nor. ed. I:54). He does not mention OSK. Halvor Østensen Luraas emigrated from Tinn in 1839 via Gothenburg and Boston and was one of the founders of the Muskego settlement near Racine, a settlement that suffered much from malaria. Mount Tabor, in Israel, is believed to be the site of the transfiguration of Jesus. OSK uses it here in the sense of a blessed place. NE I:21

1847 — LETTER 1:14

FROM: Ole and Halvor Lauransson, *Christiana, Wisconsin, 2 April 1847*
TO: Lavrants Knutsen and Knut and Tov Lavrantsen Hogndalen
Seljord, Telemark

Dear father, brothers, and relatives in Norway,

We are surprised we haven't heard from you for two years, but we won't neglect to write to you about our present situation, as there now is an opportunity to send a letter with a man from Kragerø who is returning to Norway. Last winter I was ill with the ague from September 15 and had to stay in bed for twelve weeks. March 1 I began to teach school for four months. I'm paid only six dollars a month. I have land four miles south of my brother. Here I've built a house and a shack. I have broken four acres and planted winter wheat but not much has been fenced. I haven't paid for the land, so money is tight. I live by a road that goes from a grist mill to Madison, the capital of this territory. The mill is about ten miles away and Madison about twenty miles. But there are general stores nearby. The artistry of the Americans is evident in the design of their mills, in particular the machinery. So there is much to see for a newcomer. Wisconsin was under the control of the other states but has now been declared an independent state with its own laws and defense. The constitution has been published but as the majority is opposed to it, it will probably be returned for changes in the paragraphs that the majority is against. In the south there is war with Mexico about certain borders they cannot agree on. It doesn't concern us as long as they have enough men. There have been several battles, most won by the Americans. But it costs a lot, as we'll probably notice in high taxes. This year the tax is very high, two dollars for forty acres. Pastor Dietrichson is back, which has pleased his congregation. I keep school in the southern district and Ole Knutsen Trovatn in the northern one.

I, your son Halvor, have been in good health since we wrote to you, as have my wife and two daughters Gunhild and Ingeborg. They are happy here and wish to see their cousins, which isn't possible since they are so far apart. I've paid for forty acres and if I can sell some cattle I'll buy forty next fall. We have an ox team worth about thirty dollars. We've plowed about eleven acres and fenced sixteen. Our harvest last fall was as follows: forty-eight bushels of wheat, forty-eight bushels of corn, forty bushels of potatoes, and a lot of garden fruits that all flourish here as does tobacco. Coffee doesn't grow here in any significant degree but in the southern states there is much coffee. We live by a road that goes from Milwaukee to Madison. I live to the west and Ole to the east. Madison is the seat of justice in Wisconsin. I have about twelve miles to the nearest grist mill, six miles to the nearest saw mill. Because there are difficulties here as in Norway we won't advise any to come, especially because of the ague. Nor do we advise our brother Tov to come. We cannot deny that the land is fertile and that wages are high. It would be much better for your children, but as we know your health is weak, it wouldn't be good for you to break new land. We won't advise anyone to come here. Everyone must do as he desires. If you have decided to emigrate before receiving this letter, you had better come and we'll help you as well as we can. I have thought about visiting Norway but this is uncertain. I'll at least not come until I've sold my land. I'll certainly not live in Norway since it is so much better here. We must ask you, our dear brother, to write as soon as possible and let us know about our relatives. Jorand wishes to hear of her relatives and neighbors, of Ole Fossheim, Knut and Gunhild Bringa, Egil and Else Homlid, the people at Kvistøl and Vastvet, and any news that may be of interest, if our father has married, etc. Jorand and Gunhild wish to see their brothers here if anyone is willing to pay their expenses so they can come. Your brother Halvor has sent a letter to Halvor Vehus but there has been no reply. Tell him I find this strange since he asked for a letter when we parted, but he hasn't done his duty.

We must conclude with loving regards to you, our dear father and brothers. Ingeborg sends her regards to her cousin Lavrans and says she is fine. She has learned the commandments and the articles of faith by heart. Our regards to my wife's brother, Halvor Bergsland, and to her other siblings. Also to Sigvald Løvodden if he still lives and Halvor Høgkasin, our mother's sisters Gunhild and Anne, and Tov Hegni. May God be with you!

OLE LAURANSSON, HALVOR FOSSHEIM

Our friendly regards to my father and my two brothers from me and my wife and children. We we are doing well.

HALVOR LAURANSSON, JORAND HALVORSDATTER

The address: *Mr. Ole Laverace, Christiania, Post Office Koskonongs Prairie, Dane County, North Amerika.*

> This letter has been preserved as a handwritten contemporary copy. Some parts are by OL, others by HL. The shifts between *I* and *we* are in the original. The two brothers (from the croft Hogndalen under the farm Kleivi in Seljord) went via Havre on the *Lorena* in 1843, Ole unmarried, Halvor with his wife, Jorand Halvorsdatter, and two daughters, Gunhild and Ingeborg. Their brother Tov (who, like Ole, was a teacher) did not emigrate. The process of Americanizing their patronymic has begun and "Laverace" eventually became Lawrence. The physicist and Nobel Laureate Ernest O. Lawrence (1901–1958) was a descendent of Halvor. J. W. C. Dietrichson was the first pastor ordained in Norway to serve among immigrants in the Midwest in 1844 and he established several congregations in Wisconsin. His return is from a visit to Norway, where he had attempted to persuade other pastors to emigrate. He returned to Norway in 1850. Letters by Ole Trovatn, who immigrated in 1840, were copied and widely distributed in Telemark. NE 1:23

1847 — LETTER 1:15

FROM: Gullik and Ole Gulliksen Dorsett, *Indian Creek, Illinois*
22 *December 1847*

To: Gullik Evensen Daaset, *Flesberg, Buskerud*

※

Dear and often remembered parents and siblings in Norway,

As we are alive and well in this distant continent we must write to you. First, you'll surely be pleased that we are in good health and have all we need and that we love America. We have settled here at Indian Creek where we have claimed land, set up a house, and broken three acres. We couldn't buy land because when we stopped in Koshkonong we lent our money and when the time came for repayment we couldn't get it. We were afraid we would lose it so we bought a horse and wagon for 100 dollars. We have recently been in Koshkonong and have just returned with forty dollars we'll use to pay for our land. We think we lost money by first going to Koshkonong Prairie but our loss would have been greater if we had remained there since the best land has been bought. Recently the poor land has also been bought by newly arrived countrymen who regard Koshkonong as the best place in America. But this isn't true as far as appearance, fertility, and location are concerned. First, Koshkonong is hilly, the soil is clay, the forest worthless. Moreover, it is far from towns where produce may be sold. But it's true that it's better than Norway, even though it may seem similar. It is seventy miles from Koshkonong to Milwaukee, where wheat and other things have to be brought to be sold. I must also tell you what we think of the land where we live. There are large plains, or prairies, with dry land that is best to build on and cultivate. There is land for haying and no lack of water. Nearby is a large forest that will cost quite a lot but probably not more than we can afford. We've been far from ports but now the Illinois Canal has been completed and will be in operation next spring. We live twelve to fourteen miles from the canal.

As we are satisfied here we will advise you, parents and siblings, to come. We are convinced you won't regret it if fate will be on your side, but that is in the hand of God. If you come you should go to Chicago and take the canal to Ottawa. From there it is twelve miles to us. No more, except that we have a cow and, as already reported, a horse and wagon. Ole has made one and a half dollar a day but you usually get one dollar for harvesting wheat. In conclusion, our warmest regards to our parents. Farewell. From your sons,

GULLIK AND OLE DAASET

Daaset later became Dorsett, a spelling that approximates the Norwegian pronunciation. They wrote their first letter to their parents from Koshkonong, Wisc., on 26 August 1846. In the preserved fragment they report that their journey had taken ten weeks and two days. They spell Koshkonong in a variety of ways, among them *Karskeland* and *Karskenang*. The Illinois and Michigan Canal opened in 1848. Lacking a Norwegian word for "claimed" they wrote *klemt*, which would not have made sense to their readers. »1:19 NE 1:25

1848 — LETTER 1:16

FROM: Elise Tvede, *Nacogdoches, Texas, 5 January 1848*
TO: Taale Andreas Gjestvang, *Løten, Hedmark*

Mr. Gjestvang,

You've probably waited a long time for a report, and I have long planned to send you one. But it has always been set aside for some reason or other. In the newsletter you'll have read about the difficulties I had on my journey to the Reiersens. I was finally able to leave October 4 and found J. R. Reiersen and his wife and children sound and well, which, however, was not the case for the other Norwegians. J. R. lives on land he has claimed and much of it is now cultivated. He had planted corn, wheat, rye, and potatoes, but he made his fence too low and his cattle jumped over it and destroyed everything when he was away on business. This winter he'll move to a larger prairie about thirty to fifty miles from his present home. Here he plans to run a general store. I don't think he is suited for farming. His father lives three miles from him with his youngest daughter and his son Lassen, a smith. They've been ill but are now well, except for his daughter. But they are still weak as full recovery takes a long time. They had a good harvest of sweet potatoes, corn, peas, and beans. They had wheat when I was there and I think they'll also have rice this year.

About half way between the old and the young R., an old Norwegian and his wife live in a shanty with his son and wife, his son-in-law and wife and four children, and an unmarried daughter. The old man and his daughter-in-law haven't had the fever, but the others have been ill. The son-in-law's brother, a bachelor who worked for old R., died of the fever, but he had always been weak. After he had been ill for some time he recovered and one day he walked from his home to old R. and then to some Norwegians who live three miles from R. and from there to an American, but he never got to him. In his weak state this exertion probably caused his death, which was so sudden that there was no time to take him indoors. The old man had bought land from old R. His son has moved to another county to work for a company that makes mills and machines for separating seeds from cotton owned by a Dane named Smith and two Americans. He'll have 360 a year and free board. Another young man, Terje, went there with his wife. They will board with the company at no cost and he'll have 120 dollars and she forty dollars a year. One of the Americans (Johnson) is married and Terje's wife will help her with the cooking.

In the year he's been here, the old man's son-in-law hasn't only fed his family and grown enough grain for a year; he's repaid most of his debt, more than 100 dollars, even though he and his family have had the fever. His children haven't earned any money even though they were well at the time the cotton was picked. This work may be done by children as well as by adults and the pay is half a dollar for every 100 pounds you pick and free board. Wærenskjold has made eighty-eight cents in one day picking cotton. That much isn't picked everyday, but it would have been very helpful if the two children who are old enough had made use of this opportunity to earn money. They would have had the advantage of getting far better food than they do at home and learned the language. He is dissatisfied with everything, in particular the fever and the lack of Lutherans, so his children cannot be baptized or confirmed. I think he'll move out on the prairies with J.R. A certain Nordboe and his family live there. I believe he is the Nordboe who was a friend of your father.

A family from Nes Ironworks lives with an unmarried Norwegian about a mile from old R. The parents soon died, perhaps of the fever, and their one daughter is to marry her host. This K. Olson has been well since last summer, but the previous summer he had a long bout of the fever and would neither take medicine nor move in with any of the neighbors who invited him. The girl has had the fever all summer and won't use medicine. Olsen used to live in Wisconsin and as far as I could follow him (between us, he often makes little sense), he regretted having left, but I assume he'll stay as he is now building a house. He has many strange opinions and won't believe anything he hasn't seen. He'll not even believe that potatoes grow wild in America even though this is their land of origin. He is two miles from a house that belongs to an American, Mr. Cook, who has abandoned it because the land is unhealthy and the water poor. The house has one room and a kitchen and is in as bad a shape as you can imagine. Last Christmas these moved in: an old widow with her son and three daughters, Jørgen with his wife and their children, Aslak with his wife and their children, Salve with his wife and three children, Ole with his wife, Knud with his wife, and two bachelors of whom one is the above mentioned Terje (he and the other bachelor are now both married to two of the widow's daughters)—all in all twenty-one people from West Norway. It is awful to imagine how this must have been in a year with so much illness, and several are now dead: Salve and Ole's wives and Knud. Medicine wasn't always available and sometimes they refused it when it was. They disregarded the necessary precautions for food and drink. Ole went to New Orleans in search of work. Knud's wife is insane after the fever and walks around to all her neighbors. Terje has, as already mentioned, moved to Smith & Co., as has Jensen's widow's brother-in-law. They were dissatisfied and wanted to return home when I last saw them; but before the fever they were quite happy, having enough butter and milk. Their field promised a rich harvest and they saw how easy it is to keep pigs and cows since they multiply and find most of the food they need on their own. Cook has cheated them in different ways, for instance, by showing them land that wasn't available so they will have to apply for land all over again. Old R. and the already mentioned old man will build this winter. A bachelor from Arendal has lived with Cook; he hasn't been ill and appears healthy. He went with Ole to New Orleans and they plan to return in the spring. The old man's daughter and Jørgen's sister work for American families. They've been well and are satisfied. All these Norwegians, except for K. Olsen, have only been here a year. In the Norwegian settlement, Normandy, there are two American families and one of these enjoys much respect. However, neither the Americans nor the Norwegians are doing well and they are all poor in the American sense. There are no poor here in the *Norwegian* sense.

Reiersen's oldest daughter is married to a German merchant, Vinzent, who lives out in the country twenty-five miles from here. He's a very kind man as well as industrious and wealthy, so she has made an excellent match. Vinzent likes it here and says the land where he lives is salubrious. He didn't have his own home before he married so things are not quite organized yet. He wants to plant a garden and has all kinds of fruit trees from Germany, among them some vines that apparently thrive here. A wheelwright from Nes works for Vinzent and he praises the excellent qualities of the land in both poetry and prose (he is quite a poet). As his favorite foods are pork, corn bread, and coffee, he will never want, as they are on every American's table for every meal. He was sickly in Norway but has been well since coming to Texas. Carl R., a carpenter, is also going there. He first lived in Wisconsin and at first he regretted coming here, but now he doesn't want to return. He had the fever in Wisconsin and has had it here, but was well last summer and looks healthy. He is a widower with two small children. Christian Reiersen has a general store, does well, and is healthy and satisfied. He had typhus upon arriving in Nacogdoches and was near death, but since then he only had a brief spell last summer. He lives about twenty-five miles nearer us than old R. He plans to build a house in a new town close to where he now lives. G. Reiersen (the youngest) has a store in partnership with Vinzent, but in another place and I cannot remember the name. He was also ill (probably typhus he caught nursing his brother Christian) last winter but has been well since. The watchmaker R. lives here; he often has attacks of the fever and he drinks, so he has problems. Andrew R. is in Wisconsin and I know nothing about him. All the Reiersens are glad they are here.

I forgot to mention those who came from Nes Ironworks: Jens Jensen and his wife and five or six children and Gregers, who came without his wife and children. Both had been unfortunate in getting diarrhea from drinking the unhealthy water of the Mississippi and Red Rivers along with a large amount of whiskey. Gregers died shortly after arriving and Jensen died a few days before Christmas. J. had been quite well. After he had bought some land and built a log cabin and cut timber for a better home, he went to Cherokee to build a house for Andersen, who came here with me.

He was then so careless that he drank buttermilk and ate a good portion of fat pork; this was more than his weak stomach could handle. He sickened and had to be taken home, where he died after a few days.

We are expecting a Danish family who has bought land from old R. There is no mill here so people have to go to Cherokee, which cannot be done when the Neches River floods. They can either grind corn in small handheld mills or stamp it, but both methods are awkward and the meal is very coarse. There is no school as the settlement is too poor to pay a teacher. But there are schools in more populated and prosperous settlements and the schoolhouse is also used as a church. But we have no pastors of our faith. The dead are buried in the woods, each near his own home. These are here in Nacogdoches, which is ninety miles from Normandy (the Norwegian settlement): Mrs. Grøgaard and her eight children, Røraas (a smith) with his sister and her two children, the watchmaker R. and Ørbæk. They all had the fever last summer except for one of the Grøgaard girls. Mrs. Grøgaard and Ørbæk are satisfied with their new home, but not Røraas and I believe the main reason is his personal situation, which I cannot reveal. We also have a Norwegian carpenter, Gunder, but I know nothing about him as he came while I was away. A Danish family, Lindberg, with three children, has for the last thirteen months lived partly with J. R. Reiersen and partly with Røraas. They are quite satisfied and have been in good health. He now wants to settle out on the prairies where he can have land without having to pay for it: when you have cultivated a certain number of acres for three years, you acquire title to the land. Lindberg was first in Wisconsin, but prefers Texas. As far as I can see, each of these states has its particular advantages and disadvantages. There are more Norwegians in Wisconsin, and conditions are more similar to those in Norway and most things, I hear, are more convenient. The climate, however, is harsh and it is often difficult to find land near those who have been there for a few years. Here the climate is mild and pleasant. The grass is already beginning to grow and it is so mild that yesterday I sat outside reading after sunset. It is seldom cloudy and when it rains, it rains a lot but is soon over.

All incomes are better here; but there is the major unpleasantness of living in a slave state, which makes it difficult to have free laborers. Moreover, everything here is in an early state of development. But he who has money can live in greater comfort than most here do and build a good house and a stable for his cattle (they may stay outdoors all year but as they then are cold and hungry there is no butter or milk to be had during winter), cultivate wheat and rye, and get coffee, sugar and rice direct from New

Orleans (one tires of always having the same food for every meal). It is difficult to know what one may have of fruits and garden vegetables since so little of this has been tried; but if one had good fruit trees and good garden seed, I'm sure they would thrive here. I would advise anyone planning to come here and who can afford it, to bring good apple, pear, cherry, and plum trees, as well as red and black currants, gooseberries, raspberries, and strawberries, and, if one came via a foreign harbor where vines were available, then these shouldn't be forgotten. One should also bring roots of hops, asparagus, and horseradish. I would have liked to experiment with our wild Norwegian berries and see if they would grow here. There are also many other things it would be good to bring, but I know too little about the conditions here to list them. I'm sure one should bring good bedclothes and woolen clothes, which would be useful in the winter as some days are quite cold, especially at night, and also table cloths and sheets. Linen, wool and feathers are very expensive. But cotton is a lot cheaper than in Norway. I think it would be good to bring a cooking oven as well as a stove, flatiron (I find those used here very inconvenient), fire tongs, etc., as well as a wooden chest or bureau, since furniture is very expensive here.

As far as you, most honored Mr. Gjestvang, are concerned, I would certainly not advise you to settle here, nor would I advise you not to do so. I'll urge you to make exploratory visits to Wisconsin and here as soon as you can. I'm sure a man with your means and qualities will be quite successful here if you are granted life and health; but you are also well situated at home and may therefore regret exposing yourself to the hardships of the journey and a settler's life. So you should see everything with your own eyes before making up your mind. Thus you won't risk more than the cost of travel and this cannot be much for a man in your position. If you should come here with your family without first having explored the country, you may live to regret it; and the same may be true if you do not make the journey and then perhaps with time will not see your children as well provided for as you could wish. I think you should go from Norway to New York and from there to Wisconsin—perhaps also to Iowa, Illinois and Missouri—and then go down the Mississippi to New Orleans, from where you could come here. You could return via New Orleans where I assume you could book a good cabin and board for fifty dollars to Havre. I believe this would be the cheapest route for you, but it will cost at least 300 dollars. You could visit Anderson when he comes home and he'll be in a better position to tell you everything. You may place full trust in Reiersen's account except that the health situation isn't good; however, it is apparently not any better in the other states. R. did not intend any untruth; he was here in early spring and didn't experience the health situation himself and as all said that conditions were healthy he naturally believed them.

I've still not quite made up my mind to remain here, but I've more or less decided to join company with a Dane and a Norwegian who now work for a farmer in Cherokee. I would like to live in that county as it appears to be nice and fertile, is quite densely settled, and is said to be prosperous. There are mills there and, as I've said, a small town has been planned. As for social life here I haven't yet had an opportunity to make any observations. However, I've seen that the class differences we have in Norway don't exist here: the hired hand eats at the same table and of the same food as the master of the house, and is treated with the same politeness as any other person. Indeed, if there isn't room for all to eat at the same time, the office holder will gladly yield his place to the laborer because he pays for the latter's time. If you come, you should go as early in spring as possible so you may return home from New Orleans in February after having completed your tour of the various states. You could save money by buying a horse and wagon in Shreveport, have your own provisions on your journey in Texas, and sleep outdoors at night, which is usual here and quite comfortable if you bring bedding. You should then get your provisions in N. O. such as bread, butter, flour, rice, wine, lemons, sugar, and whatever else you may fancy. This would be particularly useful if you should become ill, as these things may not be bought out in the country and hardly in the towns. Mr. Trumpy in New Orleans will give you advice when you meet him and the consul will tell you where he lives. You should take a steamboat that goes all the way up to Shreveport or else it will cost you more. Should I be here, I would very much like you to stay nearby. Please excuse me for not being able to give you a more detailed account, but as I've always been with the Norwegians and don't know the language, I haven't been able to acquaint myself with the conditions as I could wish. If you write to me, address it thus: *Mrs. Elise Tvede, Care of Mr. Georg Bondies in Nacogdoches in Texas*, and put it in an envelope to either Mr. Trumpy or the Norwegian-Swedish consul, Did. Miesegaes, both in New Orleans. My best regards to you and your family. You are welcome here. Sincerely,

ELISE TVEDE

[*In the margins*] I assume you'll have a letter from Reiersen sent with Andersen, who is going home to fetch his family next month. A. hasn't had the fever nor has he to my knowledge had any other illness. Wærenskjold had the fever for five days only and has otherwise been quite well. Staack, the Dane I may be working with, came from Wisconsin with the Lindbergs last fall and I don't think he regrets it. A Norwegian smith works in the same county. He came last summer and is doing well. There are a few other Norwegians in Texas, a carpenter Stiansen and his family, a smith Nielsen, and a former schoolteacher and brother of K. Olsen, but I don't know how they are doing. This smith is of an affluent family, but will nevertheless not return to Denmark. He too was in Wisconsin first but prefers Texas. He has had a brief spell of the fever but now appears to be well. I intend to buy land as I prefer country life.

· ⸻ ·

A selection of letters by Elise Tvede Wærenskjold is in Clausen (1961). The present edition includes letters not in that edition. Russell (2006) is a biography of Elise Tvede Wærenskjold. Elise Tvede lived in Nacogdoches, Texas a short while on her way to Four Mile Prairie, Van Zandt County, where she settled. She corresponded with Taale Gjestvang, postmaster at Løten, because of their shared interest in immigration and the United States. From Kristiania she wrote to him October 4 and December 5, 1846, and January 20, 29, and March 14, 1847 (Nor. ed. I:12, 14 18, 19, 22). The last of these letters was written the day before she left Norway and the one above is the first she wrote to him from the United States. Gjestvang had long been contemplating emigration to Texas and Elise Tvede's detailed report is intended to give him a realistic sense of life in a new settlement. Her sense of class differences is evident in her use of names: her equals have family names (Reiersen) while others are given first names. Syversen (1982) makes it possible to identify most individuals mentioned in letters from Texas (as done in Nor. ed.). The Dane and the Norwegian who "work for a farmer in Cherokee" are James Hendrik Staack and J. M. C. Wilhelm Wærenskjold, who soon became her husband.

Johan R. Reiersen may be called the "father" of Norwegian emigration to Texas. He traveled in the United States 1843–1844, beginning in New Orleans, after which he wrote a book with information for emigrants (1844), published in translation as *Pathfinder for Norwegian Emigrants* in 1981. A letter he wrote on this journey is in Nor. ed. I:6. He also published the journal or newsletter *Norge og Amerika* [*Norway and America*] from 1845 to provide information about the United States for people considering immigration. Elise Tvede became editor when he emigrated in 1846. After Tvede emigrated in the spring of 1847, she continued to send dispatches to the journal, edited by the printer until it ceased publication in 1848 (see Russell 2006, 57). Her dispatches to the newsletter are translated in Russell 2010 and some of them complement her letters to Gjestvang. Reiersen wrote a long letter to Gjestvang dated February 2 with a postscript by Elise Tvede (Nor. ed. I:27). Reiersen came to Texas with most of his family: his father Ole Reiersen, his daughters Georgine (called Gina) and Lina (married to Mads Vinzent), and his sons, Jens Lassen, Christian, Georg, Carl, Gerhard, and Andrew. A letter from the "former schoolteacher" Johan Englaugsmoen to Gjestvang December 8, 1850 is in Nor. ed. (I:47). »1:23 NE I:26

1848 — LETTER 1:17

FROM: Ellev Bjørnsen, *Ashippun, Wisconsin, 14 May 1848*

TO: Anlaug Christophersdatter, Halvor Bjørnsen, and Helge Bjørnsdatter Tonga, *Heddal, Notodden, Telemark*

Dear mother and siblings,

You've probably had thousands of thoughts about us before you receive these lines. Yes, dear mother, Torgon and I are quite well. But then you'll ask how things are with Ole and to this I must answer that I hope he, with the help of God, is in a far better state than we. For all humans, whether strong or weak, are but dust, and what can be of comfort for us on our often miserable wandering but the hope of an eternal and transfigured state after this life. Now, dear brother, you have probably already understood me: hundreds of times I've tried to take my pen and tell you this, but my feelings for our dear mother have each time kept my trembling hand from performing its duty. Oh! God of Heaven! Had I only not asked my brother to come to America! But the Lord is my witness that I meant well and it is my only comfort that no one could be more satisfied with America than he.

He was in good health all winter. He worked partly on his land and partly for others and he was always satisfied. He often wished he had come to America some years earlier since he had such great hopes for his new homeland. But the Lord in his wisdom had another land for him. On 18 April 1847, he came home from his work for an American and complained that he didn't feel well and that he was so unusually sluggish. He went to bed and as he got worse I went for a doctor the next day and he declared it was an early stage of typhoid fever and he would soon be better. But the medicine had no effect. After a couple of days I brought the doctor a second time and he insisted he was not in danger. Since I could see he had a high fever, I asked him to come again the next day. He came and continued to visit us three or four times a week for four weeks and when he asked my brother where he was most uncomfortable he was always told that he wasn't so sick and would soon be well. Ole was always asking for food, but the doctor was against the kind of food that he wanted. He said let me have this or that kind of food and I will be well again, because I am only a little tired. And it may be that we were too compliant. But he was always saying he was feeling better until he lost his voice when his fever came to a crisis on May 15. For the most part he retained his senses until his last moment and I will never forget how he set his eyes on me, smiled, and then was no more. That was at 12:30 on the sixteenth of May. Do not reproach me that I have not let you have this sad news before now. For, as I have written, it was for mother's sake that I was unable to do it. And please, dear brother, be careful when you tell our mother the contents of this letter.

I am, thank God, in good health and I can also report that my good Nella gave me another handsome boy July 15, 1847, and we have named him Adolf Oscar for my diseased sister and my wife's diseased brother Joseph Oscar. Our little boys are growing and are very handsome and big for their age. Hans Berenhard can now say what he wants and often talks of his grandmother! Torgon sends her regards. She has grown quite a lot, is healthy, and is sitting at my side writing a few words to mother! As I don't have the space to write about economic matters I will close this letter of sorrow with a prayer to God, that if it is not against his infinite wisdom, he will save us from such news as that which begins this letter. Farewell in the name of God.

ELLEV BJØRNSEN

EB expected his brother to read or report his letters to their mother. His sister Torgon's letter has not been preserved. «1:11 »1:20 NE I:28

1848 — LETTER 1:18

FROM: Jakob Abrahamsen and others, *Muskego, Wisconsin, 27 August 1848*
To: Abraham Jakobsen and others, *Tinn, Telemark*

Dear father,

We left Norway May 29 and crossed the ocean to New York in five weeks and three days and then got to Milwaukee in two weeks. I went to Hans Torgrimsen, who was in good health and doing well. We were all well on our journey, both on the ocean and going west on the lakes. I realize I will never regret my emigration. We are all glad to be here. There is no lack of food, and there are good wages for both men and women. A man earns from one to two dollars a day, a girl from five to six dollars a month, and a hired hand from seventeen to twenty-five dollars a month. A blacksmith like Nils Gjermundsen Eggerud could make from thirty to forty dollars a month. Food is cheaper than in Norway. Four bushels of wheat cost two to two and a half dollars, of rye one dollar, a pound of butter one dollar, of bacon half a dollar. A cow costs fourteen or fifteen dollars, usually with a calf thrown in. I believe that if you, my brother Halvor Abrahamsen Krokan, could come here you would live much better than you do in Norway. My wife Gro Gjermundsdatter is well and is glad she is here. Should my brothers come here they would live better than in Norway. Jacob Torgrimsen Bjørktuft and your brother Nils—you would live much better here than you do in Norway, and your brother Ole Torgrimsen should come because tailors do well here. You get three dollars to make a coat and correspondingly for other items. I see that no one has praised America too highly because things are even better than the best rumors in Norway.

To Gjermund Torjussen Stensrud,

I am sure you would do right in coming to America rather than staying in Norway; here you can have a good income and food is cheaper. Please tell my brother Thomas Abrahamsen that I am well and that I am glad I came to America. I would not wish to be back in Norway, even if

I were given the farm Nordre Haddeland. I realize that I in all ways will be better off in America without a farm than in Norway with one of the largest farms. Kittil Thovsen has repaid the six dollars we paid for Mattis Helleksen Krokan. I will conclude with regards from me and my wife Gro to you, my old father and mother, siblings, relatives, and friends.

JAKOB ABRAHAMSEN STENBØLE

To my father Ole Gunleiksen Kaasa,

Dear Father, I am in good health. I was well both at sea and on the journey up to Muskego. Eli Jonsdatter Lie from Møstrand has also been in good health the whole time. A Norwegian pastor from Bergen came here last spring and plans to stay here. We gave the pastor a half dollar to marry us as this is all that is paid here. Those of my siblings who want to come here will do better here than in Norway. I will conclude my short letter with my best regards to father, mother, siblings, friends and relatives. Sincerely,

HALVOR OLSEN

To Halvor Torgrimsen Berge and his wife Gunild Pedersdatter,

This year I have been in good health. It would give me the greatest pleasure to see you here. If you should have it in mind to emigrate, I am sure you will do better here than in Norway. Please brother, if you should decide not to come, please write me a letter when you have the opportunity. And should you not wish to write, this will have to be our last farewell here on earth. But I hope we will all be gathered with God in Heaven. My wife, Aslaug Jakobsdatter, asks me to tell her friends and family that she is in good health. A dollar is worth a *speciedaler* in Norway.

HANS TORGRIMSEN

Engebret Østensen Svadde,

I have received your letter and see you think of coming here and you ask me if I advise you to come. I will not advise you to come or not to come since you are so much in doubt. But if you had come here as you were when you returned to Norway from France, you would have been 400 to 500 dollars better off than you are now. My sincere regards to you and your mother and siblings.

HANS TORGRIMSEN

Knut Pedersen Haddeland,

I hope you don't love your possessions so much that you cannot leave them and come here to America if you want to. It is much better to live here than in Norway.

HANS TORGRIMSEN

From my son, Abraham Jakobsen: Please tell Peder Olsen Haddeland that he is in good health and is satisfied here. He works for an American and has one dollar a week.

JAKOB ABRAHAMSEN

If some of you emigrate next summer you should write me by mail as soon as possible. You should also use this letter as information when traveling, as it is not so easy when you do not have anything to guide you. My sincere regards to father, mother, and siblings, as well as all acquaintances from me and my wife.

JAKOB ABRAHAMSEN

Would you please share in paying for this letter? If any of you are coming to America, it would be best to contact C. Ove Krog in Kragerø.

· —— ·

> This is a collective letter and the use of full names for family members suggests that it was intended for a wide audience. Similar phrases are repeated as if for each intended reader. JA, his wife Gro Gjermundsdatter, and their son Abraham Jacobsen (1836–1910), who became a Lutheran pastor, were part of a group of emigrants from Tinn who sailed from Kragerø to New York on the brig *Alert* with Ove C. Krog as captain. JA had lived on the farm Steinsbøle before emigrating. His father was Abraham Jacobsen, but the letter is addressed to Ingebrigt Østensen Svadde (who did not emigrate). Hans Torgrimsen Tveito, their host in Muskego, Wisc., is one of the writers and as the one with the most experience, he was given the responsibility for mailing the letter. In 1843 Hans Torgrimsen Tveito and Aslaug Jacobsdatter Einong, both from Tinn, were the first couple married by pastor Claus Lauritz Clausen in Even Heg's barn in Muskego. Holand says he was called "Strong Hans" and praises his effort during the cholera epidemic in Muskego in 1849 (Holand 1908, 120, 122). The pastor from Bergen was Hans Andreas Stub. NE 1:29

· —— ·

1848 — LETTER 1:19

FROM: Ole and Gullik Gulliksen Dorsett, *Indian Creek, Illinois*
20 October 1848

To: Gullik Evensen Daaset, *Flesberg, Buskerud*

Dear parents and siblings in our fatherland Norway,

We got your welcome letter dated in April some weeks ago and read it with pleasure. But we are sorry to see that some of our relatives have bid farewell to this world. We will tell you a little about our situation. First, we like this country and with God's help we've had luck and progress in our work. Our health has been quite good except that Gullik was somewhat ill last fall. Second, we have what is necessary for our bodily needs such as house and home. We've paid for our forty acres, broken ten and fenced eight. This year we harvested wheat, potatoes, and a lot of *pankin* as well as other products that a Norwegian would like to see and eat but that here are used to feed the animals. We have two horses and a wagon, a cow and four pigs and with this we can thrive as farmers in our *bisnis*, or trade.

We must also thank you, dear parents, for your kind offer of money and things we may need. We know of nothing we really need except for Wexel's commentary on *The New Testament* and Luther's collection of sermons for home use. We have heard rumors that Wexel has made up a new doctrine that is not in harmony with the word of God and the teachings of Luther. This is why we would like to have these two books.

If you, my brother Even, should come, you should go to Chicago and write to us. In Chicago you'll find Norwegians you can stay with until we come to meet you to drive you and your baggage here. Address your letter to *Mr. Ole G. Daaset, Monson Post Offis, Lasall County St. Illinais.* It is best for the emigrant to exchange his money for silver *daler* coins in Norway and to exchange these for American gold money in New York. You'll then make four *skillings* on the *daler*. Emigrants have this year paid eight dollars from New York to Chicago with nothing extra for baggage. We know of nothing more of importance to write to you but will conclude with our sincere regards to all our friends and relatives in Norway and last and first to our parents and siblings. Farewell. Your sons

OLE AND GULLIK DAASET

. ——— .

> Immigrants quickly picked up new words for new things, such as pumpkin, here spelled as they heard it, *pankin*. Such words would not have been understood by readers in Norway and the brothers explain the word *bisnes*. In Norway Pastor Wilhelm Andreas Wexels was criticized for being a follower of the Danish bishop and hymn-writer N. F. S. Grundtvig. «1:15 »1:25 NE 1:30

. ——— .

1849 — LETTER 1:20

FROM: Ellev and Torgon Bjørnsen, *Ashippun, Wisconsin, 17 May 1849*

To: Anlaug Christophersdatter, Halvor Bjørnsen, and Helge Bjørnsdatter Tonga, *Heddal, Notodden, Telemark*

⇢╞◉╡⇠

Dear mother and siblings!

Because of the long distance between us we all too seldom have news from each other. I think you have long awaited a letter from me, but I've also wished to see something from you. I received your letter this spring because it had been mislaid by the post office. I see that you, praise God, are in good health, and this time I'm glad to say that we are all well. I see that you've been waiting for an account of our diseased brother's estate, but the little he had was very scattered because he had lent money to those who came with him to America. He told me this was thirty-eight dollars to Ole Nystul and eleven dollars to Ole Jamskar, who both live in Koshkonong about eighty miles from us. During our brother's illness he never explained his accounts since he didn't expect to die, especially as the doctor always insisted he wasn't in danger. Indeed, during the first two or three weeks Ole said he wasn't ill and if he would only be allowed to eat he would be fine in a few days. But in the fourth week he thought only of our Lord and Savior, whose name was constantly on his lips. When he was aware of my presence I sometimes asked if he thought he would die and he always answered no. So I have no other account of his possessions than what he occasionally told me before his illness. He wrote nothing.

I've since been to Koshkonong to see the two mentioned men, but Ole Nystul was dead and his widow insisted they didn't owe Ole more than twenty-five dollars and, what is worse, she did not have as much as a cent to pay me. But she was honest enough to tearfully implore her sons to give me a cow for fifteen dollars and a rifle for ten. They had no cash and even though the two mentioned items were valued at least five dollars above their value, they regarded it almost as a gift as I did not have any legal claim. Ole Jamskar only agreed to ten dollars and for this he demanded that I buy two bull calves, but I did not lose money on this. I don't have space for more explanations, so here is my account:

CREDIT		DEBIT	
Ragnild Thorstensdatter	50.00	Sold his land	75.00
ditto interest	1.25	ditto coat and boots	5.50
Nils Løiningen	21.12	ditto cow bell	0.50
ditto for use of land	1.25	ditto a sheep bell	3.00
Doctor Wenberg	6.54	ditto socks and coat	0.43
Peder Danielsen	1.88	ditto ditto	0.75
Sum	82.40	ditto a cap	1.00
		sold books	5.00
		From Ole Jamskar	10.00
		From Nystul	25.00
		Sum	126.18

This is an account I can swear is correct and I will leave it to you to divide the difference as you wish. And to work it out in the simplest and most practical manner, it may be best that you take your share from what should be Torgon's, for I'll pay her here and let you have a receipt so it won't create any difficulty when her inheritance is due.

As the spectacular wealth of the gold deposits in California is much talked about among our people here as well as in our newspapers, I'll briefly write a little about it. Even though, as I'm sure you know, California is a part of the United States, the distance from Wisconsin is so great that the rumors may not be entirely reliable. But as many from this state have gone there this spring, among them several I know, it should soon be evident what success they may have. However, there is no doubt that many who go to California become very rich. So I'm sure there is much gold there. But there are difficulties as with so much else. First, the climate is such that it is almost impossible for any who wish to retain their health to work from the beginning of June to the middle of August. Moreover, the rain makes the two last and the first month of the year unhealthy, but the rest of the year is said to be nice and comfortable and the land is very fertile and, moreover, easy to acquire, as the government wishes to have the land settled and are giving away 160 acres for free to those who will live there. Although the gold field is several hundred miles wide and hundreds of millions worth of gold is produced annually, I don't believe that all who go to California will become rich. Provisions are extremely expensive. Indeed, last winter it is said that there was starvation because of the enormous number of arrivals, and robbery and murder are said to be widespread.

As I'm running out of space I'll briefly conclude with loving regards to you and my mother and sister. We are all in good health and doing very well. I have another little boy we have named Otto, after Ole. Please give my regards to John Grindekaasa and tell him I am not writing separately to him this time. You must let him read this letter so postage may be saved. Torgon will now write a few words to mother.

ELLEV BJØRENSEN

Dear Mother!

I often think of you and wish to see you but I suppose this cannot be. I could perhaps come to Norway, but there isn't much for me there. So I must be satisfied where I am and hope that we may some time be gathered and never more be separated. I've worked for a year for Americans for one dollar a week and all is well. Farewell.

TORGON BJØRNSDATTER

Our little Hans and Adolf have grown a lot and talk about everything and often about grandmother and Norway. Give greetings to the family of Ingebor Halvorsdatter and tell them she is big and healthy and that she will be confirmed next winter.

E.B.

· ——— ·

As in his earlier letter, EB assumes that it is his brother who will read it. The letter is addressed to him. See the letter he wrote 17 January 1846 (1:10) about his adoption of the orphaned Ingebor Halvorsdatter Aasildrud. «1:17 »1:24 NE I:31

· ——— ·

1850 — LETTER 1:21

From: Ole Johansen Holtseteren, *Oconomowoc, Wisconsin*
 4 November 1850

To: Ingebor Olsdatter and Peder Johansen Holtseteren, *Gausdal, Oppland*

⋄⇌⇋⋄

Dear mother and siblings!

I've long waited for a letter from you, but since I haven't had any I can no longer delay telling you of my situation here in the distant West, which I hope you will appreciate. Although there has been much illness around here this fall, I have, praise God, been in good health. I'm happy here. I'm still in the same shop as before. The first two months I earned six dollars a month but then for six months I made nine dollars. For the last three months I've been paid by the pair and I've been making from eighteen to twenty dollars. Of this I have to pay for room and board. Shoes are sold from the shop at these prices: one pair, fourteen shillings (one shilling is twelve and a half cents); one pair of boots, three to five dollars. For my work I get six shillings for a pair of shoes and one to one and a half dollars for boots. Factory-made shoes are sold for much less in the stores, but they are often poorly made. Lasts and shoe pins are made in factories. It's amazing to see how the Americans work. Almost everything is done much easier than in Norway.

This town is still very small but is growing rapidly and no less than fifteen houses have been built since I arrived. I'm sorry I haven't been able to get information about Milwaukee. But I can say it began eleven years ago and that it was difficult to drive through it with an oxcart nine years ago. It is now a large and beautiful city with many factories and a population of 20,000. Many steamboats go from Buffalo to Milwaukee and from there to Chicago. About twelve and a half miles northwest of here is a town called Watertown that is growing rapidly. It was founded eight years ago and now has 900 inhabitants. The town has four grist mills, one of which is driven by steam, three sawmills, each with two saws that work night and day, three wagon factories that produce fully equipped wagons, six blacksmith shops, one clothing manufacturer, one turner's shop, one iron foundry, four drugstores, two distilleries, two breweries, and four churches, as well as eight large hotels and restaurants that receive all travelers.

The Americans are very strict observers of the sabbath and no profane work is permitted. But they don't celebrate Christmas and other holidays, and work on Christmas Day as on other days. Since my arrival there have been six services for the Norwegians at Rock River, most recently on Sunday, October 27, by Pastor Stub. The congregation doesn't have a pastor and I fear that we won't have a proper church until we get one to live in Rock River. Pastor Dietrichson has promised to find a pastor who probably won't come until next year.

When I'm not in the shop I board with Ole Iversen and he and his wife are now well but they were both very ill last fall. Ole Rødningen, who had been ill almost all the time since he came, died about a month ago, a short while after his little son. Marthe Rødningen is well. Erland Rødningen is married, as you may have heard. Many have come to Rock River from Kragerø this year and many from Hedmark and West Norway to Koshkonong, but many are said to have died of the cholera that was rife there this fall and I believe it is still active. The last I heard between eighty and ninety Norwegians had died. Nils Kjos from Ringsaker and a man from Faaberg named Christopher were among them. Carl Stene was here a few days ago and he told me he recently had attended a funeral for two victims of cholera in Koshkonong. A pastor came here and died of cholera but this did not cause an epidemic, but four have died of the disease in Watertown.

When working in the shop I board at a hotel where I pay eight dollars a month. I've heard that my sister Berthe has married Anders Føxehagen; my congratulations! I promised to let Anders know whether I would advise him to come here and I will not recommend it. Some who came with little money have become ill. They haven't done well and have wanted to return, which is quite reasonable given their situation. So I think it is irresponsible to advise any to emigrate. But as I've said before, I'm well satisfied since all work is better paid here; but much work is harder than in Norway, especially in the hottest part of summer. Tell him I'll soon write to him and give him more information as I still know so little about farming and other trades here.

There are twelve of us here who subscribe to the Norwegian newspaper *Morgenbladet,* and there I have seen that soldiers have been drafted from Gudbrandsdal and Hedmark for the war in Denmark. But I have heard they were all sent home from Christiania, which I'm sure made many happy. Many of the Norwegians here are interested in Marcus Thrane's agitation for the workers. I have heard he has been strongly criticized for having mocked religion and all that is holy and that this is why he is on trial. It is sad that Thrane should take his important cause in this direction because the worker has all reason to demand more rights. When you write to me please tell me how this case is regarded in Gausdal, as I have heard that a workers' association has been established there too.

All from Gausdal known to you are, as far as I know, well and John Loshaugen, who has been rather poorly this fall, is now better. But I've heard that Helene Holsmarken is quite ill. The weather has been nice up to now even though we had three or four cold mornings and nights a few days ago. My regards to Ole Voldslien, Christian and Ole Føxebakken, uncle Christian Sveen and his wife, uncle Gudmund Nygaardslien, and all friends and acquaintances. Finally, my loving regards to you, dear mother, and my dear sisters, and you, my dear brother, from your faithful and loving son and brother

OLE JOHANSEN HOLTSÆTEREN

· —— ·

OJH wrote to his mother from Drammen on 1 June 1849, just before his departure (Nor. ed. I:32) and from Oconomowoc on 22 October (Nor. ed. I:36, much damaged), giving an account of his journey. Here he tells that he is working for a shoemaker for six dollars a month. Ole Iversen, his wife Anne Nilsdatter, and Erland Olsen Rødningen had come with a group of immigrants from Gausdal in 1845. Ole Olsen (32) and Marthe Rasmusdatter Rødningen (26) had immigrated with their two small children in 1849. Pastor Hans Andreas Stub (1822–1907) had come from Norway in 1848. Pastor J. W. C. Dietrichson had come to Wisconsin in 1844, and returned to Norway in 1850. The word translated as shoe pin is *skopinne*, a small sharp nail, a device that held the sole to the last while the shoe was being made. Norway and Sweden were not involved in the First Schleswig War 1848–1851. Marcus Thrane began to organize workers in Norway in 1848 and in May 1850 a petition for universal suffrage with 13,000 signatures was presented to the king. The petition was dismissed and Thrane's labor movement was radicalized. Thrane was arrested in 1851 and was sentenced to four more years in prison in 1855. He emigrated in 1862.
»1:39 NE I:45

· —— ·

1850 — LETTER 1:22

FROM: Herbrand Paulsen Osland and Ole Herbrandsen Osland
Kendall, New York, 27 November 1850
To: Hellik Paalsen Aasland, *Flesberg, Buskerud*

My respected and dear brother, his wife, and children,

I must let you know that my voyage over the ocean was very pleasant. No one was sick on the entire voyage. We had no bad weather and all was nice. It took six weeks and five days to New York and about fourteen days from N. Y. to Milwaukee and for this each of us paid five and a half dollars and half of this for children. I would not advise anyone to have full board on the ship but to bring a good supply of provisions from home in a box with good flatbread, butter, *prim*, a dried leg of lamb, and good salted herring, and this would be good on the whole journey. You should also bring bedclothes but no more clothes than necessary because Norwegian clothes are not used here. Nor should you bring silverware except for tea and soup spoons, which are used here daily. Those who have coats should bring them as well as good mittens and underwear as it is cold here in winter. You should bring some good homespun so you may have clothes made in the American fashion.

I went with the others to see Wisconsin and visited Tosten Levorsen Hvashovd. Then I visited the Norwegians from our neighborhood and found they were doing well. I was there for almost two months. I worked haying and threshing for the Norwegians and earned forty cents in daily wages and then I worked for two weeks for an American and was paid five dollars and ate as at a wedding. But I didn't see any *Congress* land except for some *school* land that was for sale. But it cost more than it did before. There are many who sell their partly cultivated land and a few buildings at a profit.

I've returned to my uncle Ole Osland in Kendall and I'll live with him until I can get employment in a tailor shop in Rochester. My uncle's land and the many other large and good farms in his neighborhood are the finest and best land I have ever seen and have wonderful homes and large apple orchards and much else. They are prosperous here, but the land costs from forty to sixty dollars an acre, but that includes buildings, etc., and sometimes even the wheat in the fields. Ole and his family are in good health and are doing well. He has prospered and has no reason to regret his emigration. Old Siri Ramberg is also in good health. She is happy and sends her regards to all her relatives and friends.

You should know that it isn't necessary to exchange your money in Norway, as you may exchange your Norwegian paper money with the Norwegian and Swedish consul in New York. He pays dollar for *daler* in gold and silver. I have until now been in good health. My best regards to you, my brother, as well as the others in my family,

HERBRAND PAALSEN

Date as above!

I must use this occasion to write a few lines to you, my dear nephew Hellik Paalsen, and other relatives. We are all, praise God, in good health and doing well and we hope to hear the same from you. I haven't had any letters from you or my relatives since my old mother Siri Ramberg came here three years ago. A letter from my dear cousin Christopher Gjerde that Herbrand Paalsen has told me about, hasn't arrived yet. I cannot understand this as he says it was handed in at the main post office in New York. It may have gone west with other letters to Wisconsin.

I was very busy last summer and built a very large and good house, fifty feet long, twenty feet wide and seven feet tall with three stories. The house has more than twenty doors and twenty-four windows and all the rooms are roughcast and plastered so they are as smooth as ice on the inside and on the outside the building is painted with white lead and oil paint. It will cost me about 1,000 dollars before everything is finished and we will soon move in. Last year I built a stable for four horses and a cow barn with a large hay loft covering both. The year before I built a storage house so I have been busy building for three years.

This year I was unlucky in losing a good foal that would have brought seventy to eighty dollars. Except for this I have had good luck. We had a fairly good year. From sixteen acres I had 450 bushels of wheat and I have sold most of it for one dollar a bushel. I had a lot of Indian corn as well as oats and potatoes etc. and for this I have no proper account. I have three horses, two cows and seven good pigs. I have no particular news except that there was a big accident on Lake Erie last summer: a large steam ship burned up with 300 passengers who were going west and most of them came from Europe. I believe this happened July 17 last summer. There was much cholera in many places last summer but, praise God, not in our vicinity where we have been spared illness and death.

Herbrand says the merchants Blikfeldt from Kongsberg and Collett from Christiania have come to Wisconsin and placed several thousands of dollars in a bank in Milwaukee. So this is where they both can be found if anyone wishes to investigate, which I believe would be worth doing. I have heard that Collett has cheated Pastor Wilhelm Fangen for 14,000 dollars. He would surely benefit from having this information. In conclusion I would like to have a letter from you about your journey here, etc. The bearer of the letter can deliver it to one of these post offices, Rochester, Brockport, or Holley, which is the closest. Then I am sure it will get to me. In conclusion, my best regards to all relatives and friends. Give my regards to my good friends forestry controller Ziener and Ole Evje and Christopher Gjerde and their families. May God be with you,

OLE OSLAND IN AMERICA

Please also give my regards to my good friend Ole Narverud.

[*At the bottom of the last page*] OLE HELGESEN WROTE THIS LETTER

· —— ·

HPO sailed with the bark *Christiane* from Drammen on 30 May and came to New York on 15 July 1850. *Flatbrød* (flatbread) is crisp unleavened bread. *Prim* is whey boiled to a soft consistency. Neither the words "congress" and "school" or his idiosyncratic spellings *kongeræst* and *skolle* would have made sense in Norway. Public land was often called congress land. Since the first Land Ordinance of 1785, sections of public land were set aside for the establishment and maintenance of schools in states and territories. Siri Ramberg, Ole Osland's mother-in-law, was seventy-four when he invited her to come and stay with them in a letter dated 17 August 1846 (Nor. ed. I:11). A letter dated 8 November 1847 (Nor. ed. I: 24) tells of her arrival. The steamship disaster is probably that of the *G. P. Griffith* that went down after an explosion 17 June 1850. Another letter (Nor. ed. I:69) is dated 20 August 1852. «1:8 »1:44 NE I:46

· —— ·

1850 — LETTER 1:23

From: Elise Wærenskjold, *Four Mile Prairie, Texas, 16 December 1850*
To: Taale Andreas Gjestvang, *Løten, Hedmark*

T. A. Gjestvang!

I've had the pleasure of receiving your two letters but various circumstances have kept me from replying. Old Engelhoug is here with his friend to build a mill for my husband so they'll be living with us for some time. I hope you will follow my advice and come here to see everything for yourself before you make up your mind. It isn't easy to recommend emigration for a man who is so well positioned in Norway and surely has all necessary comforts in life. But I don't hesitate to recommend it for anyone who is in a dependent position and works for others if only he is willing and able to work. Labor is well paid here and there is freedom and equality for all who are <u>white</u>. He who is used to comfort, as for instance myself, will miss many things during the first years. But you are a resourceful person and will soon have a comfortable home and be able to grow all that we can have here, such as fruit, vegetables, wheat, rye, etc. And you will have an abundance of milk, butter, cheese, eggs, chickens, pork, etc. So after a while one may live well also here and if I'm not mistaken in my view of your character, you will soon achieve this. As for company, I think we'll have a pleasant settlement here on Four Mile. J. R. Reiersen lives two miles from us and three other Norwegian families are even closer and four families are about to settle here. Next summer we expect a flock from my hometown, Lillesand, with Mr. Erik Bache, Ørbæk's stepfather. Ørbæk says that after having visited Wisconsin, Illinois, Iowa, and Missouri, he still thinks best of Texas and is firm in his resolve to settle at Four Mile with the Baches. They plan to have a store here so we'll soon be able to buy things cheaply. We have a post office at Four Mile about four or five miles from our home as well as a good and cheap doctor two miles from us. I can truly say that this area is the most beautiful I have seen in Texas, and I've traveled a good deal.

I won't advise you to emigrate or advise against it, as I cannot possibly know whether you'll regret it or not. But if you decide to do so, I believe Texas should be preferred rather than the northern states because of its mild climate, because when one seeks a new home so far away I don't think he should choose a climate as harsh as the one he leaves. The price for land in this area ranges from two *bits* to a dollar, as this is a new settlement, but it will soon be higher. For two *bits*, or twenty-five cents, an acre you can buy a large stretch of land, but small properties of 320 acres cannot be had for less than one and a half dollars, and if there are *impruvements* it will cost more. There is still room for many Norwegians in this settlement, but since much of the land is owned by speculators I hope the Norwegians will come before all land has been bought by Americans, or the price has gone up so it will be difficult to buy for those with limited means.

You should bring all kinds of garden seeds. These are difficult to get here, but do well. I have the most beautiful cabbage and rutabagas, etc., but cannot get seeds from them. You should also bring some barley and different kinds of rye, seeds for hemp (flax is available here), kernels of apple and pear, pits of plums and cherries, some hazelnuts, walnuts and chestnuts, that all should do well here, as plums, cherries, gooseberries, walnuts and chestnuts grow wild. But these are not of the same quality as those that are cultivated. You may expect to find peach trees here; they are very easy to grow and give fruit in the third year. I would advise you to bring some small saplings of red and black currants, gooseberries, raspberries and barberries, or seeds for these plants. Their juices would be invaluable refreshment in cases of illness. I've felt an indescribable longing for the freshness of such drink when I've had fever and I don't know what I would have given for our simple lingonberry juice. If you cannot bring such plants from Norway then try to get them in New Orleans or Shreveport or on your way from there, as well as some good grape vines and figs that do well here, but are unavailable in new settlements. You should also bring some grains. I don't know whether to advise you to bring any tools, but your wife should bring a spinning wheel and a chest of drawers or a similar piece of furniture, as furniture is very expensive here. In Norway I paid fourteen *speciedaler* for the furniture I now have and I'm sure I could have sold it here for forty dollars.

I've seen Engelhoug's letter and have a few comments. Texas is far from being a wealthy state and there is a shortage of money here. Oats may be had here so you don't have to bring this. On the other hand he is quite right in what he says about provisions for your journey. You cannot bring too much fruit juice and if you don't consume it all, then bring it to Texas. If you have casks for lingonberry juice, beer or wine, bring them even if they are empty. Get some yeast in New Orleans and some hops and you can brew beer. Hops do well here if you only have some roots. Corn is now at six bits and will be higher as there is little corn and potatoes and no wheat this year because of an exceptionally cold and wet spring and a similarly dry and hot summer, and the wheat was eaten by bobolinks. Corn usually costs four *bits* and has also been sold for less. Unsalted pork and meat are two cents a pound, bacon fat eight, butter ten, a dozen eggs ten, smoked ham eight cents, etc.

You should hire wagon transportation direct to Four Mile Prairie in Van Zandt County, because your journey will be much longer and more difficult if you first go to the Norwegian settlement in Bosque County. You'll have to pay two cents a pound. If they don't know where Four Mile Prairie is in Shreveport you can say it is twenty miles this side of the town of Buffalo and in that direction. I know of no one here who is planning to visit Norway, but if you could join up with the merchant E. Bache in Lillesand, who plans to leave Norway in June, I think this would be to the benefit of both families. In New Orleans the merchant Trumpy from Bergen will help you to arrange for your baggage to Shreveport, but be sure to get a written contract, as the steam ship captains are notorious swindlers. When confronted by strangers, you would be wise to regard all people in America as swindlers out for your money. Theft, on the other hand, is very rare.

The Reiersens are doing well and I'm sure he'll soon write to you, but you should not delay your departure, as I know letters take a long time. Come straight to us with your family and we'll do our best for you. You must excuse the all too obvious haste of this letter, but I'm so busy since we have newcomers living with us and we are to have two weddings in our home on Christmas Day.

A little more about provisions for your journey: bring pickled cream (boil heavy, sweet cream with sugar, about two pounds a quart, until it is thick), citric acid, medicine for diarrhea as well as constipation, and pickled fish. If you could bring me a good *mysost*, I would be grateful.

I believe there are about 200 Norwegians here and in the Norwegian settlement thirty-six miles from our home. If you and Bache come with a party each and an expected third party comes from Oppland, these two settlements should be able to provide a living for a pastor, and most here would be happy to have a <u>good</u> Norwegian pastor. Should you happen to know of anyone fit for such a calling, he would be very welcome should he wish to come in your company. As for *Norge og Amerika*, you are quite right that it was our duty to complete the volume, but when we repeatedly sent our manuscripts to Norway and had assurances that they had been received and they were nevertheless not printed, it is only natural that one tires of it. I've sent long extracts of two German articles as well as a letter from New Orleans and three accounts from Nacogdoches, and I know that Chr. Reiersen and Reier Olsen Roa have sent manuscripts. So you can see that I'm not to blame. Best wishes and greetings from Reiersen and my husband and from yours truly,

ELISE WÆRENSKJOLD

. ⎯ .

This letter was mailed along with a long and informative letter by Johan Engebretsen Englaugsmoen dated 8 December 1850 (Nor. ed. I:47). His friend was Knud Olsen Ringnes, a blacksmith who wrote a brief letter to Gjestvang dated 30 December 1851 (Nor. ed. I:59). While immigrants in Wisconsin proudly reported purchases of forty acres, EW thinks of 230 acres as a small property. The term "improvements" has been incorporated into her Norwegian and she uses it, probably unconsciously, as a Norwegian word. *Mysost* is made by boiling the whey of milk until it acquires a solid, brown consistency. EW wrote a brief note to Gjestvang on 2 June 1849 (Nor. ed. I:33) telling him that Andreas Ørbæk was about to leave Texas for a visit to Norway. Ørbæk returned with a group of new immigrants in the spring of 1850. «1:16 »1:26 NE I:48

. ⎯ .

1850 — LETTER 1:24

FROM: Torgon Bjørnsdatter, *Ashippun, Wisconsin*
28 November–15 December 1850

To: Anlaug Christophersdatter, Halvor Bjørnsen, and Helge Bjørnsdatter Tonga, *Heddal, Notodden, Telemark*

Dear unforgettable brother, mother, and sister,

As my dear brother Ellev has exchanged time for eternity, I am now the only one you have left of us four emigrants to this distant land. But we must accept our fate and remember the words of Job: "The Lord gave, and the Lord has taken away; blessed be the name of the Lord." My brother died on his way to California, about two thousand miles from here, after six days of the disease called smallpox. He went off on this long and difficult journey in the hope of staying there for one or two years digging for gold, but it was the Almighty's pleasure to call him away before he had come to his desired goal California, about ten thousand miles from here. He left behind his wife and three sons. What hurts me most after what has happened to my brother is to see these small children who ask for their father every day. My next regret is that his wife and children are in a weak situation as he mortgaged his homestead before he left and it will probably be sold on auction. At the most his wife and children may have about 100 dollars when all his debts have been paid. He owed about 400 dollars. He used his land to buy a horse for 100 dollars and the journey cost him about 300 dollars. They were four who went together, Ellev and two sons of Hans Gasmann and one whose name is Christian Høier from Gjerpen. These four had agreed that should any of them die, the others would share their profit with their families. We now have very good news from the three survivors. They came to California around the middle of August. About two months later they had made about 700 dollars. They sent a check for 200 to their wives and children a few days ago. If these three will remain healthy and lucky the widow and children of my brother will have quite a lot of money upon their return. Nella lives with her father H. Gasmann.

I'll now tell you, my dear mother, brother, and sister that I'm in good health and make one dollar a week here with the Americans. You may feel that this will amount to high wages for a year but much is needed for clothes for a servant girl among the Americans since one must be both clean and well dressed. I'll conclude my letter with heartfelt regards to you all. Mother, please write to me next summer and address the letter to my cousin Halvor Akerhaugen. My wishes for your good health,

TORGON BJØRNSDATTER

This letter was first dated 28 November and then corrected to 15 December, suggesting the dates when it was started and concluded. In Nor. ed. this letter was wrongly placed in 1852. Halvor Halvorsen Akerhaugen, who emigrated in the same group as Ellev Bjørnsen in 1842, probably wrote this letter for Torgon. He added a note asking Halvor Bjørnsen to tell his father that he and his brother Mathias were in good health. Spelling is idiosyncratic and the meaning is not always clear. «1:20 »1:27 NE I:73

1851 — LETTER 1:25

From: Gullik Gulliksen Dorsett, *Indian Creek, Leland, Illinois*
4 *February 1851*
To: Gullik Evensen Daaset, *Flesberg, Buskerud*

—◦—

Dear unforgettable parents and siblings,

Yesterday I received your very welcome letter of May 5, 1850, for which I thank you sincerely. I'm glad to hear that that you are alive and well. I, your son Gullik, can also tell you that I'm in good health and doing well and that I'm very satisfied in this country. I've bought eighty acres and plan to build a house in the spring. I've broken fifteen acres. Before this I've for the most part worked for others since it is not so easy to manage both home and land for one without a family. I can also tell you that I have what is necessary for a farm such as a pair of oxen, a wagon, a cow, and more.

Four months ago my brother Ole went south of here to work, planning to stay there this winter. I haven't heard from him but I expect him back next spring. His luck has been very bad; he was married a little more than a year and a half when his wife was taken away by death. Her name was Anne Andresdatter, a niece of Rasmus Halstensen from Kongsberg. She died after a short illness June 9, 1850. Now Ole is a widower and has neither home nor land, but some money and a cow and a heifer. You may imagine that Ole felt he was a poor man when he had to lose what he loved most in this world.

I see that you plan to come. We would like this and think it would be useful if you could do it. As you say, it may be difficult for you, my dear parents, who are so advanced in years, so send my brothers if they have the desire to come. Since his father's death, Christopher Førle has earned his keep and clothes as well as 170 dollars in money and cattle. Imagine! He is not yet nineteen years old. He has attended school and is quite good in reading both English and Norwegian. If any of you come, go from New York to Chicago and then on the canal to Ottawa. We live a half-day's journey from there. I must conclude my simple letter with my loving regards to you all, my siblings and both first and last my dearly beloved parents. Live well. This is my wish, your son,

GULLICK G. DAASETH

To this letter Hellik C. Førle, Knut Gulliksen Kjølset, and Gunnbjørg Helliksdatter Førle have added brief notes addressed to GGD's parents. They had emigrated in 1842 and 1843. «1:19 »1:52 NE II:T10

1851 — LETTER 1:26

FROM: Elise Wærenskjold, *Four Mile Prairie, Texas, 20 February 1851*
TO: Taale Andreas Gjestvang, *Løten, Hedmark*

Mr. Gjestvang!

As I've written to General Paul Hansen Birch I'm taking the liberty to enclose this slip of paper. I assume you've received a letter I sent you last year, but there was something I forgot to make you aware of then, so I'm now correcting my error: you should bring good and large down-filled bedding and pillows. Down is very expensive here and it is such a comfort in winter. If feathers and down may be bought cheaply you could also bring this in sacks if this seems more practical. You should also buy a good cooking stove with iron pots, pans, and kettles in Norway if you can bring this free of charge to New Orleans since cooking stoves there are quite expensive and crack easily. Those who cannot afford to buy a cooking stove should bring some irons, a large cinder-box, and fire tongs. I cannot now think of more I may have forgotten.

Old Engelhoug has left us. Carpenter work proved too physically demanding for him so against all advice he went and raised a cabin near a small pond on unhealthy low land. His home is as ill chosen as his site. It is not quite six feet long, three feet wide, and has three stories. The first one has such a low ceiling that he has to <u>sit</u> with his neck bent. He is a strange man! Don't send any more of his kind to us! From old Nordboe I had a letter before Christmas. He remembers you and asks me to send his regards and to tell you he hopes that you'll decide to come. He hopes to live to see you, which would please him and give him joy. The old man is very interested in his fellow Norwegians and wants to visit us, but it is too far for such an old man. He sent a very nice pipe bowl that he has carved of white stone to my husband and to J. R. Reiersen. They have a flower carved on each side as well as the year and name. Reiersen has spoken of writing to you, but I doubt anything will come of it. He has lost the desire to write and is depressed because of the death of his wife. She died when she lost a child between Christmas and New Year.

Several Norwegian families have bought land near us so we are now twelve families in a neighborhood with none more than two miles from us. Moreover, our doctor, who is married to a Norwegian, lives here at the center of the Norwegian settlement on Four Mile. Despite all the horror stories that the Norwegians in the Norwegian settlement come up with in their attempts to keep newcomers from going to the prairies, all who came here before committing themselves through land purchase to the other settlement have bought land here. Moreover, a couple of the older settlers who have moved here as well as one of the latest arrivals are all trying to buy land here, even though they already have land there. I haven't advised any of the newcomers to settle here; I merely told them to see the prairie before they committed themselves to the brush and forests of the Norwegian settlement. Admittedly, I didn't much doubt their decision since the land here is much cheaper. The prices paid for land here may be of interest for one who is considering emigration. One farm of 320 acres with improvements for three cows and calves, a mare worth forty dollars, and work worth 150 dollars at one dollar a day; one farm of 640 acres with improvements for 520 dollars; one of 320 acres with improvements and two cows and calves and two sows for 300 dollars; one of 320 acres without improvements for 160 dollars; one of one hundred acres without improvements for forty dollars in coins and ten in bank notes; and, finally, a man was able to get 160 acres by buying the certificate for fifteen dollars, the claim rights for thirteen and a few dollars for surveying. I almost forgot a 320-acre farm with improvements that was sold for a wagon, four old oxen, and one hundred dollars. We have 1,760 acres for sale, of course not including the land we live on that we have no plans to sell. We've recently been offered two dollars an acre for this land.

I cannot think of any more and send my friendly regards to you and your family. We would be glad to see you all here next summer. Knud Olsen Ringnes still works for us for ten dollars a month and Wærenskjold is quite satisfied with him. Sincerely

E. WÆRENSKJOLD

Please send me a few lines to let us know if and when to expect you.

· —— ·

> A letter from Johannes Nordboe to Gjestvang dated February 1952 (with a brief note from EW) is in Nor. ed. I:64. EW uses the phrase "Norwegian settlement" in two consecutive sentences. The second use refers to the settlement near Clifton in Bosque County, Texas. The English word "improvements" (which she here spells *indpruvements* and *inpruvements*) seems to have become a natural part of her Norwegian. Such code switching is a regular feature of these immigrant letters but it is rare in EW's writing. «1:23 »1:32 NE I:50

· —— ·

1851 — LETTER 1:27

FROM: Nella Bjørnsen, *Ashippun, Wisconsin, 18 September 1851*
TO: Anlaug Christophersdatter Tonga, *Heddal, Notodden, Telemark*

Dear Mother,

It gives me such pain to write these lines to you. Oh! If only I did not need to tell you, poor mother, that your son Ellev is dead. My dearly beloved Ellev and I lived happily together, but our time was so short, too short for me, poor deserted wife, and for our poor little children. We had four children of whom the two youngest are dead. The youngest was born one month after Ellev had gone, so he didn't see his father here, but I have the hope that they are together in another world. May God give me strength to resist my sorrow and bring up our two little boys as well as I and my dear

Ellev would have wished. Our oldest son was four years old and the other three when they became fatherless. He loved his children and his home so much; he was so good and so kind—Oh God, had he only still been with us. How did he get the idea of going? Oh, that he never had left us. I could then have had the comfort of nursing him in his sickness. But you may not know that he had gone to California. Two of my brothers, one of my brothers-in-law, and Ellev left March 18, 1850, for California and on the way there Ellev caught the smallpox, was sick for eighteen days, and died June 13. He was buried at Salt Lake. Oh if I had his grave here—but nothing. Torgon has been well. She has grown a lot and has become big and strong. She isn't home now—then she would have written herself—but she asked me to write and send greetings to Helge and Halvor and her mother and say she is well but that she sometimes longs for you since she is like a lonely bird in the world. She comes to us now and then and I'll be as a sister for her and make things as good for her as possible. We would like to have a letter from you and hear how you are. Live well! My friendliest regards from

TORGON AND NELLA BJØRNSEN

The family in Norway had already had a letter from Torgon about Ellev's death. NB married Peter Russell in 1855. There are some later privately-owned letters to Tonga. «1:24 NE I:55

1851 — LETTER 1:28

FROM: Jacob Olsen Østern, *Paint Creek, Lansing, Iowa, 3 November 1851*

TO: His family, *Bærum, Akershus*

Dearest mother and brothers and all friends and relatives,

I know you are longing to hear from me but I have not had an opportunity to write yet, nor have I had so much to tell you since I hope you have received the letter we sent from New York. We came to New York July 10 and, praise God, we had a pleasant crossing. We left New York on the thirteenth on a steamboat to Albany or Troy, a small nearby town. Here we took a canal boat drawn by horses to Buffalo, where we arrived on the twenty-first and left on the twenty-second on a steamboat. We arrived in Milwaukee on the twenty-seventh. The journey on the canal and on the steamboat across Lake Michigan to Milwaukee was the most unpleasant part of our journey. It cost us five and a half dollars from New York to Milwaukee for each person, baggage included. Here we got horse-drawn transportation to Jefferson Prairie for me, Christine, Jacob, and Laurine and all our baggage for thirteen dollars. We left Milwaukee July 28 and came to Jefferson Prairie on the thirtieth and were given lodging by a man from Numedal named Ole Nattestad. He is a very good man and we stayed with him for twelve days so we could rest after our journey. We had decided to go to Iowa, but transportation there was twenty-five dollars and we would, moreover, have had to wait until the wheat had been harvested. But Ole Nattestad and others advised us to buy oxen and a wagon and drive there ourselves even though this, too, would cost a lot. This was what we did.

So I bought two large oxen for fifty dollars and a wagon for fifty-five and we loaded our baggage into the wagon, harnessed our two huge oxen, and set off on our journey to Iowa on August 16. Jacob Engebretsen was our driver and you may imagine he took charge. But he had no choice. He had only his mouth and a long whip to keep them going as they don't use reins for oxen here. We fastened hoops made of long rods to our wagon and covered them with four sheets we had sown into one piece and this was our house, our kitchen, our cellar, and our bedroom on the journey, and we were all comfortable. We came to Paint Creek August 24 but still had the same house, the wagon, as our home. Now we began to wander around looking for land for several days, but our efforts were wasted because the people who had already taken land were unwilling to give us any information since they were expecting relatives. But we finally found land quite close to where we had stopped and I and Jacob have taken a quarter section. This land is quite flat prairie with a small wooded hill and the largest valley is probably as deep as Jordal at Østern. We have not built a house yet but with the Dehli boys we have built a rather nice and, if I may say so, quite excellent little cabin and our wives will live here this winter.

Jacob and I have decided to go to the pinery to make some money this winter and this is about 200 miles to the north. They say the earnings are good there in winter. A good worker can make between fourteen and twenty dollars a month plus board and lodging. We will go with a boy from Sigdal who has already been in the pinery for a winter and knows what it is like. I believe winters are quite cold here because it was so cold on October 14 that there was ice on the water, so this was the first winter night. But they say it is unusually cold this fall as it is usually quite mild and nice until Christmas.

I'm very happy here and hope that God will make it possible for all good workers who in Norway have to sweat for others to come here. Then they wouldn't have to beg for a small piece of land to soak with their sweat for their daily bread, if only God would give them health and bless their labor. Jacob and I haven't made any payment on our land. It is school land as is that of the Dehli boys who have taken a half section together. The conditions are that one fourth of the price must be paid within a year. So Jacob and I will pay fifty dollars next year and after that it may be paid in installments with ten percent interest. But all has to be paid within ten years. If all has not been paid by then, the land will be placed on public auction. But we should, with God's help, be able to pay.

I suppose that some who listen to my letter will ask whether they should follow. It isn't easy to answer this question. But if one has made up his mind to emigrate and, I may add, sought council with both God and himself about entering a battle of life and death, and sincerely prayed to God for his protection, he will not scare easily, even though there is much to be worried about when confined in a ship that is played with like a ball by winds and waves. But God be praised, everything went well for us and it is indeed rare that things go wrong at sea. But many suffered diseases, also those who came here after us this fall. But if one has the necessary health there is no reason to doubt in a livelihood. A man usually makes a dollar a day and board, especially at harvest time, and food isn't expensive. A bushel of wheat costs thirty cents at Jefferson Prairie. I even heard someone say one could get a bushel for two shillings, which is twenty-five cents, and pork costs six cents per pound and butter ten cents and wheat flour is one and a half cent per pound. We didn't pay for milk because they had so much of it and only used it while it was sweet. As soon as it becomes sour it is only used to feed the pigs and I saw with my own eyes a man carry two buckets at a time to the pigs. But here at Paint Creek Prairie everything is expensive since the settlement has only been here for two years and they only have what they need for their own use except for corn and wheat. But also these things cost more here than in Jefferson.

I must note something about the journey for those who wish to come here because our route may be difficult for people with many children.

They require a lot of attention and it is worse when they are able to walk and run around than when they are babies, as there are many dangers to protect them from both on the ship and on the rest of the journey. But if they can cover the expenses, I believe lower class parents would do well here. They cannot give their children a better inheritance than to bring them to a county where they may live as free people and not have to submit to the Norwegian yoke of slavery in order to survive. For free and footloose people of both sexes there can be no doubt that they would do best in going if their future is to work as servants and in time submit to the Norwegian contract system. But I still don't know how to advise my three dear brothers Ingebret, Carl, and Lars. You must try to place your prospects for losses and gains on the scales, for here you'll have to begin with plow and scythe, in other words, till the soil. The best man works his own land here and the laborer is not regarded as a lower class of creature as in Norway. Here the laborer sits at the same table as the master even if he is the most prominent man first man in the state. But the travel costs were much higher than expected. As for oxen and a wagon, these costs may be taken care of if we have advance notice of the time of your arrival. It should be possible to meet you at Jefferson Prairie, God willing.

I promised to keep an eye on progress in the Norwegian settlements and the situation of those who've been here for a while. I'll use Ole Nattestad on Jefferson Prairie as an example since I was able to study the situation there. He had been there thirteen years and had eighty acres that were broken and fenced and planted with wheat, corn, oats, and potatoes. And as for their food, there are few homes in Norway with such abundance, certainly not in the country. And I won't tell you how much food there was in the pail of slops in their kitchen because you would believe I'm lying. His house and garden may be compared with a fine town lot except for his farm buildings; they were poor.

But I must return to Paint Creek Prairie and not speak more of Jefferson. When we came to our new home we first cut hay for our oxen. Then Christine and I went to Prairie du Chien, a small town on the Mississippi six miles from here, to buy cows. We bought two cows and paid twenty dollars for one and eighteen for the other; one will calve in April and the other in May. They still milk well so we are quite well off with milk and butter as there is no lack of good pasture. The grass on these wide plains is knee-high even when it has turned brown. I see that my letter is incomplete and disjointed as I have missed some points that I have had to repeat. But it is my way to write it all down and not use a draft.

The letter has no signature and may be incomplete. Østern was a croft owned by another farmer. Jacob Olsen and Christine Engebretsdatter Østern emigrated with Jacob Engebretsen and Laurine Olsdatter Østern, and Lars, Peder, and Engebret Larsen Dehli ("the Dehli boys") and others from Drammen on the bark *Christiane* on 17 May 1851. They were followed by JOØ's brothers, Gullik and Christen. JOØ had been involved in Marcus Thrane's labor organization. Ole Knudsen Nattestad (JOØ spells the name "Nasta" and his brother Ansten emigrated from Numedal in 1837 and founded the Norwegian settlement on Jefferson Prairie, Wisc., the following year. He wrote a small book published in Norway about his journey (Nattestad 1839). See Clausen (1982, 49-66) and Øverland (1996, 25–28). JOØ's Norwegian is influenced by English. For "steamboat" he wrote *stimbaad*, the first syllable a phonetic rendering of "steam"; pinery, spelled *peineri*, is another instance of his code-switching. He first writes the name of the state *Jova* and then adds *Eiove* so they could see how it was pronounced. Place names are spelled as he may have pronounced them: *Nyork, Troi, Milvauki, Mikigan, Pentkrekpreiri, Preiridskin*. In Norway they were used to consuming sour thickened milk. »1:36 NE 1:56

1852 — LETTER 1:29

FROM: Gaute Ingebretsen Gunleiksrud, *Dunkirk, Wisconsin, 7 January 1852*
TO: Ingebret Torstensen and Birgit Gautesdatter Gunleiksrud, *Tinn, Telemark*

In two letters you've said you would like to come to America and wish to know my views and have my advice. So I must send you a few words in answer to your request. N. N. from Hovinbygd has said there is no illness and no dissatisfaction in America. This is not true. There is more illness here than in Norway because of the sudden shifts between heat and cold and because of the large number of immigrants who often bring diseases.

But poverty as in Norway hardly exists here. I haven't seen or heard of begging since I came. On the other hand, farmers cannot generally be said to be wealthy. It's true that few worry about their daily bread since all farmers in my neighborhood have produce to sell and no need to buy food. Their major complaint is that they don't get a good price for their wheat. This year it is no more than twenty-five to forty cents a bushel. Most immigrants experience some dissatisfaction to begin with, as any reasonable person will understand. They are in a strange land, don't know the language, are separated from family and friends, and must, so to speak, learn everything all over again. No one is better suited for emigration than unmarried people who are good workers. A man who doesn't know the language and goes to work for Americans may be paid one hundred dollars a year and a single woman who has learned the language is paid from fifty cents to a dollar a week. But it should be noted that you have to buy clothes and shoes and these are quite expensive. If anyone wants to make this journey, my advice is to leave home as early as possible, late April or early May is the best time. Make sure you take a ship that goes direct to America since visits to other places will cause delay. From New York it is best to take the railroad to Buffalo. This may be a little more expensive than the canal boats, but you'll get here faster and won't be exposed to the infectious diseases and the swindlers that both follow the canal boats. Bring good homespun and bedding but don't have your clothes made in Norway since both Norwegians and Americans here use other clothes.

As I believe you'll be interested in a few words about our situation I can give you the following information: My family has grown since I last wrote. God has blessed us with two daughters, Bergit was born August 10, 1849, and the second was born January 6, 1852, and hasn't yet been baptized. We thank God for his goodness. All three children are healthy and give us happiness in our life and pleasure in our marriage. As for our property we have suffered no calamity and are in the same situation as when I last wrote. I forgot to say that if girls come they should each bring a well-made and painted spinning wheel as well as carding combs and brass combs. Please let Aslaug Sigurdsdatter Bjørtuft have the festive dress that we are selling to my mother Birgit Gautesdatter as it will be of no use to her daughters if they come here. We'll pay them whatever it may cost. It is my wish that this should be a small gift for her. In conclusion, our loving regards to parents, siblings, and friends, and our wishes for peace, happiness, and God's blessing to you all.

GAUTE INGEBRETSEN AND KARI SYVERSDATTER AND OUR LITTLE GIRLS GURO GAUTESDATTER AND BERGET GAUTESDATTER

The first part of this letter is according to *Rjukan Dagblad*, 19 June 1937, and the conclusion comes from a copy of a fragment at Telemark College. Hovinbygd is in the present Tinn. The recommended transaction may seem complicated. By selling the festive dress (which presumably is part of his inheritance) to his mother, who then gives it to Aslaug (his sister-in-law), he can repay his mother by giving the amount to his sisters when they arrive. «1:6 »1:61 NE I:60

1852 — LETTER 1:30

FROM: Onon Bjørnsen Dahle and Knud Halvorsen Dahle
Yreka, California, 12 June 1852
To: Ansteen Johnsen Næss, *Nissedal, Telemark*

Dear relatives, friends, and acquaintances!

And now an adventure story from us, emigrated pilgrims. It is long since you heard from us and you may have believed that we had long since left this world and you may have given up all hope of ever hearing from us again. Please forgive our delay. The reason is not that we've forgotten our family and our fatherland or been on a path of romance; it is our situation and special circumstances that have hindered us. Even though I'm not good at writing I'll send you this adventure story. My last letter was in 1849 and we hope you have received it. Now we'll tell you what we have done and experienced since then.

In 1848, at the time we came to America, gold was discovered in the western part of America by the Pacific Ocean in California. Rumors of this discovery were quickly spread all over America and thousands of people set off to go there since the rumors said one could fill whole sacks with gold. This area was then only settled by the wild Indians except for a few sections where there were Englishmen and Germans who hunted and fished and who had some trade with the Indians. A German by the name Sutter built a sawmill by a river in 1848 and when he dug a ditch for water for his saw he discovered gold.

In 1849 many left Wisconsin, and I too caught the gold fever. But lack of money and ignorance of the English language made it impossible to get to the newly discovered land of gold that year. We left Wisconsin in October 1849 and set our course for the Mississippi where we took a steamboat to St. Louis, where we stayed for a month without making any money. On December 4 we left the city, crossed the river, and about two miles from the city we took land on preemption, cutting firewood and clearing some of it for plowing. To begin with we boarded on a farm not so far from our land but there, as the saying goes in Norway, tramps from all over took their board so we didn't like it and left. We built ourselves a cabin where we cooked, baked, ate, and slept. We made good use of our time and worked from early morning to late night. Indeed, I was so eager that I worked in the moonlight for several nights. But I was often so tired that I couldn't eat in the evening. Our conditions were primitive but this was one of the happiest winters I've had and I regained my appetite that I'd been without for several years. The winter was mild and there was little snow except for two feet in March that melted in a few days.

In the spring of 1850 talk all around us by both rich and poor was of California. The cry was, "Hurrah for California!" We were of course affected by this fever and there was no other cure than 400 dollars for us both. That placed us in a tough spot because for we couldn't come up with more than 200. Where were the other 200? We were 600 miles from Wisconsin where we had lent some money to others, but this was so early in the spring that there was no steamboat traffic up the Mississippi. Nevertheless, I went into St. Louis one day to see what I could do about immigrating to this land in the West. There I met a doctor who would take passengers to California in a wagon drawn by four or six horses. Well, I said to him, I think this is a good enough transportation but the problem is money. We are two and don't have money for more than one. I asked him whether he would take us to California on the condition that we paid what we had now and the rest as soon as we had dug it up in California. "Well!" He replied, "I think I'll take you on such a condition. You can speak more with me about it later." This was in March and he wouldn't set out before April 20. I returned to our cabin and my work with my usual energy and was very satisfied about our income. We stayed there until April 14. We had made about 200 dollars in four months but now the time had come to turn our attention to something else.

We went to St. Louis where we stayed with a Norwegian family who had excellent news for us. Two days ago three individuals from New Orleans had come to St. Louis, two Swedes and a Norwegian, who planned to go over land to California. We talked with them the next morning and they were interested in adding some Norwegians to their party. After some talk we explained how much money we could spare for travel and that this wouldn't be enough to pay our share of all that would be necessary for this difficult journey. They said that if we let them have the sum we had mentioned they would take care of provisions as they had enough money. One of the Swedes was a tailor named Lindblom, the other a sailor named Viberg, and the Norwegian was a goldsmith named Aaberlus. We bought most of our provisions in St. Louis and planned to buy oxen, horses or mules—whatever we decided—in Independence or St. Joseph about 500 miles west from St. Louis since we could go there by steamboat on a river called the Missouri.

We left St. Louis April 17 and I've forgotten the date we came to Independence. There the tailor and the goldsmith went by land to buy some animals to set before our wagon and haul our provisions. The three of us took the steamboat to St. Joseph one hundred miles further west and if they were able to buy oxen or mules in Independence one of them was to come to us and we would return to Independence. If not, they would all come to St. Joseph and we would buy them there. It wouldn't be possible to go any further without a team. In St. Joseph we set up our tent and this was the first time we had lived in such a house. The next morning the goldsmith came and told us that they had bought three mules and a good horse, so we immediately made ourselves ready and returned on the same steamboat and landed at the town that is about three miles from the river. We met Lindblom and we were of course anxious to learn what kind of animals they had bought. We soon realized that all wasn't as well as the goldsmith had reported. We hired a man to drive our provisions to a large prairie near the town. This was Saturday evening April 27.

Sunday morning we went to see the animals and inspected them with great dissatisfaction. The sailor used his habitual exclamation, "For all my eighteen thousand devils, we cannot set out with such goats!" His comparison was apt. I have yet to see so simpleminded a deal by grown-up people. The three small and lean mules were so wild that they couldn't be taken except with a lasso, so imagine setting them before a large four-wheeled wagon to go through 2,000 miles of desert. The fourth animal was a three-year old foal. The buyers had to admit that the rubbish they had bought was useless.

Here it is necessary to go back a little in my story. These three individuals had met in New Orleans and agreed to go together to California and share in buying all that was necessary for the journey, a sum total of about 1,000 dollars. That is, the goldsmith and the tailor had to share these expenses since the tailor had promised to pay the sailor's share. The goldsmith had said that he could come up with 300 dollars and Lindblom, the tailor, who had a considerable fortune, said he would pay two thirds of the cost for himself and his friend Vibert who couldn't come up with a single shilling. And now we have arrived at a very critical period in the story. When we met them in St. Louis they told us that they had about 1,000 dollars, so we thought they had the sense and the ability to buy what was necessary and gave them most of our money. There we were on a wide prairie wondering whether our animals would grow a little and become more fit when one of them got loose and ran among the trees like a wild animal. They went for the Mexican who had sold them the animals and who knew how to use a lasso, and we were finally able to capture the mule after running around for three hours. And now we set upon the goldsmith who was to blame for our predicament. He had claimed he could come up with 300 dollars if necessary and before he had paid as much as one hundred, he said, "I have no more money." He admitted that he had looked for the cheapest animals regardless of whether they were fit for our use or not. He kept repeating the words, "This is something I understand," and had persuaded the sailor, who didn't know much about such affairs either, to agree to the purchase. So we decided to trade our goats for some oxen and there was a trader close by that had one good ox and some that were of the same quality as our mules, lean and small. The previous owner had himself been on his way to California but had realized that they wouldn't make it. Nevertheless they decided to trade with him, saying that six oxen make up quite a herd. They had heard that oxen were best and didn't at all consider their quality, only that they were oxen and that they were many. We said that they were no better than what we had and that we couldn't agree to set out with them. But the bargain was struck: we got six oxen and a very strong and heavy wagon and the American got three mules and one hundred dollars. The foal they had bought for thirty-five dollars was sold for eighteen, and three harnesses they had bought for thirty-six dollars were also sold for eighteen. So now we had a herd of six oxen. I must also tell you what happened the next night since I have already gotten so involved in this affair. To make sure that no one would come and disturb our guests during the night we took turns looking after them, and during the sailor's watch one of them had fallen, rolled over on his back, and stuck one of his horns so deeply in the ground that he couldn't get up again without our help.

The next morning, May 1, we were ready to begin our journey. But now it was necessary to learn the ox language; the three others had never heard it, so naturally they couldn't speak it. Knud and I had some practice from Wisconsin and this now served us well. We led them to the town of Independence and made a stop there since there were quite a few things we still had to buy and this was the last place where they were available. When we realized that they were quite serious about setting out into the desert in our present condition, this was the place to air our views, which we did. We said that with this team we would prefer to stay here without as much as a single shilling (and we had none) rather than go some hundred miles into the desert and then not be able to continue or return. They caught on but they were reluctant to let us go as they realized that we were better experienced than they were. None of us had the means to improve our situation except for the tailor since we had no money. But as the goldsmith had caused so much trouble, the tailor was reluctant to come up with more money and said that he had none left. Eventually he pulled twenty-four dollars out of his pockets and these were used in a new trade of oxen. We exchanged our two poorest oxen for two rather large ones. One was quite old but in good health and strong enough to begin to drag our wagon until our small ones would improve and be able to help. Now we had two good oxen and hoped the others would get stronger and that we could make the journey if we didn't have an accident.

We didn't have an abundance of provisions both because we were short of money and because we feared having too heavy a load. But we thought it would take a lot of sun to kill us and were happy and satisfied when we left in the evening and set up our tent about a mile from this nice town. On May 3 we set out in the name of God on the most difficult journey in the world. There may be expeditions like this in Africa. I know nothing of this, but I do know what this one was like and this is what I'll now tell you. At first our daily stages were short and we let all trains that came from behind pass us. There was still very little grass and we took as good care of our animals as we could, so they were fully rested every day. As long as we were near civilized settlements we could have short stages and stay overnight wherever we wanted. After about ten days we came to a river we had to cross. There was a ferry for the wagon so it was easy to get it to the other side. Knud and I led the oxen upriver to a place where it was so shallow that we could drive them across, but just then some men on horseback came with a large herd of oxen where we were going on foot. But there was nowhere else to cross the river. We had all of our six oxen tied together with a chain we took from our wagon. Knud tried to wade but the current was so strong that he had to return. Although our animals were unused to carrying anything on their back I got up on the largest one and used our five-yard long whip to drive them into the water. And we crossed the river as easily as did those on horseback.

We were now beyond the settlements and in Indian country and to make sure that we weren't killed by Indians we had to join up with a train so we would be stronger in case of an attack. There was a rumor that a company of twenty-eight men had all been killed just a few days earlier but I don't think this was true. We and thousands of other immigrants grazed animals on some large prairies and we joined up with a train that now had six wagons and thirty men. A big and strong American was elected captain and all agreed to follow his orders on where to stop for the night, keep a list of all members of the company, and appoint guards for every night, two watches with two men on each watch, the first from eight o'clock to midnight and the other to four in the morning. The guards were to walk around with a rifle on their shoulder and keep an eye open for the Indians who hid in the bushes waiting for an opportunity to rob and steal.

We traveled in daily stages of twenty to twenty-five, yes sometimes thirty miles. The land we went through before we came to the Rocky Mountains was actually an enormously wide and flat prairie as far as the eye could see except along the rivers where there were some trees. In some places we couldn't find fuel to cook our food and we burned buffalo dung. We traveled every day except Sunday and nothing much happened until we came to a large river called the Platte where there was a fort called Kearney. We followed a good trail for about one hundred miles and then we had to cross over to the north side at a place where the river was perhaps more than half a mile wide. It was a cold and rainy day. We made the floor of our wagon higher so as not to spoil our provisions and then set our oxen to pull the wagon across. The water went up to the side of the wagon and the wheels went deep down in the sand so we had a hard time getting over.

We then went along a branch of the Platte for a long stretch until we came to Fort Laramie where we again had to cross the river. It was deeper than our former crossing but not as wide. The lightest oxen headed our team. We were afraid that the current would be too strong for them and that they would be carried too far downstream and would have to swim, so we tied a long rope to the horns of the first two and then four of us crossed with the rope to the other side so we could keep them from floating down to deep water. The fifth was to stay in the wagon and yell and use the whip. And so we set across, but since we had problems standing in the strong current and feared that we would be drawn into deep water ourselves, we were unable to do much pulling. But we all got across.

Our trail was no longer smooth. It was stony up and stony down as we approached the Rocky Mountains. After some time we had to cross a third branch of this river. There was a ferry for the wagon and after a lot of trouble our oxen finally swam to the other side. The river was wide and deep and had a strong current. There was little grass in the mountains but lots of heather. The valley meadows were as heavily grazed as if they had been shaved by a scythe because thousands and yet more thousands of immigrants were on their way to California and Oregon. Every day we saw immigrants as far as the eye could see both before us and after us. At night it was rather cold and one morning I saw ice on the water. We were approaching a desert that we would have to cross, a stretch of twenty-five miles without water and grass. Before we set out on this stage we rested our oxen one day at a river. The old ox that I've mentioned had been a burden for several days. We had unhitched him from the wagon and let him go loose, and we now realized that he couldn't be of any further use to us and shot him. We were hungry for a fresh roast and our rations were low, so we ate a good deal of the old beef and packed some in the wagon.

The next day we prepared for the desert. Lindblom had a container of India rubber that we used for water for our oxen and we left the river at five in the afternoon as it was best to travel this stretch at night. There was no rain in summer and the sand was as fine as ash. There were hundreds of wagons ahead of us and behind us, so there could be such dust storms that we had to cover our faces with thin kerchiefs to protect our eyes. We went all night till the break of dawn when we stopped to rest our oxen and eat breakfast. Now the meat of the old ox began to have an effect on us and we were all more or less sick of dysentery. But we had to continue and we finally came to the Green River at five the next afternoon and were more exhausted than I can remember ever having been before.

We saw many dead oxen on our way. We had now come so far into the mountains that the rivers ran westward and at the river we now had to cross, a group had built a ferry where we had to pay seven dollars for each wagon. But some time ago we had rebuilt our wagon into a cart when we realized that it would be impossible for us to continue with our heavy wagon, so we only had to pay half the amount. Our oxen were dehydrated and exhausted after so long a journey and so little grass and we had to give up getting them to swim the river that evening even though there was no grass on this side. Now our train was divided after we had been together for two months. An old man and his son had lost all their oxen except one and he stole one from another train so he could have two, the least number needed for a wagon or cart. But the owner of the ox stopped him and the old man was in the same situation as before. We were asked to distribute their provisions among the other wagons in our train, but we had more than enough with our own affairs. We decided to continue on with three others. They had three oxen and we had five. We placed all our belongings in our cart and set off with four pairs of oxen. Our trail was strewn with dead oxen, mules and horses as well as abandoned wagons. There was a poor trail across mountains, valleys and rivers, little grass and often little water. In one place we saw a spring of water that was so hot that we couldn't hold our finger in it. We went several hundred miles with these three men until we came to the Humboldt River. Then they became impatient with the slow pace of the oxen and decided to exchange their animals for horses, hoping to make better speed on horseback. They were fine companions in the time we were together; they placed what provisions they could on their horses and let us have fifty pounds of flour and as much food as they thought they could manage without. The immigrants now came upon hard times. They were attacked by starvation, pestilence and cholera and many died. We now had provisions for about one week and we were about 600–700 miles from the settlements. This was of course too little but we didn't fear we would perish since we still had five oxen.

With a light load we drove along the Humboldt River and found grass here and there for our oxen. But then we lost one. We had no guard during the night and they had crossed the river. Lindblom swam across in the morning and found the leanest of our oxen lying in a marsh. One Sunday morning we found an ox in relatively good shape that had been left behind because he was lame. We slaughtered it and took as much meat with us as we could carry so we didn't starve as long as it lasted. According to his own wish, the goldsmith was usually our cook and one evening he cooked some dry apples along with the corn to make it taste sweeter and we all ate and drank as usual with strong appetites and everything tasted very good. We had gone on half rations that whole summer and now we had even less. The sailor had eaten quite a lot of the apples and they did their work on him during the night and he was sick in the morning. He now wanted to know why the goldsmith had made food that made him sick. The goldsmith answered that the sickness was his own fault because he had eaten too much. But because of his lies, we already held him responsible for our situation so an argument could easily have erupted into a fight. The sailor said that he would just as soon make him bleed as one of our small oxen. When two evils are joined they are both made worse. The next morning the sailor carried his rifle on his shoulder and we were afraid that he was so angry that he would shoot the goldsmith. But his anger finally subsided and they were again friends of a sort.

We followed the river for several hundred miles and the Indians were quite eager to steal horses. I once saw a train that had lost all their horses, nine in all. One afternoon the goldsmith and I went ahead much faster than the oxen at a point where the trail took off from the river for several miles and we couldn't find water. After a while we sat down to wait for the wagon, but we were so thirsty that we set off again and walked that entire afternoon before we again came to the river. There we waited till midnight for our wagon but no wagon came along. We had enough water but we waited for bread and meat to satisfy our hunger. A train that passed us told us that our wagon had stopped several miles further back, and these good men let us have food and cover for the night.

Now we came to the place where this large river sinks into some large plains of sand and again we had forty miles of desert without grass or as much as a drop of water. We rested our oxen for a day and with as much grass and water as we could carry, we started off early the next morning and continued all day and all night to daybreak when it was clear that we couldn't go any further. We had no grass or water and ten miles of desert. The only solution was to free the oxen and drive them to the river. The sailor, the goldsmith, and Knud went off with the oxen to the river and the plan was that Knud would return with as much water as he could carry and the other two would take care of the oxen and come with them when they were rested and could again haul our cart. We now had two large oxen and two small ones. The goldsmith and Knud went with the largest animals and the sailor trailed them with the small ones that were so exhausted that they couldn't run as fast as he wanted. He had heard that liquor was sold at the river so now he had little time and left the poor animals alone in the desert so he could slake his thirst for liquor. When he met Knud and the goldsmith he told them that the two small oxen had been so exhausted that they could no longer stand on their legs and that he had come to explain the situation. The next evening the sailor returned with the two largest oxen and said he knew nothing of the two small ones. In this manner we got the cart to the river. Oh, it was a delight to see the river again. For the last forty miles we had seen something that was worse than anything we had ever seen: dead oxen, horses, and mules, and deserted wagons. At the trading post by the river the price for a pound of flour was one and a half dollars, but we had no money and couldn't buy anything. We found one of the two small oxen we had lost and slaughtered it. Now we only had a pair of oxen left.

We were told that we only had 200 miles to go to California but that the trail was very rough. So Knud and I decided to leave the oxen and the cart because we feared that it would be too slow and now we had nothing to eat but meat. We fried as much meat as we thought we could carry and left most of our clothes, even our gun, and left the three others on August 24. We weren't alone. The trail was crowded with immigrants. We went in the evening and as we had so much on our backs we had to rest one quarter of every hour and walk three. Now and then we napped. At one o'clock that night, after having walked some distance, we stopped and after eating some of our meat and drinking a little from our water bottles we slept until the sun was high in the sky the next morning. Then we heard that the goldsmith and the tailor had left the wagon too and set off at high speed to overtake us, but they never did. When we had walked with our backpacks for three days we met a group who belonged to a religious sect they called Mormons and who were on their way into the mountains to look for gold. Some of them asked us whether we had any clothes we would sell them and since we had some that we could do without and that were a burden we sold them two pairs of trousers, some shirts and a pair of boots for twenty dollars. Now we were no longer paupers and had quite a lot of silver and gold in our pockets, so we could buy other food than meat, which had been our only food for three days. We bought flour, pork, rice, and coffee at one place, a few pounds of each, and at one and a half dollars a pound for everything.

We and an Irishman who also had a backpack left the wagon trail and took a shortcut over some terribly high mountains to a town in California called Georgetown. At times we were up to ten walking together in the mountains and although the Irishman had carried a backpack for more than 700 miles it was difficult to keep up with him. We came to Georgetown August 31 after having traveled for four months in a wilderness where many hundreds who had left from the same place as we now rested their bones in the desert. Many died of cholera, some drowned in the rivers, and others died in other ways. We thanked God that we had come safe and sound to the place we had desired.

On coming to the town on a Saturday evening we met a Norwegian sailor from Kragerø called Marskal and a Swede. They had come down from the mountains to buy provisions and since we knew nothing about prospecting and didn't have the money to buy the necessary tools, we asked this Norwegian to lend us money and tell us about prospecting. Although he was a total stranger he did as we asked, bought us tools for twenty dollars and some food. This Marskal had been in California for a year so he knew a good deal about prospecting. He had made about 800 dollars and said that if he knew about a place that would be good for us he would let us know. He had been traveling around and prospecting—that is looking for places with gold—and if we would like to follow him to the place he now planned to work he would help us as much as he could. But, he said, I cannot be sure that you'll make any money there. It has been long since I made any. We accepted this and followed him to a place about twelve miles from the town.

A small river ran between two high mountains and I don't believe you have ever seen such gorges and valleys. There are some in Brunkeberg but nothing like these. For the first time we were going to hunt for gold, and together with this man we began to dig a hole that I believe was eight feet square. We dug for two days before we had come to the bottom and panned whatever we believed might contain gold and then we had made two or three dollars as far as I now remember. This was poor pay for three men in two days in this part of the world and we had no great desire to continue with this uncertain work. Moreover, it was tiring and we were still exhausted after our long and difficult journey and afraid that we would spend the fall without income and that the winter or rainy season would begin before we were ready for it. So we decided to take a job that paid for the month and went to Sacramento, about sixty miles from where we were. On leaving, Marskal gave us seven dollars since he knew that we had nothing and said that if we made any money and had an opportunity to repay him this was fine, and if not that would also be fine with him. Since then we haven't seen the good sailor nor have we repaid him.

After a few days we came to Sacramento, which is built on a large prairie by a big river not so far from the coast. Three years earlier there hadn't been a single house here and now it had a larger population than any Norwegian city. We got work for seventy-five dollars a month plus meals. To begin with we were dissatisfied with this as we had heard that people were paid from eight to ten dollars a day. This had indeed been true but with the arrival of such a large mass of people, wages had been lowered and we were happy to get as much as we did. We worked on the wharf that was made higher so that the big river wouldn't flood the city. Several hundred men were at work here and we were divided into parties of forty to fifty men. After a while we had an epidemic and every day some were sick of dysentery or diarrhea. I got dysentery after a month and I was so sick that I could hardly walk. And now cholera came to the city and it became a miserable, sickly place where forty to fifty died daily. Knud had an attack and for two hours he was very sick but then it was over without any medicine. The symptoms were diarrhea and an upset stomach and if the attack lasted it gave the patient a high squeaky voice and the face turned dark blue. Then there was no hope for life.

We had been there for two months and because of all the disease we didn't want to stay any longer and decided to go to Oregon 600 miles further north and stay there for the winter. On November 2 we left Sacramento on a steamboat to San Francisco, which cost us both sixteen dollars. From there we took a sailing ship to Oregon for eighty dollars. After ten days we came to the mouth of the Columbia River and we were to sail more than 100 miles up the river to a city called Portland. We had a head wind so the ship was unable to move much, so eight of us got a man with a small boat to take us to the city for forty dollars. It was very expensive to live there so we went further inland to a town called Salem. There we hired out to a man who had a sawmill and cut logs for his saw. The first night the dam burst and he asked us to stay for some days to help him. We worked for two weeks but as he wouldn't give us more than one dollar a day we left him and began to cut firewood. We rented a room for one dollar a week. I had recovered my strength and we liked our work and were usually able to make seven dollars a day. After about a month the same man came and asked us to cut logs for his saw in the same place where we were cutting firewood and he offered us one dollar apiece for logs, large or small. Now we began to cut the big trees, a kind of fir. We cut seven logs of the largest one and the top log, which was 120 feet up from the root of the tree, was eighteen inches at the top. In eighteen days we made 180 dollars.

At the end of February quite a few left for the gold mines that were about 300 miles away. We didn't want to go up in the mountains so early in the winter. Even though this was one of the nicest winters we had ever seen, it was still winter and we kept on without work until May 8. Then there was no more work and we were not very tempted by the mines, so we discussed what we should do, stay in Oregon or move on to California. We decided to go to the gold mines and see what luck we might have there. We bought a horse for 140 dollars and a packsaddle for fourteen dollars and loaded the horse with as much food and clothes as we thought he could carry and left Salem May 13, 1851.

On our way to the mines a man was shot by Indians about eight miles from where we stayed for the night. There had been three men with fifteen horses and mules with provisions for the mines. When they stopped for the night, three Indians, two with rifles, came and signaled that they were following the same trail to the mines. They appeared to be peaceful and were given food. Then two went to bed and the third sat guard. Soon the two were asleep and as the third was tired he placed his chin in his hand and was soon also asleep. The Indians immediately made use of this opportunity, took one of the guns belonging to the three men and shot at them. One was hit and the others, having no weapons, ran to the horses and were able to escape on two of them, coming to us at one o'clock at night. We were twelve men in all and after this we kept a careful watch at night.

On May 26 we came to a place called Shasta or Yreka on the border between California and the Oregon Territory. Quite a lot of gold had been discovered here in March and soon thousands of people had arrived and the best land had been claimed. We started work and rented a machine called a cradle and in two days we washed for eight dollars in gold. This was too little and as we couldn't make more than we needed for food, we took our pan about forty feet further up. Here we panned and could see a little gold, as fine as sand. So we thought that we would be able to make some money here, bought a cradle for twenty dollars and began work. But soon the creek dried out and water is essential for this work. We dug out a spring under a large rock and had enough water to continue until the end of July, when we had made about 500 dollars. There was no more to be done since every water hole was dry and there was no rain during summer. The mining laws say that if you have running water for washing, you cannot claim more than thirty square feet. If there is no water you can dig at will as long as there is no water and no one else claims it. The first one to start digging has the right to that place as long as he isn't away for more than three days without working on it. So we dug up a fairly large area in three weeks, more than we thought we could wash out the next winter. There wasn't much gold there, but we thought we would be able to make decent wages. Then we joined four others who were working nearby. The six of us left Yreka August 20 and went over a mountain to the Humbug River about ten miles from Yreka. According to the law, a company could claim land as far from a river as it could dig a ditch with running water. So we claimed a long stretch of the river and in a week we had our ditch and cradle in place.

Now we began to pan for gold in the river itself and we had a longer stretch than we could use. Two of us removed about one or two feet of soil and gravel from furthest up in the river where panning was unprofitable. Three dug out the gravel, threw out the rocks, and shoveled the gravel up in a sluice called a Long Tom and the sixth washed out the gold, and I don't have the space to explain how this washing process worked. In the first weeks we made good money, much more than we had made before, but thereafter we didn't make more than a decent wage. Two were tired of gold mining and returned home to the United States. They boarded a ship at Ophir and we heard that it cost them 300 dollars each. Now we were only four and after a few days one of us got ill and went to Oregon. Now we were only three, the two of us and a nice fellow named Henrik Grov.

The rainy season was approaching and we had no other home than a hut, so on a rainy Saturday we began to build a log cabin. This led to the most dangerous situation we had during our entire four-year adventure. We had laid four logs on all sides and it was four to five feet high and I was standing in the inside when a huge tree unexpectedly fell over the logs. Two others were with us and one who had ten dollars worth in his pan threw it into the bushes in his haste to save himself and never looked for it again. None of us was hurt, praise God. After two days our cabin was ready and we continued to work on our claim, digging a ditch about fifteen feet long and four feet across from the river and we found 300 dollars worth of gold here. This was encouraging but we now had to throw the dirt ten to fifteen feet and one day my shoulder was so lame that I couldn't use the shovel; indeed, I could barely get on my coat. So I had to quit working. After a few days Knud was in the same condition. We felt no pain but could simply not lift our arms. We bought some Spanish pepper and mixed it in brandy and rubbed this into our shoulders, and this helped.

We left the Humbug River on Saturday, January 10, and went to Yreka to see if there was enough water to work on our claim there. There wasn't much water but we made it ready at the cost of fifty-four dollars. A few days later we met a group of seventy-five men who wanted to dig out a six-mile canal to this place. We joined them and after thirteen days we had a regular stream of water that went over mountains and valleys to this spot. A man was paid eight dollars a day to watch it, making sure that the water didn't break out. This expense was divided among us. In addition to our work on the canal we paid thirty dollars to maintain our share. Now that we had the water, we began to wash out gold. We had a man help us in the first two months and paid him four to five dollars a day. After February we worked every day except one on our claim and never had less than nine dollars in our pan at the end of the day. So we made a lot of money.

We have now washed through our claim and used up all our water and don't know of any other place to go where we can make money. But we've decided to stay in the mines for another year and do what we can. All the gold hasn't yet been dug up and perhaps we'll be lucky and find another good place. It is four years since we left Norway and two since we left the United States and one since we came to this place. The fruits of our labor these last twelve months have paid us for our four years of toil and trouble. Scoundrels are out after those with money, so our lives are in greater danger now than before. So we'll have to be on watch and be as careful as possible. The rest is in the hands of God.

We've bought a six-shooter that cost us thirty-five dollars. This is the common defense here for those who have money. But we don't depend on it. It is expensive here, especially for those who haven't had luck. We've only used money for necessities since we came here. Provisions, clothes and tools have cost us from 100 to 200 dollars. In these four years we haven't had any news from you, nor have we expected any. John has perhaps gone to America. We've written a letter to Wisconsin saying that if he comes there he may have the money owed to us there, should he need it. Now we ask you to write to us and address the letter to Wisconsin, Dane County, Clinton Post Office, so that we may have news from you when we come there, which we believe will be next year. Perhaps we'll make a visit to our homeland at some time, but this is uncertain. We'll now end our story and send our heartfelt regards to our parents, siblings, and friends, wishing you all well here and in eternity. Sincerely,

A. BJØRNSEN, KNUD HALVORSEN

At the bottom of the last page the addressee, Ansteen Næss, has written the date he received the letter: September 22, 1852. This translation is based on a contemporary copy of the original letter. Another copy of this letter was the source for a narrative in *Decorah-Posten* March 22–April 4, 1929. See also Bjork (1958, 46–50, 62–64). Onon and Knud Dahle returned to Wisconsin in 1853. Place names are often spelled idiosyncratically: *Indepense, Rokki Munton, Karne* (Kearney), *Grueelven* (Green River is a conjecture), *Skasta,* and *Vyreka.* This is also true of terms such as *kradel* (cradle). NE 1:67

1852 — LETTER 1:31

FROM: Svend Larsen Houg, *New York, New York, 16 July 1852*
TO: Ole Larsen Haug, *Aal, Buskerud*

Dear parents and sisters and brothers,

With thoughts of sending you some simple lines I'm taking my pen in hand to tell you a little about our long journey. First I must thank you all for all the goodness you have shown me from my first day to the last one I spent with you. Thanks go to you, my brother Ole, who never spared any trouble for me and thanks to you, brother Knut, for all you have done for me. And thanks to all my siblings and parents.

The last day in Drammen our son Lars was ill and his eyes were especially affected, but his health improved after we boarded the ship. On May 19 our baggage was on board and all passengers boarded the ship on the twenty-first. On the twenty-second nothing happened; many left the ship to hand over their money to the captain but Assor took care of this for me. They say the total sum was 5,080 *speciedaler*. We left Drammen at one that night and came to Svelvik on the morning of the twenty-third. We anchored for a day and those who wished could leave the ship. I and many others went ashore and this was the last time I stood on the land of Norway. At three a.m. we left Svelvik and sailed with a good wind. At nine p.m. we passed the Ferder lighthouse, which marks the entry to the ocean, but we continued to see the coast of Norway for two days. After this we didn't see Norway again.

Seasickness began on the twenty-fifth and few were spared. I and Assor were not seasick, nor were my children very affected. Halsten and Johannes were a little seasick but my wife and her mother were seasick for three weeks as were many others, in particular women, but I, praise God, was quite well so I could take care of the children and other things. I heard many who were impatient and said they should have remained home and not started out on this journey. But one cannot expect everything to go according to one's wishes on so long a journey. Till now I cannot complain of any great adversity. When so many were seasick the captain ordered us on deck as much as possible, yes, even if they needed help to get there, and if they threw up they were told to eat. They were reluctant to do this because it isn't good to eat anything. Our captain was a harsh and quick-tempered man but I think he had our best interests in mind, in particular our health, and cleanliness was very important. We had to scrape the lower deck, our floor, twice a week and six men were selected to bring us our daily water. It was poured into a barrel and one of the six had to guard it so no one would waste water. We had enough but it wasn't for washing. For this we used seawater. There was enough bed space since the beds were large enough for five men and for the most part there were only three or four in each. The cooking place was on deck but it was hardly possible for all to cook as much as they would like every day, but if you could only cook a little one day you were allowed to cook more the next.

I could have said much about the journey but there is little reason to do so as none of my siblings plan to follow me. But anyone who wants to make this journey should spend the winter in town to get some of the things they should bring. I think this would be cheaper. The grain should be dried and ground so it is ready for baking in the spring, because then there is little time. I think that half the amount of bread ordered by the captain will be sufficient. Also half of the recommended oatmeal and peas will be enough, but as for butter, one pound for each adult and a half for a child is necessary. Pork is only good if you have a well-cured ham from home. But *prim* is good to have, very little or no beer, but lots of milk in a barrel that has been used for liquor. A little vinegar, syrup, coffee, sugar and tea as one desires, but these are useful. I know that many asked me to write about this journey but I'm writing only to you. I often think of Syver Ødelien who planned to make this journey. He must be patient and attentive and then I suppose he'll do as well as others.

Now I must go back a little. We had a good sailing wind across the North Sea, entered the English Channel on May 29, and sailed in the channel the thirtieth and thirty-first at Pentecost. We had a good wind but then a headwind made us tack for four days through the channel and we saw the coast of England. When we entered the Atlantic we had a good wind for some days. Then we for the most part had a westerly wind and fog. But there wasn't really any stormy weather except June 17 at five in the evening when the wind was so strong that all sails had to be lowered. But this only lasted to the morning of the eighteenth. On St. John's Day there was a thick fog but a good wind. It was so cold for three days that we were unable to stay on deck for any length of time. On the twenty-fourth we came to the Newfoundland

Bank. This is a shallow in the ocean where a large number of fishing boats were fishing and the sailors caught many cod. On the twenty-ninth we had a dead calm; on July 4 the captain gave a sermon and baptized two children, one born in Drammen and the other on board. On the sixth we had sunny weather but little wind. On the seventh and eighth the nice weather continued and we had a better wind and then the wind turned and we had a headwind. On the twelfth the weather was warmer and on the thirteenth we had a good wind. On the fourteenth a pilot boarded the ship and at seven in the morning we glimpsed land. We came to New York on the fifteenth and the doctor came on board at six o'clock to examine the passengers and all were found to be in good health. Many others came on board, among them many Norwegians. On the sixteenth a pastor came on board and preached for us. He seemed a nice man and we bought books from him. I bought a Bible and two New Testaments, one in Norwegian and one in English, for one dollar. A man who was with him gave small books to the passengers; all were in Norwegian, ABCs and others. I must repeat what so many others have said, that strong eyes are required because there is so much to see that it is quite unbelievable. We haven't arrived at a final agreement on our passage to Milwaukee, but I think it will be six and a half dollars.

Praise God who has led us across the great ocean to this place without loss. We cannot know how he will lead us in the future. I am writing these simple words to you now but it may be that it cannot be done again. Because we don't know how long we are to remain in this world. Dear parents and siblings, if you don't receive more letters from me before others leave next year I would like to have a letter from you and know if you all are alive and how this year has been. But I plan to write once more to you if God will grant me life and health. I have written about my own experience of this journey, and others who write may agree. But they say of our journey to America that it does not often happen that it is so fortunate. We haven't had any bad weather worth mentioning.

I'll conclude these simple words with the message that I've been in good health until this day. We are all well. Don't let this letter be sent from farm to farm so it may be seen by many, but keep it at home as it has been written at various times. Please give my regards to Mikkel Hougen and Knud Tostensrud and their families, to all at Foss, and to my sister Mari should you see her. My parents-in-law send their regards and are happy to have come here. Yes, you must believe that all I've written is the truth. And with this my loving regards from your distant son,

SVEND LARSEN HOUG

Many Norwegians have come on board and spoken with us and many others who we cannot understand. A Norwegian may take us to Milwaukee. Three people have been sent from Wisconsin to help the Norwegians so they won't be cheated. A person from Gol who has lived in Wisconsin for four years has come with letters for the Norwegians who have planned to come here this summer. He had letters from my wife's brothers telling us that Syver or Halsten will meet us in Milwaukee if nothing comes in the way. This is good news. As I've said, there is much to see here. Innumerable steamboats are going to and from the city and from one end of the city to another. I must now end my letter as I have neither time nor paper for more and I have to finish it. Farewell in God. This is the wish of your distant brother and son.

SVEND LARSEN HOUG

· ——— ·

SLH wrote his first letter before the *Drafna* left Drammen (Nor. ed. I:66). The ship took this one back to Drammen after first going with cargo to St. John, New Brunswick, and from there with lumber to Grimsby in England, where it arrived on October 16. Someone, probably Ole Larsen Haug, has noted that the letter was received on 21 November 1852. The many people who came on board the ship in New York were agents for hotels and companies that carried immigrants from New York to destinations further west. Agents of the same ethnicity as the immigrants had an obvious advantage, but they were not necessarily more honest than others. Immigrants in settlements in Wisconsin established a coordinated assistance for newcomers in New York, bringing letters for those who were expected and warning against dishonest agents.

SLH emigrated with his wife Margit, her parents Halsten and Ragnhild Groth, and her brothers Johannes and Assor from Hol. Other brothers had already emigrated: Syver in 1848 and Kitil, Ola, Svend, Torkjell, and Halsten in 1849. The farm, now written Grøtt, had been taken over by Assor, who sold it before they all emigrated. SLH and his family in Aal were followers of the lay preacher Hans Nielsen Hauge (1771–1824) and his writing shows his familiarity with the language of contemporary religious literature. The Hauge tradition lived on among Norwegian immigrants in the United States, in particular in the synod that bore his name, the Hauge Synod. SLH's parents both died in 1853; he sent his letters to his older brother Ole who inherited the farm. The *prim* he recommended is made by boiling the whey of milk until it acquires a brown and fairly soft consistency. The milk would be sour and the bread unleavened. The pastor who boarded the *Drafna* was probably Oluf Gustaf Hedström, a Swedish Methodist pastor, who worked among Scandinavian immigrants in New York. »1:35 NE 1:68

1852 — LETTER 1:32

FROM: Elise Wærenskjold, *Four Mile Prairie, Texas, 26 September 1852*
To: Taale Andreas Gjestvang, *Løten, Hedmark*

Most honorable Mr. Gjestvang!

We've received all your letters and I wrote to you earlier this summer. Thank you for the three issues of *Hamars Budstikke*; the last one came Sunday. In your letter to my husband I see that you may be coming this winter and that you think a letter from us would arrive before your departure, so I'll write one now for the first mail even though I otherwise would have waited a few days, partly because several here are ill and partly because I haven't yet had an opportunity to get the certificate for Mrs. Engelhoug. Our family has enjoyed good health all summer, but last Sunday W. had the fever. Yesterday it was much milder and if we only had some quinine he would soon be well. Our lack of medicine has brought much expense and suffering on our neighbors. Emigrants must acquire quinine in New Orleans regardless of where they are going. It would also be good to have a supply of medicine for both constipation and diarrhea, which may so easily cause dehydration if you have no proper medication. For the former I believe castor oil, rhubarb, and perhaps senna tea, and for the latter laudanum and *morfin* (this word may be misspelled but this is how it is pronounced) would be good. If one has these medicines he should be able to cure himself without recourse to a physician. Almost all the newcomers have had the fever and several still have it: Brunstad's family, Dahl and his fiancée Christine, and Andersen, but I think they'll soon be well. At Qvestad's and Ringnes's they've been quite well and some haven't been touched by the fever. Grimseth, Halvorsen, Gran and his sister, Ballishoel, Anne Qvestad, and Olsen's son, who are all at Reiersen's, have also been ill now and again, but as far as I know they are now well. Reiersen had some fever for a few days but otherwise he and his family have been well. Johannes Foss and his family have had the fever but I believe they've come through now. Knud Olsen and Pedersen have had a few bouts with the fever; they are with Qvestad. Rønne is with Staack and has a fever now and then. As far as I know, none from Hedmark has died except for the elder Ringnes, who wasn't well when they left Norway. Ringnes's son, who looked as if he had only a few days to live when he arrived, is fully recovered. B. Eriksen is in the old Norwegian settlement and I don't know anything about him except that his father and a son went to Wisconsin. It is said that his father died on the journey. Bye and Graven remained in Shreveport as they had no more money. I wrote and asked them to let me know if they wished to come here. If so I would try to raise money for them. I had no reply and I've since heard that they went to the northern states.

We've had much rain here this summer and this has been very good for our fields. Now corn may be bought for twenty-five cents a bushel, the lowest price we've had since we arrived, but for the same reason there has also been more illness than at any other time since we came to Texas. Here on the prairie a very old (between seventy and eighty years) woman has died as well as a young man, Tallak Knudsen, who died of the ague and diarrhea. After he had had the fever several times he was so careless one day that he ate peaches, melons and honey and after that he had a constant strong diarrhea in addition to his fever. Had he only had medicine in time his life could no doubt have been saved. When he got it, it stopped his fever immediately but not his diarrhea, which took his life. The two old people who died last year, Engelhoug and Mollestad, were also able to break their fever but died of diarrhea. This illness also took old Reiersen's life, but he was more than seventy, and death comes to you wherever you may be. Brun, a man from Stavanger who came here from Iowa and who has lived on one of the unhealthiest farms in the old settlement, has also been very unlucky as he lost three children in the northern states and two this summer. I won't neglect to report all of this since I don't want it said that I've been silent about negative aspects. (I don't wish to waste any comments on the lies by the valley people. They are so like the stories about Engelhoug and Knud Olsen.)

My husband has set up a subscription list for a pastor and this is what we have in annual contributions: Wærenskjold $5; Staack $6; T. Knudsen $5 (he is now dead); Haagestøl, Mjaaland, Ormsen, and Aslak Nielsen $4 each; A. Vehus, Knudsen, John Paulsen, Aanon Knudsen, K. Knudsen, J. Foss, O. Fladland, Aanonsen, and Anders Nielsen $3 each. He hasn't visited any others except Reiersen. As he is a rationalist—I would call him anti-clerical—I don't think he'll care much about it. You will know most of these names from my letter. I would have liked to be able to tell you whether the people from Hedmark will contribute, but I don't know. When asked, they've avoided the issue except for Andersen, who said he will sign the list.

I wish you would come this winter. Yes, please do! If the editor of *Hamars B.* will print more of what I write, you may tell him I would prefer that my own spelling is retained. I see he has made several changes that according to my views are completely wrong. And a few important errors have been introduced: the capital is Austin, not Houston, an entirely different city, nor have I said in relation to the health situation that "...although they have their own carelessness to blame..." but: "...although they apparently to a large degree have their..." About land: Government land cannot be had for less than fifty cents an acre, but by purchasing certificates you may get it at a far lower price. Reiersen has written to you. It isn't long since I had a letter from Nordboe and he was then doing well. I'm surprised *Morgenbladet* would publish anything that was pro-emigration. An acquaintance has written to me that the cabinet minister Hans Riddervold has read my article with interest and expressed the view that something should be done to provide the destitute with the means to get started here. Oh, had they only done this to help the poor....

. ———— .

> The remainder of the letter has been lost. The newspaper *Hamars Budstikke* had published a translation of the French captain A. Tolmer's negative account of the United States and Gjestvang had sent clippings to EW, whose long response to Tolmer with an introduction by Gjestvang had been printed in *Hamars Budstikke* (see her 9 July 1851, letter to Gjestvang in *Studies* 20.) The spellings she objects to were according to one of the language reforms that eventually made written Norwegian less Danish. Her article was reprinted by the conservative Christiania newspaper *Morgenbladet* along with brief supporting statements by other Texas settlers, among them Cleng Peerson and Johannes Nordboe. In a letter to Gjestvang dated 8 December 1850 (Nor. ed. I:47), Johan Engebretsen Englaugsmoen wrote that he hoped his wife could come and join him. But he died and the certificate for his wife in Norway must be his death certificate. The letter seems to confuse him with Knud Olsen, "the elder Ringnes." Most of

the people in EW's account of the effects of the fever (malaria, then commonly called the ague) had come in 1851, while most of those on the subscription list had arrived in 1850. All of these may be identified by consulting Syversen (1982) or Nor. ed. There are letters from Hendrick Olsen Dahl and Christine Eriksdatter Furuset, who became his wife and then his widow, later in these volumes. «1:26 »1:33 NE I:70

. ——— .

1852 — LETTER 1:33

FROM: Elise Wærenskjold, *Four Mile Prairie, Texas, 21 November 1852*
To: Taale Andreas Gjestvang, *Løten, Hedmark*

—⇌⇋—

Most honorable Mr. Gjestvang!

You may already be on your way, but I have several reasons to send these lines to you; should you have left, only the postage will have been wasted. My husband had a letter from you some time ago. It had been posted in Shreveport and we also had a few lines from you brought by Johan Grimseth. Vilhelm has started a letter but I don't know when you'll have it. I fear I don't have good news as our settlement has been sorely afflicted with disease this year. As I wrote in my last letter, almost all have been ill and two, a very old woman and a young married man, died of the fever, the latter also of dysentery. As Ørbæk has a general store on J. R. Reiersen's property run by Michael Olsen from Hedmark (Ørbæk manages a store in Rusk for Reiersen's brother-in-law, Vinzent), we thought we could buy medicine at any time since this is sold at stores here. Pharmacies are only in the larger cities. This deplorable confidence that we could get medicine and particularly quinine was the reason no one thought of getting it direct from Shreveport where a one-ounce bottle can be had for four dollars. Last summer this would have been sufficient for a large family. If one can take some diuretic and a few quinine powders immediately on sensing the approach of fever, usually signaled by chills and heat waves, drowsiness and headaches, the disease may be arrested before it fully manifests itself. Once the attack is on, it may, except in a few rare cases, readily be broken, as we say, with the same means. It is necessary to take a little more quinine, usually each or every other hour, until the fever has departed. As you may know, this fever is periodic in that one is free from it in regular periods of varying length. One <u>usually</u> feels a strong chill and there is shivering all over the body and then it is good to cover up with many layers of clothes and drink hot lemonade, which I find both lowers the fever and quickly brings on a natural sense of warmth. Then follows an incredible dry heat that eventually leads to perspiration and then the fever is over for the time being. After taking quinine—ten or twelve powders will usually break the fever—one usually has one more attack of the fever and is then cured. For a permanent effect you should take a small amount of quinine mornings and evenings for a few days. You must also be very careful about what and how much you eat or drink and also avoid walking or working so you become exhausted or hot, because this may cause a return of the fever that you may break following the same procedure. Naturally, the longer you are ill without medicine, the more difficult it is to cure the illness and the more likely are complications with other illnesses, for instance dysentery, which is extremely dangerous and cannot be cured if it hasn't been possible to break the fever. All do not have the same symptoms; some may only get warm and others, more rarely, only feel the chill. Some run a fever every day, others every other or every third, indeed some only every fourth day. Moreover, the length and strength of the attacks vary considerably. With this you may better understand what follows.

This year, as I explained in my last letter, has been very unhealthy, probably a consequence of an unusual alternation of rain and sunshine. Not only Texas but the entire Union has to an unusual degree been afflicted by disease and death. The Norwegians have fared no better than others and in our settlement I believe all the Norwegians have had the fever and every tenth person has died. After I last wrote, the illness took on a more fatal character and in two and a half weeks seven Norwegians died. These were: 1. Anne Qvestad, who served as Reiersen's housekeeper and who in error killed herself with a strong poison for wolves and crows. The doctor was there when she died but unluckily he did not see the bottle of poison she had used until she was dead as it lay in her bed. 2. Johannes Olsen Foss, a very sad case as he had proved to be a kind and unusually active and hardworking provider for his family. During his illness his wife and their four children were ill, so he lacked care as well as medicine, as all his neighbors were ill. 3. A young unmarried man from West Norway, John Paulsen.

4. Margith Nielsen from West Norway, an excellent and truly Christian housewife. 5. Jørgen Vehus, an old man from West Norway. 6. Margrete Brunstad and 7. Johan Brunstad. Isn't this terrrible? You may imagine that this was a time of mourning. The burial ground is on our land and every morning I saw neighbors approaching I feared that they had come to dig a grave, and those who did the digging were often soon in need of a grave themselves. Most of these, perhaps all, could have been saved if we had only had quinine for the whole summer, but it was usually not available, as quinine rarely came to the store. When Olsen eventually acquired one or two, or at the most three bottles, he immediately sold it all to the Americans, not in small portions but in whole bottles without being concerned whether his countrymen lived or died, and for this reason quinine was only available in the store on the day it arrived. The last time he received three kinds and I believe he then had quinine from Saturday evening till Tuesday, probably the longest period he has had this article, which he only had for sale three or four times last summer. When you consider this, and also that the fever began in June and is still with us, you'll realize how inadequate our supply of quinine has been. I believe those who have neglected to supply us with this necessary article have been irresponsible. We have physicians here, but they are not very good, nor have they had quinine. Reiersen acquired three bottles and Qvestad and Ringnes one each, but this was too little for so many, especially as the illness had time to develop.

There was little care to be had as all were ill. My husband had just caught the disease when the worst period began, so my maid had to bring home the cows and calves and exposed herself to sun and rain. She also caught the fever and went home. When I was alone with everything I got it and my little Otto, who still isn't weaned, got it from me. After a few days of illness, however, we were able to get a little quinine and break the fever. Wærenskjold and I have had another visit by this unwelcome guest but we quickly threw him out the door with the assistance of quinine. Many are now well and the fever is no longer so bad. Had we had quinine, all would soon have been well. Mrs. Brunstad, who now lives with Reiersen and with whom I spoke the day before yesterday, says they have paid fifty dollars for a doctor and medicines. I'm sure they would only have needed ten dollars if they had had medicine in time and then they would also have avoided much pain and suffering in body and soul. I'm sure that I won't have to explain that many have been very careless, as you know how careless lower class Norwegians are when faced with illness, in particular as concerns <u>what</u> and <u>how much</u> they eat and drink, which is so important. Fresh, clean air is also important for the maintenance of health, but many don't care and many have lived in the midst of their corn field, let enormously large and smelly weeds grow right next to their home, stored raw wheat on their floor, and similar things that all surely have furthered the disease. We live in a fairly decent house where we never are in need of fresh air, and we had little fever. This is also the case at the Reiersens and the Staacks, where they have only had a few light attacks. All who died, with the exception of Mrs. Nielsen, are among those who arrived this year and last year, so it seems that the longer we are here, the better suited we are for the climate.

The many deaths have left painful wounds that will long be with us. They have caused a general lack of confidence so most appear eager to go to the older states if they only could sell their property. But when time has healed the pain I am sure most will prefer to remain in Texas. For my part I have not wanted to move a single moment (at least after a while, because during the first year I did have a desire to return to Norway when the fever raged). Illness cannot be avoided in any country and I would not like my son to learn to be obsequious to his betters and look down upon those below him as they do in Europe, where liberty and equality are only honored on paper but not in real life. If I were alone, however, I would just as soon live in Norway, as I never expect to live as comfortably here as I did there, both with regards to my social life and to many other spiritual as well as corporal benefits. It is quite certain, however, that this illness has been a setback for our settlement and now I regret that we can no longer think of getting a pastor. But I will not give up my hope that it may one day be possible. In the other settlement only four Norwegians have died as far as I know and in the town of Tyler two young brothers. The year I arrived, nine people died in the other settlement, but the Norwegians there were in the most unfortunate situation at that time. The disease is actually rarely fatal. Four died of dysentery, one of poison and two probably died of old age.

We have had a very good year. Grain sold for twenty-five cents a bushel, the cheapest since we arrived, when fifty cents was more common. Apart from this I have nothing to tell you and must therefore conclude with my friendly regards to you and your honored wife. Yours sincerely,

ELISE WÆRENSKJOLD

· ——— ·

> Numbers 6 and 7 were daughter and father. The Brunstads arrived in 1851. The widow, Anne Eriksdatter (1821–1903), from Furuset in Stange, married Berger Rogstad (1820–1880) in 1853 and they moved to the settlement in Bosque County, Texas, (here referred to as "the other settlement") the following year. «1:32 »1:74 NE I:72

· ——— ·

1852 — LETTER 1:34

FROM: Mari and Ingrid Helgesdatter Skare, *Spring Valley, Wisconsin*
28 December 1852

To: Helge Gundersen and Eli Andersdatter Skare, *Eggedal, Sigdal, Buskerud*

Dearest parents!

Finally, we can now tell you about our new home and our situation, what our journey was like, and how happy we are with what we have done. We know so well, dear parents, that you have longed for a letter from us and that you often have worried about why a letter never came. But you must forgive us. No one could have wanted to send you a message more than we who, as lost lambs wandering in a wilderness, have been cast around far from the home of loving parents and the pleasant company of dear brothers and sisters that used to sweeten the difficulties of life. It has been strange to leave the home of our childhood, ignorant as we were of the troubles of the world, inexperienced and untried in every way. It has indeed been strange and yet we must always have hope, a hope that must always be addressed to God. May it always be so! This is what we hope and what we wish. You are a living presence in our memory and we will never forget you and our memory of you will have a place in the hearts of your children until they cease to beat.

You may have heard of our voyage. Briefly told, we left Drammen May 15 and without difficulties we arrived in Quebec in good health July 2. Captain Tofte was competent and painstaking and all his crew were nice people. We left Quebec on the fifth and came to Milwaukee on the fourteenth. From Quebec we each paid seven dollars and a little extra to our interpreter. It took us four days to go from Milwaukee to Jefferson Prairie. We went there first and stayed for eight days. That cost us two dollars. We are now living with Erik Torstenson Lien from Numedal, where we are well taken care of.

We were both quite well on our voyage and are now in good health, for which we are grateful and praise our good Father in Heaven who has given us this and everything else. I, Mari, got ill on the way here and had to stay in bed for about six weeks. I had to have a doctor and we paid him six and a half dollars. I am now well again and quite satisfied even though dark thoughts have pervaded my soul. Ingrid has been well all the time and she went to work for some Americans seven weeks before Christmas. She was home from the twenty-fourth to yesterday when she returned to her service where she is quite satisfied.

So now you know what we have encountered till now and it hasn't been our fate to always have pleasant feelings. But we must be patient and submit all to the wisdom of Providence since we've lost the help and advice of a loyal father and a loving mother. He is the Father of the fatherless and the comfort and defender of the abandoned. He helps us and will be in your place and give us comfort and success. So we cannot say to our siblings, who may have a desire to follow us, that you must or must not come. For none may know what his fate will be. It would certainly be very nice to be united again and lovingly and happily enjoy each other's company. But you must all consider in your own conscience what it may mean to leave the peaceful and sheltered home of your parents and enter upon so long and difficult a journey. When you've done this and also sought council with God, then you may go without fear wherever you desire. This is our advice. As for the clothes we left behind, give them away because such clothes are not used here. It would be wrong to bring such things.

We haven't heard about old Beret and God knows whether she is dead or alive. Gullaug Narvesdatter says she is well and happy here. She has mostly been in service and wasn't home for Christmas. Could you tell this to her mother? Dear parents! We would so love to have a letter as soon as possible. Our friends and our home are always present in our mind's eye. Please let us know how things are at home and all else of interest and if any in our family are coming next summer. As there is nothing more of interest we will end our letter with wishes for your health. May you have the peace and blessing of Heaven! Greetings to all friends and relatives, but first and last to you, precious parents and beloved siblings! May we all once again be gathered in holy joy! Farewell!

YOUR LOVING DAUGHTERS MARI AND INGRID HELGESDATTER

Our address: *Mr. Erik Thorsteenson Lien, Springwally, Rock County, Springwally P.O. Wiskonsin of Nort-Amerika.*

⋅ —— ⋅

Mari Helgesdatter and her older sister, Ingrid, immigrated in 1852. The wharves of Drammen were bustling with emigrants in May 1852. In addition to their ship, *Christiane*, and *Drafna*, with Svend Houg on board (see his letter above), there were at least three other departures that month, one for Quebec and two for New York. The first settlers in the area around Jefferson Prairie, Wisc. came from Numedal in 1839. Ingrid and Mari's father, Helge Gundersen, lived on three different farms during the period he received the letters in these volumes: Skadeland, Skare, and Nedrum. In the usage of that time his last name changed according to where he lived. Here the name Skare is used throughout. Although Ingrid was not present at the time of writing, Mari uses the first person plural and includes her sister when she signs her letter. »1:53 NE 1:74

1852 — LETTER 1:35

FROM: Svend Larsen Houg, *Elgin, Iowa, 28 December 1852*
TO: Ole Larsen Haug, *Aal, Buskerud*

Dear parents, brothers, and sisters,

It is my fervent desire to say some simple words to you with my pen to let you know how God has led us since I last wrote you from New York. As you know, we arrived in New York on July 15 and stayed on board till the sixteenth so we could all wash up. The captain went into the city and exchanged money for us and we were given one dollar and three and a half cents for each *speciedaler*. I didn't go into the city myself as I had too much to do. Only a few crew members went and it is said to be a very big and wonderful city. On the seventeenth our journey continued, organized by a Norwegian named Holfeldt and we paid six and three-quarters dollars for each, including baggage, and nothing for children under three years. Our baggage was transferred to two barges pulled by a steamboat that pulled twenty-eight barges to a city called Albany, where we arrived on the nineteenth. Then we entered the canal, and now horses pulled the barges and horses were changed three times in twenty-four hours. We traveled night and day until we came to Buffalo on the twenty-seventh. Our little daughter got sick on the nineteenth and was ill while we were on the canal but we were able to care for her. At two in the afternoon she died just as we came into Buffalo so we were able to lay her out before we had to board a large steamboat. We weren't able to bury her there because our baggage had to be taken immediately and placed on the steamboat and when this was done it was evening and we couldn't bury her because the steamboat left that evening. On the twenty-eighth the boat stopped at another city and we buried her there. This cost us five dollars. But it so happened that a child of Arne Olson Opheimsjordet from Torpo also died that night so we could place both in one casket and we only had to pay two and a half each. It was good for us that we were treated so kindly. They came to the wharf with wagon and casket so we could place the children there ourselves. Then they went gently off with them. The next night a woman died and she was buried at a place where there was no graveyard. Our interpreter took care of all such things. His name was Iver Narum and he had been sent from Wisconsin as interpreter for the Norwegians. On this steamboat we crossed lakes that were so big that we often couldn't see land on either side. Their names are Lake Huron and Lake Michigan. All the baggage was heaped up on the deck so there was little space for the passengers, but we were in the stern where conditions were best. It was said that there were 700 people of different nations on board this steamboat.

We came to Milwaukee at night between July 31 and August 1 and our baggage was placed on the wharf. Halsten Groth found us an hour later and you may imagine how happy we were to see him. He had been waiting for us for two weeks. We stayed until August 2 and I bought two oxen and a wagon, paying sixty-one dollars for the oxen and forty-two for the wagon. Assor did the same and at the same price so we could take all our baggage ourselves. If we had had it sent to Iowa it would have cost us forty dollars, so we saved much of what it cost to buy the wagons. Old Halsten paid fifteen dollars to have his baggage taken to Rock Prairie, where his son Halsten had brought his oxen and wagon and would take his father's belongings on to Iowa. We left Milwaukee August 2 and came to Hermod Tufto in Muskego on the third and stayed there to the fourth. On the seventh we came to Rock Prairie to a man named Torkel Olsen Vammen from Numedal. He and his wife were very kind and we stayed with them for some days so we could wash ourselves and rebuild our wagons with large hoops on which we stretched canvas to protect ourselves from the rain on so long a journey. I bought a cow there for eighteen dollars and here in Iowa the price for such a cow is up to twenty-five dollars. In Beloit I bought a stove for eleven dollars and a vise for four dollars. We were ready to continue our journey on August 11 but we couldn't find our oxen and had to wait another day, and that night my wife went into labor and gave birth to a son at six in the morning. Her pain was of short duration for which we must thank God, especially since we were on so long a journey. We stayed there some days and she was soon well and the child was quiet. We continued our journey on the eighteenth and then came to Arne Solem. On the nineteenth we came to Halgrim Rotnemsjøen. On the twentieth we came to Johannes Mork. After that there were no Norwegians in our path so we slept in our wagons and these were as comfortable as houses since we had nice weather on our entire journey. We came to the Mississippi on the twenty-eighth and crossed the river on a ferry. We paid one dollar for each wagon and fifteen cents for a cow, but there was no charge for people.

On the twenty-ninth we came to Syver Groth. You have heard that Syver and Torkel were together but now Torkel has gone to California. He went last spring with several others, both Norwegians and Americans, at about the time we left Norway and their journey was much more dangerous than ours. I stayed with Syver and my parents-in-law were with Kitil and Assor with Halsten. My first task was to mow hay for my cattle, as there is an abundance of grass here. I have worked both for myself and for Syver, who harvested corn because this is done late in September and in October or even later as it isn't hurt by frost. But wheat is harvested in September. When they harvest corn they remove the cobs and the large stalks are left standing in the field. I've counted 700 kernels on one cob and I've heard that there can be even more on the largest ones, and each kernel is as large as a coffee bean. Well, don't think that I'm describing the bounty of America, but it was strange for us to see and I do believe that this is a bountiful land.

I had planned to live with Syver this winter but last fall I bought a parcel of the land that Ole Groth had taken. Many had thought of acquiring this land but had waited to see if any relatives would come. When Kitil learned that someone had bought a piece of it last spring he got Kitil Eriksen Rue to buy it either for himself or for one of us and they had me in mind. I've bought forty acres and this is enough for both field and meadow. Should I decide to plow twenty acres I could still mow hay for twenty cows. But my entire future property is 120 acres and most people claim 160 acres or even more. There are many here who have never paid as much as a cent for their land as it is possible to have land for a long time without paying for it as long as no one else buys it. This is possible because the government never comes and asks about anything. But they run the risk that someone can buy their land. However, the person who lives on the land has a right to buy it if he shows up immediately. I gave sixty-one dollars for the land I bought and I also bought a house for twelve dollars from the widow of Ole Grøth.

I moved here near the Turkey River in October. Kittil Grøth is my neighbor on one side and Kittil Eriksen Rue on the other. There are many kinds of trees here, ash, basswood, elm, and maple, and other trees for which I don't know the Norwegian names, but in many places there is only the hard oak that is difficult to use. We don't have to go far to a sawmill but it is a little further to a gristmill. But there will soon be a town and a gristmill where the sawmill is. They are now building the first store. I've planned to fence some of my land this winter so I can break some of it next spring and plant corn there, since corn but not wheat can be planted the first year after plowing. My only cattle are my two oxen and a cow. I also have a full grown pig and a little one that I bought for four dollars last fall. We have to buy everything. All tools and equipment are so expensive that it is difficult to get what is necessary if you don't have much money. So I regret that I didn't bring more iron tools from Norway because what you hear when you go to a blacksmith here is quite different from what it was in Norway. The only blacksmith is from Ringerike. Had I been able to pay the cost of setting up a forge it would have been good for others here as well, but I cannot do it on my own. We've already talked about setting up one and I cannot think of having a rake made until we have a forge.

Well, brother, you have already had much trouble with my affairs and now I have a question concerning the small account I left with you. You know that Meidel was to have three *speciedaler* and you have five. If anything remains I would like you to send it with a reliable person who is going to America next year. But I don't quite know whether I owe our sister Guri anything. You'll remember our agreement and if she hasn't received her share I suppose that what I have may not be sufficient.

I think you would ask what kind of religion we have here. My answer is that I've heard that where Norwegians have settled for some time they have Norwegian pastors and schools and things seem well organized. But they also say that people are divided in some places. Here they don't have their own pastor yet but many are members in Pastor Clausen's congregation and he will serve as their pastor and take care of necessary things until they have their own. There was another pastor here last summer and he held a service in Syver Groth's home the Sunday we arrived and he has also been here before. They know him well and say that he is truly a very good pastor. He returned October 12 and then our son Halsten was baptized. Some Norwegians here have prayer meetings.

Yes, my dear parents and siblings, I can give you the good news that I've been in good health since I left my fatherland except for a few days on our way from Rock Prairie when I had a touch of diarrhea that affects almost all who come to this country. Since then my health has been good, for which we must thank God since many of those who came with us and other newcomers have died of cholera and other illnesses. But all who set out from Grøth have been well. Nor can we speak of any adversities on our long journey as we all enjoyed good health and were given good advice when Halsten came to meet us. He is now married to Ragnil Knudsdatter Jeglum from Ustedalen who came here the same year he did. My wife and children have been in good health since we came.

I'm writing these simple words so you may see my present situation and that I haven't regretted my emigration. I'll soon have to conclude these simple words, yes, they are indeed simple but I've written them myself so you can see that they are written by my own hand. You can be sure that what I've said is the pure truth. In conclusion I must thank you for all your goodness and all your care. With this you are all lovingly remembered by me, my old parents, as well as my siblings. Yes, you, my brother's wife Kristi, are much thanked for the time I was in your company. And remember me to my sister Mari, should any of you see her. Give my regards to all who cannot be mentioned but who you know by name and to all who ask about me. And I have greetings from all from Grøth, young and old, that they are doing well and are happy here. Greetings from my wife and our small children. Live well in God; this is the wish of your distant son

SVEND LARSEN

This may be the last time I write to you. May God give us the power and strength to stand against sin and our corrupt flesh so we may love God and his holy word and be reborn in joy when our worldly wandering comes to an end. I expect a letter from you next year with an emigrant so I may hear from you whether you are alive. I'm addressing the letter to you my brother Ole but it isn't my intention that you should pay all the postage as I believe that you will all help each other in this, parents as well as siblings.

This has been a good year for corn and wheat. We haven't had potato rot as in the two previous years. Some had planted a lot and they harvested accordingly. Every year it is necessary to set fire to the grass, but on October 18 a lot more burned. After a long period without rain the grass had become quite dry. The fire burned out of control and we had a powerful wind and some lost all their hay, corn, and wheat to the fire while others were unaffected. But we didn't hear of any loss of buildings as all of this is kept out in the open. Our cattle are also mostly outdoors even though it is as cold here as in Norway. They get used to it and if the weather isn't extreme, they don't like to be indoors. But much hay is needed. I must ask you not to let this simple letter go from one place to another; keep it at home since it isn't composed or written for others. Farewell.

SVEND LARSEN HOUG

This is the address for letters that I would be very happy and grateful to receive: *Mr. Svend Larsen Houg, Elgin Post Office, Fayette County, Iowa.* If the bearer of your letter doesn't plan to come to the abovementioned place, he may hand it in at any post office so it can be sent to me by mail. This will cost five cents.

. —— .

> SLH used the post office in Elgin but lived a little further east in Clayton County, Iowa. At the end of the letter his brother-in-law Syvert Halstensen Groth wrote a few words. The agent John Holfeldt in New York had been an agent for Ole Bull's failed Oleanna project, and from 1853 he became an immigrant agent in Quebec. Commercial agents were not the only people who offered their services to new immigrants. Iver Olsen Narum, the first emigrant from Gol in Hallingdal, came with letters and followed them as an interpreter on their journey. On their way from Rock Prairie, Wisc. to Iowa they seem to have stopped at places where they were more or less expected by people whose names would be recognized in Hallingdal. Immigrants in Wisconsin had set up an informally organized support program for new immigrants. SLH's emotional difficulty in writing about the death of his daughter is evident here.
>
> When this letter was written Pastor Claus L. Clausen was still in Rock Prairie with his Luther Valley congregation. The next spring he led a group of settlers to St. Ansgar in Mitchell County, northwest of where SLH had settled. The pastor who had visited this settlement was Nils Olsen Brandt, who in 1851–1853 was home mission pastor for eastern Iowa and Minnesota. SLH writes about the local congregation in the third person, suggesting that he had not committed himself. Ole Grøth, now dead, had emigrated from Hol with his brothers Kitil, Svend, and Hallsten. Their neighbor Kitil Rue was also from Hol. Ole's widow, Gunhild Svendsdatter, could not use the land on her own. Houg tries to explain the working of the Preemption Act

of 1841, which gave settlers a right to stake claims on most surveyed land and buy up to 160 acres at the minimum price of $1.25 an acre. The rights of squatters on public lands had first been legalized in the temporary Preemption Act of 1830. Lars Meidel was a merchant in Nes in Hallingdal. The affairs of their sister Guro may relate to her share of the farm that now is owned by her brother Ole. In 1853 she married Embrik on the neighboring farm, also named Haug. Place names are as in most letters spelled idiosyncraticatically, for instance *Rokpreiriet* (Rock Prairie). «1:31 »1:40 NE I:75

1852 — LETTER 1:36

FROM: Jacob Olsen Østern, *Paint Creek, Lansing, Iowa*
29 December 1852

To: His family, *Bærum, Akershus*

My precious mother, siblings, parents-in-law, relatives, and friends,

Loving regards from your children and brothers. I received your letter May 4, my wedding day, and the day was made even more wonderful when I saw that you were all well. I was glad to see that my letter had arrived over so long a distance. In my letter of November 3, 1851, I wrote that Jacob and I were going to the pinery to earn some money. But you don't know what the word pinery means. This is forest work where they make lumber for the sawmills, and this was our work last winter. We did fairly well. We ate well and liked the work but housing was miserable. We were paid sixteen dollars a month for about five months and, praise God, we were well and healthy all the time. But you may imagine that we were anxious for our abandoned wives and the others of our company, since there was little opportunity to communicate with them. But we had no reason to worry, praise God, and we found them all safe and sound on April 19, 1852.

In my last letter I wrote that I wouldn't advise my brothers Engebret and Lars, and Carl and A. Christensen at Fossum to emigrate as they have good opportunities at home. I assumed that Gullik and Christen had already made up their minds. I long to see relatives and friends but you must note that I don't advise any to emigrate, for this is a journey that everyone must decide on his own. If you're not set on going you may lose your courage and become impatient even before you're here. But I must say it as it is, work is well paid everywhere. An able man may make a dollar a day and board. A young woman who knows the language is usually paid two dollars a week; servant girls are usually hired by the week but may be employed all year. The soil is very fertile and is probably superior to the best land in Norway. I assume that a family man with enough money for the journey and then some will in a short time be in a comfortable position. If he has children of about sixteen they can already be well paid, in particular girls since they are paid almost as well as adults, and they will thus be able to assist their parents. If God grants health, I believe that both parents and children will do better here than in Norway. When a man works on his own land and makes a living he is a free man and he won't have a tyrant who controls his time and his will as the situation is for the common man in Norway. Single people can make as much money here in a year as in several years in Norway. This year Jacob Engebretsen made 103 dollars in about seven months. I did different things last summer, I plowed some land, cut lumber, and built a house that isn't yet finished.

I cannot tell you exactly what provisions to bring for the voyage. But I do know that it isn't wise to have too much pork. Bring meat that has been well salted and dried or salted in tubs that will retain the brine so the meat will stay good. It would be a good idea to bring some spiced and salt sausage as well as potatoes and some good herring. Oatmeal bread is good to have if it is made as we made it. Our rusks were good but they must be raised and well baked and be quite cold before they are divided and dried. Loaves of bread are good for about three weeks. And, indeed, some pork as well if it isn't too fatty. But the kind of cream that we prepared is of little use. You should also have some good liquor, beer, and vinegar. On coming to New York many either sell or throw over board leftover bread, flour, and oatmeal, but this is foolish if baggage is free on further transportation because food that can be bought along the way is expensive and not the food you are used to. We still had flour and oatmeal and some oat bread when we came to Iowa. In my last letter I told you that I didn't think it would be possible to meet you at Jefferson Prairie as it would take such a large part of the summer and there is so much to do here since we don't have the houses and fences we need. But we must try to exchange letters so we can have your views on this matter. I think it would be best to buy oxen and a wagon in Milwaukee where the prices are best. A pair of oxen may be bought for forty dollars and a new wagon also forty dollars, and should you want to sell them when you arrive here you may get one hundred dollars. I told you that Jacob and I had a quarter section of school land but we were unlucky in this, as the person who was to take care of registration hadn't done it. When we returned from the pinery the land had been bought. Since there was no available land around here at Congress price that we liked, we had to buy the right to a claim, and there is still much such land available here. But we don't have the money to buy more than we need ourselves. It is possible that land of this kind will be available next year. (I don't have time to write any more about this now.)

I must take up my pen again after a long time and tell you a little more. Lars Johnsen Eeg has been to Minnesota to look around and he was quite satisfied. He was about twenty-four miles from here and saw very little settlement. So there should be land there at Congress price. Karen Østern has asked for information about clothes in case she decided to come. I think all should bring their woolen clothes, both homespun and blended with cotton, if they don't lack money for their ticket. It is very cold here and such cloth is quite expensive. I regretted that I had sold all my everyday clothes, and in particular my big overcoat, as it would have been good on the voyage. Here I have used my new duffle coat.

I have much to do and little time for writing. I wrote two letters last summer but they were damaged so I couldn't send them. I'm sorry that you haven't received any letters and this one will be late as you should have had it before Christmas. My dear uncle John Jacobsen asks for information on what the journey will cost, but I cannot say this since prices can be so different and it will also depend on what provisions are brought. It is very expensive to buy food along the canal and Lake Michigan and in Milwaukee. But in Jefferson Prairie a new supply may be bought since it isn't so expensive there. Jacob Engebretsen has gone to the pinery again for eighteen dollars a month. He left October 28 with Ole Olsen Hunstad from Sigdal, Thore Engebretsen Eeg, and Erik Lathus. Laurine and Martea are with us and are healthy and well. Laurine is with child again and expects it in March. She is quite well and asks to be remembered to friends and acquaintances.

· ⎯⎯ ·

> This letter has neither signature nor date and was written over many days. It must have been difficult for readers in Norway to understand

the legal provisions for the acquisition of land. "Congress price" was $1.25 an acre. Squatters could stake a claim of up to 160 acres on public land and have the first right to buy it when the land was put up for sale. His brother-in-law, Thore Engebretsen Eeg (the farm name is now spelled Eik), Lars Johnsen Eeg, and Erik Nilsen Lathus were in the group that emigrated in 1851. Laurine and Martea are the wife and daughter of Jacob Engebretsen Eeg. «1:28 »1:37 NE I:76

1853 — LETTER 1:37

FROM: Jacob Olsen Østern, *Paint Creek, Lansing, Iowa, 9 February 1853*

TO: His family, *Bærum, Akershus*

Dear mother, siblings, parents in law, relatives, and friends,

Loving regards from your children and your brothers. I received a note from Gullik and a letter from Karen Engebretsdatter Østern January 23, 1853. I see that you long for letters. I admit that I've been far too careless in writing, but I would prefer that whoever decides to emigrate does this without my advice. I've written two letters that haven't been sent. Last winter I wrote a letter to my parents-in-law but it advised them to emigrate and Jacob said it was far too early to advise them to come. So it is still here. The second letter has been taken by our good neighbors, the mice, and they have chewed it up. This was before we got a cat. And, finally, I wrote a letter that was posted December 29, 1852, and I hope you've received it. My dear uncle John Jacobsen asks for advice, but I cannot give a direct answer. I think it would be good for a man in his position to come here as he has children who are old enough to help him, both in his own work and working for others. The same may be said for Carl Aas if they have money for the journey. But it is difficult to work out how much will be needed. And I must add that both man and wife must be of one mind, that is they must both want to emigrate, and if there is a will there is a way, as the saying goes. It is of course convenient to have some money left over upon arriving. But if God grants health it is possible to earn money here.

It shouldn't be difficult to imagine that it takes a lot of hard work to break soil for a new farm. I haven't hired out to others since April 1852. I've plowed about thirteen acres and cut and hauled logs and set up our house. Now I'm busy cutting and hauling rails for fencing. But oak is hard to cut and heavy to haul. But I am, praise God, healthy and have the strength for hard work and I think that the time when I'll see ample returns for my labor is not far away—if God will maintain my health and give my work his blessing.

I have the good news for my dear Gullik that I have three times forty acres of prairie land so there should be field enough for both of us if you don't want to go further west. I don't have any forest land yet but I expect this will soon be taken care of. Karen asks for news of our wives and wants to know if they are expecting children. I wrote about this in my letter of December 29, 1852. My dear Christine bore me a son June 14, 1852, and we have named him Olof. You'll be too late for this great event, my good Karen. Laurine is again with child and I think she expects in March. You'll have to hurry to get here in time but I know you can make the journey in five or six weeks if you follow the mail and then you should be here in time. We'll see how serious you are about this. But you're worried that the journey is long and difficult. I won't gainsay you in this but you must remember how God led the children of Israel across the Red Sea and freed them from slavery in Egypt. I've written that I won't advise anyone to come here but I certainly won't advise anyone to remain in Wedel's slavery so long as Kyhn and his like are holding the reins.

Gullik asks for information about the journey from Quebec but I know nothing about it. I know that some have come from Sweden to New Orleans and gone up the Mississippi River to St. Paul, which is about 300 miles north of here. If you would dare to book passage that way, I'm sure it would be the simplest as well as the cheapest, but my ignorance of conditions there prohibits me from giving any advice. I've heard said that it is so warm there that a coat isn't necessary for outdoor work during winter. But if you dare to go this way, you must leave around New Year so you could get to New Orleans in early spring. Then you could go as far up the Mississippi River as the ice permits and wait for the ice to break up and continue the journey. Then you would only have seven miles from Columbus to us. But regardless of the way you choose, you should try to leave as early as possible in the spring in order to make the journey here before it gets too hot.

I've heard that malaria is said to rage here but we have avoided this disease to date. But I had severe diarrhea when we were on the canal, perhaps because we drank too much water that contained some saltpeter. It was very hot so we drank a lot of water and we also ate some white bread made with baking powder so it was as soft as a sponge. I cannot really say whether it was the change in diet or the climate that was the cause. But it is supposed to help to add some ginger that may be brought from Norway to the drinking water or to mix it with syrup that is called molasses and sold everywhere in America. By adding either of these to the water it is supposed to become a much healthier drink. But for anyone who can bring his own food, it would be best to stick to this as much as possible. Anyone coming here should bring their woolen clothes but other clothes are as cheap here as in Norway. It is very cold so thick clothes are necessary at some times during winter. But boots and shoes are as cheap here as in Norway.

Give my regards to mother and tell her that she mustn't worry about me for I live well and am happy here. I wish she too were here, but I think she is too old to set out on such a journey. If Gullik comes and wants to bring a gun, then bring a rifle. There are many deer here about the size of reindeer and you cannot shoot them with a shotgun. We have an American neighbor who shot twenty of them in January. But if you buy a rifle or any other gun, you should coat it and fill the barrel with tallow, because on the ship all guns are placed in a room where they get very rusty. Be careful of all accidents, especially while on the canal because of the many bridges. Some are so low that there is hardly any space between the bridge and the boat. There are many locks where the boat scrapes against the stone wall so it is easy to be hurt if you are not careful. All went well with us, but I've heard of many accidents along the canal. A. Christensen writes that he was sitting with Gullik drinking aquavit and punch when he wrote. Enjoy yourselves, my friends. I remember well what it was like at the mill at Bogstad, but I'm grateful for my freedom. I wouldn't change places with any of you regardless of how much I was paid. Because here the laborer is a free man and is just as respected as the office holder if he behaves well.

JACOB OLSEN ØSTERN

Long Live Liberty! Hurrah for Liberty!
[*In margins*] Please do not set a seal to your letters. I had to pay sixty-three cents for the letter I received January 23, 1853, while the letter I received May 4, 1852, only cost twenty cents.

. ——— .

This letter was received 16 April 1853. The brothers Jacob and Gullik Olsen Østern were married to the sisters Christine and Karen Engebretsdatter. Jacob Engebretsen Østern was the brother of Christine and Karen. Gullik and Karen emigrated later in 1853. Jacob Olsen's liberal views are evident in his closing declaration and in his references to the harsh conditions for those who were dependent on the two large landowners in Bærum, Baron Harald Wedel-Jarlsberg (1811–1897), who owned the iron foundry, Bærums Verk, and about one-sixth of the cultivated land in Bærum, and the Løvenskiold family, who owned Fossum Bruk, the sawmill at Bogstad, as well as a large estate. Christian Ulrik Kyn then managed Fossum Bruk. A few days later JOØ wrote to Engebret Jacobsen Østern (Nor. ed. I:78) «1:36 »1:50 NE I:77

. ——— .

1853 — LETTER 1:38

FROM: Reinert and Sigbjørn Aslakson, *Coon Prairie, Wisconsin*
24 October 1853

To: Osmund Atlaksen Ovedal, *Sirdal, Vest-Agder*

⋅⇒◉⇐⋅

Dear brother Osmund Atlaksen Ovedahl,

It is long since I had the pleasure of hearing that you are doing well. My brothers and I are doing well. Sigbjørn and I had work last spring for one dollar a day. We worked three months but then we became unwell and felt that we were not strong enough to work and returned home. It was two to three hundred miles north of here and since then we haven't worked for others but I aim to do so soon. I suppose you've been waiting for a reply but you know what the country and its seasons are like so I haven't found it necessary. I wish to know whether you are thinking of following us to America. We would be happy to have a letter with the news that you were coming. It would be best if you all came together and not one every year. I won't encourage you. You must do as you wish, but if you come I'll meet you in Milwaukee if no one else from here is going. But if anyone I know is going you can come with them and then it isn't necessary that I go. Please write me as soon as you can. I forgot to tell you that I was in the pinery last winter and worked for sixteen dollars a month. I have no news. All I know here are living well. Loving regards from me,

REINERT A. ASLAGSON OVEDAL

I must also write that I'm well. I haven't been sick for more than two weeks since coming here. When Reinert and I were on our long journey we got to see what the country is like. There is land enough even if many should come. All land is not equally good but it always bears fruit without being fertilized. I don't think it is necessary to write more about this since you have heard about the quality of the land in many letters. I am well satisfied here and I think it is better for those who can work to get along here whether or not they have a family. I won't advise any to come or not to come but I would like to see my siblings here. Sivert is doing well. He worked twenty miles from here for six months for fifty dollars. Then he got sick and now he is here. I know of nothing more to write except to send my loving regards to all my siblings. Give those at Sandsmark our regards.

SIGBJØRN ASLAGSEN OVEDAL

. ——— .

RA (then twenty-six) and SA (twenty-two) emigrated on the bark *Emigrant* from Flekkefjord on 30 April 1851. Their brother Sivert cosigned a brief statement sent with this letter where the three declared that they wanted their share of their inheritance to be equally divided between the remaining siblings. Some of the immigrant siblings from Ovedal, which they also wrote Aavedahl, who all settled in Wisconsin and Minnesota, eventually changed their family name to Allikson. In the 1880 census, however, several are also listed with the family name Aslakson. Their brother Osmund was the only sibling who did not emigrate. »1:57 NE I:85

. ——— .

1853 — LETTER 1:39

FROM: Ole Johansen Holtseteren, *Oconomowoc, Wisconsin*
20 November 1853

TO: Ingebor Olsdatter and Peder Johansen Holtseteren, *Gausdal, Oppland*

⇢≡◉⇌⇠

Dear mother and siblings,

I have long awaited a letter from you but as I haven't heard anything I don't know whether you are alive or dead. So I'll write a few lines about how I am. I'm in good health and doing well, for which I must thank our almighty God. I work at my craft and usually make a dollar or three shillings a day. Last summer I went 700 miles to a river called Mississippi to go to Minnesota and look for land. I didn't see any I liked so I returned to Rock River. Recently I've discussed the purchase of some land from Torger Vinger. This would be a good home for me. I don't have much news for you except that as far as language is concerned I know a lot more than when I was in Norway. I can speak English and I can also get by in German. Last summer, when I got tired of being a shoemaker, I went to Ole Iversen and helped him with his haying and his harvest. I was there for six weeks. When I don't have work I live with Ole Iversen and that is a good home for me.

Dear mother, I don't have more to write about now. I must conclude my poor letter with my loving regards. I've thought about seeing my birthplace once more but I've made no decision. May God lead us and may God let his light shine over us whether we may be near or far away. Write to me as soon as you can. My friendly regards to my dear brother and sister and to all my friends. The times here are pretty good. Two years ago we had hard times, but now there is work for all who want it. Those who work for the railroad have good wages and the railroad goes everywhere in the entire country. From your faithful son

OLE JOHANSEN HAALTSÆTERN

· ─── ·

Some of his spellings of place names are *Meiseiscipi, Mensota,* and *Rokreiver.* «1:21 »1:91 NE I:87

· ─── ·

1853 — LETTER 1:40

From: Svend Larsen Houg, *Elgin, Iowa, 21 December 1853*
To: Ole and Knud Larsen and Mari Larsdatter Haug, *Aal, Buskerud*

Dear brother Ole and my other siblings,

I see that you still fondly remember me and I would like to talk with you but I'm unable to express the words with my pen that I would have spoken, but this isn't possible when we are so far from each other. I received your letter of September 23 on November 22 and it made me both glad and sad. Glad because I had news from you. I hadn't heard from you since I left even though you say that you wrote to me in April last year. I haven't received it and don't know if I ever will. But I was sad, dear brother, when I read that it has pleased our heavenly Father to take our parents from their earthly life in a hope for the eternal life. I'm glad that they prayed that they would be united with our Savior in the time of grace, which is so necessary for us all, also for those who are prepared to receive the certain guest, death. But I must berate myself, a wretched human being, that the good that I would, I do not; but the evil which I would not, that I do. Dear brother, do not forget me in your prayers, as I wish to remember you when God gives me the strength to pray. It is from Him that we must receive strength both to will and to do. Except in me you can achieve nothing, says Jesus. But I'm not as diligent and vigilant in my prayers as I should be and I do not let go of my worst sins as I should even though we have just as much opportunity to fear and love God here as in Norway, as the word of God is with us.

There are Norwegian printers here and many wonderful books have been printed. We often have meetings in our neighborhood and some of us say edifying words. We also have visitors who speak at our meetings and I believe they may be called true Christians. They say there are many kinds of religion here, among the Norwegians and in other nations, but I've never heard any Norwegian here say anything about religion that isn't in accordance with Norwegian Evangelical Lutheran doctrine. Yes, praise God for his pure and unfailing word among us. This is the only true road. Clausen held a service here last summer when he and many Norwegians were going to a new settlement in the west. Elling Eielsen has also been here and spoken to us. I had heard it said that he had gone over to another sect, but he spoke and explained the word of God very well according to my understanding and urged us to hold on to the doctrine that we had from home.

Dear brother, I see you have suffered a great worldly loss in losing your dear wife. This must have caused you great sorrow. But it may be that this was her time of grace and that this is why it pleased our Heavenly Father to embrace her. But this must have been a bitter cup for you who are alone with your children. "But Jesus has counted all your sighs and tears / And gives you comfort and takes away your fears / Your Jesus who embraces your soul in all his love / And shows you the glory that awaits us all above."

Dear siblings, I've had good health since I came to this country and I'm very satisfied, for which I cannot thank God enough. My wife got sick in the middle of August and was in bed for three weeks but she was able to get out of bed on her own. Then our son Lars got the same illness and needed much care. But I must thank God for sparing me and little Halsten. By that time I had cut hay and my wife's mother was with us so I was able to do the most necessary work such as tending the animals and other chores. After three weeks my wife was tolerably well but didn't have much strength when she bore a child, a fine girl, on October 24. Now we have three children. She was quite well for a while but then had a breast infection. This was the most difficult illness she has suffered and it took fourteen days before her breast was emptied of pus and this lessened her pain. She became better little by little, so now she is fairly well and can take care of her housework.

I'll now tell you about my worldly affairs. I broke four and a half acres last spring and planted corn, potatoes, and root vegetables. Last summer I broke three and a half acres so now I have eight acres ready for use. As for animals I have a pair of oxen, three cows and a calf. I'm feeding six pigs and have butchered two. The fruits of the soil are useful for both people and animals and I have enough grass to feed my animals, which is a great advantage as they are now quite expensive. A pair of draught oxen can cost from sixty to eighty dollars, a cow from twenty to twenty-eight, a calf six to ten dollars, because fewer animals are bred than people want to buy.

You say a little about my money matters that have caused you and my brother Knud so much trouble. You think that Erik will pay but that this is more doubtful over at Rotebakkdokken. Tell him that I don't think I've done anything that should make him withhold this money from me. You say you'll send what you are able to collect with Ole Løkensgaard and this is fine. Dear brother Ole, you say you want to pay me my share of the inheritance from my parents who were called away so soon after my departure. But I have no demands on you. I received what we agreed and you shouldn't think about such things now when there is so much pressure on you and our other siblings. However, we'll see how things may look if God gives us long lives and we continue to write to each other; your situation may improve. There are so many things I could write but I must limit myself. I can tell you that we again had a good year both for corn and wheat. I hear that God has also given you this, and it is good to know that we can thank God for his gifts.

Levor Hus once asked me to let him know whether I thought he should come to America. I'll simply say that he who comes here and can acquire some land and is able to cultivate it will be able to make a living. He who works for others can also make a living as the daily wages are high. Pay is from a half to one dollar a day depending on the season. For my part I'm glad I came here because if God grants me health and blesses the labor of my hands I hope to have a fairly good return. But there is much work before your fields are fenced, so you have to keep busy with your axe.

Sister Mari has written a little in your letter, brother Ole. She says she has thought of coming to America and asks my advice. I won't advise her not to come since this could be to her benefit, and I will write to her about this. If she decides to come she must write to me as soon as she knows when she will leave Norway with the name of the ship and the captain. I must try to find her some traveling companions on her way up through the country, because when they get off the ship they stand there quite perplexed and don't know where to go. If any of my relatives or friends should come at that time they could be with my sister and give her advice. So she must write to me so I can try to get someone to go with her. But it isn't easy for anyone to leave during the important summer months. My advice is to buy a ticket via Quebec and not New York and from there to Chicago.

Brother Ole, I think you have my adz. Can you let me have it if there is an opportunity to send it here? If you can do this you must deduct a good price from what is still owed me. Why did so few people come from Aal last spring? Could it be because of the false letters that we have heard were sent to Hol or because of any of the other rumors I have heard but not been able to verify?

Dear brother Knud, thank you for all the goodness you showed me when we were together. I've heard that you were faithful in taking care of our old parents during their last illness. May God reward you for this! I must conclude these simple lines. Loving regards to my siblings from my wife and our small children and from me, your distant brother. I have greetings from all relatives here, from the young and the old from Grøth. They are in good health and well satisified. Our mother's brother has been well since he came to this county. Torkel has returned from California in good health. I believe that Kittil Grøth and his wife have a sincere concern for their salvation and this should be important for us all. My love to you all! Farewell in God. This is my most sincere wish,

SVEND LARSEN HOUG

I'm sending this with my letter to sister Mari, so she'll probably have to pay for it, but I hope you and brother Knud will share in the expense.

· ——— ·

> This letter was received on 6 March 1854. SLH's mother, Ingrid Assorsdatter, was sister of his father-in-law, Halsten Assorsen Grøth, from Hol. Torkel, who had been in California, and Kittil Grøth were among his many brothers-in-law. SLH quotes from Romans 6:19. The hymn he quotes from has not been identified. Claus L. Clausen, a teacher from Denmark, and Elling Eielsen, a well-known lay preacher before his emigration, were the first to be ordained as Lutheran pastors among the Norwegian immigrants. Eielsen formed a synod that became the Hauge Synod while Clausen took part in creating the so-called Norwegian Synod in 1853. His relationship with the Synod was never easy and in 1853 he led a migration to a new settlement, St. Ansgar, in Mitchell County, Iowa. Sven Houg's negative attitude to "sects" reflects the teaching of Hans Nielsen Hauge, who admonished his followers to remain in the Norwegian state church. In the United States, however, the situation was different and many of the more pietist immigrants joined the Hauge Synod. Erik Nilsen bought the farm Rotebakkdokken in 1852, so this may be why he borrowed money. He emigrated with his wife, Gunhild Embriksdatter, in 1857, as did Ole Løkensgaard, who settled in Minnesota. «1:35 »1:51 NE 1:89

· ——— ·

1853 — LETTER 1:41

FROM: Magrete Nilsdatter and Ole Olsen Heve, *Cambridge, Wisconsin*
19 December 1853
To: Martha Haldorsdatter Nesheim, *Granvin, Hordaland*

Unforgettable relatives, dear and loving mother,

Please forgive me for not having sent you some lines with complete information about my situation. This is not because of indifference. You, my dear and beloved mother, have often been in my thoughts. And I've known that I've also been in your thoughts and that you have longed to hear from me. But my situation has regrettably been that I wasn't able to write myself and could thus not express myself as I wished. But now I hope I'll be able to show you in a simple yet truthful manner what my fate has been since I came to this faraway country. For me as for so many others, my fortune has not always been favorable. On the contrary, my fate has at times been dark and unpleasant. A true Christian must accept adversities, however great they may be.

I'll begin my story in a city called Milwaukee, where we landed after we had passed the lakes. I had no money and was, moreover, in debt to Haldor Løne for five dollars. As soon as we arrived a Norwegian named Frøiseth offered me work as a maid. I was glad since I could go no further because I had no money. So I naturally accepted his offer and agreed to work for half a dollar a week. But to my misfortune this was so poor a service that it could be compared to slavery. Their corrupt character was known among the Norwegians and they feared that I would talk with someone and that I would be advised to leave them. So they kept me from leaving the house. Not only did I have to work under the command of this swearing and screaming woman, but I also got to try what it is to go hungry even though I had come to the famously bountiful America. I was bound in this manner for half a year when I met a Norwegian named Ole Sætre in whose company I went to Koshkonong where I was glad to find my friends again. Although I had been in Milwaukee for half a year and had been ill treated, I was only given one and a half dollar. I eventually got the rest but I was now without money. In this manner I spent my first days in this country and since then my situation has been varied.

I went to Koshkonong in the cold of winter and my clothes were too poor to protect me from the cold. So I got sick and had to stay in bed for some time. I then lived with Haldor Løne. As soon as I was well again I went to a small village called Lake Mills and worked for some nice people for one dollar a week. I was paid regularly and on time and things seemed to be going better for me. I learned the language and also learned how they work so I could get employment when and where I wanted. After my sister came here I was in their home whenever I wished. But for the most part I was employed.

I heard rumors that there was much better pay in the city of Chicago than in small villages so I decided to go there. The distance was 120 miles. I came to the famous city in October 1851 and immediately got work with some distinguished and wealthy people. I was paid ten shillings a week, a good wage, and I was happy there. But this didn't last long. (The almighty God puts people in different circumstances, all according to his wise decision. He alone knows what is good for us.) Just as I was enjoying my position in Chicago I was struck by a bad disease called nerve rheumatism that settled in my right leg up to my hip. It was at first very painful and I had to stay in bed from the beginning of January to the middle of May. I was rather depressed when my knee began to be crooked and I feared that I might become crippled. But God be praised for his mercy. He again changed my sorrow to happiness. When I began to get better I was able to begin to move my foot and by the middle of May I was so well that I could leave the house and by June I was able to walk wherever I wanted without difficulty. I got work as a seamstress until late August. In the meantime I had become engaged to the widower Ole Olson Hæve. We were both tired of Chicago and decided to leave the city. We moved in the middle of September to a little town called Cambridge near Koshkonong Prairie, and got married. Then we naturally had to have our own home. We decided to settle here and bought a house and lot for 150 dollars. Here we now are and we find ourselves quite satisfied.

I'm glad I can say, dear mother, that I'm truly happy in my present situation. Even though I've often suffered disappointments this is now entirely forgotten and I'm surrounded by a circle of lovable children. You might think that it was much for me to become the mother of three children, but they have, praise God, been more a pleasure than a burden for me and I hope that with the help of God I'll behave so they will call me their dear and beloved mother. Last June I gave birth to a girl who has been a great comfort. She is a good child and has been in excellent health and grows stronger every day. I and my family have, praise God, been healthy since we came here and I can also say that my childbirth was without complications. I'll tell you the names and ages of my children. My oldest daughter Martha was ten on July 27, Anna was six April 1, and Kari was three January 1. My youngest daughter is named Marthe after you, my dear mother.

I have now described my life since I came to this country, so I believe it would please you if I also said a little about my siblings here as I am well acquainted with their situation. Synneve and her family are doing quite well and they've been very fortunate as far as their health is concerned. They are not wealthy but they have set a little aside every year and now have cattle worth about 130 dollars. They've bought a farm with five acres of cultivated fields and six acres of good meadow here in Cambridge. It is well fenced so I would call it a good property and they paid 300 dollars for it. They are of course in debt but if they remain healthy I think they'll manage. Land in a town is always expensive.

There is a nice Norwegian church here, but it belongs to a sect called Methodist. A few Norwegians have joined this sect; there are only twenty in the congregation. I don't know what to say about this sect but I can tell you how they do things. They are zealous in their worship and live morally. They don't drink spirits, nor do they swear; indeed, they renounce all serious vices. They go to church quite often and there they confess their spiritual state. (They usually confess that they are in harmony with the Lord and that they are quite sure of his grace and that, should they at that very moment die, they are sure of the salvation of their soul.) This is their confession and all of this is good if it comes from sincere hearts, which I hope that it, with the help of God, does for some. But I fear that for others there is quite a lot of Pharisaic hypocrisy. It is not for us to judge others in spiritual matters, but according to the sixth chapter of Matthew their prayers are outward.

Mikkel and my sister live a decent life, so I believe they are converted Christians. They are happy in their situation and when people can be satisfied, this is a priceless value. They have two girls and now Synneve is on her way to give birth again. My brother Johannes is for the most part out working so I hadn't seen him since I left Chicago when he came here last fall. He had been sick for about eight days and he wasn't quite well when he came to us. But after some days he got sick from another disease called the fever and ague or the cold fever and he was weak for about three weeks, but with the help of a good doctor and medicine he became quite well and he left us after a short while to go south looking for work. My brother Lars and Nils

Olson Seim went with him. Johannes is doing well, is quite satisfied, and has laid aside some money, but I don't know how much. Lars lives with us but he has for the most part been away at work. He has already laid aside some money, has lent out fifty dollars and also had money for his journey. Lars has been well since he left you and hasn't missed a single meal. He has of course at times longed for his old home and he has often spoken of you, our dear mother, which is not surprising. But I don't think that this longing hurts his spirit because he is for the most part quite happy. We haven't heard from them since they left but we expect a letter.

I don't have more to write that can be of interest for you my dear mother. So I'll conclude my story but I won't forget to add my many thanks for the religious books you have sent me and that have been so welcome. Please accept the gratitude of your faithful daughter. There is one thing that I almost forgot. When I was sick in Chicago I lived with John Kvilekval who is married to Ragnild Nilsdatter Kvinen and they were very kind to me, especially Ragnild. I can never thank her enough for her goodness to me during my illness. I must conclude my letter with loving regards to my unforgettable mother and brother. If we are not to see each other again in this world we may be worthy of finding each other in the holy mansions on the other side of the grave. This is my heartfelt desire,

MAGRETE NILSDATTER NÆSHEIM

As your unknown close relative I'll add a few lines to you my mother and brother-in-law and let you know something about my life in America. As it is ten and a half years since I came to this country, you may imagine that I've learned more about the world than in all my time in Norway. When I came to Chicago I was only twenty-six years old. I came with my wife and child and the folly of youth in my breast. I was disappointed in my youthful hopes and my small fortune had shrunk to six dollars. I had to consider how to support my family and I hired out as a carpenter even though I knew almost nothing of this craft. But things went well. I had enough work and I still work in this trade and I've built more houses than I can count and completed them both inside and out. I've always worked as a contractor and hired helpers and have at times done very well when I've had good contracts. I lived eight and a half years in Chicago and was the owner of two houses. The first was a small cabin that I sold for fifty dollars, but the next one was a good dwelling that I paid 300 dollars for and the lot cost me about 200 dollars. After my first wife died, I sold this house for 500 dollars, which was a great mistake as such properties have now more than doubled in value and the man who bought my property has now sold it for 1,200 dollars. Yes, such are the ways of the world. We could have had this money if we had lived one year longer in Chicago. I also had another lot in Chicago that I sold last year, making fifteen dollars, and if we had kept it we could have made 130. It isn't so difficult now to see the harm done by these sales, but we may not have lived any better if we had had this money.

When God grants us our health we have riches enough. Satisfaction is the most important for a happy life. I am truly very satisfied with my young wife. She is indeed a person with a pleasant disposition. She is a natural mother to my innocent children and that is a true joy for me to witness. May God help us so we may conduct ourselves in such a manner in this world that we may guide each other on the true road to salvation. In the time I have been in this country I've often been tempted by sectarian seducers and even heard dangerous advice from infidels or free thinkers. But no one shall, thank God, ever disturb me in my faith. I will hold fast to the faith that was implanted in me in childhood and this is also the decision of my wife. We and our family are members of the congregation of Pastor Preus on Koshkonong Prairie. I'll conclude my letter with my loving regards and should you have an occasion to do so, please give my regards to my brother Viking Gjernes and tell him that all his relatives are in good health and are doing well. I know of nothing but life in God, this is my wish,

OLE OLSEN HÆVE

P.S. As this letter was laid aside for a while before it was made ready for mailing, we can tell you that we've had a letter from Johannes and Lars. They are in Chicago and will stay there this winter. They are in good health and doing well. Nils Seim went somewhere else. A short while ago Synneve gave birth to a healthy girl and she has fully recovered. We can also tell you that Asgjerd, the wife of Anders Grimestad, died after being ill for two months. A boy she gave birth to while she was ill has also died.

· ⸻ ·

> Lars Nilsen Nesheim, brother of Magrete, wrote a letter from Bergen dated 6 May 1853, on his way to the United States. He tells his mother that he has met a returned immigrant who knew Ole Olsen Hove (Nor. ed. I:80). Magrete emigrated at the age of nineteen in 1849 on the sailing ship *17de Mai* that left Bergen on May 12 and came to New York on June 26. Her sister Synneve and her brother Johannes emigrated in 1850 on the bark *Kong Sverre*, leaving Bergen on May 8 and arriving in New York on July 13. Synneve married Mikkel Sjursen

Folkedal who emigrated on the same ship. She was then thirty-two and he was twenty. In 1864 Magrete and her husband moved to Vernon, Dodge County, Minn., where she died about 1923 (Rene 1930, 509). By 1867 their family name was Hove. The spelling of place names is often, as in so many of these letters, idiosyncratic, for instance *Kæmbrids* for Cambridge. Berendt A. Frøiseth is given a rather negative characterization by Knud Langeland (1887, 64). Haldor Brynjulfsen Løne emigrated on the same ship as Magrete. He settled in Christiana, near Cambridge, Wisc., where he and his family took the name Henderson (Rene 1930, 384–388). Ole Sjurson Sætre emigrated from Voss to Chicago in 1844, went on to Koshkonong in 1845, and lived there until he sold his farm in 1856 and settled in Olmstead County, Minn. (Rene 1930, 563–564 and Holand 1908, 499). John Haldorsen Qvileqval emigrated from Evanger in 1843 and lived in Chicago (Rene 1930, 258–259 and Blegen 1931, 202). Anders Knutsen and Asgjerd Grimestad emigrated from Voss in 1846 and settled in Christiana. In the 1865 census Ole Hove's brother, Viking Olsen, is listed as a farmer at Gjernes in Voss. The Koshkonong congregation was organized in 1844 with J. W. C. Dietrichson as pastor. He was succeeded by Adolph Carl Preus, president of the Norwegian Synod. »1:71 NE 1:90

1850 — LETTER 1:42

FROM: Tosten Levorsen Hvashovd and Hellik Olson Lehovd
Christiana, Wisconsin, 14 January 1854

TO: Ole Nirisen Vangestad and Ole Helgesen Lehovd, *Flesberg, Buskerud*

Good, old friend!

Thank you for the fine letter you sent me last summer with Ole Aaslandeie where I see that you haven't yet forgotten your childhood friend. I see that you have thought of coming here and ask my opinion. Even though I know you are doing well and have a good income and that it would take a long time before you were settled here, I nevertheless say that if you and your wife desire to do this and if you fully agree on leaving the place of your birth to come here and try out your future fortune, then I'm sure that it is far easier to make a living here than in Norway; if you can be at home here. But I must add that if you should ever feel unsatisfied with your choice then I won't be held responsible for your dissatisfaction for I know of many who have come here and who have damned those they blame for leaving Norway because they didn't realize that here they come to a new and uncultivated land but had expected that everything would be prepared and ready for them. However, when they have been here a year or two they have again changed their minds because then they have experienced the great difference between Norway and America. So I don't believe that you will regret your emigration if you arrive here safely and in good health, for which God alone governs. I may be able to give you advice on where you should go, but you should come to Wisconsin and find things out for yourself. There is now no more free land here, but there are many, both Americans and Norwegians, who wish to sell their farms, and he who has money will soon be established. As for myself, I have all reason to say that I've been fortunate in coming here and I certainly don't long to return. Had I remained in Norway I would probably not have had sufficient land for our daily bread, but last fall I harvested 1,500 bushels of wheat, rye, barley, and oats as well as more than 120 bushels of corn.

Please let my brothers hear my words. Give them my brotherly regards and say that I and all mine as well as Hellik are in good health, for which God be praised! And tell my brother Levor that I'm surprised that he cannot tear himself away from home and come here and no longer remain there and waste his best years for almost nothing. For I've been told that he is working for others and if he did this here he could make as much in one year as he there can make in ten. Here the monthly pay during winter is ten to twelve dollars and during summer sixteen to eighteen dollars, and if a farm laborer hires out for an entire year the regular wage is 110 to 130, yes up to 140 dollars a year. And he can come home every night and not as in Norway have to slave out in the forest or along the roads both night and day. You may think that such a hired man is far too expensive and wonder how a farmer can have an income that allows him to pay such wages, but I have had a hired man. I paid 120 dollars for a year and I can assure you that it isn't more difficult to give a laborer such a pay here than it is to give him eight or ten dollars in Norway.

As for religion and the preaching of the true word of God among the Norwegians, we have no reason for complaint. We have a very good pastor who is active and diligent in his important calling. We have Norwegian teachers of religion for our children and regular English schools where all can send their children for free and where even adults can attend to learn the language of the country. You will understand that we, praise God, have no reason for complaint as concerns our worldly or our spiritual needs.

Please give my loving regards to Hellik Tostensen Fikkan, Hellik Andersen Aasleggen, Gullik Sjursen Vatnebrønn and Ole Olsen Ørstein and all relatives and acquaintances. My regards also go to you and to all yours as I give you my welcome to America with my wishes for all the best in your future. Farewell in God. Yours faithfully,

THOSTEIN LEVERSEN

Mr. Ole N. Wangestad,

Please excuse me for making use of this opportunity to inform my parents about my situation. Would you please be so kind as to let them have this as soon as convenient? You will no doubt find some way of sharing the postage.

HELLEIK OLSEN LEHOVD

Dear parents and siblings!

I can give you the happy tidings that I've arrived and find myself quite satisfied. I've been in good health since I left you. My voyage took nine weeks and three days from Drammen to Quebec and from there it took me fourteen days to get to Hvashovd. I was welcomed by Tosten Hvashovd and could rest there after my journey before I went out to get work. Since coming here I haven't seen anyone eat bread of oatmeal so I have been deprived of this daily nourishment; here all bread is of wheat and rye, and butter, meat, and pork are eaten daily even by the poorest. I went out among the Americans and in spite of my youth and my ignorance of their ways of working as well as their language I was paid ten dollars a month. But now I've been at home about a month for Christmas and will soon find work again. I'm well taken care of and Tosten and his wife treat me as one of their children.

I've had the honor of meeting Herbrand Osland but I fear he is the same here as he was in Norway and perhaps even worse. Even though it is easy to earn money here his income is hardly sufficient to keep him in clothes. Regardless of how much money he makes he doesn't even have decent clothes as all goes to pay for his liquor. He swears and scolds so disgustingly at those he sees that it is terrible to see and hear him. He has not yet been able to pay me for what I bought for him in Norway. He may write and boast as much as he will but this is the sad truth. In his drunken state he has fallen and dislocated his shoulder more than ten times and when the doctor has set it again he has repaid him by asking him to kiss his ass and this is all the doctor gets.

Please write to me about your situation and of other things that it would be good for me to hear. My loving regards to you all from your son and brother,

HELLEIK OLSEN

> Many of the letters from HOL were copied, suggesting that they circulated among relatives and friends. This letter, for instance, exists in the original as well as in two copies with differences in spelling and punctuation. It was stamped in Christiana on January 18 and in New York on January 28. Since people were named for the farm on which they lived, this name changed when people moved. Immigrants felt free to use either the name of a place they had lived or their patronymic as their new family name. HOL uses the name Hvashovd for Tosten Levorsen (who emigrated with his wife Kirsti Gundersdatter in 1842) and his farm while Tosten also signs himself Bergerud. In later correspondence both names are used. In the 1865 census one brother of Tosten lives at Bergerud while another lives at Hvashovd. Hellik and his brothers from Lehovd at some point began to write their patronymic Olson rather than Olsen. »1:49 NE I:91

1854 — LETTER 1:43

FROM: Gullik Olsen Østern, *Paint Creek, Lansing, Iowa, 14 February 1854*

To: Engebret Olsen Steen, *Skedsmo, Akershus*

Dear brother,

My brother Jacob has received a letter with greetings to me from you, your wife, and our dearest and beloved mother and I'm glad to see that you are all in good health. I also see that you've received half a letter from me and know that we have arrived safely at our destination. Now you are getting a complete letter so you won't have to wonder how I'm doing in my new home. We have, praise God, enjoyed good health till now, and this is the greatest good in life. As for an income, I have the best expectations. Last fall I worked nine days for twenty bushels of wheat and this will serve us well for a long time. The best pork costs five cents a pound, butter ten cents. There is no set wage during spring and summer; it depends on your contract. During haying and harvest it is mostly one dollar a day and the least a man will work for is half a dollar. Meals are always included. This winter my work is cutting rails and you may believe that this is not work for little boys as we split them from oak logs that you cannot reach around. If I have time for more I'll cut logs for a house, but this is still uncertain since so much is needed for rails. I'm happy with my situation here and have no desire to be back in Norway. But I still long for my dear mother and brothers and you are often in my thoughts. You speak of the moment when we took farewell and that was truly a difficult time. God knows how much I wanted to linger with you but I felt too weak to face the situation. My heart was near breaking when we said goodbye for the last time on the wharf and I couldn't speak because I would have cried if I tried. It wasn't the journey itself that made me so sad; no that made me glad and I'm still glad; it was the thought that I would never again see my mother and brothers.

On December 7, 1853, my dear Karen bore me a daughter. She is healthy and sound and we've called her Helga Pauline. Karen has been in good health, praise God, since the child was born. We live on a very beautiful rise of land where the air is healthy and fresh. The summer is much warmer than in Norway, but we enjoy a cool wind almost every day so the heat is not as stifling as it otherwise would have been. The winter is pretty much like the Norwegian winter. I and Jacob drove wheat to Columbus at the time you had fun at the Christiania fair. We haven't heard anything from our brother Carl. Write to him and give him our address so we can learn how he is doing. We've had a letter from brother Lars and see that he and his family are in good health. Give them our regards and tell them that we are sound and healthy and doing well in our new home. Love to mother from me, my wife, little Helga, and our foster daughter Olava, and to you and your wife from your devoted brother. There is no homespun to be had here as there are no sheep yet and this is bad since the winter is cold and warm clothes are necessary.

G. O. ØSTERN

Gullik Olsen and Karen Engebretsdatter Østern and their eight-year-old daughter, Olava, and Gullik's brother, Christen, sailed from Christiania on the bark *Zephyr*, arriving in New York on 7 June 1853. Engebret Olsen Steen was a teacher at Steen in Skedsmo in Akershus from 1847 until he emigrated in 1867. »1:50 NE I:92

1854 — LETTER 1:44

FROM: Herbrand Paulsen Osland, *Christiana, Wisconsin, 11 March 1854*
To: Hellik Paalsen Aasland, *Flesland, Buskerud*

I am greatly pleased to see in your honored letter of April 27, 1853, that you are all in good health. I see that my brother Ole came to America last summer but he has gone to his brother-in-law Knud Watnebryn 150 miles south of where I live. I've heard that he works his brother-in-law's farm, and I will with God's help visit them as soon as I have an opportunity. Their oldest daughter Boel is dead and Ole has been somewhat sick this winter but is now able to work. I can give you greetings from Hellik Lehovd that he has been in good health since he left his home and that he lives near me with Tosten Bergerud. He mostly works for Americans and earns ten dollars a month.

Will you please send this letter to those my son is living with and tell them that it would be my greatest pleasure that he came to me, as anyone may imagine that it would be good for a father to see his son after such a long separation. I and others believe it would serve him well in the future if he emigrated while young, which I hope will be next summer. Please give my regards to my brother-in-law Ole Lehovd. He would do well for his son if he let him come to America. Ask him if he would help my son come here as soon as possible and tell him that his sister's daughter Joran has been a little sick but that she has now gone to a city called Madison where she works for a Yankee. But she isn't very well paid and only earns half a dollar a week. I think she will work for Kittil Fjøse as he has bought land about forty miles further west. I must also ask you to send my letter to Ole Lehovd and see if he would send me a pair of mittens of the same kind he sent me before and also a sheepskin as they are very expensive here as well as mohair yarn for a dollar, preferably blue. We have had two good years but wheat and cattle are very expensive. A bushel of wheat costs one dollar and a good cow costs from thirty to forty dollars.

I've had a letter from my father's brother in New York State. They have had a very poor year but are doing quite well and are in good health. In conclusion I can tell you that I had an accident and dislocated my shoulder and that this has happened several times so I cannot do work other than tailoring. I now live with Anders Lindaas. Please write to me as soon as you get this poor letter. I must conclude with greetings to all my relatives and friends but first and last to my unforgettable mother. Live well.

HERBRAN PAULSEN

This is the last letter from HPO. On his death see a letter from Hellik Olson Lehovd 1:55. «1:22 NE 1:94

1854 — LETTER 1:45

FROM: Nils Ludvigsen Elvetun, *Madison, Wisconsin, 12 July 1854*
TO: Ludvig Kristiansen Elvetun, *Solvorn, Luster, Sogn og Fjordane*

Dear father and siblings,

As God has granted me health to this date I'll send you some crooked lines about my dangerous emigration to the distant land America. It is where you least of all expect to find it as it took so many unpleasant hours before we came here to our friends. We left Bergen May 1 at ten o'clock and by two we could no longer see Norway's mountains and May 2 we passed to the north of the Scotland islands where we could see the headlands. We had a good westerly wind for eight or nine days. Then we had a northwesterly gale and we had to drift without sails for eight days. But nothing was closed and none of us was seasick as that had been done with the first days we were at sea. After that we were seasick now and then. But I can write about the cold. It was colder than the coldest winter at home. And I can tell you why; 500 miles from Bergen we met large icebergs. Yes, we could see twenty to thirty around our ship all day and the captain said that the largest were one hundred feet high from the sea. When the nights were dark they had to take down the sails and let us drift and they tortured us in this manner for six days. Then we came to the Newfoundland Bank, a fishing area that is 2,000 miles from Quebec and this bank stretches for 700 miles east and west and 3,000 ships fish there every year. Then we came near land and the fjord that goes 840 miles up to Quebec. There were reefs and skerries all the way and every day we saw ships that had run aground on the skerries and ships could use as much time on that fjord as across the ocean. The current runs six hours up and six hours down and when we were 200 miles from Quebec the water changed: it became clear and we could drink it.

Eight people were left behind in the hospital in Quebec. We were four days in Quebec before we were allowed to go up through the country. Three times we had to go on steamboats through canals. Then we came to a city called Hamilton and took a train to Detroit. Then we went one mile on a steamboat again. Then we took a train to Chicago and from Chicago a steamboat to Milwaukee, and the whole way they mistreated us worse than dumb animals, and I wouldn't wish it on my worst enemy to come to Quebec. The whole way it was so unwholesome that people died every day. Tomas Solvi's wife died on the train between Detroit and Chicago and a young foreigner died of the poisonous cholera in Milwaukee. Then we took the train from Milwaukee to Madison, where we arrived on July 4. We had come discouraged to Quebec June 18.

The journey is not as people imagine. But troubles and difficulties truly come before happiness and pleasure; all concern for your well-being is gone when you come with your life and health to your friends. Every day I have coffee, tea, wheat bread, pork, butter, and cider and I sit down with knife and fork at every meal. But I'll warn you that if any plan to come next spring, they must not go to Quebec because that is the most difficult route you can go. I advise all who can earn their bread in their homeland to stay there and to those who have families I will say with certainty that it won't be nice to come here. Many who could have fed their families at home curse themselves for making the journey. I haven't enjoyed myself to this day. The homes in America are no better than barns in Norway and it is as when you come to a mountain pasture in Norway that each man sits on his own land. It is not as many have written to Norway that they become bigwigs as soon as they arrive, as when Sjur Floge and others have written that they wouldn't change places with farmers with the largest farms in Norway. Newcomers for the most part live in earth cellars and labor for their daily bread. I live with Ole Nilsen Havnen and he came with his oxen for me and my baggage and Erik Grov came for Trond and the girls from Ugulen. And now more unpleasantness. Shoemaker Hansen died of the poisonous cholera the first day we came to Erik Grov and many others got it but they got medicine that helped them. But many died. All we know arrived safely. The cholera mostly takes those who are older and many of them have died. I wish I were back when I get up every day.

My loving regards to you my dear sister Karen and to Sjur Sjursen and Amund Sjursen and Ole Sjursen. I won't advise any of you to come here yet. I'll write again in the fall. Give my regards to Synneva Olsdatter and her sister and to Peter Pettersen that I have arrived in the distant America. Address your letter to *Nils Ludvigsen Elvttun i Sand Præri i Nord Ammerika i Maddison Postofis*.

· ——— ·

> This letter is in the archives of the Dean in Bergen for the year 1854. Those who received it may have thought it should be brought to the attention of this ecclesiastical official because of its negative view of emigration. There are few such letters but we may assume that many emigrants felt discouraged. Like many others, NLE did not have a word for train and called it a steam wagon. He eventually decided that the United States was not for him: the 1865 census shows that he was back in Solvorn. He was then thirty-five, unmarried, and living with his seventy-year-old father. Solvorn was a compact village by the fjord and the fields were on the slopes. NE II:T11

· ——— ·

1854 — LETTER 1:46

FROM: Johanne Svenningsdatter Songe, *Howard, Illinois, 16 July 1854*
TO: Her family, *Songe, Holt, Tvedestrand, Aust-Agder*

⋅→≡◉≡⋅←

Dearly beloved parents and siblings!

Now that I have come safely to America I must let you know that I'm in good health and that I'm now with Mogens Sevig where I plan to live for a while. We left Risør on April 11 and came to Quebec May 30 after a pleasant voyage. We left June 1 and came to Montreal the next day. Then we were pulled by horses until we had passed the Niagara Falls and then we went by train to Buffalo. From Buffalo we went straight to Milwaukee by steamboat. It isn't worse to go by train than to use horses, but if anything goes wrong it can be dangerous since it goes so fast. In Quebec a letter from Mogens advised me to go via Chicago, but as the others in my group wanted to go via Milwaukee I couldn't do this and went with Halvor Knudsen and Hans Evensen to a town called Dodgeville where we met Svenning A. Braathen. He and his family were all well. Here I stayed for eight days until I was able to go with someone to where Mons lives. Except for the three weeks I was seasick I have been well all the time. I must thank the Almighty that he has maintained me in life and health, as many of the Norwegian immigrants have died of cholera and others have lost their lives on the railroad.

I have been very happy here and it seems that most people manage better than in Norway, so I hope that I won't regret my emigration. But I won't advise anyone to emigrate as there are many difficulties before settling down. But the pay is better here for all kinds of work. In Milwaukee I met Terje Sørensen, Salve Andersen, Jeppe Svenningsen Hofsnæs, Bent Knudsen, and John Larsen who were all waiting for letters from their relatives. I didn't meet other people that I knew. I came to Mons on June 28 and found him doing well. He has two healthy boys, Svenning who is five years and one who was born May 17 but who isn't baptized, as pastor Dietrichson hasn't been here since then. A stone church has been built in this settlement and they have the same religion as at home. They use Guldberg's book of hymns and most people have Lars Linderoth's book of sermons. It seems that people fear God more here than in Norway, but this may be because people are exposed to more illness than in Norway. Ole H. Næs was in bed with the cold fever when I came but he is now able to do a little outdoor work. It is rather hot, much hotter than at home. People have begun to cradle the winter wheat. The scythe they use to mow the wheat is called a cradle and the work is called to cradle. Some have also done their haying. Mons has cut hay for twelve cows in seven days helped by two men, and I also helped with a rake.

Please reply to this letter if you receive it and let me know how you are and whether you want more letters from me since you didn't ask me to write when I left. In conclusion, my most loving regards. May God our Father bless you and maintain you in life and health. It was difficult to leave my old and dear parents and siblings, but we must comfort each other with the hope that we will see each other again. May we live such lives that this hope may be granted. Give my regards to Gjeruld and Thore and to all our relatives, neighbors, and friends, and you my dear parents and siblings are lovingly greeted by your distant but faithful daughter and sister,

JOHANNE SVENNINGSDATTER SONGE

. ⎯⎯ .

A notice in *Morgenbladet* for April 18 says that the brig *Feyr* left Risør on April 11 after having waited for several days for a favorable wind. The newspaper also notes that there were many Mormons onboard. Mons is an informal version of Mogens. The pastor was Gustav Fredrik Dietrichson. The Danish pastor Guldberg's book of hymns (*Psalme-Bog*) was first published in Copenhagen in 1778 and was used in Norway through the first half of the nineteenth century. Lars Linderot (1761–1811) was a Swedish pastor and hymn writer. His collection of sermons, popularly known as Linderot's Postill, was widely used in Norway. The letter has *krill* (noun) and *krille* (verb) for cradle, loan words in the immigrants' spoken Norwegian. »1:56
NE I:96

1854 — LETTER 1:47

From: Christopher Jacobson, *Batavia, Illinois, 18 July 1854*
To: Hans Jakobsen Hilton, *Kløfta, Ullensaker, Akershus*

Dear mother and siblings,

You must have waited very long for a letter and the local gossips have no doubt talked of our ruin, but this is not, praise God, the case. The reason we haven't written is that we haven't been settled until now. First, I'll give a brief account of our voyage. We sailed from Kragerø on April 8 at eight in the morning and the emigrants' last farewell with Norway was a series of cannon salutes and loud cheers. We sailed rapidly across the North Sea, where nothing happened that is worth noting. On Maundy Thursday and Good Friday we sailed past England, so it was Easter when we entered the great ocean. Nothing much happened here either; we had some serious gales a few times but for the most part we had a good steady wind. We had a fiddler onboard and since the weather was so nice we could dance when we wanted to; when there are 226 passengers there are always some who want to dance. On the Day of Prayer we came to the Newfoundland Bank about 200 miles from Quebec. Here there were many large icebergs, so large that no one has so large a house in Ullensaker. No sooner had we passed these than we came to a mass of smaller pieces of ice. We had to lie there for eight days because we couldn't sail through the ice and it was terribly cold. But luckily the weather was calm; had we had a gale we would have been crushed in the ice. Several hundred ships were gathered there. Finally we were free from the ice and we sailed rapidly up the river where we had a beautiful landscape on both sides. At five-thirty on Ascension Day morning we anchored at a wharf in Quebec. Our voyage of six weeks and three days was now over. Three had died and two were born onboard. I don't find it necessary to tell you about all that can be disagreeable on an emigrant ship, how the women argue about a place near the smokestack, etc.

We were two days in Quebec. Stangeland was the first onboard and then came a hunchback named Hornfeldt. They were agents for different companies and they almost got into a fight. For, as you may imagine, both were eager to serve their fellow Norwegians. The American company's affairs were not in order and so we had to give one of these our confidence. After considering it for a long time we chose Hornfeldt's English company as it was said to be the fastest. We went on a large steamboat from Quebec to Montreal. It had more than 1,500 passengers. Then we took another steamboat to Hamilton and from there by railroad to Detroit and then on to Chicago. This went fast and the entire journey cost eight dollars and seventy-five cents. In Chicago we spent eight days waiting for our baggage as it had been left at one of the stations between Detroit and Chicago and been sent back to our starting point. This was probably the fault of the engineer. On the return journey one of the cars of the train went off the rails. There were passengers in this car and six were killed and many were hurt. Many chests were broken up and much baggage got lost, but my chest was undamaged. Kristian and I had all our baggage, as did Ole Olstad and Gulbrand Ausen.

When we got our baggage we went to Batavia where we met Haagen and immediately got work at a lumber mill that is being built here. We earn nine shillings a day. America is an extraordinarily beautiful and fertile country and I think it would be worthwhile for anyone who labors for his bread to come here. Wages are high and those who acquire enough money to buy land can do much better here. But it isn't so good to begin with, before you learn the language. I don't think that old people who can manage in Norway should expose themselves to the long journey. The sun is much higher here than in Norway but the days are shorter and the nights darker. I forgot to tell you how much we pay for our meals for a week: two dollars and twenty-five cents. All food is more expensive here; how would a farmer be able to pay such wages if he didn't get paid for his products?

The Americans have an especially well-ordered society. They never dance or have any kind of festivity on Sundays. The Norwegians can have their children well educated. We have a Norwegian pastor in a little town about four or five miles from here. I have no more to tell you except that we are all well, which is our good fortune, because newcomers seldom avoid illness as the climate here is different from in Norway. There is a terrible cholera epidemic in Chicago; 2,000 have died daily, but it isn't here. My regards to Lars and Kari and everyone at Frogner and also to you from your

KRISTOFER JACOBSEN

CJ had grown up on a farm that was part of Frogner in Ullensaker. He sailed on the bark *Inga* that arrived in Quebec on May 25. His brother Hans had the farm Hilton in Ullensaker. As recorded in his many letters to his brother, he wandered over much of the United States until he eventually settled with his nephew Jacob Hanson Hilton in New Mexico. Since so many Norwegian immigrants were entering via Quebec after 1850, there were several Norwegians working as agents there, among them Elias Stangeland and John Holfeldt, the former representing among others the state of Wisconsin (see Øverland 1989). The smokestack on a sailing ship would be for the cooking of food. The Day of Prayer, the fourth Friday after Easter, is still a holiday in Denmark. In Norway it was moved to a Friday in November and in 1950 ceased to be observed. Two shillings ("two bits") was equivalent to twenty-five cents. »1:80 NE I:98

1854 — LETTER 1:48

FROM: Elias Hansen Narjord, *Dorchester, Iowa, 4 September 1854*
TO: Hans Pedersen Narjord, *Os, Hedmark*

As I'm so far away I must tell you about our journey from Quebec with my pen. I wrote to you there and hope you have received it. We came to Quebec June 14 and after dinner on the sixteenth we went to Montreal and arrived at eight in the morning of the seventeenth. On the morning of the nineteenth we went on another steamboat to Hamilton, arriving there at three in the afternoon of the twentieth. Here we went on a train and had to pay extra for our baggage; everyone could bring 100 pounds for free and then seventy-five cents for every extra 100 pounds. We left at midnight and came to Detroit on the morning of the twenty-first and crossed a large river on a steamboat and came to the greatest railroad station we had seen on our entire journey with several thousands of wagons. In a building we saw sixteen locomotives that they were working on and they were almost finished. I don't know how many passengers were on the train as they got on at every station. We left at one in the afternoon and came to Chicago on the evening of the twenty-second. We had contracted with Holfeldt in Quebec and paid eight dollars and seventy-five cents for every adult. Children under twelve were half price and nothing for children under three. We slept one night on the train and stayed one day in Chicago until the morning of the twenty-fifth. Then we went on a train to Rock Island because the railroad hadn't been built all the way to Galena. We paid three and a half dollars for every adult and arrived there at seven in the evening. We left at nine in the morning on a steamboat to Galena and arrived at three in the afternoon of the twenty-seventh. We went on a steamboat at ten in the morning and many in our company got sick of the cholera and were taken to a hospital. Since they didn't have money they were paid for by the city. Esten Larsen and Olava Jonsdatter were sick and she died about four hours after we had left. I and several others helped to carry them to the hospital. Hendrik Sortbekken, a woman from Holtaalen, a girl who had a boyfriend who had gone to America the year before, and a two-year-old child all died. Henrik's wife was sick but she got well again and the others are well. We left that place and came to Lansing at three in the morning of the twenty-eighth and there we paid two dollars each. We met some Norwegians and went with them to where the people from Røros have settled. On the thirtieth we came to Lars Raaen and Ole Bakos and on July first we came to Bent Haanes and Tron Lang. Since then we've lived with Bent and we'll stay here through the winter. We've been fortunate on our entire journey so I must say that we haven't had problems. We haven't been sick on the journey except for a little seasickness, but this wasn't much and we must thank the almighty God. We have no reason for complaint.

At first we were very disappointed because the houses here are so poor. I can compare them to a temporary barn made of birch and with clay and gravel between the logs and we didn't believe people lived in them. But now I realize that they live better in poor houses here than in palaces in Norway. But I admit that I and others in our company wished we were back in Norway when we walked around on the first day. Things didn't look well; the sun was hot and we were tired because we were so little used to walking. But I'm certain that it will be much better when we have been here longer. I visited Jens Erlemoen on July 15 and bought a cow for twenty-five dollars. He was very happy in America and he thought he was in a paradise compared to Norway. But I didn't think so, because his house was half-finished with only three courses of logs on the second floor. This was his home, with a roof of hay, and he hasn't yet bought any land. On the seventeenth I bought another one for twenty-four dollars, and I was very fortunate and got a good price because the common price for a cow here is from twenty-five to forty dollars. And August 20 I bought yet another one for twenty-nine dollars. There is no shortage of grass for hay. Here you may have as many cows as you like and I have enough hay for them.

On July 28 my wife gave birth to a little daughter and it happened quickly. She was not in bed for more than a week but now her breasts are infected, so I haven't had time to be away at work yet. Wages are good here, for the most part one dollar a day and meals in the summer season. In winter you can get work cutting wood.

I must tell you about the landscape. The land isn't flat but has valleys between mountains and also large prairies. Most land here has been bought. There is no forest and no water and the little forest is like a birch forest in Norway and not good for building houses. But the land is fertile, all kinds of seeds grow without fertilizer and the seed doesn't freeze here. But everything you need to buy is expensive. It is quite common to pay one dollar for a bushel of wheat and sixteen or eighteen cents for a pound of coffee. There is a war in Europe and they ship as much wheat as they have in America and this is why it is so expensive. I can see that it is better to live here than in Norway even though there are many problems here that no one is aware of before they come. There are few who don't get sick with the ague or cold fever, the cholera, and many other diseases. And those who are out working for others are often in fatal danger so things can be difficult here. It is fine as long as you are well but I would absolutely advise those who have a family and a living not to come here because it is expensive. When we traveled up through the country a quart of milk cost five cents and a small loaf of wheat bread twelve to twenty cents, so it was quite expensive for those who had to buy food; twelve cents for a meal was the cheapest you could get. But we had enough food and still have food so we haven't bought much yet. Here they pay from fifty to eighty dollars for a wagon and eighty to 140 dollars for a team of oxen and from 100 to 200 dollars for a horse and forty to fifty for a yearling, so there is more money here than in Norway and he who wants to buy a small farm must have at least a thousand....

. ⎯ .

> The last page or pages are missing. The texts of the letters from EHN are according to contemporary copies. EHN was from Os, a munici-

pality in northern Hedmark, and his wife, Ane Kristine Tørrisdatter, was from the farm Paalsdalen, also called Tøresdalen, in Røros. Both Røros and Holtaalen are in southern Sør-Trøndelag. The Norwegian immigrant ship that arrived in Quebec on June 14, 1854, was the brig *Wilhelm Tell* that had left Christiania on April 19. EHN and Christopher Jacobsen (1:47) give slightly different accounts of the route between Hamilton in Upper Canada and Detroit, but the most important difference is between the journey these two had from Quebec and the more strenuous routes used in the immediately preceding years. The growing number of immigrants landing in Quebec had brought about improvements in transportation. The railroad from Detroit to Chicago was completed in 1852. Haanes and Langen are farms in Røros; Raaen is in Holtaalen; those mentioned are former neighbors. Jens Jørgensen Erlemoen emigrated from Tolga in Hedmark in 1852 and had a farm in Spring Grove, Houston County, Minn. (Ulvestad 1913, 606). The war is the Crimean War, 1853–1856. »1:54 NE I:100

1854 — LETTER 1:49

FROM: Hellik Olson Lehovd, *Christiana, Wisconsin, 12 November 1854*

TO: Ole Helgesen and Joran Paulsdatter Lehovd, *Flesberg, Buskerud*

Dear parents and siblings,

Your letter, dear father, of April 2 didn't get to me until September 20 so I had to wait a long time before I could get any reliable news about how things were at home. Letters sent with emigrants often come late. But regardless of how long I had to wait, I was happy to learn that you all, parents and siblings, are doing well and that none of my dear ones have met with any accident or grief since I left. As for myself, I must thank God who has maintained me in good health to this time except for minor changes that give no cause for complaint. But we had a time of pestilence last summer when the cholera and other diseases brought many people to their graves.

We've had a good harvest and a good income for workers as the daily wage last summer was one and a half to two dollars a day. You wonder whether I got all my baggage. I brought my things but left my box on the ship because it was much too big and heavy when they weighed my baggage, and I bought a smaller one instead. Most people bring far too much, such as Norwegian tools, which are of no use here, and work clothes that are of little value. But it is useful to bring good woolen cloth. My money was more than sufficient and I had seventeen dollars when I came here to Hvashovd. I live with Tosten Levorsen when I'm home and this is very nice. You are all lovingly greeted from all at Hvashovd, both Tosten and Hellik. They are doing well and are quite satisfied. Tosten received his letter when I got mine and he asks me to give you his most sincere thanks. I've heard that Herbrand Osland has had a letter from you father where you had some words for me but I haven't seen it and he says that he has thrown it away. You write that I shall have my share of the inheritance but I'm far from envious that the Lord has blessed your labor. I'm glad to hear of your prosperity, and should God be so good as to continue to maintain me in my health, then I do not at all long for my inheritance but rather wish that you will live long and happy lives. This doesn't mean that I disparage what may become my share, because my parents' gifts are dear to me. Give my regards to my dear uncle Ole Eilovsen and tell him that if he really wants to come here, I don't think that he will regret it if he retains his health. So say that I wish him welcome next spring. Please give my regards to my relatives and friends as well as any who wish to hear from me and tell them that I'm doing well. But first and last my regards go to my parents and siblings with my dearest wishes for your well-being, in life and in death, from your son and brother,

HELLIK OLSEN LEHOVD

Write to me father when convenient and send it by mail. Then I'll be sure to receive your letter. I will gladly pay the postage.

· —— ·

> Tosten Levorsen's wife, Kirsti Gundersdatter, was the sister of Hellik Gundersen, who was married to Tosten's sister, Marit Levorsdatter. They all used the name Hvashovd (a farm name), also spelled Washovd. «1:42 »1:55 NE I:103

· —— ·

1854 — LETTER 1:50

From: Jacob Olsen Østern, *Paint Creek, Lansing, Iowa*
9 August–26 November 1854

To: Engebret Olsen Steen, *Skedsmo, Akershus*

⇥⇒⇐⇤

Dear Engebret!

Please give my dear mother and brothers greetings from me, my wife and son, and my other relatives. I am sad to have to tell you that times are difficult here. Our relatives came to Columbus on Sunday, July 23, and I brought them to our home where we then were twenty-three people. On Thursday the twenty-seventh the cholera arrived. Haagine Engebretsdatter Østern got sick at eight in the morning and died at four in the afternoon. Jacob Johnsen Fossum got sick that same day and died on the morning of the twenty-eighth. My dear Christine got sick on the morning of the twenty-eighth and fought this terrible disease until six in the morning of the twenty-ninth. She survived the cholera— but wait! She was with child and expected her delivery in late August and her unborn baby died during her cholera. She suffered labor pains on top of her other misery and lost the child on the morning of the thirtieth. But, praise God, she is today—August 9—strong enough to get out of bed on her own and take a few steps. My little Olof was also sick. I don't know if it was cholera but he is also well now, thank God. You may imagine my state under such circumstances, my dear brother. The pain and exhaustion made me sick too and I had to stay in bed for a day.

But you must steel yourself, my dear brother, for I'm not yet through with my sad story. You know that Christine Carlsdatter Aas was married to a man from Switzerland named Mr. Drue. He got cholera in the morning of July 31 and died in the afternoon. Our dear Christen worked for him and he also got cholera on August 2 and died on the eighth. So today, August 9, we have buried a brother. But we must say with Job, the Lord gave, and the Lord hath taken away; blessed be the name of the Lord. I must tell you Christen's last words, as he gave them to Gullik. He asked us all to pray for him and to send his regards to mother. You must pass on his regards to his friends, if any are in your neighborhood.

Today is November 26, 1854, the twenty-fourth Sunday after Pentecost, so this paper has been long at rest, my dear brother. But it may be that it nevertheless will find you and my dear mother still alive, and, this is my hope, also in good health, along with my brothers Lars and Carl. Please accept our loving regards from me, my wife and son, and our relatives and friends. We are all, praise God, in good health, but Christine's mother died October 29, but not of cholera. When the time comes to leave this world, death needs no cholera. When I began this letter I was rather discouraged. It was as if I could no longer appreciate America and its climate and I saw only the negative aspects of America's many advantages. It's true that I've experienced that the climate is not as healthy as in Norway and that cholera is a disease found in all parts of the world except our beloved fatherland, so may God help us to be prepared and ready when death calls upon us.

I must tell you about this year's harvest. I had 125 bushels of wheat and 340 bushels of corn and forty bushels of potatoes. You may wish to know the prices here. For wheat we get a dollar, for corn forty cents and for potatoes sixty cents, all of this is for the bushel. I was in Columbus Thursday and sold three fat pigs and got five cents a pound. But the pigs I have are quite small. I had eight pigs, four fully grown and four small ones and then I bought seven, five fully grown and two small, at Mr. Drue's auction from his widow Christine. I will keep one of the large ones I bought to breed more, so I have eight for slaughter.

I've written that you shouldn't believe that everything stands ready waiting for you upon coming to America. In your next letter you remarked that you thought we all had to work hard for what we wanted to have. But, dear brother, let us two now understand each other. A simple laborer in Norway has to work as much as he possibly can just to have enough from day to day. But here a man may be paid seventy-five cents a day and board and for this he'll not only be able to feed a family but lay aside some money so long as he is able to work. But you must understand that all who come to America want to have their own land, and then it becomes entirely different from working for wages. You need tools and equipment, oxen, and cows. Then imagine going out on a large open tract of land and beginning to work. There are no fences, no buildings, nothing has been plowed, and nothing has been planted. On such a place you'll have to do a lot of work before you can get any money for your labor. But if you've worked under a contract you'll feel the value of being a free man. Your time and your belongings are your own and if God will only grant health you'll soon be able to enjoy the fruits of your own labor. I've always been more satisfied here, even under difficult conditions, than as an office clerk for Mr. Wedel.

I must tell you that our uncle John Jacobsen Fossum has died of cholera. He got sick in Chicago and was in a hospital there and they sent us a letter that he was dead. His children are working around here. Engebret works for an American for five dollars a month, Martine is in Columbus, Ingeborg is in Lansing, and Thorine is in Prairie du Chien. Martine earns one and a quarter dollar a week, Thorine earns five dollars a month, and Ingeborg earns one dollar a week. Lars works for a man from Hallingdal here on the prairie and works for full board and clothes and little Maren Otilie is with Thore Eeg. She is sound and healthy and has become so thick and fat that it is a pleasure to see her. All are doing well.

Please send this letter or a copy to Lars and Carl. Dear Lars, you ask me whether you should go to America. I must ask to be excused from this difficult assignment. I'm as reluctant to advise you to come here as I am to return to Norway and be a *husmann* under the good-for-nothing Norwegian farmers. Live well my dear mother and brothers. May God let you be as satisfied as I! And, dear mother, you have greetings from your brother Engebret. He is a widower and it's difficult for him to accept his fate. He lives with us.

JACOB OLSEN ØSTERN

. ——— .

In Nor. ed. the last part of this letter beginning "But here a man may be paid..." was mistakenly published as a fragment of a later letter. When he writes of working "under a contract" he is referring to the kind of contract that bound a *husmann,* or crofter, to work a specified number of days for the landowner for the right to live on and work a small piece of land. Baron Harald Wedel-Jarlsberg was a large landowner in Bærum. Christine Aas married Frans Ludvig Drue on 7 January 1854. Mari Olsdatter Aas and Gullik Olsen Østern sent a letter about the epidemic with the same mail. «1:37 »1:77 NE I:105

. ——— .

1854 — LETTER 1:51

FROM: Svend Larsen Houg, *Elgin, Iowa, 13 December 1854*
TO: Ole and Knut Larsen and Mari Larsdatter Haug, *Aal, Buskerud*

Dear brothers Ole and Knut and my other siblings,

I'm very glad to have letters from you and I received your letter of April 21 on October 10. It's the only way we now can speak with each other, we who are brothers in the flesh and cannot use our voices. We must hope to be brothers in the spirit and be so lowly and simple that the Holy Spirit may do his work in our hearts. But I often try to use my own strength even though it is of no avail for we must pray for strength from him, who is the beginning and end of faith, to begin and complete the work on our soul. I'm glad to hear that you have received such an edifying letter from our father's brother Elling, that the Lord doesn't cease to work on him, and that his son Ole has entered into a changed life. Yes, it was good to hear that he had a knock on the door of his heart so he could wake up from his sleep in sin and be united with his Savior in this world. The day of grace and salvation is upon us and it is time to be prepared.

As for the affairs of this world, I have by the grace of God always been in good health and been able to do my worldly work, which we must do as long as we are in this world. My wife has also been quite well except that late in September she and our son Lars were touched by the same disease as last fall. But this was soon over. This is the disease we call the cold fever in Norway but that here is called the ague. Now all are well; may we understand that this is all due to the grace of God. For our daily needs we also enjoy God's abundant blessing: we again had a good year. I don't have much to sell, but I've broken new land this year so I will be able to sow more wheat. So if God gives us the same yield as in the past I will have more to sell. Breeding cattle pays well here but since I haven't been here so long, I haven't had much to sell even though I now have ten cows.

My dear brothers Ole and Knut, thank you so much for all the trouble you have had concerning my account. Because of your attention it has become much larger than I had expected. And I see that I've also received a brother's share in our parents' chattel, something I didn't deserve. But now it will all be very welcome since I'm short of money because I'll have to pay for my land. You say that you don't know how to send me this money since so few from Aal are planning to emigrate, but I have some good advice. There is some money here after the deceased Ole Syverson Reinton from Hol that will be collected by Kittil Grøth, who will send it to his relatives at Reinton. So now Kittil and I have agreed on the following: I'll be a party to this and you'll give the amount of forty-eight dollars to his relatives and be given a receipt. I don't know for sure how much I am to have since I don't remember the amount owed to me by Nils Dokken, that I hear you have now received. I also see that I am awarded the costs in the case with Ole Dokkmyrane, something I haven't thought about but hope was a just decision. If there is a surplus you can keep it until there is an opportunity to send it with someone you trust.

Dear sister Mari, thanks for your letter of September 21 that I received November 24. I was sad to learn that you have suffered so much from your bad health. But I'm glad you believe that our merciful God will make you well again. Yes, it would be good if we could appreciate God's goodness and how he makes use of many means to call us to our conversion. Dear sister, I hope you see that all things of this world will soon come to an end. I can see how far behind I am on the road to life, but I'll pray sincerely to God that he will maintain in me a small spark so that I may not altogether stand still but with the help of God continue to progress so that I may find the road to life. This road and none other is the one of which Jesus says, I am the way, the truth, and the life. Yes, dear siblings, may you pray with each other and for me your distant brother. I see that you haven't given up on your thoughts of coming here and I would like you to do this, but you must consider this matter on your own. But don't delay your decision. If you come, I would like you to bring the things I wrote about in my last letter with the exception of Guldberg's book of hymns because it is now printed here and I have it. I'll conclude with loving regards from me and my wife and our three children, Lars, Halsten, and Ingrid.

Brother Ole, you can forget the adz that I asked you to send to me; I have now set up a smithy and can make things for myself as well as a little for others when I have time. I must soon end these simply written words. Yes, my words are simple and God grant that I may become simple, for it is written that we must become simple as children in order to enter the Kingdom of God. Yes, it pleases me to learn that the Holy Spirit is at work in your heart, for we cannot have faith in Christ through our own reason nor can we come to Christ except through the working of the Holy Spirit. May the grace of God be with you! I also have greetings from your relatives from Grøth, young and old. They are doing well and are in fairly good health. Assor moved to a new settlement eighty miles west of here and there he was married to Kirsti Jakobsdatter Søndre Mork. He moved last spring but he and his wife were here last fall. Johannes has lived with me for a year but he now wants to have his own farm. The little gift that is enclosed is for your children Ingrid and Lars as a souvenir from their relatives here. It is from my wife who got it from her brother Torkel when he returned from California. We often see gold coins here; indeed they are quite common. But they are round; those made in California are like this one. Faithfully,

YOUR BROTHER SVEND LARSEN HOUG

In many letters from Norway it is said that things are just as good in Norway as in America; but those in Norway have not been to America but we have been in Norway. We know something about what it is like here. This is not to rebuke you, for you have never said this, but one should not talk about that of which one has no experience.

. ——— .

> This letter was received on 16 February 1855. The envelope tells us that twenty-six cents were paid in Elgin and that two *daler* and one *skilling* were paid in Aal. SLH has evidently preempted land that he now has to buy in order to formalize his claim as a squatter. Preemption rights were included in federal law through the 1820s and 1830s, were at the center of the Preemption Act of 1841, and were affirmed by the Homestead Act of 1862. Assor Grøth moved to the new settlement of St. Ansgar, Iowa, founded the previous year by Pastor Claus L. Clausen. In her journal entry for 7 July 1862, Gro Svendsen notes that she was welcomed by Assor Grøth upon arriving at St. Ansgar. A later letter makes clear that many newly arrived immigrants stayed with him (Svendsen 1950, 26, 30). Ole Olsen lived on the croft Dokkmyrane, since then deserted. He and his wife Margit Eivindsdatter emigrated in 1886. He was then seventy-three; she was seventy-nine. Guldberg's book of hymns was published in Wisconsin by *Den skandinaviske presseforening* (the Scandinavian Press Association) in 1854. Those mentioned in the concluding paragraph are his wife's brothers. «1:40 »1:76 NE I:106

. ——— .

1854 — LETTER 1:52

From: Juul and Ole Gulliksen and Susana Halvorsdatter Dorsett
Earlville, Illinois, 20 December 1854
To: Gullik Evensen and Tostein Gulliksen Daaset, *Flesberg, Buskerud*

⇥⟹⟸⇤

Dear Father, mother, and siblings,

As I have arrived safely I can no longer delay writing to you about how I am. Our voyage was quite contrary and it took nine weeks from Norway to America. We had a head wind almost all the way across the ocean. We were all in good health until we had gone 800 miles up into the country to a city called Buffalo. There we went onboard a steamboat where many had died of cholera before it had been made clean. Many immediately became sick and twelve had died before I left the group. It was very difficult to find my brothers. I first came to Clemet Stabekk and lived with him for a month before I found out where my brothers were. The reason was that I had lost my chest with all my papers. From Clemet I went to my brothers, first to Gullik and I found him doing well. Then I went on to Ole and found that he too was doing well. I have been there since then.

I've been in good health the whole time. As for the letter Andres Gjømle had from Clemet Stabekk about the climate here and in Norway, the difference is as great as between night and day. This is the reason for this illness. One must be careful with food, in particular during summer. Because of the climate it is also necessary to avoid being soaked. The climate is the worst thing in America, and this is true.

As for my own situation, I'm not all that satisfied. I've longed to be back and the reason is that I'm in a strange place. It is worst before learning English. I'm working for an American and am now making ninety cents a day. In summer a man can earn from one to one and a half dollars. So you can see that it's easy to make money here. I won't advise any to come to America; you must do as you wish. I must now conclude my letter with many regards to you my dear parents and siblings and to all friends.

JUUL GULLIKSEN DAASET

As there is more paper I'll make use of this opportunity to inform you, my dear father and mother and siblings, about my situation. I can tell you that last summer I was remarried to a girl whose name is Susana who was born on the farm Brenna in Tinn. This was July 14, 1853. We had a girl we named Ambjør who was born August 16, baptized August 27, and died in late September 1854. I've bought land and built a house with four rooms in the first floor. I've been a little sickly through the fall and till now. Otherwise I'm quite satisfied. I have all that is needed to maintain life and have no worry about my income.

I cannot say how glad I was when I could receive my dear brother Juul in my home that is so distant from you. You cannot know how glad I was to welcome someone in my family into my home and that I could have information about you and learn that you are doing well. I've received the gift that you sent with Juul. It is a pleasure for me to have such a remembrance from my father and mother. I cannot give you anything in return except my thanks from myself and my wife.

Dear brother Tostein, when we parted you asked me to write and tell you whether it would be better for you here. Since you have a farm that gives you a living, I think it is better that you stay in Norway. A man has to work hard in America in order to make a living. It is also difficult to have the health necessary for work. During summer it is very hot so work is difficult. At times it is 100 degrees here in summer.

Hellik Førle and his wife Mari died of cholera last summer, leaving behind four children, the oldest nine years and the youngest eighteen months. Several neighbors died last summer. We will conclude our letter with loving regards from me and my wife to our dear parents and siblings. We are in good health and hope to hear the same from you.

OLE GULLIKSEN DAASETT   SUSANA HALVORSDATTER

I must ask you to write to us by the first mail. Send it by mail so it will come right to us.

· ——— ·

> Syntax, spelling, and punctuation are idiosyncratic, at times making interpretation difficult. The Norwegian letter uses "kontralig," a misspelling of "kontrari," an anglicism with the same meaning as the English word contrary that is no longer used. «1:25 »1:72 NE II:T12

· ——— ·

1855 — LETTER 1:53

From: Anders Helgesen Skare, *Decorah, Iowa, 7 February 1855*
To: Helge Gundersen and Eli Andersdatter Skare, *Eggedal, Sigdal, Buskerud*

My dear parents and siblings,

I can no longer delay letting you have a little report about us. We are all in good health to this day for which we must thank our almighty God. Ingrid and Mari are working in homes in Decorah, about five miles from Steinar Olsen Hellerud, where we have our home. I cannot give you a complete report about this country since new immigrants don't know much about it. I will tell you a little about the times. A bushel of wheat costs eighty-eight cents, pork four cents a pound, coffee seventeen cents, and sugar seven cents. A pair of good draft oxen costs from eighty up to 120 dollars, a wagon from fifty to sixty dollars, a breaking plow from thirteen to fifteen dollars and a cow from thirty to forty dollars. Prices are very high. But you can also get a good daily wage, ten to fifteen dollars a month for a hired man during winter and from fifteen to twenty a month in summer, so I think it's easier to make a living here than in Norway for people in a modest position, if they have health and can work. I wouldn't advise those who have a good living in Norway to set out on this long journey, but the laborer who has the opportunity of coming here would be happy. All should expect difficulties at first. There are some who haven't gone through as much as they say, and it is from these that most of the loud complaints come. Those who have many small children and those who have reached a high age will be exposed to many difficulties as well as illness on the journey and I would not advise them to set out on this long and difficult journey. At present I don't have any news, so I must end my short and simple letter. Our regards to my beloved parents and siblings and to Uncle Halvor Skadeland and his wife and children, as well as all relatives and friends. May God's blessing and protection be with you! This is my wish and that of your faithful children, Ingrid, Mari, and Ingeborg Helgesdatter Skare. Farewell.

ANDERS HELGESEN SCHARE

PS. I forgot to tell Ole Eriksen Skareeie about money for travel to America, and I cannot give him a meaningful answer, as I wouldn't advise him to set out on this difficult journey. With so many small children it would be a difficult journey, especially with the illnesses that newcomers so often get on their way here. As for Lars Olsen Skareeie's request for advice on whether to go or not, I don't think it would work for him, because here work is not as easy as he is used to in Norway as he has weak health.

I would like to have a letter from home at the first opportunity with all the news you may have.

Did you receive the letter I sent last summer after my arrival to America? When you write to me address the letter thus: *Mr. Anders Helgesen Schare, Decorah P.O. Winneshiek County Iowa, North Ammerika.*

Greetings to all from Jacob Johnsen Jellum.

· ——— ·

> AHS and Ingeborg Helgesdatter Skare emigrated in 1854, two years after their sisters Ingrid and Mari. The letter he wrote soon after his arrival has not been preserved. As Anders writes in his next letter, Jacob Jellum, also from Eggedal, was his partner. «I:34 »I:65 NE I:107

· ——— ·

1855 — LETTER I:54

FROM: Elias Hansen Narjord, *Dorchester, Iowa, 30 March 1855*
To: Hans Pedersen Narjord, *Os, Hedmark*

Dear parents,

I've received your very welcome letters, the first, dated August 8, on November 4 and the second on February 20. We are so glad that you remember us here so far away. We must also thank you for your hair that was enclosed. We were very glad to see it.

I must inform you about our situation in America and how we're doing.

I'll begin in early September when I bought a stove that can be used for baking and some copper pots—a large kettle for washing clothes, two pots, a coffee pot, a tea pot, and more—and for this I paid eighteen dollars. In late October I went with Esten Larsen to look for land and we shot three deer. Esten has killed fifteen this winter, and they are as large as big reindeer and quite fat and the meat is like lamb. Nils Mikkelsen Syl has shot five deer. But we haven't found any suitable land yet. We plan to go further into the country and look because there is nothing for us here as most land has been bought. But there is enough land in Minnesota and you can live on it for two or three years without buying it until it comes to market, that is when it is to be sold. They survey it three to four years in advance and a date has been set for when we can buy. Esten Larsen and I have planned to be together, as it isn't good to be alone when making a new start.

We've had a harsh winter after New Year. But during Christmas there was nice weather and no snow. Recently it's been so cold that I haven't felt so cold a wind in Norway. It's terribly cold on the prairie, so we need as good clothes here as in Norway. But it doesn't last as long. There has been a lot of snow, it has gone up to the hips. But now the weather is nice again. They have poor buildings for the animals and many Americans have no buildings for them and they freeze so the ears and tails fall off. Now many have too little hay and they pay from three to eight dollars for a ton of hay, and half a dollar for a bushel of corn, and one dollar for a bushel of wheat. One of our cows has calved and the others will soon follow. A good cow gives about eight or ten quarts twice a day. The milk is fatter than in Norway so you get a lot of cream and one quart of cream makes about one pound of butter. They usually don't have more than two cows. They don't need milk for their own use since it is so hot during summer and the Americans never eat sour milk.

But they eat many kinds of game that we don't eat, squirrels and prairie dogs that are similar to foxes, and they have a lot of game birds, and animals, and fish if you are close to a lake. Rivers with fish are few and far between. But there are good springs all over. They only build where there is a spring or they can dig a well. There are no sugar trees here. This is a tree called sugar maple that looks like a large birch and they bore a hole in it and tap the sap that they boil to make syrup and sugar. Corn is mostly used for cattle and pigs and it is a remarkable plant. It grows on tall stalks, about four or six feet tall and with two or three ears on each stalk and with three to four hundred kernels on each ear. Tobacco grows here and wild plums, probably better than in Norway, and oranges and many other fruits. They have as many pigs as they wish. Tron Lang sold 100 last summer. The most common food is pork and wheat bread. Those who've been here a while have all they want of food and drink so I can see that it is better to live here than in Norway. No one needs to fear poverty here. So for my part I don't regret my journey to America, nor does my wife, if we can only stay well. But there are many difficulties here too.

And then I must tell you about religion here. We don't have a pastor yet, but I think one will come to us next summer because we have a large Norwegian congregation. But many of the Norwegians don't want a pastor, for there are so many kinds of sects that it is almost impossible to know whom to approach. The Norwegians are members of all the sects here. There are Baptists and Frankeans and Quakers and Methodists, as they call them. These say they are without sin; when they are together and pray they confess to their pastor how long it is since they sinned. They select one who has gone the longest time without sin and they say that some haven't sinned for two or three years. And there are many other sects that I don't know about. We don't have a church yet but we have decided where it is to be and I think we'll have a pastor next summer. They have written to Norway for one but some have written to Røros asking Derek Iversen to be pastor here, and these were Bernt Haanes, Tron Lang, and three or four other men. They say they don't wish to have an ordained pastor from Norway because such pastors don't have the right Lutheran doctrine. They've had Elling Eielsen here and he is not a real pastor but one of those they call readers in Norway. He says that the Norwegian pastors are not real either. They don't baptize children correctly, in the third article the word "common" should not be used, when they have Holy Communion he doesn't give them absolution, and he does not lay his hand on them. They say that he confirms children even if they are ignorant if they only say they want him as their pastor. He doesn't wear a cassock because he says that a pastor's gown is a papal vestment. He is not a parish pastor but has a flock here and a flock there and he doesn't enter the baptized into a register nor does he sign any certificates. He baptized my daughter because they said he was a real pastor and they said that a pastor's gown wasn't used here. But the Norwegian pastors here are like those in Norway and there has been one here since we arrived. They don't wish to see him or hear him, but he will be here this spring too, because there are many whose children have been baptized by Elling Eielsen and the Norwegian pastors won't accept his baptism.

[*In the margin*] You must send this letter to Tøresdal so they can see it. We will soon write to them because we have also received their letter.

The text is according to a contemporary copy and has no signature. Tøresdal was where his wife's family lived. It is not always easy to follow him and he is unclear in his explanations of both the preemption system and the theological differences between Elling Eielsen and the pastors in the Norwegian Synod. He has evidently been discussing the correct wording of the Apostles' Creed, where he has been used to hearing the phrase *en hellig alminnelig kirke*—a holy common church. The translation used today in American Lutheran churches is "Holy catholic church." Previously American Lutherans referred to the rendering as "Holy Christian church." The problem with *alminnelig* may have been that it was a translation of "catholic." Followers of Hans Nielsen Hauge were often called "readers" because they read so much in the Bible. The stove EHN bought was so different from those he was used to that he used the English word, spelled as it sounded to him, *staav*. He found it strange that Americans did not eat thick sour milk with a spoon. «1:48 »1:63 NE 1:108

1855 — LETTER 1:55

FROM: Hellik Olson Lehovd, *Christiana, Wisconsin, 14 April 1855*
To: Ole Helgesen Lehovd, *Flesberg, Buskerud*

As I haven't had an answer to the letter I wrote November 12, I must tell you how I am. You may not have received it or you may have written to me and I haven't received it. Actually, I don't have much new to tell you except that I was rather sick last winter around Christmas. But I'm now quite well and will go to work again next week. In my view it is good to be here because the wages are good. As long as you are in health you have a good opportunity to earn money, so I think I'll be quite satisfied here.

I had a letter after New Year that my mother's brother Ole died November 28 last year after having been bedridden for about two to three months.

Herbrand Paulsen is in good health and continues as before. He has written to Norway for his son. Well, this shouldn't be so bad for his son, but he won't have much support in his father. I cannot think of more to write except to give my loving regards to all relatives and friends in Norway and first and last to my dear parents and siblings. Tosten Hvashøvd sends his most friendly regards. Both he and his family are in good health, for which we must thank God. I have greetings from Anders Lande and his family and from Gudbrand Holtan and his family. They are all in good health and doing well. With this I will ask you most sincerely to write to me as soon as you receive this and tell me if my brother Ole is confirmed.

HELLIK OLSEN LEHOVD

Confirmation marked the passage from childhood to adulthood. His brother Ole's first letter after emigration is dated 10 June 1862. «I:49 »I:59 NE I:109

1855 — LETTER I:56

FROM: Johanne Svenningsdatter Songe, *Howard, Illinois, 28 May 1855*
To: Her family, *Songe, Holt, Tvedestrand, Aust-Agder*

Dear parents and siblings,

You may be longing to know how I am. As for my health, I haven't been ill except for three days last week and that was only a cold. I'm keeping house for a man from Drammen for one dollar a week and have agreed to be here until fall. He isn't farther from Mons than I can walk there on Sundays. I often go to him because it is my greatest pleasure as there are no others in our settlement that I know from home. Please thank Uncle Halvor for writing to Mons about me. I got a letter from Mons in Quebec about my further journey and telling me to go by way of Chicago. But I didn't dare go that way because those I was traveling with were going to Milwaukee. So I went with them to Dodgeville and from Dodgeville I came here with a Norwegian with horses and a wagon. I don't know more about my cousins from Nes than I was told in a letter this spring from Svenning Braaten. Halvor Knudsen bought a house last fall. Hans Evensen and Gurid also live there and they were all healthy and doing well. Karen Svenningsdatter Braaten was married last fall to Lars Olsen Mo from Gjerstad. He had bought eighty acres about one and a half miles from where Svenning lives and built a log house. They are moving there this spring when the cows have been fed through the winter. I see in a letter from Nes that you want to know whether I came with all my baggage. I only lost my featherbed. It was in a sack that was lost on a train from Milwaukee to Madison. Johanne Nes lost her spinning wheel.

It is very cold in the winter, colder than in Norway but it doesn't last as long. This spring they began to plow in early April. The land is used year after year without fertilizer and things grow very well. The plant that grew at my father's house the summer before last is called corn and it is mostly used for pigs. They grow corn, wheat, and potatoes.

At Christmas I went to the wedding of Mons's brother-in-law. His name is Gunder Aslaksen and I was there for two days and many were there for three days. There were many guests and they were married at home. Our pastor is Dedriksøn, a son of Dederiksøn who was in Ramlet. He is a very good pastor. If you write, please let me know your ages as I am not quite sure of the exact year. Torbjørn Sævig writes that you have been to his wedding but that mother had to stay home because of a swollen finger. Time doesn't permit me to write more. Please give my regards to all relatives and friends.

JOHANNE SVENINGSDATTER SONGE

I must ask you not to let this letter go anywhere else as it is so simple that I want you to keep it at home. Please write to me. It doesn't have to be about important things but I so look forward to hearing something from home. I must also give you regards from Mogens Sveningsen and his family. They are in good health.

· ⎯⎯ ·

> JSS received a letter a few days after she had mailed this one. She wrote the letter herself and place names are even more idiosyncratically spelled than in her first letter: *coebec*, *cecago*, *Milvok*, and *Mædissen*. She has heard the American word railroad and writes *reilvogn*, blending the English rail with the Norwegian word for wagon. Apparently, Mons (also spelled Mogens) had sent some corn kernels to his

father who had planted them by his home. Their pastor was Gustav Fredrik Dietrichson. Ramlet is in Holt. «1:46 »1:58 NE I:112

. ——— .

1855 — LETTER I:57

FROM: Sigbjørn Aslakson, *Coon Prairie, Wisconsin, 12 July 1855*
To: Osmund Atlaksen Ovedal, *Sirdal, Vest-Agder*

⇢⇒⇐⇠

Dear brother Osmund A. Aavedal,

I must use this opportunity to let you know that I and my brothers Reinert and Sivert are in good health and doing well. We hope that this will find you in good health. In your last letter you asked for a receipt signed by a Norwegian pastor. I wrote you about this last spring and you may now have received it. At that time, however, none of the men who had been appointed were here to sign it, so I was unable to fulfill your wish. Our pastor came in the middle of June. To begin with the agreement is for one year. We went to him a few days ago and got him, Stub, to sign as you had asked, so now I hope that everything will be according to the law and that it will go your way without further difficulties.

Apart from this I have no news for you except that the people here on Coon Prairie are as far as I know in good health. In conclusion I have greetings to you from those here who know you. And finally, regards from me and my brothers,

SIGBJØRN A. AAVEDAL

. ——— .

In a letter dated 24 October 1853, the three brothers had relinquished their claim on any inheritance from Ovedal. Hans Andreas Stub was pastor in Muskego, Wisc., 1848–1855 and Coon Valley, Wisc., 1855–1861. «1:38 »1:109 NE I:113

. ——— .

1855 — LETTER I:58

FROM: Johanne Svenningsdatter Songe, *Howard, Illinois, 7 October 1855*
TO: Her family, *Songe, Tvedestrand, Aust-Agder*

⁂

Most beloved parents and family,

Thank you so much for your very welcome letter of May 6 that I received June 12. It gave me an even greater pleasure to see that you are all doing well. This is a gift for which we must never cease to thank him from whom all good comes. He has protected me from illness and accidents except for the minor incidents that always happen in life. I was a little sick a few times last summer and once I had three swollen sores on my hands so work was difficult, but I'm now in good health. All summer I worked for a Norwegian for one dollar a week, but I left yesterday and will live with Mogens Sevig for a while and do some weaving and then I'll go to his parents-in-law for more of this work.

You ask for information about the state of religion, about pastors and such, so I'll try to explain things as well as I can. The Lutheran church is the most common one among the Norwegians. There are now ten Norwegian pastors in America and our pastor's name is Gustav Fredrik Dietrichson, an excellent man in his conduct of services. We must thank God that he sends us teachers who preach the pure and unadulterated Lutheran doctrine. The pastors and the congregations have formed a synod that meets every other year and there is one elected representative for every hundred confirmed members. Such a meeting was held last week at Herman Preus's congregation in Spring Prairie and we had one representative from our congregation. Mogens has twice been a representative and this year he was a substitute. The synod is called the Norwegian Evangelical Lutheran Church in America. We have a church service eight to ten times a year and as far as I can see, God's word is explained and all church matters are conducted in the same way as in Norway. There is a religion school for the children and all members of the congregation contribute according to their own will. No one can be forced, but surely if one refrains from contributing to such a matter he cannot have a Lutheran spirit, nor is it in keeping with the teaching of Luther who said that one must begin with the children. People generally speak more of religion here than at home. But some depart from the Lutheran church, as is to be expected. In a country like America where there is freedom of religion and where so many sects flourish, there will always be restless minds who do not follow the church and its teachers and such people will hold on to whatever comes to mind and this will often be at the expense of the church and its members, and especially its pastors. But when one has a strong faith from childhood and stands firmly on the Holy fundamental principles, then one may with good reason use the glorious words against tempters: "Get thee hence, Satan." So I am satisfied with religion and other things, so it is doubtful that I'll ever return to Norway. Let us all strive to pray with a humble heart that God will help us on our way though this sinful world to the goal he has set for us. The battle is hard and the struggle is heavy. There are many who will tempt us with the allurements of the world but they must be fought if we are to achieve salvation. If we but do what we can, then he who leads us on our path will also help us in his grace, for he does not wish the death of any sinner but that he may be converted. God in his mercy has promised to help us in this, so we may live in such a manner that when we have come to the end of our worldly wandering, we may be gathered in the heavenly mansions.

Dear parents, write to me when you receive this letter and tell me all that has happened since you last wrote, how long brother Ole has been away, and such things. Mons asks me to send his and his wife's and children's regards. They are doing well. He says that it will soon be twelve years since he was at Songe but that if the conditions are good for skis or skates, he'll visit you for Christmas. I also have greetings from Ole Nes. He is in good health and works for a Norwegian near us. I will conclude with the warmest and dearest regards to my parents and siblings and my other relatives and friends. Your loving daughter,

JOHANNE SVENNINGSDATTER SONGE

This is the last preserved letter from JSS. «1:56 NE 1:112A

1855 — LETTER I:59

From: Hellik Olson Lehovd, *Christiana, Wisconsin, 12 December 1855*
To: Ole Helgesen and Joran Paulsdatter Lehovd, *Flesberg, Buskerud*

Dear unforgettable parents and siblings!

I received your letter of May 4 on June 23 and I was glad to see that you are doing well. I can also please you that I'm doing well and am quite satisfied. I live with Tosten Hvashovd when I'm not working for the Americans and I've been with Tosten since last Pentecost. Last spring I worked six weeks for a Yankee. I can speak and understand English quite well and I can even read a little since I've gone to school these last two winters. You ask how much money I've earned here but I cannot be accurate because it is impossible to save all one earns. Clothes are very expensive and it is necessary to dress as they do here when out among people. My capital is now a little more than 180 dollars, which I have lent out at seven to eight percent. Interest rates vary greatly and you can demand just about anything between seven and twelve percent. As for me, I think I'm now fully grown and a little taller than you, father, because I know that I am sixty-seven inches. As for my strength, I haven't really tested it, but you know that you get stronger until you are fully grown.

Dear father! Isn't it good that we can tell each other about ourselves even though we are so far apart? I've agreed to work for Tosten Levorsen for a year. I began December 10 and will be paid 130 dollars. I think it's better to be in one place with people I know than to wander among the Yankees. Even though I could get more a month for part of the year I would have to pay for the journey to and from home. There are hotels in every town where travelers sleep and eat. Here you cannot lodge for the night with anyone, as you do in Norway, and at these hotels it usually costs one dollar a night with supper and breakfast. Anders Lande died September 9. His daughter Kari was married the fall before last to a man from Hallingdal and she now has a son Levor named after her husband's father. Last spring Anund Anundsen Braata married Berit Julsdatter Buin. Last fall Hans Hansen Dyrebo married a girl from Sogndal named Gjertrud. Ole Koppang has married a girl from Hallingdal. Old John Ribrud has died. When he and his family came to Gulbrand Sætre they were all well but he was laid in bed after fourteen days and it was thirteen weeks before he died. All his children and grandchildren except Ragnhild have been sick but now I think they all are well. I've heard that Tosten Vingestad is dead. He was about 1,500 miles south of here in a city called New Orleans where the great Mississippi River runs into the Mexican Gulf. Many Norwegians go there to work during winter but during summer it is too hot there for Norwegians. But he must have found the wages good and he decided to stay for the summer and became a victim of the cholera.

I must not forget to give my warmest thanks to brother Ole for being so eager to acquire knowledge. He is now better than I am in writing and I understand that he must have been good in reading as he had the first place on his confirmation Sunday. As for Uncle Herbrand, it pains me to tell you the truth: he still drinks and swears so it is terrible both to see him and hear him. My regards to you my parents and siblings and may God protect you and guide you in life and in death. Your unforgettable son and brother,

HELLEIK OLSEN LEHOVD

Honored friend!

I owe you thanks for the dear greetings and news in your letter of May 11. Please give my regards to my brothers and tell them that I and my family are doing well and that it pleased the Lord to call home my youngest daughter last spring on June 6. Her name was Kjersti and she was about ten months old. You should also tell my brother Levor that I am rather surprised that I haven't had a single word from him about how he is doing or about anything else that could be of interest for me to know about the land of my birth. I cannot believe that he has forgotten his brother and sister on this side of the Atlantic. Yes, it really hurts me that he doesn't write to me, and I ask you to tell him this. My most friendly regards to you and your family from your always faithful friend!

TOSTEN LEVORSEN

Write by John Ingebrigtson. Claerke to the Norsk Lutherske Church an Koskonang.

> It is difficult to know how many wrote their own letters but in this case the person who wrote either just for Tosten or for both has signed his work in English, a language he evidently cannot write as well as

he does Dano-Norwegian. Pentecost (*Whitsun*) is the seventh Sunday after Easter Sunday. At their confirmation the boys and girls stood in line in the aisle of the church, the boys on the right and the girls on the left, ranked according to how well they had done when they were examined in their faith, in particular in the catechism. It was accepted that placement could be influenced by class. «1:55 »1:64 NE 1:117

1855 — LETTER 1:60

FROM: Holger Petterson Helle, *Leland, Illinois, 28 December 1855*
TO: Hans Ormsen Øverland, *Nedstrand, Tysvær, Rogaland*

My friend!

Thank you for your letter of October 21 that I received two weeks before Christmas. It is truly a great joy for one who is so far from his fatherland, family, and the friends of his youth to hear about them and their well-being. The Lord has granted us good health since we last wrote. As I then wrote, we had a small test of illness and since then we have not been ill a single day. I will briefly answer your questions: Since my last letter I have for the most part harvested corn and potatoes, mainly corn. For a month after St. Michael's Day I worked for a Norwegian for fifteen dollars. Since then I have worked for Americans and I have been paid sometimes one dollar and sometimes eighty cents a day. I am quite satisfied here because I see many people from the Stavanger region every day and I do not at all regret that I left Norway's grey and unfertile mountains and sought America's beautiful and fertile fields. Nevertheless I often think of Norway and of my relatives and friends there, but without longing and dissatisfaction.

You ask whether I'm married and my answer is: I am happily married according to the rituals of the Norwegian church and the laws of America. We were married around the time of St. Michael's Day by pastor Ole J. Hatlestad, who is the Lutheran pastor here. Ten years ago he was schoolteacher in the western district of Nedstrand. We are living with a Norwegian whose name is Ole Rogne from Voss. He lives close to P. Helle. We both worked for others until Saturday before Christmas. I don't know whether I will hire out now during the coldest winter as it is quite cold and the wages are low. It was rather cold during Christmas. Wages are quite good in summer and one may have from one to two dollars a day. If you hire out for the entire year you may also have fairly good wages. I was offered 150 dollars for a year, but I didn't want to commit myself for so long a time. Those who hire out for the whole year can get from 150 to 200 dollars. You can dress yourself well for fifty dollars, so if you are hardworking and careful you may save from 100 to 150 in a year. For 3,000 dollars you can buy an area of government land with a circumference of several miles. Cultivated farms in this area cost quite a lot. A well fenced farm of 160 acres with a house costs about 3,000 to 4,000 dollars or more. But you can also make good money farming. On a farm of about eighty acres you may harvest for more than 1,000 dollars a year. The profit from a farm of eighty acres, after wages, necessities for the home and seed have been deducted, is from 500 to 600 dollars. A house like yours would cost about 1,000 or more. Those who don't own land have no other tax than two days of road work each year. Those who own land pay accordingly. The man I live with has a property valued at about 3,000 and he paid ten and a half dollars in tax this year. Pastors are not paid according to any regulations but according to an agreement between pastor and congregation. This is divided among the members. A horse team costs 300 dollars, an ox team more than 100, a new wagon from seventy to eighty, a foal fifty dollars, a cow from twenty to thirty.

Thank you so much for the news you sent me. Some things surprised me, not the least that Ole Johan had left home and become a seaman. If you see him, tell him that I think it would be just as good for him to come here as to be at sea. I forgot to include the prices for food but will give them here: a bushel of wheat costs from one dollar and twenty cents to one and fifty, a bushel of potatoes twenty cents, butter fifteen cents a pound, pork five cents. Anders Ubø lives near us and he and his wife are in good health. They have a son.

Please write as soon as possible and tell me all the news you can think of, and not least how things are with Dietrichson and whether you have been able to get rid of him. Please read or bring this letter to my mother, with dearest regards from me and my wife. Ask her not to let our separation sadden her too much, because even though we are separated I will never forget her. Give my regards to my siblings as well as my friends and those who ask about me and to my wife's family. Ask all to write often to us.

HOLGER PETTERSON

Letters to Hans Ormsen Øverland from his son Hans Andreas Martin Hansen Øverland are published in Zempel (1991). This letter is mailed from Waverly Station, a post office created along with the new railroad in 1853, but the name was changed to Leland because there was another Waverly Station in Illinois. St. Michael's Day is 29 September. Even though it ceased to be officially recognized by the Lutheran church of Denmark-Norway in 1770, it was long an important day in rural Norway. It marked the end of harvesting and was a day for thanksgiving. Ole Jensen Hatlestad was from Skjold, a part of which is now in Tysvær, and taught school there before coming to Nedstrand in 1842. He immigrated to Jefferson Prairie, Wisc. in 1846 and was a schoolteacher there until 1850. He was ordained in 1854 and was pastor for some years in Leland. He played important roles in the immigrant society both as a pioneering newspaper publisher (*Nordlyset* and *Democraten*) and, later, as president of the Augustana Synod (Malmin et al. 1928). Ole Larson Rogne emigrated from Voss to Leland in 1844. He lived there till his death in 1905 (Rene 1930, 157). After returning to Norway from Wisconsin, J. W. C. Dietrichson was pastor in Nedstrand. NE I:119

1856 — LETTER I:61

FROM: Gaute Ingebretsen and Kari Sigurdsdatter Gunleiksrud
Dunkirk, Wisconsin, 28 January 1856
TO: Ingebret Torstensen and Birgit Gautesdatter Gunleiksrud, *Tinn, Telemark*

To my dear parents Ingebret Torstensen and Bergit Gautesdatter,

I have recently received your letter of May 1, 1854, and must ask my father's forgiveness for not having answered earlier. I can only blame my own neglect. I see in your last letter that my parents were then in good health, and this is the most important of all and I sincerely hope this is still so. I and my wife and children are, thank God, in good health. I can tell them we have had good harvests and prices have gone up both for what we sell and what we have to buy. We get good prices for our grain. Wheat is one dollar and twenty cents to one and fifty for a bushel, barley one dollar a bushel, oats and corn fifty cents, and potatoes seventy-five cents. Luxury articles are about the same price as in Norway. A good horse costs 150 dollars, a cow from twenty to thirty dollars, and a team of draft oxen 100 to 112 dollars. I must also let you know that land has become much more expensive recently. I could probably have sold my 120 acres for one and a half thousand dollars. But I improved it quite a lot last year. Last summer I broke thirty-three acres and improved our house for about 214 dollars.

I must add some words about John Gunnuldsen who lives with us when he is not out working. He has worked three summers for me. He is an excellent worker. Last fall he went to Minnesota where he has taken land he is working on this winter. He hasn't paid for the land yet since it hasn't been put on the market. He has saved about 200 dollars and has a good team of oxen. You must tell his father that he is waiting for a letter from him as he wrote to him last fall before he left us. I can also tell you that Sigrid Nilsdatter lives with us when she is here. She is in good health and makes a good living. She has been with an American for more than a year. She was with us for a short while last fall and she is setting aside money every day and now probably has 140 dollars of her own. She works about thirty miles from us and earns one and a quarter dollars a week.

I also have greetings from Østen Pedersen Gollo who has agreed to work for me for one year for 150 dollars. Holje Grimsrud and his family are in good health and doing well. Enclosed is my receipt for the money I was given on my departure from Norway as well as my waiver of my allodial rights to the farm Gunleiksrud. As I don't have further news of importance for you, I will conclude with loving regards to my old father and mother, my brothers Hans and Erik, and my sisters Kari and Margit. I must congratulate Margit on her new state as I have heard that she is married. Our regards to my wife's siblings, to Gunnuld Grimsrud and his wife, and Aslaug and Kittil Bjørtuft, and to all our relatives and friends. We wish that you may all live happily in your different stations. Sincerely

GAUTE INGEBRETSEN AND KARI SIGURDSDATTER

«I:29 »I:73 NE III:TII

1856 — LETTER I:62

FROM: Lars Nilsen Nesheim, *Chicago, Illinois, 28 March 1856*
TO: Martha Haldorsdatter Nesheim, *Granvin, Hordaland*

Mareta Haldors Dater Nieshiem,
Dear unforgettable mother and brother,

As I now have the opportunity I must not neglect to write a few lines about how I live. I've been in good health, for which I must thank the almighty God, because life is easy as long as we have health. My brother Johannes has been sick with the ague some times this year, but has been at work almost the whole time. I hope that he with the help of God will be cured by summer. He says he likes it here in America. We are working in Chicago. Iver and I are working together. My brother works somewhere else but we see each other every Sunday. Six days ago we had a letter from my sisters. They live about 150 miles from here. They are in good health and are very satisfied in America. Mikkel and Ole have bought land in Cambridge in Wisconsin but I don't know how much. I left my sisters six weeks before Christmas and went to Chicago where I worked for Klaus Skjeldal and Nils Grimestad from Voss driving milk into the city. I was paid twenty dollars. I've had good pay since I came here so I cannot complain. I pray that God will grant me health. When I left my sisters I lent Mikkel fifty-three dollars and I've made more money since then. I think I can make more here than in Norway so I don't have to work so hard. I haven't been without longing for the place of my birth. You mustn't think that nothing is lost when you go to America for there are as great difficulties here as in Norway.

Tell my uncle that his son is in good health. He is with his sister in Iowa. I haven't met Niels Olsen Laiem since last fall and he then said that he was in good health and well satisfied in America. I must end my simple letter with loving regards to you my dear mother and brother. Don't forget to write to me.

LARS NIELSEN NESHEIM

LNN's sisters, Magrete and Synneve, live in Cambridge (*Keinbres*), Wisc. with their husbands Ole Olsen Heve and Mikkel Sjursen Folkedal. Klaus Knutsen Skjeldal emigrated from Voss to Chicago in 1844 and Nils Oleivsen Grimestad followed in 1850 (Rene 1930, 327–328, 453). «I:41 »I:71 NE I:120

1856 — LETTER I:63

FROM: Elias Hansen and Ane Kristine Tørrisdatter Narjord
Dorchester, Iowa, 26 December 1856
TO: Hans Pedersen Narjord, *Os, Hedmark*

To our parents and siblings in Norway!

As time now permits, I can no longer delay giving you a report on my situation. When I wrote to you in May I told you what it was like then. For a long time I haven't been working as I had an accident taking a rifle down from the ceiling not knowing that it was loaded. It went off and the bullet went through a toe on my left foot. It was very painful at first and I was mostly in bed for six weeks. But I'm now quite well. Otherwise, I and my wife and children have been well all the time and are enjoying our new home and do not regret our emigration. Our thoughts often go to the old home and we would like to visit, but we may compensate by using the pen. We are so happy for the gifts you sent us with Christen and Berit. They were so welcome and we lovingly remember you who are so far from us that we probably won't see each other more in this world. But we hope that we may be able to live in such a way that we will see each other when we are with our God and our savior Jesus Christ. I've recently heard that my sister Sigri is dead and this makes me very sad even though we have taken farewell with each other in this world. Also other friends are said to be dead and I expect that you'll tell me about this when you write, for I've waited a long time for a letter from you. I haven't had a letter since Christen and

Beret came here. They are living with us and are in good health and are doing well in America. They have a little daughter who is twelve weeks old and she is big and healthy.

I've heard rumors that you have hard times in Norway. This is, praise God, not the case here. We had an average year last summer; we didn't have much rain, so it wasn't a great year, but certainly not hard times. We have to buy most of our food. We didn't produce much because our newly plowed field was too dry. We had about fifty bushels of corn and I don't know how much wheat since we haven't threshed yet, but it isn't much. One bushel of wheat costs seventy cents and a bushel of corn fifty cents. We have for the most part bought flour since it costs from one to one and a half cents a pound. When they grind wheat they get two kinds of flour; one is like the finest rye flour in Norway and the Americans don't care for it and give it to the animals. The finest flour costs three cents a pound. A pound of pork costs five or six cents and a pound of meat from four to eight cents. We have slaughtered two pigs so we can eat pork and wheat bread every day and often say that we should have been able to send you some Christmas bread and a little pork. There is no lack of food because the wages are also good. In summer a man may be paid a dollar a day and for some kinds of work you may have two dollars during harvest. In winter the wages are not so high, usually ten to twelve dollars a month, but those who are unmarried and can go away for work can have from twenty to twenty-five dollars all year. Right now we have a harsh winter with snow and cold weather. We have about two feet of snow, and winter came about eight weeks before Christmas.

Last summer I worked for Jens Erlemoen building a house and I made about forty dollars. Since I cannot be so far from home I cannot make all that much money. Now I don't have much to do. I take care of the animals and do a little around the house. Esten Larsen sometimes goes hunting and he has shot nine deer this winter. We share our land as I wrote in my last letter. I'll answer some of your questions. We have 120 acres with a fairly good forest of oak, ash, elm, basswood, sugar maple, and black walnut that has a black-gray wood. There are three good springs and the land is dry and healthy without any swamps. There isn't much difference between the climate here and in Norway except that the summer is a little warmer. The winter is at least as harsh as in Norway. The wind is as cold as in the mountains and it blows all the time, winter and summer.

We had our land on preemption as they call it for one year when we didn't have to pay anything, only fulfill the requirement of settling on the land within thirty days after we got our papers. You can have it without fear for one year, but then you have to pay or else you lose it. It costs fifty dollars for forty acres of government land. All around here are Norwegian; many are from Holtaalen and most are from Hallingdal, Hadeland, Valdres, and Bergen. We are four miles from the nearest store, mill, and sawmill, and it is about twenty miles to Decorah, which is growing fast. It is about six years since the first inhabitants came and now they have fifteen stores and several kinds of workshops. It is about twenty miles to Lansing on the Mississippi. This is a great river and has many steamboats in the summer. A railroad is being built about thirty miles from us. We don't have a Norwegian pastor yet but I think we will soon have one because they are building a parsonage. A Norwegian pastor visits us a few times a year because there are so many Norwegians.

If you know of someone who is going to America this year I wish you would send me a hymnal. I cannot get one here and would like to have one. Some who came from Norway last summer have died. Johannes Lien from Brekken and his oldest daughter are dead and Christen Jokumsen Tamnes and his sister have had the ague since they came. Most of the others are well now. Bent Haanes sold his land for 800 dollars. This winter we have had five pigs and seven stabled animals and a plentiful supply of hay. We give corn to the pigs. Pork is the main product here and we also produce wheat and corn. The market has been good because of the large number of immigrants in Minnesota. Sometimes as many as a hundred wagons pass here in one day in spring with people who are going to find new land. They have white tents over their wagons. We haven't had news from Elev Toresen so we don't know whether he is alive or dead. Our loving regards from me and my wife and children and in particular from Ane Kristine for all the gifts that you sent to her. It makes her glad to look at them and she is using her stockings this Sunday.

ELIAS HANSEN

· ⎯⎯ ·

> This letter is to the families of both Elias and Ane Kristine and they have received gifts from the latter's parents in Røros. Like the other Narjord letters, the text is that of a contemporary copy. EHN writes that his last letter was in May. It is dated 30 March, but it may well be that it had taken several weeks to complete. These immigrants came from farms in quite high altitudes where the summers were too short for wheat and the common grain for bread was rye. In Iowa, the second-grade wheat given to the farm animals was better than the best rye flour used in Os and Røros. «1:54 »1:70 NE 1:129

· ⎯⎯ ·

1857 — LETTER I:64

From: Hellik Olson Lehovd, *Christiana, Wisconsin, 24 January 1857*
To: Ole Helgesen and Joran Paulsdatter Lehovd, *Flesberg, Buskerud*

Dear unforgettable parents and siblings,

I received your letter of October 29 on December 13 and saw to my great pleasure that all is well with you, for which we must praise God. I can please you with the same news. I've had no difficulties since you last heard from me, but I must send you some lines. I see that you've heard the sad news that Uncle Herbrand ended his earthly life on a day of celebration, July 4, when a kind of shooting contraption made of two iron rings exploded. One of these and a three to four inch long iron splint went in on one side and out the other and through his guts. He lived three or four hours. Ole Olson Lia helped him and he was conscious at the time he died as he wasn't drunk. This happened in a little town named Clinton about four miles from here where there are no less than four liquor stores where he stayed most of the time. I came there the evening before his funeral but wasn't able to see him. Arrangements were made for a very decent funeral as he didn't have any means himself. This will probably be the last time I have anything to write about him.

As for myself, I don't have much to tell you about my income beyond what you saw in my last letter. I've been here with Tosten Hvashovd since I completed my year of service on December 11. I'll go to Minnesota next spring to buy land, but since I don't know where I'll find land to my liking, I cannot tell you how to address your letter. If you write, send it to Tosten Hvashovd. We see that you've had a poor year in Norway and that you have hard times. But here in America it's been a fairly good year, not quite as good as the year before, and the price of wheat is lower than last year. I don't have any news as there has been no illness or deaths. Tosten and Hellik Hvashovd are doing quite well and Tosten had a daughter named Anne on Sunday, November 30, and Hellik Gundersen had a son on July 6. His name is also Hellik. They've been quite busy this year as they have each built a house of brick. Each house is twenty-eight feet long and twenty feet wide, with four rooms, two downstairs and two upstairs. The kitchen addition is twenty-two feet long and eighteen feet wide. Each building has fifteen windows and seven doors and they were ready in November. They have their land in common and the distance between their homes is as between Upper and Lower Lehovd. Last year they bought a machine called a self-raker and reaper that rakes in sheaves by itself so a man and four horses can mow ten to twelve acres a day. And T. and H. Hvashovd and A. Anunsen and T. Anunsen Braata also bought a threshing machine that we used last fall. I've learned to run the machine and we threshed 200 to 300 bushels of wheat and 400 bushels of oats a day.

Thank you so much for your welcome letters. We enjoy hearing from the home of our forefathers as there haven't been any immigrants from our parish this summer. Your good friend Tosten Levorsen asks whether you could send him news about his brothers as he hasn't had a reply to the letter he sent them last year. I will end my letter with greetings to all relatives and friends and first and last to you my dear, unforgettable parents and siblings, with the wish that the protection and guidance of Our Lord may be with you in life and in death, from your unforgettable son and brother,

HELLIK OLSON LEHOVD

There is one thing I must ask you, either father or brother Ole, that if you can read my letter, then please rewrite it, as it is very poorly written and put together, as the pen has been held by me myself, the below signed,

Norways Gjentleman HELLIK OLSON

. ⎯ .

>Tosten Hvashovd has helped him write before, but now he proudly announces that he has written this letter himself. The self raker was fastened to the reaper so that the wheat was left in same-sized heaps. The word "self raker" has not been recorded earlier than in 1857, so they have bought a new invention. Tosten Levorsen Hvashovd was married to Kjersti Gundersdatter, the sister of Hellik Gundersen Hvashovd. HOL also wrote 14 on May 1856 (Nor. ed. 1:123). «1:59 »1:66 NE 1:132

. ⎯ .

1857 — LETTER 1:65

From: Anders Helgesen and Ingeborg Helgesdatter Skare
Nerstrand, Minnesota, 4 February 1857
To: Helge Gundersen Skare, Eggedal, *Sigdal, Buskerud*

⇢≡◉⇇⇠

Dear parents,

I received your letter dated April 16, 1855, on October 2, and your last letter of May 21, 1856, in late September. I was so glad to hold it, because I saw that you all are in good health, and I can send you the same joyful message in return, that I've been in good health to this day, for which we must thank the almighty God. I see that you wrote to me in 1854 and I still haven't received it, so it has probably been lost.

Now I'll tell you what I've been doing. Jacob Johnsen Jellum and I have bought land together, 160 acres with forest and 160 acres of good prairie land, and we bought our jointly owned 320 acres from the government for one and a quarter dollar an acre, which made 400 dollars altogether. Further, we have recently sold sixty acres of our forest for 800 dollars. Well, now I've started my story and I'll tell you a little more. We've bought three five-year-old ox teams for 405 dollars and two milk cows for seventy dollars. And for myself I have a milk cow and a two-year-old heifer. We've also bought a wagon for seventy-five dollars and the necessary implements for farming. We've built a fairly good house as well as a building for the animals for the winter. In this country the animals are not kept in buildings during summer. Moreover, we've broken eighteen acres that we'll plant with wheat next spring.

I, your daughter Ingeborg, have moved here to my brother's home. I came to him April 21, 1856. And as I just now have come home from work I must tell you, my dear parents and siblings, that I've been in good health since we last wrote to you, and for this we owe thanks to God. I see that my sister Ingeborg wishes to know what I do when I'm with the Americans. I do the usual work: washing and ironing nice clothes, baking bread for the family everyday, and keeping the house nice looking. Well, if I should try to tell you about all my chores it would be a long list and I cannot do this with my pen. Consider that this country is not like Norway, because here the women only do indoor work, what is usually done in a home. I earn three dollars a week when I'm working for the Americans. I have now learned to speak so much English that I can be paid in full like others. Because you must understand that when people come to this country they at first cannot be paid the regular wage since they don't know the language. Since I came here to Minnesota I've been away at work almost all the time, except for a few weeks when I was home last summer. Now we are talking about changing things because we have some...

> The last page has been lost. Ingeborg later married Ole Johnsen Jellum. It was not uncommon that siblings had identical names. Tradition required that children be named for their grandparents; if two grandfathers or grandmothers had the same name, it would be used twice. «I:53 »I:93 NE I:133

1857 — LETTER I:66

FROM: Hellik Olson Lehovd, *Christiana, Wisconsin, 10 April 1857*
TO: Ole Helgesen and Joran Paulsdatter Lehovd, *Flesberg, Buskerud*

Dear parents and siblings,

I sit down to write you some lines with sincere love to tell you about my situation. I can please you with the news that I've been in good health and had no accidents since you last heard from me, for which we must thank our good God who does all so well. And I hope that these lines find you in good health. You've probably received the letter I sent you in January. There I told you about my decision to go to Minnesota in the spring. Now I must tell you that it pleased the Lord to take away our good friend, Tosten Levorsen Hvashøvd, who died March 5. He was very weak all winter. It began with an infection in one of his legs after he was cut for bleeding and he had to stay in bed most of the time from late November last year. But when I wrote to you last winter he didn't want me to mention it until it was better. Lately his leg was so much better that he could sit up now and then, but he died of an illness he has suffered from for a long time called cancer of the stomach. But he wasn't really weak until a few days before the end. This has been a sad loss for his grieving widow and his children as well as his dear brother-in-law Hellik as they lived together in love as brothers. Because of Tosten's death I had to sign on for seven months with Hellik and Kjersti, from April 15 to November 15, and for this I get eighteen dollars a month, which makes 126 dollars for seven months, and this is surely a good wage. For a whole year I could have made 160 to 170 dollars, but from this must be taken money for good clothes, something I haven't saved on because this is necessary to stay in good health in America. And I must say that I'm glad I've come to this free country as I'm at the age when I would have had to be a soldier. Here all above twenty-one who have been in the state for one year have the right to vote for candidates for all kinds of office.

I must also tell you about what is not so worthy of praise. First, the large amount of unstable paper money that is circulating here, as there are many hundreds of banks in America. There are no less than fifty-five banks in Wisconsin and as some occasionally go bankrupt it isn't safe to hold on to paper money. And we don't have as nice a climate here as in Norway. There is a strong heat in the summer interrupted by thunder and lightning and powerful rain that comes with a strong wind because the country is so flat. And last winter in particular we had a very cold and severe winter and much snow. But early in this month we had good weather and on the third some started to plow, but now we have snow again. So the weather is changeable—one day summer and one day winter.

Now I must tell you that I didn't work for more than room and board when the winter was at its coldest. Since I completed my one-year contract I've made twenty-five to thirty dollars. We've had a letter from my companions Ole Helliksen Landeiet and Gulbrand Toreson Dokken in Minnesota who lived here at Washovd until last spring. They bought land for 400 to 800 dollars with the money they had for a year's work, and I think that is a good income. But for him who is alone and without either brother or sister it is almost impossible to buy and cultivate land. I must now end my poor letter as I have no more news for you. Please write to me as soon as possible and let me know how you are doing and whether you have any news. In conclusion, my friendliest regards to all relatives and friends and those who may wish to hear from me, but first and foremost to you my parents and siblings with the wish that you may have the Lord's protection and guidance both in life and in death, from your dear and unforgettable son and brother. Sincerely,

HELLIK OLSEN LEHOVD

The next time you write let me know if you pay anything for my letters in Norway as I have paid for all my letters from here, which is forty-eight cents.

«1:64 »1:69 NE 1:138

1857 — LETTER 1:67

FROM: Torgrim Olsen Lee, *Black Earth, Dane County, Wisconsin*
24 July 1857
TO: Anders Olsen Lie, *Hedalen, Sør Aurdal, Oppland*

To our dear parents and siblings in Norway,

Now that we've arrived and I have the opportunity I'll write you some simple lines and tell you about our journey to America. We were at sea for seven weeks and six days and we stayed on board the ship for four days after anchoring in Quebec before we arranged for our further journey. We had one price from Quebec to Madison but had to change conveyance four times: thirteen and a half dollars for every adult and half price for those under twelve. We went by railroad, a very fast transportation. It was more than 700 miles and it took us four days and nights. In Madison we bought tickets to Black Earth. It was a happy moment because there we were met by old friends, all the Skindingsrud boys, Knut, Petter, and Ole Brager, Gulbrand Berg, Halsten Norby, Arne, Ole, Andreas, and Anders Stensrud, and many more and each took care of his own. Some went here and some went there. Knut Jøranbyhaugen lives with Gjermund Hesjebakken and he received us as his own family. We stayed with him for three days and then I went to Aslak Lee and spoke with him, and the next morning Aslak came with a wagon and two horses for my baggage and drove me to his home. He received us as welcome guests and we can live with him for some time. We were happy to meet him and he lives well in all respects.

I'll now tell you about our health. Marit was sick for about three weeks during the voyage but I and the children were well all the time and for this we must thank the almighty God. I've been somewhat ill for five or six days since we arrived but it isn't much if we understand the difference between pain and health. And I'll tell you a little about others in our company and some deaths. Siri Moen became mad again as soon as we came on board so they had to make a cage for her and it was a great punishment for us all. Both of Iver Grytelia's children died at sea and the youngest of Jon the Fiddler's children died and Ole Paulsen's youngest and one of Ole Skalshaug's children who was ill when he left home died at sea. The oldest daughter of Ole Bonli died after we came to Black Earth, as did Mikkel, son of Mikkelsen. Marit Jørandby died after she came to Harald Stugaarden and one of Palmesen's children also died.

We attended church service in a schoolhouse one Sunday and were very pleased to have such a clever pastor. I've hired out to Anders Lund from Aurdal for seventeen dollars a month and Marit has taken service with Levor Lien's brother-in-law. Tell Rønnaug Sølibakken that her brother-in-law Torgrim came to Levor and got the spinning wheel and books before they moved. We had a letter from Ole Høvolne with greetings to you all. They are in good health and doing well. Ole Dolven came to Aslak Lee and I went home with him and he gave me a pair of pants, a shirt, and a jacket.

I, Ole Dolven, send my regards. I'm in good health and doing well and I'm satisfied because here you need not worry about having enough to eat and we don't have to eat salted herring and gruel every day as in Norway and an adult man may be paid from fifteen to thirty dollars a month depending on whether he knows the language. To Herman H. Klemetsrud: it would be good for you to come here. If you wish to come next spring and someone is coming who can lend you ten dollars for your travel expenses, I'll repay them when they come to me. I'll conclude with greetings to all relatives. Farewell,

OLE DOLVEN

We haven't met Tord Amsrud or heard anything from him. I have greetings from Anne and Levord Lien. They are in good health and doing well. If any of you decide to come to America you must bring an illustrated Bible for Ole Dolven and I'll pay you for your trouble. Tell Kari Olsdatter Brakahagen that we've arrived safely and in good health. No more now. Regards to all at Jonsrud. I must end my poor letter with friendly greetings to all relatives and friends from your distant son and daughter Torgrim and Marit. Farewell. Please write to us when you can. Give our regards to Karen Lia and tell her that Marit often thinks of her. First and last, regards from us all,

TORGRIM LII

· ——— ·

This is the first of many letters from two generations of immigrants from the farm Søre Li in Hedalen in the municipality Sør Aurdal in Valdres. This correspondence is discussed in Øverland (2002). The Norwegian spelling of their name was Lie, but members of the family wrote Lee in the United States, thus retaining the pronunciation. The letter is also meant for his parents-in-law, and the "we" and "us" in the letter include TOL's wife, Marit. Ulvestad (1908, 778–779) has an account of the early emigration from Sør Aurdal to the area around Blue Mounds and Black Earth written by the sons of Levor Lien, who emigrated in 1849. A more recent study is Joranger (2000). Arne Stensrud came from Valdres around 1850 with his sons Ole, Andreas, and Anders. Aslak Lee emigrated in 1848. Holand writes that "his enthusiastic letters to friends in Valdres was the most important factor in the growth of the settlement" and that his "home was a common stopover for strangers" (Holand 1908, 187). Ole Dolven emigrated from Sør Aurdal in 1852 and later moved to Morris, Minn. (Ulvestad 1913, 586). »I:100 NE I:142

· ——— ·

1857 — LETTER 1:68

From: Ole Hansen Rustand, *St. Ansgar, Iowa, 28 September 1857*
To: Elling Olsen Elsrud, *Aadalen, Ringerike, Buskerud*

To my relatives in Norway!

About two years ago I had a letter from my brother Nils Viker to which I soon replied. I hope he received it and I haven't heard anything from any of you since then. It then seemed that my brother was thinking of coming here, but as I haven't heard from him I assume that he has changed his mind. It would be best for him to remain where he is. As information for those who consider emigration I'll note the prices of farm animals, etc.: for a cow the price for the last two years has been from thirty to forty dollars, an ox team from 120 to 150 dollars, a team of horses from 300 to 400 dollars, a good farm wagon from eighty to one hundred dollars. All farm implements have correspondingly high prices: a plow for the breaking of new land costs from twenty to forty dollars depending on size and a regular plow from fifteen to sixteen dollars, so you'll see that it isn't easy to come here if you don't have the means. It's quite different for free and independent people as the wages are good. An adult man is paid from twenty to thirty dollars a month and sometimes during haying and harvest the pay can be from one to one and a half dollars a day. This is for simple labor; a craftsman is paid more. An adult girl who knows the language is paid from one and a half to two dollars a week.

My son Eric went to Australia three years ago and we had a letter from him a short time after he had arrived, but since then we haven't heard anything. My son Ole the younger went to California two years ago. We've had letters from him and he neither praises nor criticizes the place. My son Ole the elder has been here till now but this summer he sold his and his brother Ole's land for 2,400 dollars. On the ninth of this month he went to New York but we don't know whether he then went to California or Australia. If Ole finds his brothers I think they'll all return to Norway. My sons have lent 6,000 dollars for three years at an interest of ten percent and Ole took with him 1,100 dollars for his journey. What remains here is forty acres of forest land belonging to my son Eric and I think this is worth a lot as the price for forest land has gone up. If Eric decides to go to Norway before Ole finds him and if he doesn't plan to return here, he should send me an authorization to sell his forest and I'll then send him an account of the matter.

Eric Slimsen told my son Ole that Torgrim Haugerud was in danger of losing a lot of money. But he was unable to give me any real account of the situation, so I would like to be informed when you write to me. Eric also told Ole that Syver Storrusted and his wife had changed their will and had excluded all their heirs in America. If this is true I don't think they have done the right thing and I think it should not make a difference for them where their lawful heirs lived. But it may be that their heirs in Norway have greater need of what they may get than do those who have come to America.

As for the land here, it cannot be denied that it is both good and easy to farm. Here it is as convenient in all respects as it can possibly be, but there are of course difficulties here too. The most important are the so-called prairie fires every fall when all grass is burned, and this causes great damage for many people as it often happens that a good deal of hay burns and that the harvest is destroyed. Yes, it even happens that homes, animals, and people are in danger. Winters are very cold, especially the last two winters, and I've never felt so severe a cold in Norway. The snow drifts over the prairies with more power than in the mountains of Norway. The last two winters several people have died and a large number of animals have frozen to death.

When you see relatives of Endre Gulbrandsen Øymoen, give them his regards. I was with him and Peder Lunde last summer and worked on a claim I had near them. Endre has 160 acres and twenty-eight head of cattle, including eight draft oxen.

My wife left this life for eternity July 25 after being ill for only two days. She had weak health the last two years of her life. I don't know whether I'll stay here or return to Norway for the rest of my days. To my dear brothers, Nils Viker, Hans Rustand, and Torgrim Haugerud, my son-in-law Elling Elsrud, Kari Sand, her husband Erik Gulrud, and my brother Simon Sørum: my friendly regards to you all with the wish that you may live well.

OLE HANSEN RUSTAND

I can tell Elling Elsrud that Irgens, who had a general store at Enger, and his brother have come here and settled in St. Ansgar, one mile away, where he also has a store.

OHR (who also uses the name Haugerud) probably addressed his letter to Elling Olsen Elsrud, married to OHR's daughter Olia, but it addresses members of his family in general, among them his brothers, Nils Hansen Viker (who was sixty-seven in 1857) and Simon Hansen Sørum (in Gran, Oppland) and his sons, Torgrim Olsen Haugerud and Hans Olsen Rustand. He had divorced his wife, Guri Torgrimsdatter (who lived at Rustand in 1865), and emigrated with his second wife, Berct Olsdatter Olshullet. He had two sons named Ole; the older Ole had been in Iowa but was on his way to Australia; the younger Ole had gone to California from Wisconsin in 1855, and at the time of this letter went on to search for gold in British Columbia (Nor. ed. II:32). He eventually returned to the United States. Letters from England, Australia, and Canada by these three, who use the name Haugerud, also appear in *Fra Amerika til Norge*. Ole Haugerud the elder wrote to his sister and brother-in-law at Elsrud on 8 October 1857, from Liverpool on his way to Australia. He writes a little about the poor health of his father and also (in case he should not survive his journey) gives a detailed account of his debtors in Fillmore County, Minn., and Mitchell County, Iowa, to a total of $5,713, roughly half of which were his brother Ole's (Nor. ed. I:145). According to Holand, Peder Lunde and Endre Gulbrandsen emigrated from Aadalen in 1856. After searching for land in western Minnesota they settled "in Hayward, Freeborn County, where they became the first settlers" (1908, 434). OHR's troubled relationship with his family may be reflected in his delayed mention of the death of his second wife. »I:78 NE I:144

1857 — LETTER 1:69

FROM: Hellik Olson Lehovd, *Christiana, Wisconsin, 25 November 1857*
TO: Ole Helgesen Lehovd, *Flesberg, Buskerud*

⋅⇌⇌⋅

To my respected and unforgettable father Ole Helgesen Lehovd,

I received your letter of May 24 on July 6 and I was glad to hear that all is well. I can give you the happy news that I have been well and healthy all summer, for which we must thank our good God who does all so well. There was less illness and death last summer than ever before. First I must ask your forgiveness for the long time that has passed since my reply to your letter. This is partly due to negligence and partly because I haven't had time. You must realize that there is much to do when large farms are run properly and all sowing and harvesting must be done at the right time. My main work is to run the machines, first the reaper or mowing machine that is drawn by four horses. We didn't begin to cut the wheat until August because of a late spring. But it has been a good year and at Hvashovd they harvested 1,124 bushels of wheat and 1,270 bushels of oats and a lot of corn. Since early September we've been running the threshing machine that is drawn by eight horses and we've threshed all kinds of grain, in all, 14,273 bushels. At Hvashovd they own half the machine and have made a lot of money this fall. We thresh with eight horses and four men and charge five cents a bushel for wheat, four for barley and two and a half for oats. It is dirty work in dust that makes both seeing and breathing difficult, but I've learned how to run machinery that many others cannot, not one in ten.

Many here have married and I'll mention some that we know. I was in two weddings last summer, first for Ole Andersen Lande and Helena Olsdatter Raaom, and then to Hellik Gulliksen Hamre and Maret Amundsdatter Braata from Lyngdal. And Ingebør Toresdatter Dokken has married Ole Veggar from East Norway. I've heard that Niri Sjulsen Stykop has married the widow Jøran Sjulsdatter Berget, but I'm not sure, as they have moved many hundred miles from here. On St. John's Day we had a grand celebration when a Norwegian Evangelical Church here in Koshkonong Parish was consecrated. No fewer than eleven pastors were present and the church is octagonal and made of bricks and it took five years to build it. We have two other churches near here.

I now have more relatives here as Maret Teksle and her children came last spring and live with Kittil Kampestad. They are all in good health. You ask for information about Jøran Granstuen, but I haven't spoken with her for three years. I've heard that she is alive and works in a city called Madison. When I see her I'll write to you about it. The times here in America are fairly good, but the price for all produce is lower than last year. The price for a bushel of wheat is now forty-five to fifty cents, for barley thirty-five to forty cents, for oats eighteen to twenty-five cents, for potatoes twenty cents. And when the price for what they sell sinks then wages follow. And because of the large immigration, land is now so expensive that it is almost impossible for a man of modest means to become the owner of a piece of land, so I must say that I believe that the rumor in Norway that America will never be filled up is untrue.

I don't know more to write about that would be of interest for you. In your last letter you thank me for having paid for my letters, but I must say that this is not much, as a letter to Norway costs forty-eight cents, and one from Norway, forty-six cents, and I'm glad that you don't have to pay for any of this. I must now end my poor letter with regards to my parents and my brothers Ole, Paul, and Knut, and my sister Jøran, and to all relatives and friends that it would take too much space to list here with my wish that God will protect them and guide them both in life and in death, from your absent son and brother.

HELLIK OLSEN LEHOVD

And I must give you greetings from all here at Hvashovd. They are in good health. And the one thing I will ask you is that you write me when you have the time and opportunity. I would also like to have a letter from my brother Ole.

· ——— ·

> Lyngdal is in Vest-Agder. Ole Veggar moved to Olmsted County, Minn., in 1854 (Holand 1908, 499) and had probably returned to Koshkonong, Wisc. for his wedding. «I:66 »I:75 NE I:146

· ——— ·

1857 — LETTER 1:70

From: Elias Hansen and Ane Kristine Tørrisdatter Narjord
Dorchester, Iowa, 7 December 1857
To: Hans Pedersen Narjord, *Os, Hedmark*

Dear parents and siblings in Norway!

As I haven't written to you for a long time I must now briefly and, as well as I can, reply to your letters. I've received five letters from you since I last wrote. I had two letters at the same time last winter in March, one from my brother Jens, dated July 13, 1856, and one from my brother-in-law Peder Tørrisen, dated November 29, 1856. When Simen and Ingebor-Anna Syl came here last summer I got one from my sister Maret and one from Tøresdalen. I received your letter of April 25 late in August, and we were glad to see how you are doing in our old home.

I must tell you about our situation. We are now well, even though we have both good days and bad. In July last summer I was in bed for three weeks with the bilious fever. Nils Mikkelsen Syl was here and he went for a doctor who charged one and a half dollars and since then I've been quite well. My wife and our two girls have been well all the time. They often speak of their grandparents, especially when putting on the socks that you sent them. They say that they are going to Norway, to Dala Granny and Narjord Granny. They thank you many times a day and go to the door saying they are going to visit you. But I think it is too far for them to make the journey. And Hilla sends greetings to Aunt Mali that she is very like her. She is big and full-bodied with reddish-yellow hair and those who know Mali say that she has come to America when they see Hilla. And Anna Maria is like her mother and Aunt Eva. We like it here. This year's harvest is modest, 400 bushels of corn and as much as we need of potatoes and different root vegetables and herbs. We don't have wheat because we don't think that we have enough cultivated land to get enough to make it worth renting a machine for threshing. I was away cradling or mowing wheat last summer and I earned almost all the wheat we need. I got two and a half bushels of wheat a day. A bushel costs fifty cents, a bushel of corn costs thirty-five cents, and potatoes twenty-five cents. We had thirty wagonloads of pumpkins that we for the most part use for the animals or boil for syrup. I have four large pigs and four small ones and one that we have slaughtered. Three that will be slaughtered for Christmas get as much corn as they'll eat. Corn is mainly used to fatten pigs. I have four oxen, two that are fully grown and a team that I'm about to begin taming, two fully grown cows, a heifer that will calve in the spring, and two calves. I bought a cow and a calf last summer for thirty-five dollars because I lost one of my cows last spring when she sank in a hole in a bog. She was to calve three weeks later, so I had to buy one. Butter costs twenty cents a pound, pork six cents, coffee fifteen cents, and sugar fifteen cents. But I think that all prices will be lower because the price of all grains has gone down because we had a good harvest but not much export.

I'll answer your questions even though I think I've written about some of this before. We share a house with a loft and we have chinked it with plaster and sand as we haven't decided whether to sell the land or divide it because the land around here has been bought by speculators and our land is too little for two. We could of course buy more, but it is expensive. But much of the land around us is unsettled so we use it for pasture and hay. We haven't decided what we should do. Everyday clothes here are like those the members of the higher classes use in Norway, but people use the clothes they have. It would be good to bring your best winter clothes. Americans usually buy their clothes ready-made in the store and then they throw away their old clothes and put on the new ones.

We now have a pastor from Norway who will stay here. I haven't heard him yet. He has conducted one Sunday service since he arrived. We live about seven miles from the parsonage. This is a large congregation so I think our pastor will have three churches. We don't have a Norwegian school yet but there are English schools here. There is a good arrangement for the English schools. The land is surveyed in squares and one sixteenth of a section is set aside by the government to pay for the building of schools. The English school has no religion. Everyone can have his own religion. It is for learning reading, writing, and arithmetic; they use the Bible and geography for reading.

Most of our neighbors are from Holtaalen and on Sundays we often have meetings. Last Christmas Bør Olsen from Holtaalen and some of his neighbors visited us and one month ago Jokum Nilsen and Elisabeth Maria Østhus from Røros came on a visit and she asked me to remember her to my sister Marit. Last Easter we visited them and we are often visited by our friends from Røros because they come past here when they go to the store. Christen Olsen Buk will teach school this winter about four miles from us. Christen Tørrisen is away working and won't return until May 1. Beret lives with us and their little daughter died fourteen days ago and was buried last Sunday. It is about a mile to our burial ground. We haven't had many deaths. A man was killed by lightning last fall while in bed at night with his wife and two children who were not in the least hurt.

I see that my brother Jens wishes he were here, and so do I, as I know that his situation cannot be good, but I don't advise him one way or the other. For my part I can say that I'm glad I went. When Peder Abrahamsen Dille visited us last Sunday he thanked God for giving him the decision to come here and get away from Røros. Even though he didn't like it to begin with, he now sees that he easily makes a living here and enjoys himself. But I cannot advise anyone to come or not to come. I can tell you as well as I can about my situation and what it is like here, and then you'll have to decide for yourself. If any are coming next summer then please send me the hymnal that I asked for in my last letter, and also Guldberg's book of hymns as it is used for church services here.

We must thank you so much for all that you sent us last summer with Simen from Tøresdalen, from our mother and sister-in-law Kirsti, to whom Hilla sends her thanks. When she puts on her stockings she says she is going to Granny Dala and Kirsti Dala, and they often argue and say Granny is mine, no she is mine. And we gladly invite Kirsti to come and take care of our children. Indeed, we could often have had use for her. She'll get good food, delicious pork, and wheat bread, because there is much such food in America, and the rest may be discussed when she arrives. You want to know what a letter costs. It is usually forty-six cents and you shouldn't have paid for any of the letters I've sent you. I haven't paid for receiving letters from you other than the last one. I assume you have paid for the earlier ones. People say that you now have to pay at some post offices when you deliver the letter, so when I send this one I'll note what I have paid on the letter. The next time you write you must tell me what you pay.

As I've been writing on this letter for several evenings I'll now take farewell with you and send my friendly regards to all friends who ask about us. To father and mother both at Tøresdalen and Narjord, we are often with you in our fond thoughts. If any plan to come here, they mustn't make their chests too large. It is better to have several. It is good if two can easily carry it. Good clothes chests can be very useful here and all good things are useful here; preferably good woolen clothes, woolen skirts, coats, and cloth.

We have had winter for about a month. It rains now and then, so we don't have a hard winter.

ELIAS HANSEN AND ANE KRISTINE TØRRISDATTER

Hilla Eliasdatter sends a lock of her hair and enclosed is her letter in her own hand. You must write to me as soon as you've received this and tell us whether there are any who are thinking of coming next spring and whether there is any news since we left you.

· —— ·

> This letter is for both Elias Hansen's family at Narjord in Os and Ane Kristine's family in Tøresdal (also called Paalsdal) in Røros. Elias's father, Hans, has noted that he received it 26 January. The copy was written by Elias's brother, Peder. When the children are reported as saying that they want to go to Dala Granny, they are referring to their grandmother in Tøresdal, Ane Kristensdatter. The two aunts are Mali Hansdatter and Eva Tørrisdatter. Ane Kristine's sister-in-law, Kirsti Olsdatter, married her brother, Peder Tørrissen. These two had the farm Paalsdalen in 1865. Kirsti was then fifty and they had no children. Bør Olsen had a farm in Hesper, Winneshiek County, Iowa, and in 1860 he and others from Holtaalen, Røros, Tolga, and Os moved to Jackson County, Minn. But after the U.S.-Dakota War of 1862, they returned to Winneshiek County, Iowa (Holand 1908, 519; Ulvestad 1907, 99–100). Elias Hansen's partner was Esten Larsen. This is the last letter from him in this edition. «1:63 NE I:147

· —— ·

1858 — LETTER I:71

FROM: Magrete Nilsdatter and Ole Olson Heve, *Cambridge, Wisconsin*
4 *January 1858*

To: Martha Haldorsdatter Nesheim, *Granvin, Hordaland*

Dear and unforgettable relatives,

We are ashamed of our negligence. Much too long a time has passed since we told you about our situation. You may think that we have forgotten you, but this is not so. There are reasons for our silence. The summer before last you, dear mother, had the great expense of sending us a large quantity of nice homespun and a religious book and this was much more than we expected. We thank you so much for these welcome gifts. But we also want to tell you that it took a long time before we held them in our hands. When the emigrants who brought them came to this country they let us know that they were going to Iowa. We waited for the letter we hoped you had sent with them and were sure that he who had the letter would send it to us by mail. But we waited in vain. Then, after a long time had passed, we wrote to Lars Medaas asking if he could find out whether one of the emigrants from Granvin had a letter for us. It didn't take long before he wrote and let us know that he had been told there was a package of gifts for us. Lars Iversen went to get the package and took the trouble of bringing it to a person we know well from Voss who lives in Decorah who sent it to us as soon as an opportunity arose. We got it a short time before the emigrants came last summer. But there was no letter.

We now have your letter of April 16 and have read it with great interest. We sent it on to your sons in Minnesota. Since then we have waited to hear from them, but we can no longer let this delay our letter to you even though we had planned to give you news about their situation. We had a letter from Lars last spring but it failed to explain things as he had written an earlier letter that never arrived, but we've heard that both Lars and Johannes have bought land and we hope that they'll soon be prosperous farmers.

We have enjoyed good health since we last wrote to you. And we have nothing to complain of in other matters as we have an abundance of both food and clothes and all that we need for our comfort. We can actually say that we are doing very well, especially in the good relations between us and in our pleasure in our well-behaved children that all contribute to our happiness. Since our last letter we have again received a daughter. Her name is Susan and she is one year and one month old. We now have half a dozen girls who are all equally loved by their mother and their father. We don't have great worldly riches nor do we desire them. There are so many who seek their all in this world and who regard wealth as the greatest prize. But the world makes its demands on the heart that is too busy with its affairs. The world will dominate our senses and distract our soul and thus actually keep us from true renunciation and from loving and serving God as we should. If we are to consider the true imitation of Christ, then he was not only poor, but in true renunciation he labored in prayer to God. Oh! May we be filled with desire to imitate him in his divine attributes and do good deeds. Oh, how happy we then would be!

We could have written much about the affairs of this country but we don't think this would be of much interest for you, our dear mother, so we'll end our simple letter with loving regards to you, our unforgettable mother and brother from your faithful

MAGRETTE NILSDATTER AND OLE OLSON HEVE

. —— .

Lars Iversen Medaas was from Granvin. His son, Iver Larsen, became a businessman in Decorah, Iowa (Ulvestad 1913, 796). «I:41 »I:134 NE II:1

. —— .

1858 — LETTER I:72

From: Gullik Gulliksen Dorsett, *Leland Station, Illinois, 21 January 1858*
To: Torsten Gulliksen Daaset, *Flesberg, Buskerud*

Far distant brother Torsten Gulliksen Daaset!

Much and long time has passed and many things have happened since I last wrote to you and since I heard from you. I hope you'll excuse me for not having answered your previous letter but I assumed that Ole and Juul wrote. I received your welcome letter dated December 1 on the eighteenth of this month and now I owe you thanks and a reply. I can please you with the news that I've been in good health, God be praised, almost all the time, but it saddens me to hear of my mother's death and my sister's troubled situation. You tell me of your great difficulties with our mad sister, but you must comfort yourself that he who rewards the good will reward you for your good work. My brother Juul went further west to a newer and less settled state, Minnesota, last fall and he bought 120 acres that he is now working on. As far as I know he is in good health. My brother Ole lives nearby and is in good health and doing well.

I suppose you wish to know about my situation as well as that of my brothers. I have cultivated forty-five acres. I haven't been able to use all my land and have leased parts of it. You may wish to know about my harvest. This year I harvested 340 bushels of wheat, 100 bushels of oats, forty bushels of potatoes, and some corn. Income on land has been low this past year because of the low prices for grain and the high wages the farmers have to pay. We were better paid for grain in previous years but this year we have had to sell wheat for half a dollar a bushel and oats for twenty-five cents. This low price has brought about a scarcity of money that cannot last.

I had a house built last summer. It was twenty-four feet long, sixteen feet wide and twelve feet high. The kitchen is an addition to the building. It is fourteen feet wide and fifteen feet long. I have fourteen windows: three in the kitchen, three in the living room, one in each of two bedrooms and one in the pantry. The loft has five windows. I have a team of draft oxen and a team of horses but only one cow. I've also built a stable that is twelve feet wide, eighteen feet long and eight feet high. Barns are not used here as in Norway. It has been a great advantage for people here that a railroad that goes west from Chicago passes by us. Before we had to haul everything we had to sell all the way to Chicago, about eighty miles from here. We also had to go there for building materials and such. Now I live merely two miles from a depot where we can sell our products and buy our necessities. Soon there will be a little town there as people are building and settling there one after the other.

You write that you often think of coming to America. I cannot say anything certain about this as it is a very important and difficult question. In such a matter there are circumstances that are beyond human understanding and it isn't possible to predict that others will fare as well as one's self. For an honest laborer there is more money than in Norway, but there are also many difficulties, especially in the beginning and for the impatient. But this is something one gets used to. There may be more illness here than in Norway but the country is as healthy as most places in Norway. Further west, in Iowa and Minnesota, the climate is healthier and the land cheaper. I cannot say more. I think it would be good for you to come. My loving regards to my father, siblings, and relatives,

GULLEIK G. DAASET

> The brothers from Daaset were poor writers and this letter, including the signature, has been dictated. The style is formal. Their sister, Maret Gulliksdatter, lived with Torsten at Daaset in 1865. She was then forty-six. «I:52 »I:79 NE II:3

1858 — LETTER 1:73

FROM: Gaute Ingebretsen and Kari Sigurdsdatter Gunleiksrud
Dunkirk, Wisconsin, 15 March 1858
To: Ingebret Torstensen and Birgit Gautesdatter Gunleiksrud, *Tinn, Telemark*

Dear parents and siblings,

I've had two letters from you. The first, dated February 12, 1857, I received April 1 that year, and I send you my loving thanks. Please forgive me for not writing before; this has only been due to my negligence. I'm glad to see that you are in good health and I can also, praise God, please you with the news that I and my family are in good health and doing well. I must tell you how much I harvested in 1857. I had 620 bushels of wheat, 620 bushels of oats, 100 bushels of barley, and 150 bushels of Indian corn. A man broke land for me, so 150 bushels of the wheat were his. This was a good harvest but prices were not so high this year. For some years we have received a little more than a dollar for a bushel of wheat and this year we only had half as much. I don't have more animals than I need to run my farm. I have two very nice brown mares that will be five years old next spring.

I see that my brother Hans is thinking of visiting us. This would indeed make us glad. This will be expensive for you but if you stay with us for a while I'm sure you would be able to learn much that would benefit you if God gives you health. I've often thought of visiting you but you may imagine that it wouldn't be good for me to leave my wife and children. I can also report—if you haven't already heard it—that Helje Syversen Grimsrud died May 30, 1856, and his wife remarried a man from Solør March 20, 1857. I must also report that for the year 1858, I hired a man from Hardanger for 110 dollars.

I got the letter dated April 16, 1857, that you sent with Halvor Endresen Tufto, late last August, but I haven't received the money you sent with him because he went to Minnesota where he lives about 200 miles from me. I hope I'll get it when I go there, but this will be expensive. The man who brought me the letter you sent with Halvor Tufto said you thought there would be a larger share of the inheritance for me. If such is the case and if my father permits, some of my or my wife's family may wish to go to America and then they could have this money and repay me when they arrive. If they don't have enough for their expenses they could earn money here and then repay me. Should none of them come, my brother Hans could bring it if he comes. And if he is not planning to come either, the best and cheapest way will be to send me a bank draft. My loving regards,

GAUTE ENGEBRIGHTSON AND WIFE

Loving regards from my children

GURO GAUTESDATTER, BIRGIT GAUTESDATTER, GUNIL GAUTESDATTER

·⎯·

Guro and Birgit have written their own names but Gunil is so little that she cannot write yet. The two oldest are now attending English school. Earlier that winter they also attended Norwegian school.

At the end of the letter are brief greetings signed by Sigrid Nilsdatter, Ole Vetlesen Berg, and Østen Pedersen Gollo. «1:61 »1:81 NE III:T12

·⎯·

1858 — LETTER I:74

FROM: Elise Wærenskjold, *Four Mile Prairie, Texas, 16 October 1858*
To: Thomine Dannevig, *Lillesand, Aust-Agder*

⇢≡⇠

My dear good Thomine!

Your brother, to whom I've written a few times this summer, has probably told you that I was expecting a little boy again and now I can—God be praised!—tell you that the little person arrived happy and healthy on the fourth of this month. I cannot describe my happiness when all was over: for I'm old, as you know, and was afraid that I would have to leave my beloved children. Neither Vilhelm nor I have relatives in this country so it isn't easy to say what Vilhelm would have done with the children if I had died, as it is quite contrary to the custom of the country that a white girl keeps house for a widower, and a stepmother—well they are rarely good. But—thank God—I'm well and hope that the Almighty will grant me some years with my three sweet boys. I began labor just after noon and our little boy arrived in the evening at ten minutes past eight. His name will be Thorvald August, after your dear Thorvald and a little German friend I had on the ship. I wish that my little Thorvald will be as good and clever as your Thorvald—then I couldn't wish for more. Thorvald can probably not remember me much beyond what you have told him. You must tell him that I loved him almost as much as my own children and that he now has a namesake in distant Texas. I wonder whether the two will ever meet! I've been well all the time, better than after the two other births and I only had someone at my bed the first three nights. Since then I've had my little boy with me and taken care of him myself. He is so nice, he never cries; but he does keep me awake at night. Our neighbors are very good in such situations; they sit by the bed all night and bring food to each other. But this is only true of our country neighbors; the town ladies follow American customs.

Please, dear Thomine, give my regards to my correspondents in Lillesand, your brother, Kaja, Anne, Stina, Mrs. Fredrichsen, and Mrs. Thorkildsen, and tell them that all is well with me and that I would be glad to hear from them. Now I don't have the time or the desire to write to them all because this would be to repeat the same and then the same again. I wrote to Hansen a few months ago about a pastor who wished to come here. I cannot say how much I wish that we could have a pastor here again, a pastor who had the ability to instill a love and respect for the Christian faith in our young people. If Crøger is the man Schøth claims he is it would be wonderful for us to have him here. You must give my most friendly regards to your old parents, your children, and all my other friends and acquaintances. Your acquaintances here are all doing well. I suppose you know that the Baches have a hotel here in addition to their store. They are said to make good money but it is more than I can understand that they want to serve travelers when they have no need to do so, especially as they have no children to lay aside money for.

Recently a company of riders and other artists were in Prairieville and Mrs. Bache made quite a lot of money. Among them was a living skeleton, a mulatto who, except for his head and neck, was nothing but skin and bones. They said he was an awful sight but I would have liked to see him because there is probably no other person like him in the world. Vilhelm and the boys went to see it all. Sigurd has lived with us for two or three months. He teaches our boys and has room and board with us. Some neighbors' children also attend his school. It is nice to have Ørbæk with us. Ouline hasn't been well this summer. For a while we thought she was in a family way but that was regrettably not the case. She is visiting the older Norwegian settlement with her husband. Ole Johan is with Reiersen and building up quite a fortune. Andreas' widow didn't get nearly as much from her husband as she had expected. He believed he was worth 3,000 dollars in all, but I now hear that he only owned his house and some cattle. This would, to be true, not be insignificant had only the property had a greater potential and had she been used to simpler circumstances. Storekeeping may be more profitable than farming but I've often thanked God that we haven't gotten involved in it; it is a very uncertain source of income. If the man dies it all goes apart since wives here never run a store and probably couldn't do so under our circumstances. But I could continue farming should Vilhelm die and as we have very little debt and very little is owed to us, I wouldn't have to let others take over. I know how to take care of our cattle just as well as my husband since I am the one who keeps an account of our cows, horses, and sheep. I write down all that are bought and sold, slaughtered, die, or get lost, and I work out our profit at the end of each year. What makes storekeeping so uncertain here is that almost all do their purchases on credit and many cannot or will not pay. So when an estate is settled large amounts are lost and I believe that those who do the settling know how to line their pockets.

When Pastor F. last visited us he told me that his mother would send me some newspapers with a man named Albertson from Holt who lives in Tyler, a town about forty miles from here. I looked forward to receiving letters from all of you and the portrait of Thorvald. But Albertson came without anything for me. Could he have been unwilling or how else explain it? When you see Mrs. Fredrichsen ask her to please me with another letter. It is now one and a half years since I last had a letter from her. You must tell Bina that Helene and her husband have visited us. They are doing very well; Helene almost too well as she is so lazy that she is becoming much too fat. Their marriage is said to be an unusually loving one. Christopher died of pneumonia in Shreveport and Helene was with him at the end. Lise's little boy is also dead. The others are well. Poor Bina who lost her son! How is her remaining little boy? Please do me the kindness of putting the enclosed letters in envelopes and mailing them. Send me a long letter and tell me everything you think may be of interest for me. Live well! My most friendly regards to you and yours from Vilhelm, the little boys, and your faithful friend

ELISE WÆRENSKJOLD

EW was a prolific correspondent but most of her letters have probably been lost. Except for two letters to Thomine Dannevig in 1852 and 1857 and one to the newspaper *Morgenbladet* in 1857 (all in Clausen 1961), there is an eight-year hiatus between the letters to T. A. Gjestvang, where she mainly wrote to inform about the situation among the early settlers in Texas, and this letter to her friend Thomine Dannevig in Lillesand. Most of the known letters by EW are in Clausen (1961), and some were also included in Blegen (1955). In both editions, however, parts of letters have been omitted, for instance references to people in Lillesand and passages that may have seemed detrimental to EW's reputation. In a note (40) C. A. Clausen explains that his edition's text of letters to the Dannevig family is from a local newspaper publication in 1925, and it must be the editor of this publication who is responsible for the cuts and changes.

Thomine Dannevig's brother was Samuel Hansen. In 1865 he is listed as S. N. Hansen in Lillesand where he was a merchant. Some of the people mentioned are Erik and Ingeborg Bache, Anton Schjøth (in Lillesand), Ouline Reiersen, Sigurd Ørbæk, Johan Reinert Reiersen, Ole Johan Ørbæk, Andreas H. and Gina Ørbæk, Bina Grøgaard (in Lillesand), Helene and Peder Georg Reiersen, and Conrad Claus Christopher Grøgaard. Pastor Anders Emil Fridrichsen had left Texas the preceding year and gone to Minnesota. He later became a pastor in Portland, Ore. (Clausen 1961, 47 and Bjork 1958, 303–319). There were several brothers named Albertson in Tyler. A letter from Elef Albertson is in Nor. ed. II:175. «1:33 »1:85 NE I:12

1858 — LETTER I:75

From: Hellik Olson Lehovd, *Christiana, Wisconsin, 28 October 1858*
To: Ole Helgesen Lehovd, *Flesberg, Buskerud*

Dear Father,

I have your letter dated April 5 and I was glad to hear that you are doing well, and I can now please you with the same news, that I have been in good health since you last heard from me and there has been little illness and death. Some of our acquaintances have died since I last wrote: old Anund Braata and Ingebør Thoresdatter Buin, who both died last summer. Knut Klemetson Juvelie has married a girl from Hov in Rollag.

I made a journey last summer. I left Wisconsin in May and went to Minnesota to claim a piece of land. But when I got there almost all Congress land had been taken and some had been given by the government to the railroad companies. But I traveled several hundred miles around in the country and took some prairie land without a single tree. In Minnesota there are large prairies and little forest and it is very expensive and you have to haul lumber five to ten miles. So I think I'll sell it and take work in Wisconsin. Minnesota is not a fertile place as it is almost as cold there as in Norway and little forest. There is a great shortage of money and people pay from thirty-six to seventy-eight percent interest and I have lent some money there at thirty-six percent for the year. And I experienced a storm such as I have never seen with rain, wind, and thunder and a hail storm July 30 over a stretch of several miles. The hail measured from ten to thirteen inches around and weighed from three-quarters to a pound and killed pigs and sheep and beat the wheat and corn down to the ground and broke all windows to the north and west. I didn't like it there because there are no pastors, churches, or schools, except for occasional itinerant pastors. There was one there last summer and the service had to be held under an open sky with confirmation, communion, and baptism. Children who were almost two years old were baptized, so I wouldn't advise anyone to go to Minnesota. But Wisconsin and Illinois are good places and everything is organized there with churches and schools so those who can buy land in W. or I. can do well. Workers can make more money in these places. I traveled between 500 and 600 miles last summer and returned here about two weeks ago and I am now ready to go again. When you write send it to the same post office as before and I'll be sure to get it.

It was a poor year all over America as blight caused great damage to the wheat. There is a great shortage of money, so according to the newspapers you've had a better year in Norway. Now telegraph wires are stretched all the way from England and across the ocean and up through the country so that we can read the news from London two or three days earlier, and I believe that soon a wire will go all the way from Norway to America. I must end my letter with greetings from all here at Hvashovd. They are doing well and are in fairly good health. Give my regards to my relatives and friends such as Ole Ellefsen, Anund Bergerud, and Knut Ørsten, and tell them that I'm doing well here. And finally, greetings to you, my dear and unforgettable siblings, from your brother and to you, my dear father, from your son with the wish that the Lord will guide and protect both your life and your soul and that you will hold to our Lord Jesus Christ so that sometime we will be gathered in our Almighty God where there is everlasting rejoicing and happiness. This wish is from your unforgettable brother and son. Live well in the Lord.

HELLIK OLSEN LEHOVD

HOL also wrote home 10 April (Nor. ed. II:9). Knut Klemetson Juvelie emigrated from Flesberg in 1853 and in 1858 he moved to Zumbrota, Goodhue County, Minn., where he farmed (Ulvestad 1913, 736). After an exchange of telegrams between Queen Victoria and President James Buchanan in 1858, the first transatlantic cable failed. A new one was ready for use in 1866. «I:69 »I:83 NE I:13

1859 — LETTER I:76

FROM: Svend Larsen Houg, *Elgin, Iowa, 18 January 1859*
To: Ole Larsen Haug, *Aal, Buskerud*

As God has maintained me in life and health to this date, I must again write some words to you. These have not been delayed because I have forgotten you but only because of my own negligence. Nay, the heart of your brother in the flesh is not so cold. I received your welcome letter of April 24 on June 18. Thank you for telling me about so much. It was good to hear of my siblings and of the home of my fathers that I so often recall in my memory. In particular I often think of you my siblings and of how you are in the world and of whether the chastising Lord is allowed to remind you to have the word of God as your law and guidance for your conduct. Oh, my dear siblings, I cannot admonish you but it has often been edifying to receive your kind admonitions. I am but a poor sinner who must bend his knee before God in humility and pray for his forgiveness for my sins and transgressions against so merciful a God. For I have disobeyed him since my childhood. Nevertheless he has been so good that he has maintained in me a longing to seek him. Oh, that I may be more sincere in my faith and in my prayers and remain awake so that when it is my time to exchange this world for eternity I will come to the shores of heaven. Oh, how good it would be if we see each other again on that day when all is revealed, if we then may be saved. Help us in this, God the Father, the Son, and the Holy Spirit.

I've been in good health since I last wrote. The children and my wife have also been quite well, considering the frailty of woman; there is much work with our growing family as we now have six children, five of them boys. The youngest is called Assor and they are all healthy. As for other matters, we have to be careful as money is short because there was a low price for wheat last year and this year the harvest was poor. But we have what we need and even a little we can sell. I had 105 bushels of wheat and that was about half of the usual. Corn did better and there was an abundance of hay. I'm feeding seventeen head of cattle this winter and six sheep, but I only have eight pigs. Cattle have become so much cheaper; the price is less than half of what it was two years ago. I would like to sell a team of good oxen and a cow or two but I don't think I'll be able to sell them for much more than the price of the meat, but this can change quickly.

I've received the money you say Ole Bratager asks about. Thank him for his trouble when you meet him. In your last letter you wrote that Knud Knudsen Houg wanted to visit me if possible. I was glad to hear this and I thought that I would do what I could for him, but I soon heard that he went to Minnesota with the others in his company as he likely didn't want to leave them. But I don't think he did right in this if he had planned to work for others, because it is better here than in Minnesota for anyone seeking employment in these times. You ask me to tell you what your last letter cost me and it was as usual forty-eight cents. I sometimes think of you, my brother Knud, and of how you are doing since the times are so uncertain. But the times are not as uncertain here in our state of trial as they will be when we exchange time for eternity: that will be a great change. Oh, then we would certainly all wish to be a friend of Jesus so that he could clothe us in his righteousness as we do not have any righteousness in ourselves.

My loving regards go to you, all my siblings. Although I don't mention all of you by name you are all included. Perhaps this may be the last time I write to you. You are lovingly greeted from me, my wife, and our children,

SVEND LARSEN HOUG

To you brother Ole,

In your letter there are many things that you wish to know about. It is no easy matter for me to answer you but I will nevertheless try according to my poor understanding. You wish to know whether we received the pastor I had mentioned. I have probably written about P. A. Rasmussen, who has been as a leader of the true believers for some time. He came to us and led us in meetings and church services, but we cannot have him as our regular pastor as he lives far away from us and has a large congregation where he lives. He has promised to visit us twice a year for the necessary church services. He also travels around in the country for prayer meetings and church services among his brothers in faith. He was converted when he came from Norway as a young man and lived among his believing friends here. Then he was appointed to be their teacher and he studied for some time at a school run by the German Lutherans, so he is well versed in the German language. He has translated many good books from German, among them Johann Arndt's homilies, that we now have. He has also in the last two years published several pamphlets in defense of Lutheran doctrine, and we get one every month. They contain much that is edifying and in them we can learn about the state of Christianity in many places.

Elling Eielsen lives far from here but I know him and I know what people say of him. I think he has been the greatest instrument in this country for the maintenance of true Lutheran doctrine and the pure gospel. And this is why he has been derided and lied about as are almost all those who teach without fear and who reveal false doctrines and the evil of man. And we know that Jesus said to his disciples that you shall be hated by all people for my name's sake. Elling Eielsen was with us last summer and held prayer meetings and church services. He told us that he had planned to go to Norway but that he had received several letters from believing Norwegian brothers in a state called Texas. So now he'll go there and from there to Norway, God willing him to still make such long journeys.

I have more. A Norwegian by the name of Arne Boyum from the Bergen diocese has traveled among us the last three years preaching the word of God. He truly has the gift of explaining the word. He has been here three times and the last time was at the time we celebrate the birth of Jesus and he then held a prayer meeting in my house on Christmas Day and at another home nearby on the Second Day of Christmas. He has been elected pastor of many small congregations both here in Iowa and in Minnesota. Several of us have talked about having him as our teacher but I don't know how this will work out as he is so far away. But on his travels he sometimes passes nearby.

You ask whether we have a church. We don't. The congregation is small and it isn't necessary to build a church yet. Church services are held in homes until we can build a church. The pastors don't wear a cassock but everything is done according to the word of God and without any superficial ceremonies. As for the organization of the church and congregation, this would be far too much even though I have it all in print. Those who are elected must teach according to the word of God and the unaltered Augsburg Confession and they may serve as long as they remain in the living faith. The majority here have a church and a pastor with a good salary. They invoke the doctrine and the name of Luther but do not follow him. We must thank God who woke up a man like Luther who could take back the pure and clear word of God from the darkness of the papacy so that we can have it among us and that we may have the light if we walk in the light. The Norwegian pastors have a publication called *The Church Times* where they hold forth with wonderful praise of the Lutheran church and say that they alone are the Lutheran church, and meanwhile the true believers who are the true limbs of the church are proclaimed sectarians and instigators. I've often read these publications and I think that for the most part they serve to lull the majority in their dead faith and to trust in the superficial church service and that if you only live a decent life then your Christianity is sufficient. But much more is required, the entire human being, both body and soul. But I must conclude. I have spoken as I believe.

You would like to hear about those who are called Frankeans. I don't know much about them as there are none in these parts, but apparently there are enough of them in this country. I don't know their origin but they proclaim the Lutheran doctrine. But they are remarkably wrong about Luther; I've heard that they eschew the doctrine we have grown up with. They differ from us in their view of the baptism and Holy Communion. They say that the bread and wine merely symbolize Jesus, but Jesus says that they are.

You ask how far it is from Iowa to Minnesota. These two states are side by side, northern Iowa and southern Minnesota, but when you go far north in Minnesota it is much colder than here. Both are large states. I haven't received the money that you sent me with our former neighbors, nor do I know when it will be done. I wrote a letter last year to O. M. S. about how he should send it to me but haven't had a reply. I'll write again. But to go there would cost me almost as much as they brought. I must now conclude my poor letter and set my name to it,

SVEND LARSEN

· ⸺ ·

SLH also wrote 31 March 1857 (Nor. ed. I:135). This letter was received 7 March. It presents three central actors in the early immigrant church. Peter Andreas Rasmussen, who had emigrated in 1850 as a schoolteacher, became pastor in Lisbon, Ill. from 1854 to his death in 1898. At first he was a prominent member of the Eielsen Synod but broke with it in 1856 because of disagreement with Eielsen. Remaining a Haugean in his theological views, he eventually joined the Norwegian Synod. The German school was the Concordia Theological Seminary at Fort Wayne, Ind. In 1856 Rasmussen organized a publishing society in Lisbon and among his many publications is the translation of a book of homilies by the German theologian Johan Arndt (1555–1621). Elling Eielsen was a well-known Haugean itinerant lay preacher before his emigration in 1839 and was central in forming the first synod among the Norwegian immigrants in 1846. He traveled extensively among the Norwegian immigrants and visited Texas in 1859. Arne E. Boyum emigrated in 1853 and became a pastor in Fillmore County, Minn., in 1858. He was in the Eielsen Synod but in 1876 became the first president of the new Hauge Synod. The standard history of the Lutheran churches among Norwegian immigrants gives this brief description of the principles associated with Hans Nielsen Hauge and his followers, among whom were these three pastors as well as Svend Larsen Houg: "Christianity is something to be *experienced*, which experience involves a spiritual awakening, conversion, and a separated life; worship is simple and informal, in contrast to ritualism and formalism; lay activity, the practice of Christian testimony in public as well as in private, is to be encouraged" (Nelson and Fevold 1960, 126).

Ole Person Bratager (1811–1868), was from the farm now spelled Brattegard in Aal. Knut Knutsen, on the northern of the two Haug farms in Aal, was married twice and had four sons who reached adulthood named Knut Knutsen. Three of these emigrated and this is most likely the youngest, who emigrated in 1858. *Kirkelig Maanedstidende* [The Church Monthly] was published by the Norwegian Synod; *Kirkelig Tidende* [The Church Times] was edited by Rasmussen 1856–1861. The Frankeans were named for the German Lutheran pietist, August Hermann Francke. There was a Franckean Evangelical Lutheran Synod of New York and some Norwegian immigrant pastors affiliated themselves with this synod in the late 1840s and eventually entered the Scandinavian Augustana Synod in 1860. The last sentence in the penultimate paragraph is somewhat cryptic in the original letter as well. He seems to intend that Jesus says he is in the bread and wine. «1:51 »1:90 NE II:17

1859 — LETTER I:77

FROM: Gullik Olsen Østern, *Paint Creek, Iowa, 18 January 1859*
To: Engebret Olsen Steen, *Skedsmo, Akershus*

⋅⇒○⇐⋅

Dear beloved mother and brothers,

It is a long time since we heard anything from you or you heard from us. So I long for news from you. I would be glad to know how you are, whether our old mother is still alive and if she is up and about. I can, praise God, report that we are all healthy and well. You know that our oldest daughter is dead and our second will be three on March 3. Our youngest daughter, Helga Pauline, was one year on October 23; she is big and clever and right now she is busy organizing our pots and pans, so you will realize that she makes herself useful in our home. I almost forgot to tell you all that Caroline can do; she can wash, sew, and iron, and she also helps her mother to spin and she can sing English children's songs. You may think she is just as clever as your Laura, Engebret.

This year's harvest is modest. On the same acreage I had 200 bushels last year, I now had 100. The reason was rust that kept the wheat from ripening. Potatoes didn't do well. Corn did better. This summer I broke seventeen acres. I'm still not used to horses. A little while ago I almost traded my oxen for horses but now I've decided to stay with oxen for the time being, especially since there now is a shortage of money. The railroad goes to Prairie du Chien on the Mississippi and we expect that it will soon reach us. They say it will come along Paint Creek about five miles south of us. So there will be fast transportation here and I assume you'll visit us. It will only take three to four days when the black horse is harnessed. We are four miles from the Mississippi and thirteen miles from Prairie du Chien.

I have three cows and a heifer, eleven pigs to be slaughtered in a few days and six that will live until fall. I have greetings from the Aas people; they are in good health and doing well. I, Jacob, Jacob Engebretsen and our families, and old Uncle Engebret celebrated Christmas together and had a very good time. Sunday after New Year we were all at our brother Jacob's where we also met Anton Larsen Skillebekk and his family.

We don't see much of Maren Skillebekk, as she is married to a son of a virtuous and very well-known family here on the prairie. She is forced to live in a convent, much against her nature, I believe. Without asking your permission we took it upon ourselves to give Maren Larsen Skillebekk what was left by Christen. It was then our intention that it would simply be her possession, but this is no longer the case. After a short while the girl married this abovementioned holy person, and he has in all ways and to his utmost shown us his respect—but note! this has been with lies and slander. Indeed, he even planned to honor us with a visit by representatives of the court. Our brother-in-law, Carl Aas, had borrowed about 100 dollars from Christen and it wasn't easy to raise such a sum in a short time, but he repaid about half of it. But this didn't satisfy the important man who went straight to a lawyer and authorized him to collect the rest. The lawyer was well known to us all and let Carl know what to expect. Carl could have had the sheriff at his door. But it didn't go so far and Nils got his money without this extra entertainment. We are so furious because of this shameful behavior that we'll do what we can to get this money back. Just send us mother's signed power of attorney to collect the money. And please have it done as quickly as possible with all necessary details and the required signatures. I look forward to visiting him next spring, and it won't be as pleasant in his ears as when he heard that he was to inherit the fruits of our brother's labor. Enough of this! If all goes according to plan, we'll send the money to mother if she needs it or to our dear brother Lars who we sincerely think deserves it. Write the authorization on a separate piece of paper, as it will be used in court, and send it with your letter.

We would like to hear from our brother Carl as we have only had one letter from him. But ask him not to use as heavy a paper as he then did because it cost us two dollars. Give him our love and tell him we are doing well. Please tell us about our relatives. Is Lars still in the army; does he still suffer from that nasty sore throat he so often used to have? I would be happy to hear that it no longer bothered him. Please ask him to write to one of us and give us his complete address; there are so many with his name that we cannot write until we have his address. Anton Larsen Skillebekk tells us that it is long since you had a letter from us. It is very regrettable that letters with precise addresses are not delivered. I can say from Jacob that he sent a letter to you in the spring of 1858 and enclosed in this letter was a note with greetings from me and my wife to you and your family.

And I can give greetings from my brother and his family. They are all in good health and doing well and his wife will soon be adding to their family. Hans Arnesen List and his wife are in good health and doing well. Ingeborg Johnsen Fossum visited us from Minnesota for Christmas. Her brother's two oldest children are confirmed, so he has good help on his farm. He has told Ingeborg that he wants to sell his farm and buy one near us. Torine Aas, Andrine Østern, and Martine and Torine Østern work in Prairie du Chien where they earned two dollars a week until last fall. But now they earn one and and a half and don't like it. So girls make money here, but they also spend it. They are so well dressed that you cannot see any difference between a servant and a daughter of her employer if you should see them walking side by side. I must now conclude my letter with the sincere wish that it will find you all in good health and satisfied with life. You are all greeted from all of us. Yours faithfully,

G. O. ØSTERN

. ——— .

Bottolf Bottolfsen had emigrated from Norderhov in Ringerike, Akershus, in 1850, and was one of the first settlers in Allamakee County, Iowa. His son, Nils Bottolfsen, who married Maren Skillebekk, had a farm near Harpers Ferry, Iowa (Ulvestad 1913, 554). GOØ's sister, Mari, was married to Carl Aas. As their dead brother, Christen, had neither wife nor children, his mother was his legal heir. So Gullik, Jacob, and Mari now want their mother to demand a return of her inheritance that had been given to Maren Skillebekk, now Maren Bottolfsen. There is no further mention of this affair in later letters. There is a letter from Hans Arnesen dated Mabel, Minn., 30 July 1854 (Nor. ed. I:99). Here he is given the name Østerneie. The name used here, List, may be short for Listuen, where his brother, Torstein, lived in 1865. Hans Arnesen and his wife, Haagine Johnsdatter, emigrated on the bark *Christiane* in 1851 with Jacob Olsen and Christine Engebretsdatter Østern and many others from Bærum. «I:50 »I:97 NE II:19

. ——— .

1859 — LETTER I:78

From: Ole Hansen Rustand, *St. Ansgar, Iowa, 24 January 1859*
To: Torgrim Olsen Haugerud, *Aadalen, Ringerike, Buskerud*

My dear son Torgrim and family,

After I had received your last letter in 1857 I immediately wrote back. This is more than a year ago and since then I have written both to you and to my other family. This was last summer, but as I have not had any reply I fear that they have not arrived. I have waited for letters from you, in particular to learn about the results of the case between you and Meinik and the outcome of the deal between Erik Gullerud and Ringnes as I have heard a rumor that it has cost him 15,000 *speciedaler*. I would like to know the reason for your dispute with Meinik since I am unable to fully understand the situation on the basis of the information I have received. I have had to assume that an act of carelessness set it all off.

I don't have any particular news except that this last year has been the poorest since the Norwegians began to emigrate to America. Crops seemed promising in the spring but then a continuous massive rain lasted through the summer and when the time for harvest was near we had a powerful rainstorm with hail that beat down the fields. There has hardly been any wheat, which is our main crop. Here and there the corn did well but most places there was less than usual. We've also had a shortage of money for the last one and a half years, so times are hard. There has been an increase in taxes and they are twice as high as the year before. The tax on my land—about 200 acres—is more than thirty dollars and we have to pay taxes on everything we own, cattle and all.

I haven't heard from your brother Ole the Elder who went to Australia about one and a half years ago except for a letter written just after he had arrived. If you have a letter from him then write to me immediately. Last summer I had a letter from your brother Ole the Younger and another one just before Christmas. He left California last summer and got to a place called Fraser River in the British lands and his purpose was to dig for gold.

He says that he plans to return in two years. When you write I would like to know about the division of the estate at Finsand and how much your brother Hans and his wife inherited. I haven't heard anything about this. I am, praise God, in fairly good health. I will end with loving regards to you and your wife and children,

OLE HANSEN RUSTAND

This is the last letter by OHR in this edition. He died on 2 July 1861. He wrote a brief note dated 24–30 January 1859, saying that he had received a letter from his son, Ole the elder, in Australia when he was at the post office to mail this one. In this brief note he is concerned with a rumor that he has said that he would rather be a beggar in Norway than remain in the United States. Hans Olsen Rustand and his wife, Inger Olsdatter, had the farm once owned by his father. She was from one of the two Finsand farms, now owned by her brother, Mons Olsen. «I:68 »I:82 NE II:20

1859 — LETTER I:79

FROM: Juul and Ole Gulliksen Dorsett, *Earlville, Illinois, 22 February 1859*
To: Gullik Evensen and Torstein Gulliksen Daaset, *Flesberg, Buskerud*

Dear brother Thorsten Gulliksen Daaset,

I am taking up my pen to write you some lines about our situation. We are doing well and wish to hear the same from you. I'll give you a brief account of our harvest. This has been a rather hard year. Most of the wheat was damaged by rust and the potatoes rotted so we have hard times for both farmers and farm laborers because the farmers cannot grow anything and the bachelors cannot get work as there is a shortage of money. It is not that there is no money in the country, but people have no expectations. I've had work almost all the time since I came here. As for your thoughts about

America, I'll tell you that if you cannot make a living there I know that it would be better that you come here because you must not think that it is always like it was last year. No, we have had an abundance of work and money. If you come, don't bring your work clothes, only bed clothes and blue and black woolen cloth. Nor should you bring things of silver except spoons since they have no value here. But if you come then you should come next summer if you cannot come now. You must let me know, for I have sold my land to be ready to go with you when you come, because we should go further west where land is cheaper. We can get land for one dollar and twenty-five cents an acre and as much and as good land as we want. And to you, Hellik, I'll say that if you don't have enough money to buy a farm there, then it is best that you come here. But it isn't good for me to advise anyone to come. You would perhaps not be satisfied or perhaps get sick, and then you would blame me. But I have no doubt that it is better here. I'll end my letter with loving regards to all. I'm in good health. Write to me as soon as you receive these simple but well-intended lines. We would like to know whether you are coming or not. Our best regards from me and my brothers to our old father and our siblings and friends who ask about us. Farewell.

JUUL GULLIKSEN DAASET

Dear Father,

As so much time has passed since I wrote to you I won't let this opportunity go by. I often think of you but you know I'm not good at writing. Dear father, we are so far from each other that we cannot talk with each other, so I'll use my pen to tell you that we, praise God, are in good health and have what we need to sustain life. I must also tell you that we have a little girl who was born September 12 and baptized on Christmas Day. Her name is Ingeborg after my wife's mother. She is growing and thriving. I have no further news. Yours sincerely,

OLE GULLIKSEN DAASET AND FAMILY

«I:72 »I:94 NE II:27

1859 — LETTER 1:80

FROM: Christopher Jacobson, *Ogalla, Wisconsin, 13 March 1859*
To: Hans Jakobsen Hilton, *Kløfta, Ullensaker, Akershus*

―――

Dear, dear brother!

Even though I have no more to tell you than I wrote in my last letter I'll write these lines to thank you for the letter you sent me last year. Yes, you had indeed collected a lot of news for me. It pleases me so to hear about the doings of the friends of my youth. The most remarkable was what you said about "Karine Luften" who had been so cleverly fooled even though one may easily commit errors while asleep. But everything you wrote was of interest and gave me much pleasure. I'm glad to see that you have accomplished so much since I left you, that you are married and have two happy sons who will, I hope, in time give you happiness. I'm sure that you'll give them a good upbringing.

I'll answer some of your questions. My modest education hasn't made things easier for me as I haven't tried to make use of it. It may have been different if I had gone to the Norwegian settlements but I have little interest in doing this. My many friends and acquaintances are a varied lot, good as well as bad, and I don't put much trust in friends whoever they may be. There is little entertainment here as it is settled quite recently. There are occasional dances or balls but as I haven't learned to dance like they do here I rarely attend. I now understand and speak English quite well so the language is no longer a problem. As for marriage, it has never yet occurred to me; but a young person who wanders from one place to another and who stops in different towns and villages will of course try to get a girlfriend among the many lovely and attractive girls, so why should I not also have one now and then. Finally, you ask whether I've ever thought of coming home. Well, it would have been the nicest thing I could imagine to see you and my dear Norway again, but it would be difficult for a man to come back to Norway and try to make a living after he has been in America for some years. Oh, dear brother, don't wish to have me back, for I lack nothing and you must remember that no one was pleased with me when I was there. I was unmanageable and loved both women and wine and I may have become worse had I stayed at home and even put you all to shame. I know that mother is sad that I'm so far away from home but if she thinks it over she will be happy. Now no one will whisper in her ear: "Last Saturday night Christopher was at a dance and he was so drunk that he almost began a brawl and then he went home with some loose girls, etc." You see how things would be for our mother. Now she may find pleasure in the letters she occasionally has from me and I believe that I may thus cause her and all of you greater pleasure than if I had been with you. In a few years—if I remain healthy and keep on working—I suppose I could have a few hundred dollars saved, but I haven't yet wandered enough for my satisfaction. I would have liked to be in a place where there is gold but first I will need about three or four hundred, and this won't be possible until next year as money is short now and wages low, at most sixteen dollars a month. Since I came to America I have been ill for almost two years and you know that this set me back quite a lot. But since I last came to Ogalla I have, praise God, been well.

Dear brother, we may never see each other again but I hope you won't forget to write to me now and then so I may have news of what things are like in dear old Norway. Is mother well enough to walk as far as to your house and is she pleased with her sons? Write to me as soon as possible and tell me everything; even if it seems of little value to you it will be of interest to me. Give my regards to your Jakob and Oluf from their unknown uncle. You and your wife are lovingly remembered and you will also, I'm sure, give my love to my old mother when you see her. Farewell. Your

CHRISTOPHER JACOBSON

Write my name as I write it and use a W in Wisconsin.

. ⎯⎯ .

> There were post offices with the name Ogalla in both Chippewa and Dunn Counties in Wisconsin in the 1850s. Hans Jakobsen Hilton was married to Anne Olsdatter, and their two sons in 1859 were Jakob (5) and Oluf (3). CJ concludes his letter by insisting on his new identity: he is no longer Kristofer Jakobsen but Christopher Jacobson. «I:47 »I:137 NE II:28

. ⎯⎯ .

1859 — LETTER 1:81

From: Gaute Ingebretsen Gunleiksrud, *Stoughton, Wisconsin*
25 August 1859

To: Ingebret Torstensen and Birgit Gautesdatter Gunleiksrud
Tinn Telemark

⋙◦⋘

Dear parents and siblings!

Your letters, one dated January 28, 1859, and one undated but probably written earlier, were sent with Sivert Gunnufsen Grimsrud and I got them both last winter. I was glad to see that you were all in good health and doing well. Praise God for this! I can also please you with the news that I and my family have been well since I last wrote. Let us thank and praise the Lord that he each and every day and year shows his grace, love, and fidelity to us poor, weak, and miserable beings. I would like to make a proposal to my brothers; one of you may wish to visit America. You mustn't think that I'm urging you to stay here for life. No! That is not my intention, for in this you must act according to your own free will. I'm only suggesting that one of you should come here and visit us and in addition see the so widely famed America. It may be most convenient for Hans to make this journey. You may wonder why? Well, because of your trade; you could learn much here that would be of use and benefit in Norway if you stayed for a year. However, even if I believe this to be true, I'm not suggesting that you would make a lot of money by doing this, only that here you'll see many things that are done much better and much faster than in Norway. I'm sure that you could, on your return to Norway, introduce them and perhaps find them both better and more convenient. I know you have the money for many such journeys and I hope you'll come, if for no other reason than to see a loving brother.

You may be assured that I've often thought of visiting Norway and that I still would like to do this. But if you try to understand my situation, you will see that such a long journey is almost impossible for me. You may ask why, and the answer is that I am the provider for a family and it would not be easy to leave so beloved a family behind. You may also be pleased to know that my three children now have come as far in reading Norwegian as I may expect. The two oldest ones are beginning to read English. There has been little rain here all summer and I haven't threshed yet. In this area we have had little better than a mediocre harvest.

Last fall I received some of the money you sent with Halvor Endresen Tufte and the rest around midsummer. So I've now received fifty *speciedaler*, for which I send you my most heartfelt thanks. Our most friendly regards from all here. May the blessing of Heaven be on you all, my parents, siblings, relatives, and friends! You are also sincerely and lovingly greeted by Sigrid Nilsdatter who says she lives well here with me.

GAUTE ENGEBRETSON

GIG appears to have dictated this letter but signed it himself. «1:73 »I:150 NE III:T13

1859 — LETTER I:82

FROM: Ole Olsen Haugerud the Younger, *Yale, British Columbia Canada, 3 November 1859*

To: Guri Rustand, *Aadalen, Ringerike, Buskerud*

Dear Mother and siblings,

I haven't written to you since I left four years ago so I'll take up my pen to tell you that I'm still alive. In order to tell you how I've been I'll have to begin with the beginning. In late November 1855 I left Wisconsin with my companion Andreas Sørensen from Nes in Romerike and we came to San Francisco January 6, 1856. I went to the mines and when I had come to my destination I had already spent 300 dollars. I began digging for gold in the hope that I had come to a land of gold but instead I found myself in the greatest gathering of scoundrels on earth. But I continued my work in good faith. I tried in different places and found nothing but finally I had a little luck and made a few hundred dollars. Then a letter from our brother Ole told me that he had emigrated to Australia and I decided to go there to see him. I began my journey June 23, 1858, but in San F. no passage was available as all ships and steamers were going to British Columbia because of the rumors of the gold discoveries there. So I decided to go there and got passage on a steamer that left July 10. But what terrors we encountered! Early one Sunday morning it began to storm without pause from the northwest so the ship was awash with waves and the wind continued to increase until the ship foundered and a hole was knocked out of the bottom. There were 500 people on board and we were all kept busy until we got to land after five days without food or drink. I was in grave doubt about what I should do but I decided to continue my journey and took passage on a sailing ship. I came to my destination after six weeks and this cost me 250 dollars. Here I began mining again and as for my profits, I have sometimes made a day's wage and sometimes not.

Last spring I, my companion from Wisconsin, another Norwegian, and an Irishman decided to go up the river with a small boat for provisions, which we bought for all the money we had. But we had many difficulties and our boat was overturned by a strong current and we lost about 500 dollars' worth of provisions. We went on with the little we had left until we came to our destination. I began digging in May but there is no point in telling you how much I made last summer because you wouldn't believe me. I'll tell you what I have to pay for provisions. Wheat is thirty cents a pound, smoked bacon forty-five, meat thirty-seven, butter 100, coffee sixty-five, sugar sixty, potatoes twenty-five, tea 125, and everything else accordingly; so board, clothes, and tools come to about two and a half dollars a day so you can see for yourself how long you can remain on your feet without making money. Dear friends, I have no idea how long I'll stay here as digging for gold is such an unreliable employment. You mustn't believe that digging for gold is like digging for potatoes in Norway. You can work one year after the other without finding anything but you have to keep going all the same and hope that luck will be on your side. I would strongly advise all, whether they are near or far away, against going after gold. There are many difficulties to be endured: first the journey, then the swindlers and murderers, and thirdly the wild Indians.

I've had a letter from our father since I came here. It was dated December 12, 1858. But I haven't heard from our dear brother Ole, so I don't know whether he is dead or alive. And I've had two letters from Ole Viger and Lars Lindelien.

Dear mother and siblings, if God grants me health and life for so long I hope that I'll see you again in this life, and nothing could make me happier than to see my dear mother and siblings after so many troubles in these heathen lands. At present I'm in good health, which is the best one can have in this world. Now I have no more to write about or perhaps I have too much, but I will regardless end my letter with loving regards to you all and the wish that God may be with us, because without him we can do nothing. Your loving brother

OLE OLSEN HAUGERUD THE YOUNGER

«1:78 »1:88 NE II:32

1859 — LETTER I:83

FROM: Hellik Olson Lehovd, *Mantorville, Minnesota, 30 November 1859*
To: Ole Helgesen Lehovd, *Flesberg, Buskerud*

To the honorable Ole Helgesen Lehovd in Flesberg parish,

I've received your letter dated April 30. It was addressed to Christiana and the people at Hvashovd paid for it so they could break the seal and see the news about their people. They sent the letter to me in June without extra cost and October 31 I received a letter dated September 18. I see that you are in reasonably good health and doing quite well, and it is my greatest pleasure to hear a good word from you, my close relatives. I can also tell you that I've been in good health since you last heard from me, which is the good work of God for which we should always have him in our thoughts and be grateful.

This has been a good year, in particular for wheat, barley, oats, and potatoes, but corn didn't do so well since we had early night frost. In some of the eastern states such as New York, Indiana, and Ohio they had a much poorer year because of a drought during summer. But money is still short as there is no market for wheat until the railroads will come further into the country. The price for wheat is now only forty-five to fifty cents a bushel. In Wisconsin there is a fairly good price for wheat, more money, and good wages.

This fall I've been running the threshing machine and we threshed 11,000 bushels. I was paid thirteen dollars a month by a man named Nils Ellefsen from Drangedal. You ask how much land I've bought. I didn't buy my land from the government because the land was not yet on the market; I only bought the preemption right for 160 acres from an American who has set up a small house on the land, and I paid him fifty dollars. The government price per acre is one and a quarter dollar but a railroad has been staked out nearby and the company was given land by the government, six miles on each side of the railroad. Now the price is two and a quarter dollars per acre. I've had expenses plowing some of the land and fencing it for more than fifty dollars not counting my own labor, as lumber is unusually expensive here in Minnesota. Moreover, I lost all the wheat I had harvested because there are often fires on the prairies in the fall that burn all grass and there was one on October 13 that burned my wheat and part of my fence so my harvest was only forty-eight bushels of potatoes. I must say I've been unlucky since I left Wisconsin; there things always went well for me and I increased my savings, so I've now decided to be a hired man whether I'm paid little or much. I know that I won't be able to get back the money I've invested but I'll nevertheless return to Wisconsin in the spring. I'm glad that I owe nothing to any man and that I still have so much money lent to others that I can have fifty to sixty dollars a year in interest; the interest rate here is now fifteen to twenty-five per cent.

I see that my brother Ole plans to come here, and I think this would be to his advantage if you can do without him at home, as he is at the age where he will have to serve as a soldier and here we are free from this. I think it's better here than in Norway for those who come in their youth and have good health. If he wants to go he should go with some reliable people. The best time to leave Norway is late April or early May because those who leave early have the shortest voyage. You don't have to bring more clothes than you need on your journey, but if you have enough money you should bring some black or blue homespun, both thick and thin, so that you can have clothes made according to American fashion and also bring blue gloves because here they cost one dollar a pair. Buy a book called catechism songs because this is not to be had here. I won't make a list of provisions because you know what you'll need of butter, dried leg of lamb and pork, etc. Bring a coffee kettle and a little aquavit for your health. You don't have to bring as much bread as I did since I didn't use more than half of it, but it's good to have milk on the ship. As a single person, it is good to have a simple box for your provisions on board that you can leave behind when you disembark because it's expensive to have a lot of baggage when you go inland as you have to pay by weight. You should have a small but strong and well-made chest where you can place all your clothes and a little food, because when we went our baggage was handled very roughly in some places and when we came to stations or towns everything was thrown into a big pile and on the steam ship our chests were stacked from floor to ceiling so that we at times could not get to our provisions and had to buy food. As for money exchange it is best to have a reliable captain and give the money to him to exchange for American money. When we arrived we were given one dollar and three cents for one *speciedaler*. You should try to travel with someone you know for the bed on board the ship and you must also bring bed clothes. And make sure at once that you'll have a good bunk by writing your names on it. The best places are either in the middle of the ship or in the stern because this is where there is least movement. And you must remember that you have an important voyage and an almost as long and important journey in through the country. But you must be steadfast in your faith and not begin to have regrets should you meet illness and adversity because then things will be difficult for you. Pray to God that he will guide us and be with us and when he is with us what can then be against us. You should go to a town called Fulton on the Milwaukee and Mississippi Railroad in Rock County, Wisconsin; Jul Torgersen Koppangen is a storekeeper there and it is ten miles from Hvashovd.

I see that you expect me home next summer but I cannot go since my brother is coming and I've had no reply to my letter. But I cannot forget Norway and I would like to see my old home and birthplace and see and speak with my parents and relatives. I also have a desire to travel around in the world while I'm young to acquire knowledge and see and experience much. I see that you have sold some forest land at what seems to have been a good price. I'm sure that timber will have a high price in the future in Norway but as times are difficult I realize that you had to let it go. I must tell you that I'm taking it easy this winter as there is no work to be had. I'm living with Ole Helliksen Flata. There are only the two of us and I sit indoors and smoke my pipe and we are very comfortable. I don't have any more news except that Ole Klemmetsen Juveli has married Kjersti Helliksdatter Flata. There has been little illness and death and we have had fine healthy weather all summer and there has not yet been any snow.

I must now end my simple letter and send my dear father and mother greetings from their distant and unforgettable son. I wish my brother Ole a good journey. I hope that we'll soon have the pleasure of seeing each other here in good health. Say to my siblings that they must not be sad that their brother is leaving them; nor must my parents be sad but let him go in the name of the Lord. In conclusion I wish you all the best in body and soul and the guidance of the Lord in life and death from your son and brother,

HELLIK OLSEN LEHOVD

· —— ·

A long paragraph of this letter is addressed to Hellik's brother, Ole, with advice on how to prepare for his journey to the United States. Ole is first referred to in the third person (he) and then there is a sudden shift to the second person (you). In the next paragraph "you" again refers to Ole Helgesen, their father. The best known book of catechism songs is by Petter Dass (1714). «1:75 » 1:87 NE II:33

· —— ·

1860 — LETTER I:84

FROM: Erik Theodor Schjøth, *Sturgeon Bay, Wisconsin, February 1860*
TO: Christian Fredrik Wyller Schjøth, *Oslo*

My dear and beloved son Frederik!

I've received your two welcome letters and they made me very glad. From them, as well as in the letters from your uncles and aunts, I see that you are still the good and kind Fredrik and my dearly loved son as you always were when I was at home. I'm so glad that Uncle Christian is taking care of you as I'm sure that he'll be good to you and that you will make sure that you are deserving. In letters from your aunts Rikka and Frederikka I see that your new Aunt Alvilde is as good and kind to you as a mother and for this the gracious God will reward her and you will surely be a grateful son. Give them both my regards and also N. P. Dahl and his wife. You say that they too have been good to you and I'm sure they are because they were also always good to me and Dahl is one of my oldest and best friends there at home. I often wish that I had such a friend here so far from family and friends.

When you hear that someone is going to write to me you must ask their permission to include a little letter, even if it is only three lines, so I can be sure that you are alive and well. I would like your siblings to do the same since this is my best comfort in my grief and longing for you. It is my highest wish to see you, my dear son, and your siblings again, but whether or when this can be depends on our gracious God. I'll do all I can and leave all in the hands of Him who decides what is best for us. Farewell my beloved son. In my next letter I won't forget to include a letter to you from your devoted and loving father.

E. T. SCHJØTH

For some reason ETS (1808–1888) left his upper middle-class family in Christiania around 1854, four years before the death of his wife

Olava Sophie in 1858, and settled in rather primitive circumstances in Sturgeon Bay, Wisc. The son he writes to here was fourteen in 1860. In 1868, at the age of twenty-two, Christian Fredrik Schjøth went to China to work for the Department of Customs and was promoted to Director of Customs in 1890. In 1877 he visited his father in Wisconsin. His diary covering this visit is in the Norwegian National Archives. Christian Schjøth, a younger brother of ETS, was a merchant in Christiania and was remarried to Alvhilde. Frederikka, a sister, was married to Gulov Gulovsen. »I:86 NE III:T14

1860 — LETTER I:85

FROM: Elise Wærenskjold, *Four Mile Prairie, 25 March 1860*
TO: Thomine Dannevig, *Lillesand, Aust-Agder*

Dear Thomine!

Now that I have such a good opportunity to have it sent I will write to you all and see if it may not be possible to wake you up so you could send me a letter as well as the portrait of Thorvald that you have so long promised me. I wish that you would also send me portraits of yourself and Niels. It's so terribly long since I have heard from any of you. Tell Bina that Marie is here with me and that I've spoken with Nicolai, who is a nice and clever boy. He understands English, Greek, and Latin, but not a word of Norwegian. He is to be a schoolteacher where Emma lives and will have thirty students who will pay two dollars each a month. Emma is doing well and has two little boys. Marie is very thin and looks old. She says she will write to Bina. She talks a lot about Bina and Grøgaard as well as the Hammers, in particular Lina and Marie. Helene is with her husband in New York and they are both well.

My little Thorvald is unhappy as I am weaning him. It makes me sad too. He'll be one and a half April 4 so I could have breastfed him a little longer, but the maid I've had this winter is leaving me next week and I would like to have it done before she goes. My new maid, Emilie Andersen, the daughter of our traveling companion across the Atlantic, has already arrived. Both are excellent. It would make me very happy if your Thorvald wrote to me. He may not remember me. My regards to your husband and children from us all! Please write soon to your old friend

ELISE WÆRENSKJOLD

. ——— .

This letter is not in Clausen 1961. A fragment is in Blegen 1955. EW wrote a letter to her mother-in-law on the same day (Clausen 1961, 52–53) and the day before to friends in Lillesand (Nor. ed. II:40, most of which is in Clausen), thus making good use of the opportunity to send letters with the returning immigrant. There was no correspondence with Norway during the war. The people mentioned are Thorvald and Niels Dannevig, Thomine's sons, Bina Grøgaard in Lillesand, Anne Marie Grøgaard, Keyser Grøgaard, and Emma, formerly Grøgaard, now Matthews. Helene and Peter Georg Reiersen were in New York. Her traveling companion was Torger Andersen. «1:74 NE II:39

. ——— .

1860 — LETTER 1:86

FROM: Erik Theodor Schjøth, *Sturgeon Bay, Wisconsin, 2 June 1860*
TO: Gulov Gulovsen, *Oslo*

My dear brother-in-law, G. Gulovsen!

I received your welcome and friendly letter of 21 October along with the others on November 24. You may imagine that it was a pleasant surprise for me. Thank you so much and please give my regards to all these blessed correspondents who have remembered me with such kindness. You and Anton wrote that my other brothers would also be writing and this is why I have waited so long; but when nothing arrived I wrote to brother A. and my children February 17. Since then I haven't heard anything from home so my letter may not have arrived. This is why I'm now writing to you, asking you to let me hear from you. After I received my last letters I've so longed to hear from you again and you must be so kind as to write to me when your time permits. This longing and waiting is unbearable and *my hard work* is difficult. I'm planting potatoes. In your letter I see that there have been many significant changes there at home, many acquaintances are dead and I suppose more have followed since then. May God grant that you are all well.

There is not much I have to say about myself except that I am, praise God, well and in good health. I'm in the same situation as last year when I wrote to your good Frederikka. Last spring I could have acquired a good business by taking over a ferry landing, but I didn't have enough of the almighty gold and had to let that bird fly, but not too far. My neighbor got it for the time being, but as the distance across the lake there is twice as long as here where I am and also a lot more dangerous when there is a strong wind, there is a lot of talk. If the gracious God and kind people will give me a little help I should be able to get it again *pretty soon*.

Last spring I had two baths that *pretty near* put an end to all my grief and worry. The first one was on March 11, rather early for a bath. Mr. Hjorth, the carpenter, was visiting and I was going to follow him home, prodding his sleigh across the ice. My plan was to follow the road on returning home. We had been told that the ice was weak but in my experience it has never been as treacherous at this time of year as it turned out to be. First we hit a crack in the ice and the sleigh tipped over, but there was a lower layer of ice so we only got wet on one side. But as we approached land we had a more serious accident; we sank, Hjorth sat in front and he crawled up on the ice with thick boots on his feet because of his rheumatism. I sat behind him, my legs were stuck, and I went down with the sleigh. There was open water near land where a large cedar was lying out on the water. I chose it rather than the edge of the ice since I luckily could swim, climbed up on it like a squirrel and ran up to a man from Jutland who lived close by, tore off my clothes, put on some dry ones, packed my own on my back, ran the two miles home, jumped into bed, went to sleep, and didn't even get a sniffle. The second one was two weeks ago. I had been away and had let someone have my boat in return for a small canoe that I used to paddle myself home. As I was sitting there philosophizing and thinking of my old home and family, I suddenly got on my feet, thinking that I was in my own sturdy boat, lost my balance, and went head first out of that damned canoe, that looks much like a trough for pigs, crawled ashore, went straight to bed, and thanked God for my salvation. I have been near death several times, but the almighty God has protected me.

Every now and then I am given a little reminder not to be too careless.

As for America, you will be better informed than me since you have access to good newspapers. I read *Emigranten*, a miserable newspaper that is filled every week with politics and nonsense, embezzlements, frauds, and murders, advertisements and quacks, enough to make a man sick if he doesn't have a strong constitution. There is little about my dear Norway except now recently about the Swedes again making threats, which doesn't please me at all. About America I will only repeat what an old and wise German said to me in Quebec. He had traveled and tried out much here, was satisfied, and wanted to return home. I thought he could tell me a little about America. *Amerika ist das grosse Europeische Zugthaus*, he said, and that was all he wanted to say on this subject. And the old man spoke the truth.

The cold weather and grasshoppers caused great damage all over Wisconsin last year and I'm sorry to say that it doesn't look as if it will be better this year. These guests have already appeared in company with an even worse plague: slugs. They eat all garden plants as quickly as they can grow as well as rye and wheat. If you dig under a corn stalk you can pick up a handful of these nasty animals that are one to two inches long, so we are very concerned for our harvest.

I was glad to see that both you and brother A. wanted me to come home. I know you are sincerely thinking of my own good, but my situation is like that of the other Norwegians here. All wish to be home again but this is almost impossibile as they have used what they brought with them and are unable to sell their land and miserable huts, at least for the time being. Some have been offered assistance from their families if they would return but they are ashamed of coming home in a worse state than when they left. This is pretty much the way it is with me too even though I have the advantage of being alone, and however much, as you may imagine, I wish to see my children and all of you again, I see no possibility except, as I wrote in my letter to brother Anton, if I had something I could develop here for another couple of years so I at least had so much that I would not become a burden for you, my dear brother-in-law and others, as I have been in the past. I must stop writing for now and thank you again for your brotherly letter where I saw that you haven't changed in your friendship and goodness and are as you've always been since the first day I saw you thirty-five years ago. Give my regards to my dear siblings and my good children who I hear are behaving themselves so well. Farewell, my good Gulov. My most friendly regards from your faithful

E. T. SCHJØTH

The German may be translated: America is the great European jail.
«1:84 »1:103 NE III:T15

1860 — LETTER I:87

FROM: Hellik Olson Lehovd, *Christiana, Wisconsin, 4 November 1860*
TO: Ole Helgesen Lehovd, *Flesberg, Buskerud*

Dear unforgettable father,

I received your letter dated April 27 on June 20. So now I cannot make further delays and must take up my pen to write you some lines even though they may be clumsy since I do not often use the pen, but I hope you will be able to read it. I know that it gives you both pleasure and comfort to hear from your distant son, so I must ask you to forgive me for my long delay as we have so much to do here during summer that it is not often that time permits.

First I must let you know that I sold the work I had done on the land I had claimed in Minnesota and returned to Wisconsin in April. Since then I have worked regularly, often at Washovd. I worked one and a half month for Kittil Kittilsen Teigset during harvest for thirty-six dollars. My regular wage has been ten dollars a month except during haying and I worked for twenty-five days on the threshing machine for seventy-five cents a day. I am happier here than in Minnesota where I often longed for my home in Norway. But I am now living in the best and most fertile part of America with large farms and good houses and more money among people. The railroads cut across the country in all directions so it is easy to sell all products and there are flourishing towns and churches and both English and Norwegian schools.

We had wonderful weather last winter and little snow, but around New Year it was so cold that it was difficult to be out on an open field for thirty minutes without getting frostbite in the face. We had an early spring and most seed was in the ground in March and since then we have had favorable weather but little rain except for a little in June that gave good growth so we had one of the best harvests since I came here, in particular for wheat which is one of the most important products in this country. When we have a good year and fairly good prices for wheat, as now when it has been from seventy to seventy-eight cents a bushel, a worker may make more money than in poor years when farmers don't hire more help than necessary to harvest their fields and pay little. Then a working man cannot do better than to keep himself in clothes and survive the winter when there is rarely work to be had. But it is better here than to be in Norway and haul coal during winter.

I've been in fairly good health since you last heard from me except for a week last month when I was sick. But such minor changes in life are of little concern now that I'm well again. We must thank Almighty God that we may enjoy good health which is one of the best things that a human being may enjoy in his life! We have had little illness and death here since the heat was not severe last summer and there was no cholera. I don't know of recent deaths among people we know. Tosten Anunsen Braata and Ingebor Olsdatter Rebrud were married last summer and I have no other news, as I cannot remember that anything out of the ordinary has happened here. I have heard rumors that two of my cousins, Paul and Hellik Granstuen, came to America last summer but I haven't seen them and don't know where they may be. It is so good for me to have letters from you since this is the only way we can speak with each other and it is no matter for me to pay for the letters. I was happy to see in your last letter that you were all in good health, but I also see that you have hard times in Norway as you first had a poor year and then a harsh winter. According to the newspapers there was a large flood in Norway last summer that caused water damage in many places.

Since times are so difficult for you some may ask why I don't ask you to come to America. Then I must reply that I indeed wish that my parents and my siblings could all be together in one place in this life. But you are too old and weak for such a long journey and you don't have the means to buy a farm here in the good part of America that would be large enough to feed a family. You would need a lot of money to cover all expenses as the land is very expensive and you would have to buy both cattle and farm equipment. So I think it would be better for you to remain at home and be satisfied that you have a good home. We must be satisfied with what the Lord gives us of good times and bad. And no one should plan to go to America to be free from all troubles in life, because nowhere on this earth is perfect. So I will certainly not ask anyone to come, but each may do as he wishes. So should anyone come and be dissatisfied, then I will not be criticized.

I have no more to write about except that we will have an election on the sixth of this month. Then we will elect a President of the United States who will be the most powerful person in this country for four years. Two have been nominated. One is for the expansion of slavery and the other is for its limitation as we here have two competing parties. All who are twenty-one years old and have lived in the state for a year can vote. I must now conclude my letter with the hope that you will write to me when you have an opportunity and send the letter to Christiana as I am at present working for Hellik Gundersen V. In conclusion I send greetings to all my friends and relatives and, finally, to my parents and my brothers and sister wishing you all good for body and soul and the protection and guidance of the Lord in life as in death, from your unforgettable son and brother,

HELLIK OLSEN LEHOVD

. ⸺ .

Enclosed was another letter to Ole Helgesen Lehovd from Hellik Gundersen Hvashovd. A note at the bottom of the last page says that the letter was received December 16. «I:83 »I:89 NE II:51

. ⸺ .

1860 — LETTER I:88

FROM: Ole Olsen Haugerud the Younger, *Albert Lea, Minnesota*
12 December 1860

To: Guri T. Rustand and Torgrim Olsen Haugerud,
Aadalen, Ringerike, Buskerud

To my dear mother and siblings in my abandoned land of birth.

Dear brother Torgrim Olsen,

As my wandering in the corrupt lands of the far West has now come to an end I feel it is my duty to let you hear from me. I am, praise God, in good health and I wish you the same. I'll first tell you a little about what happened on my last journey to Fraser River in British Columbia. Last winter I stayed in a small town called Fort Yale from where I went about 600 miles with my friends up to a place called Quesnel River. We saddled our own horses, that is, our shoulders. We had to carry our bedding, provisions, mining tools and cooking equipment, which consisted of a coffee pot and some cups made of birchbark. At night, when we sought rest, we laid our bedding, that is, our woollen blanket, on the snow to rest our tired limbs for the next morning. And in this manner one day followed the other, over high mountains and deep valleys; at times we could walk and at times we had to crawl, because the land was a wilderness where we could not see paths or roads. But what we did see was unpleasant, the wild Indians fighting among each other like the wolves one may see in Norway. They were as naked as they had entered the world and tried to hide behind rocks or trees or wherever they could because they were like wild animals running in the forest.

You mustn't think that there was any pleasure in this work, but that was not to be helped because as one has come out into the world one must also put oneself to the test. So in good spirits we continued on our way until we finally, after three weeks, came to a little town called Fort Alexandria about 525 miles from where we had started. Here we rested our tired and weary limbs for two entire days but after this rest we had more in store as we had not yet come far enough into the wilderness. Here I bought more provisions for quite a nice price: wheat flour at 125 cents, smoked pork 175, beans 125, coffee 200, sugar 250 a pound and everything else accordingly. I took my 130 pounds of provisions, including my tools and set out across a mountain for seventy-five miles. It took me ten days to get to my destination that I had thought would please me with its beautiful scenery, but I was soon disenchanted. All I could see were high mountains and deep valleys, eternally covered with snow and forests of fir. It was so cold that one could almost freeze to death and there was no place where I could earn my keep. Then I had a strange notion: how would this work out with no money, little food, no house and no more of a home than a hare in the woods and all of this many hundreds of miles into the lonely valleys where the echo of the forest is your only answer! I placed my trust in the hands of the Almighty, who up to now had led me on all my dangerous paths and hoped that he yet again would sustain me. So I wandered from place to place in the valley and finally I found my little treasure hidden away far down between the rocks and there I began to work. The least I made in a day was thirty dollars and there is no need to mention how much I could make. I worked until the sun rose above the steep mountains and an unbelievable mass of water flooded down into the valley and soon washed over my mine. There was nothing more to be done and I decided to go home. I left this place May 18 and after a long and difficult journey I came to our dear father September 12 and have lived here quite comfortably since then. My journey home cost me 475 dollars.

Dear siblings, I can give you greetings from our dear brothers in the far South, in Australia. Their letter was dated Inglewood, Colony of Victoria, August 21, 1860, and they wrote: "I know, dear friends, that you are expecting us to return but you may lay such thoughts on the shelf. We cannot return at present. We cannot deny the truth: We really have no money! Nor do we have any expectations of making any if our luck doesn't change. You mustn't believe that digging for gold is like digging for potatoes there at home, but we must continue our work in good faith and believe that all is for the best." It's a long letter but there is nothing of interest that needs to be mentioned. They were in good health at the time they wrote, for which we must thank the almighty God. Ole Viger is still in California and rumor has it that he is making good money. Lars Olsen Lindelien still lives on his farm in California.

Our dear father has sent you three letters without receiving any reply. Here he told you what you should do concerning his money in Norway. So he would like some information about this when you write to me. He is in fairly good health and lives quite happily here in the distant West. I have greetings from Peder Lunde and Gulbrand Jonsrud and from other people you know. They are in good health and are doing well. Should God let us live yet some time, dear siblings and mother, we may perhaps be gathered again in this life and talk with each other. I now have no more to write about and will send these simple words with my loving regards to you all. And I wish you all the best. Yours sincerely

OLE OLSEN HAUGERUD THE YOUNGER

· —— ·

OOH's two brothers in California are Erik and Ole (the elder) Olsen Haugerud. Their father in Minnesota, Ole Rustand, was divorced from their mother in Aadalen, Guri Rustand. «I:82 «I:92 NE II:54

· —— ·

1861 — LETTER 1:89

From: Hellik Olson Lehovd, *Christiana, Wisconsin, 18 January 1861*
To: Ole Olsen Lehovd, *Flesberg, Buskerud*

My good friend and brother,

I wrote to our father November 4 and promised I would write to you, so I should keep my promise even though I have been delaying it. A short while ago I saw in a letter from Ole Gjerde to his father Ole H. Gjerde that you have had a poor year in Norway and that winter again came early. There is such a difference between Norway and America where our summer lasted to November 22 when it got so cold that there was ice on the ground and since then we have had a little rain and snow and we could use our sleighs at Christmas.

As for your often mentioned thoughts of going to America I won't tell you to come or not to come since I know that my father may need you at home and I don't know whether you are in good health and able to work hard. Because this is necessary in order to earn money here. When you come you will have to find work because you know that I don't have a home of my own. But I am quite satisfied here. I'll give you some information about the situation in this country. We have freedom of religion and anyone can join any sect he wants to. There are Catholics, Presbyterians, Methodists, and Lutherans here and nearby there are Americans who are Jews and who have Saturday as their holy day rather than Sunday. But we Norwegians are for the most part Lutherans and some are Methodists. We must pay taxes even when our money has been lent out and we don't own land. In the last two years I've paid three to four dollars in capital tax and every man between twenty-one and fifty has to pay a road tax of one dollar. Taxes are considerable and Hellik and Kjersti Washovd pay forty-five dollars a year in capital tax and eighteen dollars in road tax.

Now I will tell you about the prices for clothes that we mostly buy ready-made. A pair of boots costs three to four and a half dollars, nicer ones three to six dollars and a pair of shoes one and a half to two and a half, plain trousers two to three dollars, nicer ones three to six dollars, a plain vest one and a half to two and a half dollars and of silk three to six, plain coats cost from three to ten dollars and if made of cloth from ten to fifteen dollars, overcoats cost from five to fifteen dollars, a nice shirt one to two dollars and a plain shirt one dollar, and stockings cost one half to one dollar.

But we earn more money than in Norway; in the six to seven months from mid-March or early April we are paid twelve or thirteen dollars a month. Many of the farmers here have from 300 to 500 acres under the plow and when the wheat is sown the pay is mostly ten dollars a month, but during the haying season it is fifteen to sixteen dollars a month or three-fourths of a dollar a day. But then you have to cut about 2,000 to 4,000 pounds a day. And when the wheat is harvested you can get from twenty to thirty dollars a month or one to one and a half dollars a day but for a full day's pay you have to cut or bind eight acres a day and this presses the sweat out of a man as I've seen that the thermometer shows ninety degrees in the shade. This is a time when everyone who is willing and able must work. The wheat harvest begins in the middle of July and we work from sunrise to sunset. On June 21 the sun rises at 4:22 a.m. and sets at 7:40 and on December 21 it rises at 7:26 a.m. and sets at 4:30. Here the day is not as long in summer and not as short in the winter but we have dinner about seven hours later than in Norway. We live well in this country and have pork, meat, white bread, butter, and coffee every day, but the Americans eat only three times a day. It should be noted that the wages mentioned above cannot be expected the first year after arrival as all work has to be learned all over again. The first year among the Americans is difficult when you don't understand a word of English, but it's easier to learn when you are young.

Here we are free from military service as soldiers are recruited. But in times of crisis all who have sworn loyalty to the country may have to serve. According to the newspapers it seems that we are going to have a civil war as some of the southern states want to leave the Union and have their own laws and government as they don't want to be under the new president, who will be inaugurated March 4, 1861, because he wants to abolish slavery. I cannot know how far this will go but according to the latest news a revolution is feared.

As for myself I can tell you that I'm in good health and doing well. I was employed until November 25 and since then I've worked now and then, enough to pay for my room and board here with Hellik Gundersen

Washovd. I have no more news as there has been neither illness nor death and all here at Washovd are well and in good health.

Dear brother, I've given you an account of the conditions in this country and now it's up to you to decide. I'll add on my own account that it's an advantage for a young person to wander out into the world to see and to try out many things, but it is not as easy for men as it is for women to come here as they only have to work indoors with cooking and cleaning and are paid from one to two dollars a week. If you want to go next spring you must write to me in advance. The name of the town of Fulton has been changed to Edgerton, Rock County, Wisconsin and this is where you must go. With this I will conclude my letter and send my father and brothers and sister loving regards from their son and brother.

HELLIK OLSEN LEHOVD

The text is according to a contemporary copy signed with the initials H. W. Ole emigrated later that year and at the bottom of the letter he has written: "The last time I wrote here at Lehovd 21/4 61. O. Olsen." In the Norwegian edition there is a letter from Hellik Gundersen Hvashovd dated 5 March 1862 (Nor. ed. II:77). «I:87 »I:99 NE II:56

1861 — LETTER I:90

FROM: Svend Larsen Houg, *Elgin, Iowa, 27 February 1861*
To: Ole Larsen Haug, *Aal, Buskerud*

My often remembered brother Ole and all my siblings,

As so many days of our lives have passed since I sent you any news I must take my pen in hand to write you some lines. I received your letter of May 9, 1859 on June 22 and that of December 10, 1860 on February 1,

1861. I'm grateful that your brotherly heart still remembers me and that you have told me about so many things from the place of my birth that is still dear to me. Before I received your last letter I had often thought that my siblings may have believed that their brother in America was dead since you hadn't had any letters from him. But this is not so. The reason has been my negligence, but there have also been some other obstacles that have held me back.

You'll remember, brother Ole, what you wrote about Syver Groth on an enclosed slip of paper. At that time I didn't know anything about it and you only wrote that it had been kept from you. Since then a trustworthy man has told me that I had also been included in that group, and I then realized that this had troubled you. But it caused me no concern as I knew that I was innocent. God has preserved me and I hope he will continue to preserve me from such errors. It is sad that one who once knew the path of truth should blindly spread rumors about people whom he doesn't even know by sight and far less knows of their faith and their conduct. But who may twist the truth more than one who has shared in it? I won't write his name here but I'm sure I know who he is. This shows how all who won't keep up with the world are proclaimed to be sectarians. Such is the world, that all who would live with God on earth shall be persecuted.

I now think you would ask me about the present state of religion. It's difficult to say much about this since there are so many who write about it. Many newcomers want to say something about religion and they may not know anything about it; indeed, I can safely say that they don't. So there is much to explain. My only hope is that the Lord knows his own and that we have the word of God, pure and free from falsehood, even though some are at work to smuggle in some sourdough both here and in Norway. You well know, my brother, that I and some others here have not had the same pastor as the majority and this is why we are called a sect. We have had the well-known pastor Rasmussen to conduct services for us but we have been trying to get a permanent pastor of our own. We've now been successful and will have John Nilsen Fjeld, who you know so well, who emigrated last summer. He has been here twice and we are now expecting him back. I hope that he with the help of God will become an instrument for the promotion of the glory of God also in this country. He lives in Wisconsin but he will visit us every sixth or seventh week. Indeed, he may become pastor for the entire congregation here, as the others don't have a pastor either. But I don't know anything about this now. As for myself, I am merely a poor sinner and I often anger my Lord and God in many ways, but he has never deserted me but chastises me and reminds me that I should be more diligent in seeking grace in Christ, he who alone is the salvation of sinners and has established the word of reconciliation among us. Yes, may God in his grace make me praise him from my heart and not alone by my mouth. May God help me in this.

I must again thank you for the news about the home of my fathers as well as about yourself. It is good to hear that God has blessed the work of your hands and even more so to hear that you continue to seek the Lord so he may succeed in his aim, which is to save us. I hear that our brother Knut has married and that his health is better now than when you last wrote me. I hope he will love the Lord who has bought us so dearly. I see that the Lord has visited our fatherland with his chastising rod: an unusual flood and a poor harvest. His purpose in this is to call us to conversion but it may happen as the Lord has complained, I have chastised you but you would not feel. We have had a very good harvest in these northern states but we have hard times in some places in America too and who knows how long He will spare us. He may already have lifted his whip over us too.

I can imagine that among the things my siblings would like to ask me is that you who have been so long in America, you must be doing quite well. My answer is that I'm not exactly well off but neither can I lie before our Lord and say that I'm poor. He has given me as much as I have needed till now. I have a good farm even though I still owe some money on it. I have not yet cultivated so much of my land, not more than twenty acres, but this is enough for my use. Last year I had 280 bushels of wheat and more than 300 bushels of corn. This winter I am feeding twenty head of cattle, eleven pigs and seven sheep. These are all undeserved gifts from God.

What you write about having heard that I was ill in the fall of 1859 is true. I was sick for some weeks but since then I've been in good health and my wife has also been quite healthy. Our children, now seven, are all well and lively. The youngest is called Knud and will soon be two. I see that you send greetings from uncle Elling. Please send him my loving regards should you write to him again and say that I hope I will continue to pray and have faith until the last. You always have greetings from Knut Torsteinsrud, the faithful friend of my youth even though we led a sinful life. When I read that you hope he'll continue to live in truth, I was deeply moved. It was truly good to hear that someone continues to struggle as there is no promise of a prize for he who only struggles for a time but that he who is faithful till the end shall have the crown of life. Please tell Knud that I'm glad that he is progressing on the road to salvation. Give my regards to those who knew me and who ask about me.

Don't bother to send me my small share in the inheritance from our father's sister Torand Foss. I leave this to you to do with as you find best. I'm sure there is a poor person you can give this small sum to. It's strange that the old man should marry again. I must conclude these simple lines with loving regards to you and your family. All my siblings are lovingly greeted from me and my wife and children.

SVEND LARSEN HOUG

You ask about the price of postage. Your 1859 letter cost forty-eight cents as usual and the last one in 1860 cost seventy-six cents. This was probably because it was slightly over the set weight and then you have to pay double. I've always paid for my letters as the postmasters say. But I fear that things are not done right in Norway. I pay as much for the letters I send as for those I receive.

I send greetings from my mother-in-law Ragnild Groth. She is in fairly good health although she feels her age. I also have greetings from all at Groth, but in particular from Kittil and Syver who have experienced a conversion. All are doing well. Birgit Veslegard lived with me from the time they came here until last fall when they moved to their own land not far from here. Both she and her husband were very nice people. This letter has many errors and is unclear but you must read it with the best intentions. Regards from your brother

SVEND LARSEN HOUG

God knows whether we will be able to send more letters to each other.

· ——— ·

> This letter was received on 15 April 1861. Sitting at his table, SLH tried to imagine himself in a conversation with his siblings, recalling words from letters and imagining their questions for him. Our reading of these letters should include that which is omitted. The only implied reference he makes to the Civil War is his phrase "these northern states." John N. Fjeld had been an itinerant lay preacher in Norway before emigrating in 1860. He was a pastor for several congregations in the Norwegian Synod in Wisconsin from 1861 until his death in 1888. That Haugeans were considering joining the Norwegian Synod congregations if they could have Fjeld as pastor speaks of a fluid situation among adherents of the various synods. Knut Larsen married Ragnhild Sveinsdatter Hestebrekk in 1860 and they bought the farm Rud in 1861. Elling Olsen had moved around and had settled in Meland in Hordaland, just north of Bergen. Torand Olsdatter had died at

Foss in neighboring Hol in 1855 and had no children. Birgit Mikkelsdatter Veslegard married Torkel Torkelsen Hoff in 1859 and emigrated. From 1863 they farmed in Norseland, Minn. «I:76 »I:112 NE II:59

1861 — LETTER I:91

FROM: Ole Johansen Holtseteren, *Watertown, Wisconsin, 11 November 1861*
To: Peder Johansen Holtseteren, *Gausdal, Oppland*

Dear brother,

It is many years since I heard from you. I've expected letters but haven't received any. So I could not wait any longer to write and tell you how things are with me. Dear brother, I am in a deep grief that is indescribable. My dear wife has passed away after a brief illness. She has gone from the world to heaven. She left behind a son who is with my father-in-law Ole Kaarfeld. He'll be four on February 24. They love him and he is taken care of and brought up as their own child and this makes me glad as I must be away and work in my craft. I've thought of leaving my craft and beginning work on my land but after what has happened I have no desire to do this alone. But I must say with Job, The Lord gave, the Lord took, the Lord's name be praised. The world is but a place for a brief stay. I am, praise God, in good health for which I owe thanks to the almighty God.

My brother, I would so much like to have news from you. Write me simply how it is for you and how your sons Anders and Johan are doing. Have you taught them a craft or are they still at home with you? How are my sister and brother-in-law? I would like to hear from all of you. It would make me happy to have news from you. Write to me. You don't have to pay for letters. I'll pay for them when they arrive. I've heard that mother has become a widow again. Is she with you or where is she? Friendly regards to my old mother. I have no more to write about. Greetings to you and your wife from your loving brother,

OLE JOHANSEN HAALTSÆTEREN

OJH was a shoemaker. In 1865 Anders and Johan Pedersen were at home at Holtseteren as was the widow Ingeborg Olsdatter. «1:39 »1:143 NE II:67

1861 — LETTER 1:92

FROM: Ole Olsen Haugerud the Younger, *Albert Lea, Minnesota*
23 *December 1861*

To: Guri T. Rustand, *Aadalen, Ringerike, Buskerud*

Dear mother and siblings!

As I have permitted time to pass for so long without writing to you I feel that it is my duty to let you hear from me. I have received a letter from you dated at Elsrud April 22, 1861. I'm glad that you are all in good health and doing well in spite of the hard times in Norway these last years. We cannot sufficiently thank our Lord and Savior for every crumb we so undeservingly receive from his gracious hand. First I will tell you that our father has left this world of sin. He passed away the night before July 2 after having been ill for only two days. He was as a different person in his last days and thought much about all the wrongs he had done to his wife and children, as he once said to me soon after I had returned from my adventures in the lands of temptations. Our father gave his widow, that is his third wife, his land and all that is on it but as their marriage was not legally confirmed before he died this is of no significance. As I am the only one here I have an obligation to see that we get what is due to us as this is the only way we can have our expenses repaid. The amount due to us is more than 300 dollars, almost as much as it all, including the widow, is worth.

I have had two letters from your brothers in Australia dated June 16 and July 24. They say they live well and are in good health and not much more. I assume they are satisfied with their luck. Although they would like to return they cannot afford it. Erik is the partner of an American and Ole is with an Englishman. I know that it is not music in the ears of Norwegian farmers when people in lands of gold complain that they cannot earn the money for the voyage home. People shouldn't believe that it is so easy to come by money honestly. Those who believe you can pick up gold from the streets are bound to be disappointed in their expectations. No, it is quite different. First, patience is necessary in order to survive failure as well as success. Second, both thrift and hard work are required. And third, it is necessary to think more of the soul's salvation than of the sinful ways of the world, which the tempter always keeps before your eyes. What would you think if you came to a country where Sundays are spent in adultery, murder, theft, drunkenness and card playing and where people mistreat each other in the most dreadful manner? You would then soon discover the meaning of the striving for worldly goods in foreign lands. People must be on their guard here more than in a civilized country. In greatest need the help is near—this was my experience.

I have heard that Nils Viker came to America last summer. He is at present with his sons in Fillmore County, Minnesota, about eighty miles to the East. I have decided to visit him there in the spring and I'll then do as Elling Elsrud has requested and ask him about his clever arrangements for leaving the country. I send greetings from Ole Viker the younger and Lars O. Lindelien. They are still in California, in good health and doing fairly well. The wheat harvest has failed in many places in the Northwestern States because of the long period of incessant cold rain since early spring followed by a long drought. This made the soil hard as rock in many places and because of this most of the wheat withered away.

As for the war, there are quite severe losses on both sides but it seems that the North will win over their enemies. A short while ago the Union Army had a glorious victory over their enemies. The fleet went into a harbor in South Carolina named Port Royal and the Rebels had to retreat from their three large forts as well as a series of fortifications along the coast. Our people captured large stores and much ammunition. The rebels must have left their camps in great haste because their tents remained with all their equipment so it was as if they had all been carried away by a whirlwind. And their cannon were all ready to shoot at the enemy had they tried an attack. The rebels' losses are unknown but 200 Negro slaves who had escaped from their masters told that the loss was great. Now people who wish to visit their relatives in Europe have to have a passport. Anyone who is a citizen of the United States may have one on payment and demonstration of their loyalty. The system of passports has been introduced in order to cut off the rebels' relations with Europe.

I'll now end my poor letter and hope that benevolent Providence will govern and advise us all on the true path to eternal salvation; this is the wish of your devoted brother. Sincerely,

OLE OLSEN HAUGERUD THE YOUNGER

Guri Rustand lived with her daughter Olea Olsdatter and Elling Olsen Elsrud. The widow in Minnesota was Anne Hansdatter Svensrud. This is the beginning of a long legal battle that can be followed in letters in Nor. ed. II and III where Guri Rustand's unwillingness to compromise is one factor that eventually leaves most of the money in the hands of lawyers. «I:88 »I:156 NE II:68

1861 — LETTER I:93

FROM: Ole Aslesen and Ingrid Helgesdatter Myran, Elling Ellingsen and Mari Helgesdatter Wold and Ingeborg Helgesdatter Skare
Decorah, Iowa, 27 December 1861

To: Helge Gundersen Skare, *Eggedal, Sigdal, Buskerud*

To Helge Gundersen!

We have received your letter of April 6 and are glad to see that you are all doing well there at home and that the times are both good and bad. Dear friends! We can give you the same good news about us, that we are all in good health and doing well, for which God be praised. This year has been neither abundantly good nor terribly bad. Furthermore I can tell you, my friends, that all things that we farmers have to sell are very cheap. Thus one bushel of wheat is fifty or sixty cents and pork is two or three cents a pound. But what we have to buy for our own use is expensive. All cotton material is quite expensive. Coffee is twenty-five cents a pound and all we need for our home is expensive. This is because of the war.

As far as we know nothing decisive has happened in the war and the situation continues to be unstable. So you may realize that times are not so good for us, even though we have no reason for complaint compared to those who have had to leave their homes because of the enemy. But the position of the North, that is the Union, is better than that of the South. I can tell you my friends that about 640,000 men have gone to war to fight for and defend the Union. They have not been forced but have gone of their own free will urged by their own hearts to defend, maintain and expand liberty and the laws and government. The reason for the war between the Northern (Republican) States and the Southern (Democratic) States is that the South wants to spread slavery all over the American states and destroy their good laws and government. We Northerners are against the Southern States because of their heathen slavery and un-Christian treatment of the slaves.

We are all doing well and neither illness nor misery has visited us or our neighbors. As for religion, each and every man can have the religion he wants and we and our Norwegian neighbors have a Norwegian pastor and school so we are confessors of the pure Norwegian Lutheran Evangelical Christian Religion. So we will without doubt wander happily from this life to a better one. With this I must end my short and simple letter to you my unforgettable dear father-in-law Helge Gundersen and family and all my other friends. Sincerely,

OLE ASLESEN AND FAMILY

I will also send you a few words about our situation. Reading your letter I am happy to see that you are healthy and what more could we wish for in this life. Although sister Ingeborg Skaalen has by an act of our gracious and almighty God lost her dear husband, we are nevertheless glad that she is in an improved position. But for her this will surely not be much compared to the loss of a good and loving husband. However, her great comfort is that God, in whom there can be no deceit, has promised that he will be a father of the fatherless and the protector of widows. This will be so if we pray to him truthfully and believe in him. Then he will also do it.

Dear father-in-law, I will send you the glad news that I and my beloved wife are doing well, for which we praise and thank God. I should also tell you that the times are more or less hard for us all because of the war. Concerning the advice you want from us, we think that the best and the most correct is for the father to divide his property between his children as he sees best. So I'm in full agreement with you and I'll send you the authorization you mention as soon as you need it. Also I, Ole Aslesen, declare that I agree that you should divide your property and will send you my authorization when you need it. Also I, Ingeborg Helgesdatter, declare that I agree that when the situation demands that you divide your property, you should then divide it as you see best, and I'll send you my authorization when it is needed.

With this I will end my short and simple letter with my wish that you write us immediately. May we all enjoy the help of God and be strengthened and maintained in the word and the faith until death. Greetings from your faithful,

ELLING ELLINGSEN AND MY WIFE MARI HELGESDATTER

Dear unforgettable father!

You will be happy to learn that I too am in good health and have all that is necessary for this life, which is good health, which I have by the providence of God. I have worked as a maid till now and at present I'm at home with my sister and brother-in-law E. Ellingsen. Thank you so much for sending Lars Linderot's book of homilies. As for your question about my income, it has varied. I don't think that I could have saved more in Norway and this is all I can say about it. I'm very happy in my situation. I would like to have a letter from you, my sister Ingeborg, about your situation. Please accept my childish regards from your daughter,

INGEBORG HELGESDATTER

. ⎯⎯ .

> In 1858 Helge Gundersen became a widower, and part of this letter concerns the inheritance of his son and daughters in the United States as he is about to be remarried to Marit Helgesdatter and move to the cotter's farm Nerdrum. His youngest son, Halvor Helgesen, became the new farmer at Skare. His sons-in-law speak for their wives in this matter since Norwegian laws still denied married women the right to control their property or capital. Beginning in 1839, however, the legal situation for women had been improved in the United States. Their pastor was Ulrik Vilhelm Koren. Ingeborg had been married to Knut Nilsen Skaalen. The letter refers to Psalms 68:5: "A father of the fatherless, and a judge of the widows, is God in his holy habitation."
> «I:65 »I:98 NE II:69

1862 — LETTER I:94

FROM: Juul Gulliksen Dorsett, *Newburg, Minnesota, 23 January 1862*
To: Torstein Gulliksen Daaset, *Flesberg, Buskerud*

Dear unforgettable family and friends in Norway,

I can no longer delay letting you know how we are. I am in all ways healthy and well satisfied, for which we owe thanks to God. And I have been successful in everything. I bought my land and I live here alone and work on my land. I have fenced and broken about sixteen acres. I have four oxen and a cow and two steers, as they say here. I have excellent land for haying and more land to cultivate and about fifteen acres of forest land and all of this is as conveniently located as one could wish and I have a well near my house. A creek with different kinds of fish runs through my land. I haven't heard from my brothers since last summer when I had a letter saying that all was well.

We are building a Lutheran church that we will complete next summer and we have a schoolhouse that costs us a little, but not more than we want to give. We also have a good market here. We can go to a large city one day and return the next. There are towns along the Mississippi River and we have both steamboats and railroads, and there one can buy what one needs and sell what one has.

We've heard that some who have wanted to come don't dare do so because of the war, but there is no reason to fear. It doesn't disturb us and no one has to be a soldier who does not want to serve for pay. There are enough who want to go to war. Moreover, the war is so far south that we like you in Norway merely hear rumors of the war. It is 1,400 miles to the nearest battles so we have a good laugh at those who want to come but are afraid of the war. The reason for this war is that many don't want to work but only want to hold office as in other states in Europe and therefore we have strife both in the church and in society. There are many sects among us. Some are Frankeans and some are Methodists. It's not unusual that the husband goes to one pastor and the wife to another, so it seems that they have lost their senses, but most hold on to their old Lutheran church. We have a good pastor by the name Jensen. He is a good man and we hope to keep him.

It's difficult to make money now that all we have to sell is so cheap. The daily wage for a hired hand is half a dollar. Wheat is a half dollar a bushel. Butter is six to eight cents a pound, pork two and a half cents, and the prices are this low for all things. Here it is not as in other places; the more people who come the more there is for all. When the land is cultivated there is more to sell for every year and all who come here in need of their daily bread can find all they need. Here they can live well and have liberty. I remember the books I saw when I was in Norway. I have experienced that it is quite true that the work here is hard, but it is better to work for an American than for any others. Things are far harsher in Norway. Here, if one's employer doesn't come then there is no work to do, but if one has been there as long as agreed then one is paid for the day one stayed indoors without working. Should anyone be coming next spring I ask you to be so kind as to send me Luther's Catechism. This would make me very glad. This has been disorganized and I will end with friendly regards to you all. Live well in God. Friendly regards,

TORSTEN DAASET

. ⎯⎯ .

For some reason Juul Daaset signed with the recipient's name. His post office was in Newburg but he was a member of the North Prairie congregation in Rushford, where Nils Edward Schancke Jensen was pastor. The church was completed in 1863. The Norwegian Synod was dominant in this area, but there was an Augustana Synod church in Newburg (these may be the "Frankeans") and his own congregation was not affiliated with any synod even though their pastor was also pastor for a nearby Norwegian Synod congregation. Juul Daaset's naive attempt to explain the Civil War illustrates how little some immigrants knew about the society they lived in. «1:79 »1:108 NE II:72

. ⎯⎯ .

1862 — LETTER I:95

From: Ole Jesperson Taksdal, *St. Louis, Missouri, 2 March 1862*
To: Tobias Tørresen Kvia, *Nærbø, Haa, Rogaland*

Dear cousin,

I thought I should send you a few words and tell you how I am and that I, thank God, am in good health. I wish to hear the same from you. May the grace and peace of God our Father through Jesus Christ and the Holy Ghost be with you! Oh dear relatives, it is difficult for a pilgrim to be alone in a foreign country without a friend to speak with. But this would not be as difficult as to be forgotten by family and friends and not to hear any more from Norway, my fatherland, so I long to have a letter from you. I will let my pen move over the paper again to talk to my dear family and yet once more try my luck. I trust that you will write me some words in return if God grants you life and health. I hope that you will urge my parents and siblings to write to me as I would so love to hear from you all and have news from Norway.

I must tell you that I've signed up for the war for freedom here in the United States to liberate the slaves. There are two parties here, one wants to trade people, the Africans or Negros, just like we trade cattle and they want to spread this as much as they can and they had already gotten quite far. So now this costs us a lot, in people as well as in property. Where this goes on is called the Southern States and where we are is called the Northern States. But all of it is under one law and one king. But the Southern States have broken the law and it is now our purpose to stop the slave trade and liberate the poor souls so that they may seek the Christian faith and become Christians so that, as it is written, they may be plucked like brands out of the fire so that the wounded may with the power of God be cured.

And it is so with each and every one of us that when we discover that we are ill we go to the doctor to be cured. And it is the same in spiritual matters: when we realize that our soul is ill there is no other way for us than to go to our heavenly Father and doctor. May the Lord give strength to me as well as to you and to all who wish to go through the narrow gate where we may be forgiven all our sins, errors and transgressions against our dear Father in Heaven who is always there with his wide loving arms ready to embrace any lost son or daughter. May God give us strength to do battle for the glory of God so that when we fight against our external enemies we will not forget the inner and spiritual enemies that we have to do battle with every day. For it is said that the Devil walketh about as a roaring lion, seeking any whom he may devour, and this is something we often experience in so many thousand ways. So it is indeed necessary to stand guard with the victorious weapons of prayer so that Heaven may ever hear our cries by day as well as by night.

We marched into a fort called Benton Barracks. There were twenty to thirty thousand soldiers in this fort and on the first of January I experienced a great pleasure. In this large host of soldiers I found my dear uncle Ole Olsen Skjæveland. He was a soldier and we talked several times until January 13, when we had to go our separate ways and we haven't seen each other since. Tønnes Hansen Gilje and Engebret Jonnasen Serigstad and Andria's husband are also soldiers. I and my two friends Anders Nilsen and Ole Olsen Nesberg signed up about three months before Tønnes and Engebret and Hans, Andria's husband, and we are about thousand miles nearer the front than they are but it won't take them more than three days to come here. We are with a battery that is called the First Minnesota Battery. We are soon ready to go against the Southerners. We are only three Norwegians in this company; the others are English and German. We were enlisted November 21, 1861 on two conditions: that we were either to have fifteen dollars a month and no clothes included or thirteen dollars and free clothes and we chose the latter. Meals are always free and we have enough of both food and clothes. But our houses are but tents with stoves.

I must now stop with this and tell you what it is like to live in America, and it will be good as soon as liberty returns to us, which it has, but as you can understand, it has been very limited by the great rebellion we now have. But we hope it will soon be over. Craftsmen can make good money in America. Yes, I can say that it is good for anyone who wants to work. But there is a great difference in pay for different kinds of work. And now I will give you evidence of how fertile America is: no one here begs for bread as far as I have seen and my friends agree. One of them has been sixteen years in America and the other six and they have not seen a poor person because anyone who will work in America may support a family of any size. I have heard that some write from Norway that they are afraid of coming because of the war but this should not keep them from coming as the war is far from the places they want to go to. So there is no more danger now than before and there is no reason for fear. Soldiers are not forced into service, not a single one, they are all volunteers. We do not go with protests and regrets but in good spirit and a light mind because we want to have our freedom returned. I had a letter from Sven Undene in Chicago on February 19 and he says that he has not had a letter from Norway since I came to America and he would like to hear about his family's situation and about how things are in our old fatherland Norway. And so do I.

I must end my letter with the warm and heartfelt wish that God's blessing—spiritual and temporal—may be upon you and your children. Oh, wake and pray and struggle and fight. The road is long, our time is short. The groom will soon arrive in state and we must stand at Heaven's gate. My most friendly regards from your devoted

OLE J. TAXDAHL

· ——— ·

> OJT was a soldier in the Minnesota First Battery of Light Artillery and fell at Shiloh 6 April 1862. His uncle Ole Olsen Skjæveland is probably the Ole Olsen listed as a soldier in the Minnesota Second Battery of Light Artillery and also died in the war. Ole O. Nesberg was also in the Minnesota First Battery of Light Artillery (Ulvestad 1907, 289, 312, 318, 333). Tønnes Hansen Gilje, in the artillery during the war, settled at Hanley Falls, Yellow Medicine County, Minn., in 1867 (Ulvestad 1913, 669). The other soldiers have not been identified. The "English" soldiers are English-speaking Americans. The letter quotes from Zechariah 3:2 and 1 Peter 5:8. NE II:76

· ——— ·

1862 — LETTER 1:96

From: Knud Ivarson Vike, *Fifteenth Wisconsin Regiment near Island No. 10, Missouri, 29 March 1862*

To: Dordei Knutsdatter Vike, *Spring Prairie, Wisconsin*

Dear wife and children,

I must straight away write you some brief words. I am, praise God, well. I sent a letter March 9 from the camp at Bird's Point but I don't know whether you have received it. I've had no reply. I am now further south than before. We are close to New Madrid. We are on this side of the river and the rebels on the other side. Our cannon boats have been firing on the rebel fortifications for eleven or twelve days. They cannot hurt them but they are now surrounded. There are forty thousand Union soldiers and five miles further up there are fifteen to twenty thousand rebels, but now they cannot get supplies of provisions, gun powder or bullets. They will soon have to give up and we will with the help of God take them as prisoners. I have heard that New Orleans has been taken by the Union army but I don't know if this is true.

I must tell you that the lists for the families were not sent to the governor in Madison. The adjutant forgot it but our captain has now returned to Bird's Point where the protocols are kept and when he has completed the lists he will send them to Madison and then you, my dear wife, may receive your money. I must tell you that it is two weeks since I talked with Gulleik. He was a little sick with diarrhea and I haven't heard from him but I hope that he will soon be with me. Almost the entire regiment has diarrhea but I hope it will soon be over. This is not a healthy place and the river is mixed with soil and the water is unhealthy. We have a lot of pork and meat and coffee and sugar, peas and grits, but we don't eat much.

I must now end my poor letter. I don't know when we'll be paid. If you, my dear wife, are in need of money then you should ask Brynjulf, because I want you to live well and you should buy pork and butter, coffee and some sugar and molasses. I hope you have enough fresh milk. I must stop, my unforgettable wife and children. Dear children, obey and respect your mother! My regards to all relatives and friends! Give my regards to Anders Lee, Lars Møen, Amund Graue, Odd Himle, Styrk Vike and all our friends. I will soon write again.

KNUD IVARSON VIKE

I have seen Ole Stangeland. He was well, but I must remind you once more to please send me a letter. When we left Madison we were given a little whiskey but since then whiskey has not passed my lips. I must tell you that we see many slaves every day, big and small, women and children, and it is not a nice sight. Our chaplain holds service for us twice a day.

· ——— ·

> The two letters from KIV to his wife in Wisconsin are exceptions to the rule that this edition presents a selection of letters sent to Norway. He and Dordei Knutsdatter came to his brother Styrk at Spring Prairie in 1853 and he volunteered in January 1862. He died on 31 December 1862, of wounds he received at the battle of Murfreesboro (Rene 1930, 520). The Fifteenth Wisconsin Volunteer Regiment was primarily recruited among Norwegian immigrants and Norwegian was the language of command. The leader of the regiment, Colonel Hans Christian Heg, was killed in battle in 1863. One of his letters to his wife is also dated 29 March (Blegen 1936, 68–70). Pastor Claus L. Clausen was chaplain of the regiment. The camp at Bird's Point on the Missouri side of the Mississippi, opposite Cairo, Ill., was the regiment's main quarters in early March (Blegen 1936, 57). New Orleans was taken by General Butler on 26 April. This captain was Frederick R. Berg. Gulleik Ivarson Vike came from Voss to Muskego in 1843 and moved to Spring Prairie around 1845 (Rene 1930, 213). Anders Nilson Lirhus (later Lee) married the widow Dordei Knutsdatter. Lars Johannesson Møen (later Johnson) came from Voss to Muskego in 1841 and moved on to Spring Prairie in 1845. Amund Christofferson Graue (later Christopher) came from Voss with his parents in 1850. Along with Lars Møen and others he moved to Emmet County, Iowa, in 1866. Odd Johanneson Himle came from Voss via Gothenburg in 1837 and moved to Spring Prairie in 1845 (Rene 1930, 105, 191, 213, 304–309, 456, 519–520). »I:102 NE II:78

· ——— ·

1862 — LETTER I:97

FROM: Jacob Olsen Østern, *Paint Creek, Lansing, Iowa*
later than 15 March 1862

TO: Engebret Olsen Steen, *Skedsmo, Akershus*

⁂

Dear brothers, mother and other relatives,

Good Engebret, I received the letter you sent me last fall a few days before Christmas. I've forgotten the date and Gullik has the letter. So I cannot see when you sent it. I received the other letter March 15, 1862. Here I see that you are in a difficult financial situation and this makes me very sad. I am sorry that I'm not in a situation that makes it possible to be of any assistance. My own finances are not brilliant at the moment. I owe about 500 dollars at ten percent interest which means that I have to pay fifty dollars a year in addition to taxes and my other expenses, not the least at the store. The prices have gone up significantly because of the war in America. But the prices for farm products are poor because of the blockade of the Mississippi. I was in Prairie du Chien with two good pigs some time ago. One was 382 and the other 380 pounds and I only got two dollars and forty cents per hundred pounds. Wheat is now at sixty cents a bushel and oats twenty. But there is talk of better prices next year when they believe that the blockade of the Mississippi will be lifted.

I had 600 bushels of wheat last summer and 240 bushels of oats. I still have 300 bushels of wheat left to sell and it would be helpful if I'm paid one dollar per bushel, which is what people say, but I am not so confident. Moreover, together with Arne Knudsen, a man from Hallingdal, I have endorsed a 500 dollar loan for my neighbor, an American. But we have been given eighty acres as security, so I don't think we will lose anything on this deal.

One year ago I lost a three-year-old mare. She died of the bots, a kind of worm that is found in horse stomachs. I do not know any name for it in Norwegian but it kills horses by biting into the horse stomach and eating until it has made a hole, whereupon the horse dies, and this took only twenty-one hours in the case of my mare from the time I noticed that she was sick. The mare was worth one hundred dollars. I bought another horse of the same age some months later as I only had one left and paid one hundred dollars. I have bought a machine to mow my wheat and timothy and this cost me 137 dollars. The machine is pulled by two horses and does excellent work. I have heard it can mow twelve acres a day, but then you need two horse teams so that one can rest while the other is used. Two men are then needed, one to drive and the other to remove the wheat from the machine as soon as there is enough for a sheaf. Both sit on the machine. So you can see how I have made it much easier for myself than when I walked with a scythe and can now sit and mow my hay and my wheat.

I cannot remember whether I've told you that we have twins. They were born November 1, 1860. They are girls and are, praise God, well and healthy. Their names are Maren Christine and Karen Elise. So now we have six children, two boys and four girls.

I have some information from Aas. I went there when I had received your letter and asked them to write to you individually to explain what they could do about the loans you had written about. Lars Olsen Saga and Christine are doing well even though they may not have any ready money at the moment. He has sold eighty acres to a German for 800 dollars and last fall Anton Skillebekk bought eighty acres for 600 or 700 dollars. He now has 120 acres of Drue's land but it will be sold next spring. He cannot have a deed in his name before it is sold at the highest bid, so he has decided to have an auction. The land was heavily mortgaged and he has paid neither interest nor taxes, so it now has to be sold. If the price isn't too high he will of course buy it himself. But he is not greatly concerned as he has bought 160 adjacent acres in his own name and has begun to build here. If he buys the said land he will sell it as soon as convenient and when all of this has been done he said he will write to you.

As for Carl Aas and his sons I can tell you that they are doing well. They are in good health, the parents as well as the children. The boys work at home, they have 200 acres and no debt and they have all of last year's harvest still unsold and probably some ready money. So I don't think it should be difficult for you to get some money from these two families. If I had been in their situation, that is, without debt, I wouldn't have hesitated to borrow 400 dollars in my own name and send you the money. But, regrettably, this is not possible. My children are not yet of any use and they are expensive.

Two of the Fossum girls are married: Martine to a man from Land in Norway and Thorine to a German. Andrine Østern is married to a man from Ringerike. You asked me how far we are from each other. From my house it is about two miles to Aas but not more than one and a half to where Lars now has started building. To Dehli it is two and a half. To Helene Nordvolden it is half a mile. To Gullik it is three-quarters of a mile. To Jacob Nordvolden one and a quarter, to Jens Larsen Økri a quarter mile. To Jacob Engebretsen Østern one and a quarter and to Thorer Eeg one and three-quarters. To the place where Andrine Østern lives it is seven miles, to John Østern thirty miles, to Hans Arnesen Fossum forty miles and to Maren Skillebekk one mile. As far as I know, all is well with them at present.

· ⎯ ·

> The rest of the letter has not been preserved. As noted on each letter, this and another letter dated 31 March (Nor. ed. II:79) were both received on 3 May 1862, but they were mailed separately and this undated and unsigned one, which gives the date when the letter with the bad news was received, was probably written first. The feared economic disaster has not yet struck. Much of this letter explains why he cannot send money to Norway but it must, ironically, have served to convince his Norwegian family that he was doing very well. The fact that he is not sure whether he has written about his twins born in November 1860 suggests that correspondence is no longer frequent and this is the last Østern letter in the collection. As people in Norway used the name of the farm they lived on as a last name, immigrants in the Midwest often used their last name to refer to the farm they lived on. So here Jacob, referring to members of the Aas family, uses Aas as a place name, as he in the next letter calls his own farm in Iowa Østern. Christine Carlsdatter Aas was the widow of Frans Ludwig Drue, who died in the cholera epidemic of 1854. She is now married to Lars Olsen Saga. Hans Arnesen Fossum has also been referred to as Østerneiet and List. The letters often do not reveal the official family name in the United States. Maren Skillebekk was married to Nils Bottolfsen. «I:77 NE II:80

· ⎯ ·

1862 — LETTER 1:98

FROM: Anders Helgesen Skare, *Minnesota, 8 April 1862*
TO: Helge Gundersen Skare, *Eggedal, Sigdal, Buskerud*

⇢⇥◯⇤⇠

Dear and unforgettable father and siblings,

I have received your honored letter dated January 15. Please, dear father, let me know of your and my siblings' situation and health when you write your next letter. It is such a pleasure for me to learn how you all are. You ask whether I'm satisfied or unsatisfied with the already executed division of your estate. To this I will briefly say that I am satisfied and that what has been done may for my part be considered binding. But I don't wish to conceal from you, dear father, what I have earlier brought to your attention. I think that, as the oldest son, and considering that the Norwegian allodial laws give me the right to have my father's farm, I should have been granted a small mite in compensation. This may not be entirely according to your view but I have the hope that both you and my brothers who are at home will see that this request is reasonable. I think that my brothers have been given so good a price for the farms that it could be considered reasonable that I was given some compensation for my legal right. You must understand and I hope you believe that I would be glad to hear that my brothers who take the farms will be able to succeed and that it is absolutely not my intention to, so to speak, throw a stone in their chain, but they are there and I am here. They can help each other while I am alone and if I have more work than I have the strength for I must use my money and hire the help I need to get the work done. For this reason it should be recognized that just as my brothers may seem to need the money they have received, I also need what should have been allotted to me. If you, my father, will not take anything from what should be regarded as your separate property in order to fulfill my request, then I think that my brothers who are to take over the farms should in all reason do it, especially since they have been given these farms at what must be said to be a very low price even though I certainly do not envy them this. If you and my brothers should be opposed to my request and find that my right to have the farms is not worth any compensation, then I will with this make known to you that I will not give away my allodial right for nothing. I will let it for the time being stay open. It may be that I at some time may make use of it. I would like to have your views on this as soon as possible.

With this I will end my letter since I at present don't have any particular news to tell you. Please give my regards to all friends and in particular to my siblings and tell them that I would be glad to hear from them. It would be a pleasure to pay for your letters and read them even if I received letters from you several times a year. You need not excuse yourself with your inability to put together a letter because I can easily get at your meaning.

We've heard that many have wanted to come here from Norway, but that they've been discouraged by the war. But that would not cause any difficulties for immigrants. It is true that the war now is raging in this country, but it is not near the route used by immigrants. I think it is 800 miles or more from here, as it is in the southern part that they fight this war. And I'll tell you a little about it. Here you are not forced to be a soldier, but you are bought or recruited. Each soldier is paid thirteen dollars a month from the day they are recruited and until the war is over, and then each soldier is to have his recruiting money, 100 dollars! And those who are hurt during their service and damage their health or become crippled will have a pension for life. The war is mainly about slavery, as, for example, two big ones cannot be placed in a small cage and both will then try to win power. A president (or king) cannot be in power for more than four years before a new one has to be elected, and there are two different parties here and both have different platforms or laws. One is called Democrat and the other is called Republic! And now there has been a Democrat president for a long time and this Democratic platform is that they want to spread slavery over all the United States. The southern states are slave states and they have bred so many Negro slaves that they do not have enough work for them! So you may imagine that they would like to have slavery developed so they could sell their slaves at a good price. So the slave owner is like a farmer who has more cattle than he needs! And this Republican platform or Republican president or king who now governs in the United States is opposed to the Democratic one and they do not want slavery to be spread but want the slaves to be free so that every slave will be master of his own body. And the southerners who live in a slave state and want to keep slavery have also elected a president as they did not want to be under this president whose name is Lincoln! During the government of the former president they stole most of the weapons from the Northern states and gave them to the slave states as they have been expecting a war between the states for a long time.

It is said that the Northerners have nine hundred thousand soldiers and the Southerners between four and five hundred thousand soldiers and they are said to have drafted almost all who were fit as they take them as soldiers from the age of seventeen to sixty. And it is said that the Southerners have lost every battle this winter. Six weeks ago they had a large battle, but they have also had many small and large battles and it was 30,000 from the South and 40,000 from the North who fought for about three days and the Northerners took 15,000 prisoners and killed 10,000 and the remaining 5,000 were able to escape. And the Northerners also took all their provisions and they had 1,200 horses and mules and 600 four-horse wagons and more than 100 for two horses, and all their cannon and guns. In short, the Southerners had to leave everything they had to the Northerners.

I will bring my scrawls to an end. You may not even be able to read them since I so rarely make use of a pen. I'll repeat that we all are in good health for which I must not forget to thank God! I haven't paid for my last letters since I have often heard that the letters that are paid for do not get to Norway because the postmasters use the money themselves and burn the letters. Please be so good that you greet Jakob Gulbrandsen Skare and his family from me and ask him to write me because I would like to have a letter from him because he was my good old friend. I will reply to his letter. I must now end my poor and simple letter with my best and loving regards to you my father and siblings, relatives and friends. Write back immediately and tell me about your situation. Regards to all my siblings there at home, and to you in particular, my dear father, from your faithful son,

ANDERS HELGESEN SCHARE

> AHS does not give his address. He may either still be in Nerstrand or he may have already moved to Norway Lake. His main concern is his right to have some monetary compensation for his right as the oldest son to inherit his father's farm or farms. His father is in the process of remarrying and has obviously wanted to settle the inheritance of his children before he establishes a new family. In order to redeem the farms, AHS would have to return to Norway within ten years. As seen in his next letter, it was his youngest brother Halvor Helgesen who took over at Skare. AHS's sisters readily accepted their father's decision. Such issues, conflicted or not, must have been common in immigrant communities. He had no Norwegian word for a party

platform. First he wrote *førm* and then *platførm*. Neither would have made sense to his readers. They may, however, have understood the name of his new country, *yunaitisstet*, and his president, *Linken*. Such spellings may suggest that he gets news by word of mouth. The great battle must be that of Fort Donelson in February. «I:93 »I:101 NE II:82

1862 — LETTER I:99

FROM: Hellik and Ole Olson Lehovd, *Christiana, Wisconsin, 10 June 1862*
TO: Ole Helgesen and Joran Paulsdatter Lehovd, *Flesberg, Buskerud*

Dear parents,

We got a letter you sent last fall and one dated April 27 and we are grateful as it is good to hear from our faraway family. I must first of all ask you to forgive us for our thoughtlessness in not having replied to your letters before. You'll be glad to hear that I've been in good health since you last heard from me and have been doing well in all ways. I went to Minnesota last fall and returned about two weeks ago and I'll be going back next week. I'm using Ole Helliksen Flata's land there this year and have bought cattle from some people who owed me money. I came here in order to collect money I was owed for work and to visit my brother. And I must tell you my dear father that I have been entrusted with three offices in the town of Canestio, Dodge County, Minnesota: Supervisor, Justice of the Peace, and Clerk for School District No. 5. In Norwegian the first is a member of the town council and the second is about the same as a tax commissioner, but I have more authority as I am authorized to marry people according to the laws of this country as a chief magistrate does in Norway, and the third is a treasurer for a district of the English school. For two of these offices I am elected for one year but as Justice of the Peace for two.

Last year we had a hard winter with much snow after Christmas and many storms and a few days with harsh cold in between. At the end of

February and early March there were thirty-four inches of snow and it was not gone until early April. And we didn't begin to sow until April 22, but now we have nice weather and the fields and meadows look good. We have enough food as we had a good year and all products are cheap. This is because money is short. In this country the best times are when there is a high price on products such as wheat, pork and butter. But now much transportation has stopped, especially shipping from abroad, because of the war. Unlike in other countries where food products are expensive because of war, here we have enormous amounts for export every year. I see that you think it's good that food is cheap but here it isn't as in Norway where almost all need to buy it.

I'm sad to see that both you and mother are in poor health. We are sending you our likenesses so you can see us and in particular me who you have not seen for so long and I think it will please you. For this reason we must make our letter short so that it won't be too heavy. Our most loving regards from me and all my family. May you live well in the Lord!

HELLLIK OLSEN LEHOVD

To my dear and unforgettable parents and siblings,

We have received your two letters and I must send you a few words to tell you that the good Lord has kept me in good health since I last wrote to you, for which both you and I should give thanks to God. I am now at Hellik Hvashovd's and plan to stay here until November as I am hired for a year and will be paid 135 dollars and I have also received some clothes that are not included in my wages. And this winter I haven't had so much work so I've attended school and visited some of the towns around here. In Madison last winter I met several of my companions on the voyage who had volunteered for the war. I see that you are in poor health for which I am heartbroken and will remind you that it is necessary to seek the Lord Jesus at all times and finally to die with faith in him. And then, my dear parents, you may have your blessed rest in the name of the Trinity in the graveyard at Flesberg Church. I can do no more than to pray to God for you as I hope you will also do for me. Farewell,

OLE OLSEN LEHOVD

The hand is different in the two parts of the letter. «1:89 »1:107 NE II:87

1862 — LETTER I:100

From: Guttorm Olsen Lee, *Blue Mounds, Wisconsin, 25 July 1862*
To: Anders Olsen Lie, *Hedalen, Sør Aurdal, Oppland*

To all our family and unforgettable friends in Norway, whom we have left but never forgotten,

I must now in my great grief sit down and take my pen in my stiff and heavy hand to write you some simple and incomprehensible words, briefly and simply, but nevertheless sincere and well-intentioned. But my hand is too heavy and my tongue is dumb. This is the best I can do. I would be so glad to see you and talk with you, even just for a moment, but as this is impossible because we are so far from each other we will have to speak with each other in writing. We received your letter dated April 10 on the second day of Pentecost and we read it with great pleasure and we see that you are all in good health and doing well. We have also received this blessed gift from our gracious God except that we now have met with an adversity that places a great and heavy burden on us. May God help us in our infirmity! We should be as happy in bad times as in good, for he who wounds us will also restore us.

I must, with a heavy heart and tear-filled eyes, tell you that our brother Torgrim has passed away and has left the great ocean of this world and that his death was both quick and unusual. He went on the morning of July 18 to a small town about four miles from home with a man who was living with us. In town they met Knud, son of Aslak Lie at the mill. He was there with grain and he told them that he had a letter to our brother from Ole Dolven at home. So they went home together until their roads parted about one and a half miles from town, and then our brother decided to go with Knud to get his letter and said goodbye to his lodger. Then Knud and our brother were suddenly met by a powerful thunderstorm and the thunder killed them both, not the thunder but the lightning that comes with the thunder. They were driving with two horses and a wagon and one of the horses was killed but the other one was unhurt. When people found them they were both sitting as if they were alive except that their heads were leaning backwards. Such was our brother's departure from this world. Oh God, grant us for the sake of Jesus our Savior that we may in this mirror be moved in our hearts of stone so that we may say with the hymnist that nothing shall tear me away from Jesus.

I see that you wish to know how mills are run in America. We have many mills in our neighborhood. One is four and another is five miles from us. The mills always make flour of the wheat and the miller takes one-eighth of the flour as his fee. As for water, we have excellent spring water that comes up from the ground as if it is boiling. In some places there are three to four springs in one square and the water runs into brooks, and those who don't have springs have to dig wells. Some have to dig 160 feet and some from ten to twenty feet. We have very hard times and a poor harvest because of a fly that destroys the wheat so many don't bother to cut it. But the barley and potatoes look pretty good if God does not decide to show us who provides our harvest. As for the war, it is sad that they cannot agree, because people do not die in the hundreds in the war but in thousands. And now 300,000 men are to be drafted into the army and God knows when this destruction will come to an end. We have a new law that says that anyone with a family may have free land of the land that belongs to the government. But this free land is far from here so it will cost money to go there.

I don't have more news but I must ask you to write to us as soon as you get this letter. I see that you my dear brother Ole have entered into matrimony, so I will wish you happiness and that you will want to come over to this country. I think it would be easier for you to support a family here without land than in Norway with a little farm. I think that you have the money to go far enough to get land for nothing. I would have told you to come if I had been sure that you would have liked it here, but I will not say a word either for or against. I must now end this poor and simple-minded letter with my regards to you all from all of us here. I'm grateful for every moment we have had together and for every word you have sent us since we left. So farewell our friends in the Lord. There is peace for our soul in the Word and in prayer. Sincerely,

GUTTORM OLSEN LIE

> GOL's brother in Norway, Anders, did not emigrate. He became the next farmer at Søre Lie and all but one of his sons emigrated. When he wrote a "square" (*rute*), he probably had a surveying unit in mind, for example, a section or a quarter section. The new law is the Homestead Act of 20 May 1862. «I:67 »I:128 NE II:89

1862 — LETTER I:101

FROM: Gunder Helgesen Skare, Ole Aslesen Myran, Elling Ellingsen Wold and Ingeborg Helgesdatter Skare, *Decorah, Iowa, 13 August 1862*
TO: Helge Gundersen and Eli Helgesdatter Skare, *Eggedal, Sigdal, Buskerud*

⋅⇌⇋⋅

Dear Father,

Now that Providence has brought me well and happily here to Iowa in America I must send a few lines to you about my journey. We left Svelvik on the morning of April 16 and arrived in Quebec June 21 from where our ship went up to Montreal on June 23. It took us two months and one week so it took us a very long time to cross the great Atlantic, which was because we had a persistent head wind that several times threatened to turn us back. I was a little seasick to begin with but except for this I've been in good health. Two died, a woman who was taken ashore at Aasgardstrand to be buried and a small child who was buried at sea. We left Montreal on the twenty-fourth and came to Prairie du Chien July 1 where I was lucky to meet Elling Vold who happened to be in town when I arrived. Our chance meeting was celebrated as a happy occasion for both of us and I left my group and came home the next day. As I don't have more to write about I will conclude these lines by sending my loving regards from a distant son,

GUNDER HELGESEN

Dear father-in-law,

As we now enclose this authorization giving you the right to divide your property, we can also tell you that we are all in a fairly good health, for which God be praised. And we, Ole and Ingrid, have by Providence been given a girl child who has been baptized with the name Eli. Our harvest does not seem very bad, nor does it seem very good, in particular as concerns the wheat as a small insect, a kind of fly, has settled on it and wasted it so that in several places it dried out before becoming ripe. As for the war, it doesn't seem that it will be decided soon. Our government has demanded an increase of 300,000 soldiers and consequently the prospects for a quick end to this hard war are slim. As we wish you the best of luck and God's blessing in your new position, you and your dear wife are most lovingly greeted from us all. Your faithful sons-in-law,

ELLING WOLD AND OLE MYRAN

To my dear sister Eli,

I'll send you a few words to let you know that if you have thoughts of coming here you shouldn't bring more everyday clothes than strictly necessary and you must not have any new ones made in that fashion. You should rather bring the material. And you can leave your brooches behind and rather bring both small and large silver spoons. You are lovingly greeted from me,

INGEBORG HELGESDATTER

· —— ·

In Eggedal, Helge Gundersen had married Margit Helgesdatter and settled on the farm Nerdrum. Eli emigrated in 1866. «1:98 »1:104 NE II:90

· —— ·

1862 — LETTER I:102

FROM: Knud Ivarson Vike, *Fifteenth Wisconsin Regiment*
Nashville, Tennessee, 20 December 1862

TO: Dordei Knutsdatter Vike, *Spring Prairie, Wisconsin*

I'm glad to again take up my pen and send you some poor words about my situation. I'm doing quite well all things considered. I'm covered with boils all over my body, my thighs and legs and my arms. They swell and it's good when they empty because I'm quite miserable at times. We lie on frozen ground and sleep under the open sky. I don't say this to make you sad but neither is it something to be happy about.

Today on the twentieth I received your dear letter dated the sixth of this month and when I read it I was both glad and sad. I'm glad that you are all well but sad that you have had to sell our oxen at so low a price.

But it doesn't matter; I am now far away. I have sent you money but I don't know whether you have received it. Please write to me as soon as you get the money and I would also like to know how much state money you have received. And I would also like to know how much you, my dear son, made last summer and also what the prices are for wheat, pork, butter, and hay. I must stop—

I haven't had news from my dear brother Gullik for three weeks and he then said he was getting better. I'll now end my poor letter to you my dear wife and children. I am well and I'm so happy that you are in good health and for every letter I get. My loving regards to you all as well as to all my relatives. I have made many mistakes. I can see it now. Live well.

· —— ·

> This unsigned letter is written on paper made for Union soldiers and has the following heading: *"The Soldier's Guardian Angel* / Times of joy, and times of woe / Each an Angel's presence know. / Guardian Angels hover round / Peaceful Home, and Battle Ground." KIV died eleven days after he wrote this letter. «1:96 NE II:93

· —— ·

1863 — LETTER I:103

FROM: Erik Theodor Schjøth, *Sturgeon Bay, Wisconsin, 14 January 1863*
To: Jens Rudolph and Christian Schjøth, *Oslo*

My dear brothers, Jens and Christian Schjøth!

All good things come in threes. I've written to you twice since I received your welcome letters and I'll now try a third time, hoping it will meet with better luck than the others that probably haven't arrived as I would then certainly have heard from you. So I will repeat my heartfelt thanks for your letters, the blessed portraits and the draft that I received one month after it had been dated. Four days after receiving it I went to the bank in Green Bay where I was paid money on the draft as I could prove that I was the rightful owner. I wrote my first letter to you there and I now believe that it went down with a steamboat that was lost on Lake Michigan. When I received your latest letter of April 26, 1861, my good brother Christian, I also wrote immediately and this letter has probably suffered the same fate. The mail here in America is as honest as the banks and the courts. If you pay the postage to Europe the postmaster will as a rule put the money in his pocket and the letter in the stove.

May God grant you all a happy and healthy New Year and may God grant that these lines will come into your hands so I may have the pleasure of hearing from you that you are all alive and well. I am still, praise God, in good health and your help has been a blessing. I used it to improve my house and my land and along with my own work and thrift it has made it possible for me to live independently and not have to work for others in my advanced years. I still live alone. I have an old white horse that I bought two years ago for twenty-four dollars and that I use on my farm, a good hound, a cat and plenty of chickens. I run a little store that provides for my daily bread and keeps me in good clothes. I do my purchases in Green Bay, in summer on my boat and in winter on a sleigh with my old John (my horse). I am going there in a few days as we haven't had snow for sleighing until now this winter.

These last two years have been good and bountiful but a bad money crisis began two years ago. You couldn't know if the dollar you had one day would be worth a half or a quarter dollar the next. I suppose you hear about our unfortunate war there at home that I think will ruin the entire country and that costs us thousands of our own men and millions of money daily. Many a Norwegian boy has lost his life, not so much because of bullets and sword as because of illness and the poor nursing available at the front. I was too old to join (you have to be between eighteen and forty-five) and had to stay at home to protect the women and children should the Indians become restless, as they have in some places. Around where I live there are many who fish and hunt but I'm not afraid of them (even though many are). I'm their friend because I trade with them and don't insult them. I have a name among them that I am not ashamed of. They call me the good man because I've often shared my bread with them and permitted some to stay overnight in my cabin when the weather has been poor. Men who have wife and children would not dare to do this. You may imagine that many of them are hardly created for the sake of beauty.

Enough about America and myself; tell me, my dear brothers, how you and your wives and children are, and how are my blessed children? This question brings bitter tears to my eyes. Oh, how happy you are who every day and night can kiss and cuddle your blessed small ones while I, poor man, have been separated from mine for nine—nine—long, long years. Oh, I would willingly die tonight as I write these words for a single kiss, a caress from them. Last spring I had a great desire to make a little visit but it would have been too expensive. My financial situation won't allow it and it would put me too deeply in debt, so I'll have to wait some years more. I have one good thing here: I'm respected and liked by all and this soothes my grief and my longing. I must now stop writing for now; my eyes cannot take any more tonight and the mail leaves at six tomorrow morning. Farewell and God bless you all and give regards to all who may still remember me from your devoted and grateful brother,

ERIK T. SCHJØTH

«I:86 »I:125 NE III:T16

1863 — LETTER I:104

FROM: Elling Ellingsen Wold, Ole Aslesen Myran, and Ingeborg Helgesdatter and Gunder Helgesen Skare, *Decorah, Iowa*
19 *January 1863*
TO: Helge Gundersen, *Eggedal, Sigdal, Buskerud*

Dear father-in-law Helge Skare,

We have received your very welcome letter dated in Drammen December 12, 1862 and see that everything is well with you. We see that we may be able to have an exchange of money with Kitil Folsaas from Numedal, and this is something we appreciate. We have received his money from his brother here, Halvor Folsaas, and have drafted the following authorization for Kitil Folsaas: We have on the sixteenth of this month received a sum of 470 dollars which we divided according to your wish: first, Ole should have his part, 337 dollars, and Elling the remainder. The latter requests your agreement that this remaining amount is shared with your daughter Ingeborg who is with us.

You seem to fear that we are in danger from the Indians. But this has, praise God, not happened to us since we live almost 200 miles from there. As you have heard, they indeed revolted and in the most horrible way they murdered men, women and children. It's been calculated that no fewer than 800 people were killed by the Indians and that a large amount of property was destroyed. The state of Minnesota has suffered much damage in this war. An army was immediately sent there and it soon overpowered this wild enemy. Some hundred were taken prisoner and after an inquiry thirty-six who were the worst criminals were hanged. The ropes were arranged so that they all fell at once. We don't yet know what will be done with the others. [*In the margin*] These were hanged on the second day of Christmas.

Late last year I, Elling, sent you a letter that I assume you have received. We hope to have a letter from you as soon as these lines are in your hands and that you will tell us when you wish us to receive the remaining amount. We may meet some here who may wish to have money there in order to help their relatives come here, and now we don't know what to say to them. As the money now gathers interest we assume that it would not make any difference for Halvor to whom he paid this interest, while for us it would be an advantage to have the money sent here. Should you wish to send it as a draft, it must be on a New York bank and be in American gold. You must take care that this is on the draft; otherwise we may be cheated.

To conclude, we all give our most heartfelt thanks to God for his blessing that he has given us through a dear father's hand as an inheritance and gift. You are much greeted from us all. Live always well in God. Your faithful sons-in-law,

OLE ASLESEN MYRAND AND ELLING ELLINGSEN WOLD
AND YOUR DAUGHTER INGEBORG

Dear father and siblings,

I see that you wish to have a message from me. I've been here with Elling and my sister Mari since my return. I am, praise God, in good health and well satisfied. I've planned to visit my brother Anders as soon as I can get someone to go with me. My loving regards,

GUNDER HELGESEN SKARE

> The transfer of money between immigrants and the home country was often arranged without the help of banks. Helge Gundersen has paid

money to Kitil Folsaas (probably to finance his emigration) and his brother in the United States gives a corresponding amount to members of Helge's American family. But, as seen in the next letter in this series, all members of the family were not happy with their father's arrangements. The basis for these transactions was the sale of the farm to the younger brother Halvor Helgesen for 2,400 *speciedaler*, some of which was to be divided among his siblings. «I:101 »I:106 NE II:96

1863 — LETTER I:105

FROM: Barbro Tollefsdatter Sando, *Estherville, Iowa, 10 September 1863*
TO: a sister, *Aal, Buskerud*

Dear Sister,

I can finally write a few lines to you and tell you that I received your letter of April 11, 1860 after it had taken more than a year to get here. Thank you so much. I was so glad to hear that all was well with you and that you are happy. I am so far away that it will never be possible to see or speak with you so it is good to receive an encouraging and enjoyable letter. I see that there have been many changes, in particular in the Skottebøl family. Your letter brought the first news of my sister's death and my mother's illness and later I heard that she too had passed away. I hope they both had fought the good fight and were rewarded on the other side of the grave. I cannot but shed my sad tears for those who have crossed over and wish peace on their dust. I can tell you that our brother Nils died two years ago in September after having been ill for almost a year. The doctors said it was dropsy and he wasn't bedridden for more than three weeks. He was fully conscious to the very end. He often used the word of God and we understood him to be united with his Savior and God granted him a peaceful end to his worldly pilgrimage. I am telling you this here as you may not have been informed. His grieving widow and two children send greetings to you and all his family in Norway.

We and our children are in good health and are quite satisfied. Our six children are doing well; even though I have had eleven childbirths only six live, five sons and a daughter named Berthe Maria. They are all big for their age, gifted, and eager to learn. They can read both Norwegian and English well and they can write and do a little arithmetic. Berthe will be seven on February 4; she can also read and is a good little girl. I'm enclosing her portrait as a reminder of her as well as of us. I could have so much more to tell you but I won't even begin since I'm unable to tell you all. Remember me to my brother Haakon and tell him that it is two years since we received his letter that we have not yet answered. Please thank him from us. And tell our brother Ole the Younger that it would be nice to have a few lines from him too. Give my regards to all my siblings and to Knut Tretterud and then to all our relations and friends from us and our children. Farewell and may we all be gathered where there will be no more separation. This is the wish of your far distant sister,

BARBRO

· —— ·

BTS then had two living sisters: Guri Tollefsdatter Bøygard and Randi Tollefsdatter Opheim. She and her husband Ole Eriksen Sando emigrated in 1845 and first settled in Rock Prairie, Wisc. Aagot Tollefsdatter Skottebøl was born in 1810 and died at Christmas in 1858. Her mother Margit Olsdatter Opsata died in 1860. Her husband Tollef died in 1848 and their son Ole Tollefsen the Elder was the farmer at Opsata. Ole the Younger had emigrated and lived at St. Ansgar, Iowa. Nils Tollefsen Opsata emigrated in 1845 and died in 1861. He was married to Kari Tollefsdatter. Ole the Elder emigrated with his family in 1866 and sold the farm to his youngest brother, Haakon. «I:7 »I:117 NE II:103

· —— ·

1863 — LETTER I:106

From: Anders Helgesen Skare, *Norway Lake, Minnesota, 27 September 1863*
To: Helge Gundersen Skare, *Eggedal, Sigdal, Buskerud*

Unforgettable father,

I'll take my pen in hand and tell you my view of the authorization that you asked of me some years ago. You wrote that you had requested one from Elling Wold and your children who live in Iowa and that you received an authorization from them. But about one year after you had received my authorization I had a letter from Elling E. Wold that he had just sent you an authorization. So it seemed to me that you hadn't spoken the truth to me, your son, and I resent this, my dear father. Yes, dear father, I'll now let you know my unconcealed opinion. The rumor is that you wish to limit my inheritance rights in favor of my brothers. As I am your oldest son I think this is unreasonable. If you will recollect the situation at the time I went to America you know how this started. I could have stayed home and made use of my right to the farm. But I left my home, where I had received so many harsh words, in sorrow and anger. I don't think I had done this if I had been given work. It would have been nicer to live on my father's farm than to settle in such a faraway place. But thank God, I and my family are in good health and I'm doing reasonably well. Yes, my dear father, when I was with you, just try to remember, I asked you to help me in two different ways, either give me some money so I could start a business or let me have some of your land, but my requests were futile. So I'll say it as it is: you decided that I had to leave home. When you asked me for an authorization you told me that each of your daughters would have 300 and each son 400. But nothing came of this and what you said is worthless. I told you what I thought about this some years ago. My view was that you should demand 2,800 *speciedaler* for your farms, but you said that this would be unreasonable and that 2,400 would be sufficient. But with what Gunder now has been given, I think that the price I suggested would have been right. Gunder says that he was given 700 *speciedaler* and then Halvor surely has received a similar amount and it then seems that you will forget me. And Gunder says that you, my father, have said that I should pay interest on the money I've been given, and that is unreasonable.

I must now end my letter. I have no news and for news about the situation in this country you should write to Gunder Johnsen Moen and Ole Hellerud. This was an average year and the prices for what the farmer has to sell are average. Gunder and Ingeborg are with me and are in good health. Many regards to my father and his family and my brother and sisters from me and my family. Give my regards to Gunder Moen and ask him to write to me. And now I ask you my father to respond to this letter as soon as possible. Farewell. Sincerely,

ANDERS HELGESEN SCHARE

> AHS evidently had a more troubled relationship with his father than did his younger siblings. The farm Skare was sold for 2,400 *speciedaler* in 1863. «I:104 »I:141 NE II:104

1863 — LETTER I:107

FROM: Ole Olson Lehovd, *Christiana, Wisconsin, 28 December 1863*

TO: Ole Helgesen and Joran Paulsdatter Lehovd, *Flesberg, Buskerud*

Dear unforgettable parents and siblings,

We have received your letter of October 27, dear father, that you addressed to Hellik Hvashovd. I see that you are worried about the long and devastating war that rages without pause and that is beginning to create more and more fear in men of the age for army service and their families. There was a draft again last fall, but the call is not for men but for money: every drafted man who has sworn an oath to this country has to pay 300 dollars to the government in return for being free from the draft for three years. And even they who haven't sworn the oath but who have voted in a public election have to pay this amount. In this town twenty-one men were called up, eighteen Norwegians and three Americans, but as some paid and others were let go because they hadn't voted and some because they had old parents or others they were responsible for, none had to go. I can please you my dear parents and friends with the information that I haven't yet dressed up in Uncle Sam's blue suit, as I see you feared. My name has not yet come up and they cannot make me go since I haven't voted. I can say that I have no fear of the war as so many have and if I have to go I'll go freely and bravely, even though I know that this decision has laid many thousands in their graves.

As for your suggestion that we should come back to Norway, I wouldn't like to come back so soon after having left. Then the ignorant and crude Norwegians would assume I was enormously wealthy and powerful since I had been in this country where there is gold aplenty, where the pigs walk around in the woods ready roasted with knife and fork in their backs, and where roasted pigeons fall out of the sky. I can remember that there were many who told me when I left Norway that things wouldn't go well for me here since not all in my family wanted me to go and I think this has made me less happy.

I've been in good health since you last heard from me, for which we must thank God. I've had work most of the time since I came here and these last nine months I've worked for Americans. It's useful for those who intend to stay here to learn the language, and I can understand it quite well. I worked for an Englishman for two months but I was dissatisfied with him because I couldn't understand much of the language, and they were unscrupulous and had a very ungodly home. Then I worked for a Yankee named C. H. Brown for seven months. I was paid sixteen dollars a month and liked it as most Yankees have clean and comfortable homes, something the Norwegians still have to learn. So in my view, if you are healthy and work up an appetite you can go with pleasure to the Americans' table, so nice and clean and set with many dishes, so I enjoy being with the Americans more than being with the Norwegians. I've agreed to work for this Yankee for 175 dollars including two weeks free, so I can now be better paid than before when I at most was offered 140 dollars. All I've worked for have asked me to return. I can truthfully say that I haven't become such a one as those at home thought I would and I haven't fallen to dance, card playing, drink, idleness or other vices. My occupation here is as ordained by God; I go to work in the morning and to rest at night and on Sundays I have for the most part been to church. The Yankee I worked for is the neighbor of Pastor

Ottesen in the Koshkonong church one mile from Hvashovd. Ottesen was on a visit to Norway last summer. Anne Fjøse lives nearby and there will soon be an auction there of the belongings of Ole Lindboe who passed away in a hospital on August 27. He was wounded in his right hand last year. I said goodbye to him for the last time in Madison two years ago, the day before they went south. I know, father, that you knew Andreas Osland! He is also a soldier in the Fifteenth Wisconsin Regiment and a few weeks ago he was here with a month's leave. I hope that you know all those from our area who are in the army so I won't make a list here. Ole Olsen Holtan, Knut Kleve, and Kari's foster son have been in the war against the Indians in the west and have now gone south to shoot the so-called rebels.

My brother Hellik and his family were in good health when he wrote to me November 16 that he had bought the land of Gulbrand Toresen Dokken—160 acres prairie land and, two and a half miles from there, five acres of forest land—for 800 dollars and he moved to his new farm September 1. They have a daughter born September 16 and baptized October 28 named Julia Oline and she is growing and is healthy. But he's afraid of the draft that was held in the town where he lives on November 10. The names of six Norwegians and one American were drawn but not his, but then came a message that the draft would be postponed to January 5 and that this would be a new draft if there hadn't in the meantime been a sufficient number of volunteers. I think he'll try to pay if he's drafted if this is still possible. The draft is for three years. In our town there will be a draft of twenty-one men on January 25 and those who wish to pay will have to pay 300 dollars. So the war first makes a man poor and then he may still be forced to go to war as it seems quite uncertain who will win. The North has done better than the South, but the Northerners would have been more successful if they had been united. Many here think the South is right, and the war is slowed down because there are so many betrayals by Northerners who support the South. I wonder who will win this war and when.

I spoke with Paul and Hellik Granstuen a year ago but I haven't seen Jøran as she is working in Madison. There is a rumor that Paul has married an American girl. He is, as you know, somewhat wild and he was sentenced in court to marry the girl. The rumor is that they had tried to kill the child. I must conclude my poor letter with loving regards to my father, mother, brothers and my sister Jøran. I wish that these words may find you in good health and I hope that you will write to me when convenient. I haven't heard from you for more than a year. You must tell me about things that have changed since I left and about all who are dead and those who are married, both rich and poor. It would make me glad to see news from Norway which I believe I've seen for the last time, as I don't wish to return. I would like to know whether Ole Kjølseteie and Anders Tidemansen have come here and how Ole Herbrandsen is getting on with his merchant tours. While I was at home he seemed to be seeking the company of the worst kind of people in the valley. I don't feel sorry for him, I would merely like to know where the poor man lives.

Father, when you write please address the letter to me at *Salems P.O., Almstad County Minnesota* as I plan to go to Minnesota this winter. In these last days we've had a harsh cold that none of the Norwegians has experienced since coming here. If I haven't gone to Minnesota my brother will pay the letter for me as this is also his post office. My kindest regards to you my parents and siblings. I hope you will live honest and loving lives and help each other in all things and not have as many disagreements as when I was home. And I ask you my brothers to help our father as much as you can now that he is getting old and weak. You must not in any way feel sorry for me as I haven't suffered any want. The two things here that I appreciate the most are first that one may enjoy learning a new language and second that one may earn more money than in Norway. I have much more money than I had at home. I have 343 dollars in my pocketbook and have more owed to me. My best regards to my unforgettable parents and siblings. Please give my regards to Lars Trollerud and Kjersti if they are living. I wish them well both here and in the life to come. Farewell,

OLE OLSEN LEHOVD

I have greetings to you father from Hellik Gundersen who says that he and his family are in fairly good health and that his old mother lives much as before and that Kjersti and her children are all in good health. Give his regards to Lars Engerud and to Ambjørg and Hellik Bergerud and their family and to Levor Fikkan and his family from all here at the Hvashovd farms. Please let us know how they are when you write to me and I will then send it to them as they haven't had letters from them since they last wrote. I am now with Kjersti Hvashovd and have been here since two weeks before Christmas. I'm paying for this letter so you don't have to pay for it in Norway as you have done sometimes before.

. ——— .

> Kjersti (also spelled Kirsti) Gundersdatter Hvashovd, a widow, had been married to Tosten Levorsen Hvashovd and was the sister of Hellik Gundersen Hvashovd. The two had adjoining farms. Regarding

Ole Olsen's reference to roasted pigs and pigeons, he has probably read or heard the popular song, "Oleanna," by the Norwegian journalist Ditmar Meidell (1853). Translations by Martin B. Ruud and Theodore Blegen were the basis for the folksinger Pete Seeger's version in the 1950s. Jacob Aal Ottesen was pastor at Koshkonong from 1860 to 1891. Ole Lindboe was wounded in the battle of Stone River and died in Nashville, Tenn. (Ulvestad 1907, 307). «I:99 »I:110 NE II:107

· ——— ·

1864 — LETTER I:108

FROM: Juul Gulliksen Dorsett, *Newburg, Minnesota, 5 September 1864*

To: Torstein Gulliksen Daaset, *Flesberg, Buskerud*

⇢⇌⇠

Dear brother Tosten,

Since I haven't written to you for a long time I will take up my pen and send you a few words to let you know that I'm in good health. Praise God for his goodness. I don't have any news that would interest you except that we have war and rebellion in this country, but this hasn't hurt us in the North as the war is in the South. There has been a draft here twice but we have hired people in our places and thus bought our liberty. What mainly hurts us is that the prices for what we have to buy, in particular clothes, are high, but we are paid quite well for what we have to sell. The government has no right to draft a person who has come to this country and who has not sworn allegiance, so I would advise you dear brother to come next summer. I have a home where you can stay. I'm not married and I have a family of strangers living here to farm my land next summer. I do wish that you would come. Wages are good for a man who wants to work. If you come I would like you to farm my land since I'm a bachelor. I believe that the war is soon over and that we will have peace. Dear brother, if you still have your farm I would advise you to sell it and come here. Should you wish to buy land here you'll be able to buy it at a lower price than in Norway and I wish you would come. And if you come, I would advise you to bring as much homespun and other cloth as possible, but no more readymade clothes than necessary. You can have them made here according to the custom of the country. If you can, bring some fine linen cloth. The price for clothes has gone up so much that you should bring as much as possible. And please bring a nice piece of silk for me. I'll pay you for it when you come. I must now end my poor letter with friendly regards to you and my siblings and in particular to my old father as well as to all who ask about me. As far as I know, Ole and Gullik are doing well. Dear brother, write to me as soon as you get this letter.

JUUL DAASET

«I:94 »I:123 NE II:113

1864 — LETTER I:109

From: Sigbjørn Aslakson, *Coon Prairie, Wisconsin, 10 October 1864*
To: Osmund Atlaksen Ovedal, *Sirdal, Vest-Agder*

Dear unforgettable siblings,

Thank you for your letter of April 2 that I received in May. I'm glad to hear that you are all well in every respect and I can tell you, thank God, that we are all in good health and are doing more than well in worldly things. I haven't spoken with our brother Reinert since last spring. He lives 200 miles north of here where he has land and does well. Nor have I spoken with Sivert since last spring when he went about 200 miles further west and settled there.

It is four years since the terrible civil war between the northern and southern states began and since then there have been continuous battles with varying luck and many thousands of brave soldiers have fallen on both sides. But now everything suggests that the war will soon be over. The southern states have used all the men they have who are capable of bearing weapons while the northern states still have many able-bodied men who haven't yet done military service. Moreover, the war with all its destruction has been fought in the South and several of these states have been taken by the North. The army of the North has recently won many important battles and taken important forts and cities along the coast. We live, thank God, so far from the war that we don't feel it as much as you may believe. We have recently drafted 500,000 new solders in addition to the soldiers who are already serving and every state and every township had to raise a certain number of men according to their population. In the township where I live, as in so many other townships, we collected enough money to hire the number of men we had to provide. Those who are hired get from 600 to 1,000 dollars a year plus money for their provisions and clothes.

Should any of you wish to come to America I don't think that the war will make things difficult; only those who are citizens have to serve in the army and wages are now as high as they have ever been. This has been an average year. I had 1,100 bushels of wheat, barley and oats. I must now end my letter with my regards to you all from me, my wife and my two children, Berthe, who is three and a half, and Alexander, who is one and three-quarters years, and regards to all my relatives and friends. I wish you will write to me and let me know how you are and whether any of you are thinking of coming here as it is uncertain that I will ever come to Norway. So live well and it is my wish that God will be with you and us in life and death. Farewell. Sincerely,

SIGBJØRN ATLAKSON

. —— .

SA's brother, Reinert, wrote from East Eau Clair on 20 October (Nor. ed. II:115). He and his brother Sivert (who lived in Minnesota) had been visiting SA when the letter from Norway arrived. «1:57 »1:114
NE II:114

. —— .

1864 — LETTER I:110

FROM: Hellik Olson Lehovd, *Salem, Minnesota, 26 December 1864*
To: Ole Helgesen and Joran Paulsdatter Lehovd, *Flesberg, Buskerud*

Dear parents and siblings,

Your letter of March 5 to my brother Ole arrived three days after Ole came here from Wisconsin. So I can no longer delay writing a few words to you as I know that you long to hear from us. Please forgive me for having waited so long. It is partly because of my thoughtlessness and partly because the war has had such a great impact on us. Imagine living in a country where about one million able men a year are needed to keep up the war. And I've been waiting for an end to the war that would make you happy. But I'm sorry that I have no such news. But I must write the truth about our situation and not make it worse or better.

First I must tell you how I've been since I last wrote to you. I have, praise God, been in good health. I was married September 19 to Britha Olsdatter Rørvig from Vik parish in the diocese of Bergen. She was born April 7, 1841, and came to America in the summer of 1858. We have a daughter named Julia Olina born September 16, 1863, and she is healthy and is growing big and strong and she is good and kind in all ways. My wife is also in good health. Her parents came to America in the summer of 1862 and they now live with me. All their children are in this country, two sons and five daughters. One son and three daughters are married and two of my brothers-in-law have already been in the war and one died there and the other lost his left arm in a battle last summer. The first year I was married I used Ole Helliksen Flata's land but the summer of 1863 I bought 165 acres from Gulbrand Toresen Buin for 800 dollars. He had built a house, broken thirteen acres and fenced a good deal. My farm is in a Norwegian settlement and is near the parsonage. Our Pastor Steen is the son of the Pastor Steen who was in Rollag parish.

When I bought my land I had a debt of about 300 dollars and you will understand that much is needed for a new home, cattle, and farm implements. Prices are very high and the huge war taxes get worse year by year so I've had to sell forty acres and now have 125. We had an average year here but in the eastern states they had a poor year. This year I harvested 186 bushels of wheat, forty-five of oats, ten of barley and potatoes. My brother Ole came in May and he bought eighty acres of uncultivated prairie land six miles from me for 325 dollars. He worked nearby and made more than a hundred dollars. In September he worked on a steamboat on the Mississippi for seventy-five dollars a month. But in October I had a letter from him saying that he had signed up to serve for one year in the place of a German from La Crosse in Wisconsin who had been drafted and that he was to have 700 dollars that would be sent to me. I haven't received anything yet so I believe he has been fooled into the army, and this is sad because he hadn't sworn an oath of loyalty and therefore could not be drafted. I recently had a letter from him that he is in a training camp in Madison in Wisconsin and that he's been ill for a month and in a hospital. But he's now better and will soon be going south to do battle. He was sworn in on October 17 for one year and he writes that I must give you greetings and say that you mustn't be worried because he will come home well with the help of God.

The war is a terrible thing because of the drafts. They are held every three or four months and from 3 to 4 to 500,000, yes five hundred thousand men, are called up at a time and every town has to provide its share according to the population. The draft is done in the following way. All names are written on small slips of paper and put in a box and a man who is blindfolded draws as many slips as are required from the town and if your name is drawn you either have to go or have someone who hasn't sworn an oath of loyalty go in your stead, because the law that made it possible to pay 300 dollars to be exempted has been revoked. No one has been drafted from our town because in this year alone we raised about 8,000 dollars to pay for volunteers to take our place. But 300,000 men will be drafted February 8 and we haven't raised money for our share both because it's difficult to find volunteers and because we are now taxed so heavily that we first squander our savings and then have to go to war. Our country's debt is so enormous that I cannot describe it. The war takes more than a million dollars a day. So now the good times are over and everything has become expensive and there is a war duty on almost everything. I'll mention what some things cost before the war and what they cost now. Coffee was fifteen and is now sixty cents, sugar eight is now twenty-five cents, tobacco was thirty-five to forty and is now one dollar, and liquor used to cost thirty to fifty cents a gallon and now costs two to five dollars. Cloth was ten cents a yard and is now eighty to ninety cents. And you cannot write a valid receipt without a stamp called a revenue stamp. There is even a war tax on matches. You may not know the reason for this war. There were thirty-three states that were united and governed by one president who is in office for one year. But every state has its own government and takes care of its own state affairs. Slavery is the reason for the war. In 1776, at the time a part of North America separated itself from England and was called the United States, the constitution allowed Negro slaves in the Southern States up to a certain latitude if the people in the state voted to have slaves. But in the Northern States people couldn't have slaves even if they wanted them. Since 1776 we have had presidents from the Democratic Party who supported the constitution and protected foreigners, and everything flourished. But then came a party called the Republican Party and they came to power in 1860 and elected Abraham Lincoln as President. When he took office he made a declaration that all Negroes who were held as slaves should be made free and taken from their masters without compensation. For this reason all the slave states left the Union and went to war against us because they didn't want to have their property taken from them since many of them owned several hundred Negroes. I don't belong to the Republican Party and I haven't elected Lincoln who has now been reelected for another four years so the prospects for an end to the war are not good. Even though slavery is a bad thing and should be abolished, it should not be done in such a manner. It would have been much better if we had bought freedom for the slaves, yes given their weight in gold, and not started a war. England supports the South as they believe that the South has a right to secede and have their own government. The North wants to force them but we must ask if this is possible because we still haven't won a major victory even though there have been battles that have lasted for three, four, yes even six full days and in some twenty to thirty-five thousand men have been killed and even more have been wounded and entire regiments have been terminated. The Scandinavian Fifteenth Wisconsin Regiment has been almost terminated and many people from Flesberg have died in the war, such as Levor H. Letmolia and Ole Gulbrandsen Sætra and many more that I cannot remember.

    Then we have the wild Indians in the West, in the Dakota and Nebraska Territories, who rebelled two years ago and murdered about 900 white people in their homes and ravaged and burned wherever they went. They were only 100 miles away and we have been afraid and have had to keep an army against them. They have now been forced further west so that we have no more reason to be afraid. The reason for this rebellion was that the government did not pay them their annual pension as they were once the owners of the entire country.

Our money system is weak. There is no other money than that issued by the United States and everything is in paper, yes even a cent. There is no circulation of gold and silver and in New York a gold dollar costs two dollars and twenty-five cents. But the worst of all is all the widows and orphans and cripples that are the result of this terrible war and these are a just punishment for our great sins and our godlessness. God grant that it may serve to make things better and make us reflect and pray that God may make things better than they now are. And we must thank God for bountiful harvests so that we have had enough for our daily bread. Many go to Canada to avoid the draft and I think that I may have to do this because I don't want to go to war if I in any way can avoid it. Imagine becoming a cripple for all my days, but as the adage goes, in greater need the nearer help, so the Lord may make things better than they now seem to us mortals. I will advise my relatives and friends that it is better that they stay at home in the land of their birth until things change here even though wages are significantly higher now and a hired man is paid twelve to fourteen dollars a month in winter and twenty to twenty-five dollars a month in summer, and during harvest the pay is two to four dollars a day.

I have no news for you as none of our acquaintances have married recently. Gullik Andersen Lande is dead. I had a letter from Hvashovd a month ago and they are all in good health except that old Kjersti had been ill for some time but was then getting better. I must now end my letter and pray to the almighty God that we may one day be joyfully gathered in our heavenly home where there will be no separation. I hope that these lines may find you all in good health and well-being in body and soul. Nor must you my dear father grieve for us and nor will we in any way blame you should we be taken by the storm of war, because we emigrated of our own free choice in the hope of finding a country where it would be easier to earn our daily bread, as it indeed has been up to now. No, no one can know what is to be. Finally, our regards to my father and mother from me and my wife and daughter, to my siblings and to all friends and all who wish to hear from us. I wish you all well in this world and the next. Farewell in the Lord from your unforgettable son and family,

HELLIK OLSEN LEHOVD

· —— ·

Noted at the bottom of the letter: "Received 5/2 65." Lauritz Steen was pastor in Rock Dell, Minn., 1861–1868. «I:107 »I:III NE II:116

· —— ·

1864 — LETTER I:111

From: Ole Olson Lehovd, *Madison, Wisconsin, 29 December 1864*
To: Ole Helgesen and Joran Paulsdatter Lehovd, *Flesberg, Buskerud*

⁂

Dear unforgettable parents and siblings,

As I now have time and opportunity I must write you some lines. I've received your letter dated last March but as I've now moved from where I lived last summer I cannot remember the exact date you wrote it. We see that you are doing well and I'm glad that you were in good health and that you had made improvements on your houses, for which you must be glad. I also see that you've had to cut down your forest and this is a great setback, but it may be as God has intended and it may be that Gulbrand G. Haugen was acquainted with God's intention when he began cutting in your forest at the time I was about to leave my home for what I assume was the last time. I have no news except that my brother and his family were in good health and doing reasonably well, but he may have written to you and you'll then know more about his situation and he will have told you what you asked about. I recently had a letter from him. As I have enough paper and I don't have much to write about I can let you know that Hellik's wife is named Brita Olsdatter Rørvig. Her parents came from Norway two years ago last summer with three of their children and they all live with Hellik. At the time I left, the old man was building a house next to Hellik's and old Ole Rørvig is married for the third time and has all his children in this country. I believe they are eight in all and they all except one live in Minnesota. Two girls and one boy are unmarried and they live with Hellik when they aren't working so it is quite nice for him with all his wife's people around him. But as far as I could gather in the short time I was there he won't be burdened by his share of his wife's inheritance. Ole Rørvig was once a wealthy man in Norway but because of drink and negligence he is now a man who depends on others for support. But all this is of course none of my concern one way or the other. I recently had a letter from Hellik where he told me that he had harvested 186 bushels of wheat, forty-six of oats and ten of barley and that he had sold forty acres of his poorest land last summer but had enough left for the work of one man. Gulbrand Toresen is a neighbor but he doesn't have a regular home and goes around from one to the other, mainly at Ole Flata's, a very outspoken Democrat who now wants to escape to Canada because Lincoln has been reelected and he doesn't want to serve him and his administration. Ole Flata has become wealthy in Minnesota and has been lucky in acquiring land and has a large and good farm with forest and meadows and nice buildings and good fields, but he's very weak and has someone use his land every year.

I left Wisconsin and moved to Minnesota in April of last year and bought eighty acres, all of it prairie and without a single tree but with excellent soil. Last spring I went further west where there is government land to be had but the land with forest was taken. I was where the Indians had gone to war so I saw much destruction where they had been. They had not only destroyed farms but also burned down important towns. Last summer an innumerable mass of people moved west to take land as you can have 160 acres for twelve to thirteen dollars. I worked there for some time last summer on the railroad that has been completed to a town named Rochester about twelve miles from where Hellik lives and the land is increasing in price for this reason. Minnesota had a good year last summer, while in Wisconsin the crop failed on many farms because of a kind of fly that settles on the wheat before it is ready and destroys most of it. Minnesota hasn't been visited by this plague and there was good work to be had in the wheat as I had from three to four and a half dollars a day for four weeks, and this is because of the war as so many have gone. Last fall I worked for a time on a steamboat on the Mississippi and the boat I was on went between La Crosse in Wisconsin and Winona in Minnesota. This is very hard work both night and day, carrying loads that are heavy enough to kill you. And most of those who work on the boats are Irish who are the worst kind of people you can be with and who do nothing but drink and fight and live like pigs in the dirt so their homes are a terrible sight. They live for the most part in towns along the railroad where they set up sheds made of boards and in winter they pile cow dung on the outside of the sheds halfway up the windows. And you may imagine that this decorates the towns. So you can see that I've tried a lot of hard work in this country so you shouldn't think that I have just enjoyed myself here.

But it's not only the hard work that I have found difficult here but also other troubles and hardships because the world has its worries here too. I enjoyed myself more in Wisconsin than in Minnesota, but I don't want to tell you about this as I may not see Minnesota nor those I knew in Wisconsin any more in this life as I am behind locked gates and fortifications and cannot go where I want. I have in other words been recruited and the almighty God is my witness that I've been sworn into the United States Army. This was on October 17 in La Crosse and I'll have to serve for one year, which is what I agreed to when I was sworn in. I haven't been drafted but I'm what they call a *substitute*, one who has signed up instead of a drafted man, a German from Dunn County, Wisconsin. I came out from a saloon and met this man who asked me what I would take to go in his stead. I said 700 dollars and he said I'll give it to you. Then it was *all right* and we were taken to Madison on the nineteenth. But I got sick right away and was brought to the hospital November 1 and I was sick for a long time. In English my illness is called *Pleurit Fever*. It gave me pain in my chest, mostly on the right side and an intense pain in my stomach that I still have since anything I eat makes me sick and weak so when I come to the South I fear that my life will not be long if I cannot be cured. I was almost well a while ago but then I got sick again and he who had this room made it worse rather than better but he has now been fired from the hospital. This doctor was a Norwegian fake who is now said to have gone to hell. We can see many of the consequences of the war here, a lot of wounded men, some have lost a leg and others an arm and many have wounds in their legs and arms and shoulders and it isn't nice to see so many wounds. There are many here who have to use crutches and we often see those who are in the throes of death. On Christmas Day there was one who had his throat cut as when an animal is killed and had a tube inserted there so he could breathe. The sick are taken quite good care of here with nice and clean bedclothes and a good bed. The rooms are long and there are two rows of beds, one along each wall and with a passage between them and each bed has a number. On the wall above each bed is a piece of paper where the name, age and much else is written. When my illness was at its worst I had a letter from Hellik that he hadn't received my money for going to war and this made me sad. I wrote to those who were supposed to send me my money at the office in La Crosse and I was answered that my money was there and that it would be sent that very day. I wasn't called up at the time I was to go from La Crosse but when some soldiers came a few days later I was called up. The reason, they said, was that they didn't know where I was. But I was afraid of taking my money to Madison as I was almost sure it would have been stolen from me as 1,600 dollars have recently been stolen from men who have gone instead of some who were drafted. There is a lot of theft here and they steal money and clothes from each other and many have escaped from the camp. This camp is a large area fenced with a high board fence and with guards all along the fence. But if you really want to go over the fence you can do so. You may imagine that in these four years many who have been here are now resting in their graves as the last regiment formed here in Wisconsin is the forty-fifth. But many soldiers have gone into the old regiments and all who were drafted last fall were placed in old regiments and now 3,000,000 men have been drafted to meet February 15, and I believe this will continue.

I enjoyed reading that Christopher Hovengen was such an oaf. I can imagine that Beret Bergrud would sniff her nose when such trouble came upon her daughter. I remember when our family was said to have started the rumor that Ole Ellefsen was wooing her, which I have heard people here say was true, but those imps who are dishonoring her with their lies are also slandering us. But I don't think there is much honor in being as she now is. And now the rich man's daughter at Gjellerud is also comforting her baby on her lap while looking for its father, but the rich must also suffer some adversities. And Paul Høymyr has now entered into holy matrimony and thus put the other brave bachelors to shame. I've heard old Anne Tullerud say that Paul would never be married because he was too fond of this world and that Ole Høymyr had practiced usury on her. She holds on tight to her money so you may believe that I asked her to forgive him his sins but it didn't seem that she could, so I said forgive and you shall be forgiven. I sent your letter on to Hvashovd as they cannot well afford to pay for a letter so it's better that the one who has to slave for every cent should pay for it.

Times are good for farmers as the prices for wheat as well as for butter and pork are good, so it's better for farmers than it will be for me next year when I'll probably be exposed to hunger and suffering in bad weather and illness and being killed or wounded with great pain and crippled for life. I would rather die than be severely wounded. But I'll pray to my God that he for the sake of Christ's blood will make my last hour good. The soldiers don't think much about their salvation, except perhaps a few, and they commit the gravest sins imaginable. I've heard that when dying in battle they can let out streams of curses. I'm not saying that I'm going to die in this war and I may come back unharmed, so you must not grieve or in any way be anxious for my sake. You should rather work as usual and take care of each other. If I have committed any sin that has brought harm to any of you I must ask your forgiveness for my offense as I know that in the wildness of youth I let the devil govern me as he so often may govern a human being and I may have mocked you and even led you into sin. So I'll ask both you and God to forgive me. Since these may be the last words I write to you I'll thank you for the time I spent with you. May you live together in harmony and peace so you'll have better days in this life as well as in the next. You can write to Hellik when you receive this letter, but you must write on thin paper as the letters from Norway are so expensive. Hellik will send it on to me. And you must write about many things.

    I may have scared you in writing that food is expensive as I saw in an earlier letter that you were glad that food was cheap. But when food is expensive there is money to go around as it is all brought to the towns. Here they haul wheat like coal is hauled at home and they have built large buildings to store the wheat by the railroad and there is an open chute outside the building where they can drive their wagons of wheat and empty them. I send greetings from Marit Teksle and her children. They are all well and they moved from Wisconsin to Minnesota last summer and they are living with some people from Hallingdal quite near Hellik since they haven't yet built on their own land. They bought eighty acres of prairie land close to my land last summer. Ole Teksle is now in debt even though he is an important person, and he doesn't work hard, as his mother doesn't want him to do much. Beret and Joran are working in Rochester. I've had a letter from Hvashovd and they are all well and you can tell their relatives that they are quite successful. You don't have to copy this letter and remove anything but let every iota stand and let any who wishes to see it see it as it is, because it is written by a soldier. I wish that these lines will find you alive and in good health,

OLE LEHOVD

> Letters were often copied so they could be shared with others and, as the conclusion of this letter suggests, parts of letters that were considered private may then have been omitted. «I:110 »I:113 NE II:117

1865 — LETTER I:112

From: Svend Larsen Houg, *Elgin, Iowa, 17 April 1865*
To: Ole Larsen Haug, *Aal, Buskerud*

My often remembered siblings,

I should have written a long time ago, but I must confess that my indifference and negligence have caused this delay. But now I will use my pen to tell you that God in his grace has kept us all in good health since I last wrote. When we speak with each other we usually ask whether your family is in good health and when the answer is yes, we say that God is owed thanks—and this is true. Oh, may we fully appreciate his grace, for it is in the days of our bodily health that we should seek the health of our soul, but I often feel that worldly matters are at the center of my attention and that the spiritual is set aside as less important. Oh, that I and all of us may hold to the Lord and seek the grace that is offered us all in Christ, for there is no other name given to us for salvation than the name of Jesus Christ.

I will now tell you brother Ole that John Fjeld ceased to be our pastor last spring because of the long distance and his poor health. You may imagine that we feel a great loss since he was a preacher of repentance. We had to have a congregation so we saw no other solution than to join the others even though we don't think much of the pastor. The majority praises him as a good preacher as he doesn't make the road to heaven very narrow, nor does he make it difficult for people to be Christians. But we must follow the eighth commandment and forgive and speak well, etc. But it would have been good to have a pastor who could give us the correct word of truth. We now have a school teacher for ten months of the year, but even this is not enough as he is responsible for such a large area. The law requires us to have an English school. My two oldest sons have learned a little English as it is necessary for the coming generation to learn the language of the country and not be as simpleminded as us. I won't say much about my worldly possessions even though I now have had a good income. But God has confided in me a greater possession in my children, and so many souls bought with the blood of Jesus are far more than any worldly property. I have ten children, eight boys and two girls. The youngest is one year old and is named for our uncle Elling. Oh, what a responsibility for me as a father for the upbringing of these young souls.

The harvest was quite good around here but somewhat variable. They say that it was a very poor year in Wisconsin and that a small fly destroyed the crop. It was here too but it didn't cause much damage. As for the war, I cannot tell you anything about it because it would be too complicated for me even though we have newspapers so that I have the news every week. The war is still going on, but this winter much has happened and it seems that the South is sinking further and further to their downfall. Note that it is some time since I last wrote on this letter and we have now had more news from the war and the latest news is that the top general of the South has had to surrender with his whole army. There were bloody battles before this so we have good reason to hope that the war will soon be over. I wish that the Lord would at some time visit the south for its barbaric deeds. — I heard some terrible news from the war this morning but it was only a rumor so I won't mention it.

I must conclude these simpleminded lines as I am such a poor writer. I send greetings from your relatives from Groth and they are all doing well. Three of them are still at the age where they may be drafted but this has not yet been their fate. My old mother-in-law is alive and lives for the most part with me. I recently had a letter from Assor where he tells me that three of his children have been called by the Lord. They died one after the other of a throat disease and he expresses his grief. You are all lovingly greeted from me and my wife and all our children. May God in his grace help me and us all through his Spirit that we may labor for the Salvation of our Soul now when we still have time.

Some words for my brother Lars.

Some time ago Assor Groth sent me a letter saying that Svend Skrattegard and his sons have sent documents to Nils Gudmundsrud claiming their allodial right to Skrattegard and I assume that this case has already been taken far. According my view as well as that of many others here, Svend Skrattegard's oldest son has no right to property in Norway as he has taken land here and has taken an oath under this country's constitution. So he cannot have any rights in Norway. The younger sons haven't taken land yet, nor have they taken an oath. But in his letter Assor says that they all intend to do this, so I don't think Lars should pay for the allodial rights. It may be that Nils Knutsen has or will get the authorization of the younger sons to apply, and he may have the right to do so. But I cannot understand that he is so powerful a man that he can do this. These lines may not be useful but I wanted you to know.

SVEND LARSEN HOUG

Since I have some space left I'll tell you what I didn't wish to write about in the middle of my letter. That was three days ago and now we know for certain; our dear president was shot in front of his house either on Wednesday or on Thursday before Easter, we don't know for sure yet. This is a sad happening as we cannot expect to have another man like him to govern our country. God alone now knows.

> SLH wrote this letter over several days. The date is most likely the date it was sent: by that time the "terrible news" that had been a rumor had become a certainty (Lincoln was assassinated on April 14). Evidently SLH began writing the second half of the letter just after he had had the news of the surrender at Appomattox on April 9. Congregations, particularly in the Norwegian Synod, often had a parochial school, usually as a complement to the public school that immigrants called the English school. This teacher would have moved around from congregation to congregation, teaching a month or two in each. SLH could not read English. The newspapers he could subscribe to at this early date were *Emigranten*, published in Wisconsin from 1852, and *Fædrelandet*, also in Wisconsin from 1864. They merged in 1868. The transactions implied in his note to his brother Lars may seem complicated. In Norway allodial law ensured the right of the oldest son to acquire the undivided farm. This right would descend to younger brothers should the older one die or not wish to have the farm. Svend Olsen, farmer at Skrattegard, sold his farm to Lars Larsen Haug in 1862 and emigrated with his family. As a soldier, Ole Svendsen, the oldest son, had sworn loyalty to the United States whether he then was a citizen or not. The question raised here is whether he then had the rights of a Norwegian citizen. Nothing came of this and Lars Larsen continued to have Skrattegard. Nils Knutsen Gudmundsrud was mayor of Aal from 1840 to 1863 and this is the reason he was involved. He was the father of Gro Svendsen, whose letters are well known, and the pastor Ole Nilsen. He was the grandfather of Sigrid Nilsdatter who married a son of Gro Svendsen and who has many letters in this edition. SLH also wrote on 30 April 1866 (Nor. ed. II:133). «I:90 »I:147 NE II:119

1865 — LETTER I:113

FROM: Hellik and Ole Olson Lehovd, *Salem, Minnesota, 8 June 1865*
TO: Ole Helgesen and Joran Paulsdatter Lehovd, *Flesberg, Buskerud*

⋅→≡◉⋐⋅⋅

Dear parents and siblings!

I've read your letter of February 19 and see that you were in good health for which we must thank God! I must tell you that I've returned to Minnesota as I was discharged from service on May 4 in Madison. But I didn't get my last month's pay until May 31 and I didn't get my money from him I had gone to war for until the Eve of Pentecost, when I received my 700 dollars in La Crosse. I was given an honorable discharge and I don't think it can be said that I did anything wrong. I did my duty, obeyed the officers and went where I was told. But I admit I was lucky. When I got well I was sent to another hospital to take care of sick soldiers, so I didn't have to go to the South. Actually, I was taken from the hospital at the end of April and placed in the Wisconsin Fifty-First Regiment, K Company. We were given guns, but just as we were ready to leave orders came that no more solders were needed and we were all discharged. I worked mostly in the kitchen as there were three to four hundred men in the hospital. Many died while I was there, almost three or four every day. Most died of the measles.

You'll be glad to know that I'm quite well, just as good as before, and that I have more than 850 dollars in money and clothes for these seven months, so I made good money for risking my life. I had better luck than I had expected; many of those who went when I did have died and many have been crippled for life. I had to pay for my ticket home since the government pays to wherever you enlisted. And I had a nice trip in the wonderful railroad car at great speed over the American prairies as a free man. I was happier when I went home than when I left, not knowing whether I would ever come back.

I must end my poor letter as I don't have much more to write about. I hope that these lines will find you in good health. I hope that you'll soon write to me or to Hellik as I'll pay for the letters even though you say that you'll pay. You probably have enough expenses and your income may not be much more than your expenses in your poor old mountain country. And as for my coming back to you as your son and brother, it may be a good thing. But I am not so eager to do this yet as I now have survived the worst and have acquired a fair fortune considering the few years I've been here; it's only four years since I was on the blue Atlantic. It is worst when you first come to this country where any ignorant and crude Norwegian who has been here a while—even if he cannot speak a word of English— may act the gentleman and lord it over the poor newcomer. But times have changed and I can be as clever as any other. I'm grateful for all your kindness and if we live as we should in this life we may be together after this life is over. You must live together in harmony and love, and I'll certainly forgive any sins you may have committed against me, but I believe that my own sins against you are greater than yours against me. I hope that you'll write and tell us what is new. Give my regards to those at Bergerud and to Levor Fikkan. First and foremost, greetings to my dear parents and to Paul, Knud, and Joran! I wish you health and all that is good. Farewell in God!

OLE OLSON LEHOVD

Dear parents and siblings,

On this occasion I must sit down and write a few lines far more glad in my heart than I was before because my dear brother has returned to me in good health. He has been very lucky and made more money in these few years than any we know in this country. We must thank God that the war has come to an end and that so many soldiers have already come home to their dear family and friends. I can tell you that I and my family are well and in good health and my daughter is growing big. I don't have much new to tell you except that Niri Hansen Dyrboeiet was married last winter, after he came home from the war, with Maren Sørine Testman from Land parish, born in Christiania and the daughter of a merchant there. She has been in America since she was quite young and is well educated, in particular in the English language, as she has been teacher in a regular English school. As for the times here, the prices for the products we sell have fallen significantly since the war changed in favor of the North, as money in gold has fallen in value and paper money has gone up. And the products we have to buy have also fallen in price but not as much as the prices for what we sell. Wages too have fallen. But our taxes are enormous. Last winter was nice and mild and we had little snow, but spring was late and we didn't have grass for our cattle until the middle of May. But now fields and meadows look good. Levor Torstensen Hvashovd was here in April to have a look at Minnesota. His family was in good health except for his grandmother who kept to her bed last winter. They were very glad that you remembered them in your last letter and for the news about their family in Norway. I must now end my letter with loving regards from me and my wife to all my family and friends, to you my unforgettable father; and to you my brothers Paul and Knud and my sister Jøran even though it is now so long since you saw me that you may not remember me as you were so young when I left. But I know that your thoughts of your brother in a distant country never will be extinguished in your hearts. Finally, my regards to you my dear mother and my thanks for your last letter where you ask our forgiveness for any resentment we may have. I will of course forgive you as it makes me glad to hear that you have your God and Savior in mind and regret your past sins and that when the hour of death is upon you, you will be ready to leave this earthly life and enter the eternal mansions and enjoy the happiness of being with our dear Lord and Savior where there will be no more grief and worry. This is your son's wish. I hope that this letter will find you all in good health.

HELLIK OLSEN LEHOVD

HOL wrote on April 18 and May 29 (Nor. ed. II:120 and 121). In the first he wrote of his joy at the surrender of General Lee on April 8, and in the second he told his father that he had sent him some newspapers and offered him a subscription if he would pay the Norwegian postage. He had not then heard from Ole. Maren Testman was the daughter of Wilhelm Testman who emigrated in 1838 and came to Iowa the following year in a group that included Hans Barlien and Cleng Peerson (Semmingsen 1941, 58). «I:111 »I:122 NE II:122

1865 — LETTER I:114

FROM: Rakel Tonette Aslakson, *Coon Prairie, Wisconsin, 22 June 1865*
To: Osmund Atlaksen Ovedal, *Sirdal, Vest-Agder*

My good friend Osmund Atlakson Ovedahl,

As I now have an opportunity I'll write you some lines about our journey and our situation in America. All went well across the ocean and also on the train up through the country. We're doing well, are in good health and are quite comfortable. We've liked America very much in the time we've been here. We came to Coon Prairie June 9 and our voyage across the Atlantic took thirty days in very nice weather. We had all we needed and were in good health on the entire voyage as well as on the train up through the country to La Crosse where Sigbjørn met us and drove us home to Coon Prairie. Apart from this I cannot give you much information since we haven't been here long enough, but we can say that America is better than Norway in how people live and other things, and we can say that all the letters that are sent from America to Norway are true as we find everything to be much as it has been described.

Reinert lives about 150 miles north of here and he will soon visit us. Sivert is in the war and Sigbjørn had a letter from him saying that he was doing well and was in good health. We think he'll soon be home. He has land in Minnesota about 200 miles further west where Thron Hoversen lives. At Sigbjørn's they have a little girl named Olene and all in our family are well. We couldn't recognize any at Ovedal or Metfjelds since everything has changed in the last years. They all live well at Metfjelds as do all others around here. Please give my regards to Skibeli and Konstali and let them know that we have crossed the ocean to America in good health and are enjoying ourselves. We haven't been long in America but we don't wish to be back in Norway. It may be that we will change our mind in the future but we cannot know this now. We waited about four hours in La Crosse before Sigbjørn came to us but we got a message that he was on his way. I have no more to write about except for greetings to all acquaintances. Ask

Olene and Siri Skibeli whether they'll come to America since I like it so well here. I know that Siri will confirm my words that America is a great country, most of all for women since the work is much lighter. Tell Anna Haughom that we met Lars Elias in Quebec and that he went with us to La Crosse were he got work. We have greetings from Siri Gabrielsdatter to Osmund Gabrielsen Ovedal that she is in good health. Until I get to know things better I'll live with Hover Ovedal. I've been here too short a time to say anything of importance except that I like what I've seen of America so far. We don't know of any more to write about now except to send our regards to all acquaintances. Farewell,

RAKEL TONETTE ASLAKSDATTER AND HER SISTER

. ———— .

Rakel Tonette (twenty-four) and Siri (twenty-eight) Aslaksdatter Ovedal and Siri Gabrielsdatter Ovedal (thirty) emigrated on the bark *Hebe* from Stavanger on 28 April 1865 and arrived in Quebec on May 29. Their brothers in Sirdal, Osmund Atlaksen and Osmund Gabrielsen, each had one of the six Ovedal farms in 1865. In Norway patronymics had masculine and feminine forms. In their new country, however, women soon adopted the masculine form so that Rakel Atlaksdatter became Rakel Aslakson. Rakel calls the immigrants' farms by the names of the farms they came from in Norway: Ovedal and Metfjelds (Midtfjeldsaa). After coming to Coon Prairie she lived with her mother's brother Hover Sigbjørnsen Ovedal. «I:109 »I:116 NE II:124

. ———— .

1865 — LETTER I:115

From: Elise Wærenskjold, *Four Mile Prairie, Texas*
spring or summer of 1865
To: Thomine Dannevig, *Lillesand, Norway*

⤛═◉═⤜

My dear Thomine,

As you see I'm in a hurry to write to you; we haven't yet had any mail and we don't know when it will come, but I'm confident that it cannot be much longer and therefore I write to you now in the hope that it will find you well and alive. I long to hear from you. I have at times amused myself with reading old letters and I took up one of yours where you tell me about your boys and promise to send me a portrait of Thorvald. My dear Thomine! You must not forget this promise but send it as soon as possible. I don't know whether Mr. Trumpy still lives in New Orleans but I should regardless receive your letter if it is sent to the Norwegian consul there. I suppose Thorvald doesn't remember me at all. He was probably about five when I left and I can remember from when I was three and a half, so he may remember me, especially since he was such an exceptionally intelligent child and was so fond of me. How strange it would be if I should see him again as a young man and in a way a stranger even though I have loved him as my own child. My eyes still fill with tears when I think of you. It was far from my thoughts when I said farewell to you that it would be for so long, perhaps forever. How many pleasant hours we had together in the home of your brother! Hours that will never be extinguished from my memory. And as part of this memory, the image of the sweet little angel, who now apparently has grown up to be an equally pleasant young man. Perhaps Thorvald will please an old lady, who loved him so and who will always remain his motherly friend, with a few lines from his hand? As for you, my dear friend, I hope you will send me a long letter as soon as you receive this. After my children, my greatest pleasure is to have letters from my loved ones in Norway and Denmark.

I cannot forget old friends and don't put much effort into establishing new friendships. I don't seek company; I go wherever I have an errand, especially when Wærenskjold is away from home, but rarely when he is here. We have many visitors but there are few who interest me. Two Germans who were here last winter were an exception to this rule. They reminded me of the time I lived in Norway when I so often could take pleasure in the company of well-bred and well-informed men. But this was only true of the nobleman. The baker was no better bred than people are here; but he was much more polite. I would have liked Wærenskjold to be home but he was then enjoying himself in Bosque. People made quite a fuss about him there and he is much better at striking new friendships than I am. Vilhelm and the children and Miss Frederikke are with one of our neighbors today but I preferred to stay home.

We never all leave the house at the same time. There has been more theft since the war began. The war brought so much nastiness, for instance scab. The soldiers got it in the camps and brought it home to their families and now it is widespread. The children and I had it last year. It is said that troubles never come singly and this seems to be confirmed now: when the war began the grass disappeared from our prairies and we got weeds that the animals won't eat instead. This wasn't only unexpected; it had great consequences as it destroyed our most important industry. In the winters of '63 and '64 we lost forty-seven milk cows and many more calves and heifers. We lost so many sheep that we had a smaller number at the end of the year than at the beginning. But we haven't actually regressed, merely stood still. It was much better last year, partly because the winter wasn't so cold and partly because I fed the cows more corn. I bought corn for cloth as our own crop was far from sufficient. Wærenskjold was away so I did as I found best. I let the sheep graze in the rye and they did very well. We had an unusually wet winter with steady rain for more than three months so we could hardly use the roads. This made it difficult to work in our fields. Last year was exceptionally cold and the thermometer showed four degrees below zero on New Year's Day and the ice stayed a long time so the animals were thirsty as well as cold and hungry. God knows why they didn't all die!

We would have liked to move if we could sell for what our property is worth, but I doubt this will be possible. Vilhelm has talked about going to Oregon, but I would rather go to the northern states where there are many Norwegians and better communication with Norway. I would love to visit Norway in a year or two and have Otto and Niels confirmed there. Niels is almost as big as Otto; but Otto is more handsome. Niels is the one who looks most like me. Thorvald is a very nice little boy and mommy's pet. Otto and Niels are very good at herding cattle and pigs and you must know that this is not an easy thing to do and requires a very practiced horse rider, not merely because it so often has to be done at a full gallop, but even more because the animals try to get away by running into dense brush, crossing over deep streams etc. The cattle are almost wild. I wish I could boast of my boys as good scholars, but there has been little school during the war and they have regrettably not inherited their parents' interest in reading. Vilhelm reads as much as I do.

My loving regards to your husband and your two sons as well as to your old parents if they still are alive, and your brothers and their wives, in particular the good Alida who might send me a few lines. Give my most friendly regards to Bina Grøgaard and all those you talk with who may still have friendly thoughts of me. There may not be many. And you my dear Thomine must send me a long letter with information about you and yours and our common friends and all else that you know will interest me. The day I receive your first letter will be one of celebration. May it only not contain too much sorrowful news! Farewell, dear Thomine, and remember your always devoted

ELISE WÆRENSKJOLD

· —— ·

This letter (not in Clausen 1961) is one in a batch of the first letters EW wrote after the war. Thomine Dannevig was married to Lars Tellefsen Dannevig. James Trumpy was Norwegian consul in New Orleans. In a sentence on scab in the family some words have been cut out, making it unreadable. «1:85 »1:119 NE II:125

· —— ·

1865 — LETTER I:116

FROM: Siri and Rakel Tonette Aslakson, *Coon Prairie, Wisconsin*
20 December 1865
TO: Osmund and Berent Atlaksen and Sara Atlaksdatter Ovedal
Bakke, Sirdal, Vest-Agder

⋆⇒◦⇐⋆

Dear siblings,

I'll take my pen in hand to let you know that we now are in good health. It has been up and down. Siri was so sick that we thought she would die. She got sick September 28 and was in bed five weeks. But she is now well and we are all well and Sivert has come home from the war. He came November 10 but he had first been to Minnesota. Reinert hasn't been here yet even though he said he would be here as soon as we came. But we expect him before Christmas. When we wrote to you June 22, Olene was in good health but at six in the morning of the twenty-third she got sick and was dead at six in the afternoon. Life is very uncertain. So it is important to seek what is certain and what never fails. I am quite satisfied here. We asked Sivert if he wanted to go home, but he answered that he didn't want to go to Norway.

We would like to know if any of you want to come here and if you do you should either all come or none. If you come you'll be welcome. Bring scarves and wooden clogs because they are very useful on the voyage and not available here. Have warm clothes on the journey. We sailed among huge icebergs and it was so cold that we almost died. We were sick for a day but then all was well. If any neighbors are thinking of coming they should bring blue, red and green cotton thread since they only have white here. We'll pay for it when you arrive. But you must keep an eye on everything on your journey inland. If you have anything new you should either sew a patch on it or have it among old clothes because we were inspected by customs officers and it cost a lot to have it with us. Pack your things in old barrels or strong wooden boxes. In new chests you should have old things. Both old and new are useful here. Bring large headscarves. Here they cost eleven or twelve dollars and we haven't seen small ones. It doesn't cost anything extra to bring things whether you have a lot or a little. When you come to Quebec you should take the train and not the steamship.

Siri says that she likes it here. I haven't longed for home since I came. There is work to be had indoors and outdoors. I've mostly been at Sigbjørn's but Rakel has been many places. When I was sick she came here and was sick for two weeks but was for the most part on her feet. There has been much illness here and a lot of typhus. Many have died and others have become well after a long illness. Karen Tonette was sick for sixteen weeks, Nils Tobias six weeks, Sara two weeks, Henrik five weeks, Rakel Tonette Trondsdatter five weeks, Anna Berte was sick for three weeks and died October 2, Regine and Severine for seven weeks, and Ole Tobias for five weeks. Stine Maria is also sick and now Johannes Vermunsen is very sick. All have been sick at Gabriel's since Peder Christian died. Sivert thinks of going to work in the forest. Sigbjørn's harvest this year was 300 bushels of wheat and 400 bushels of barley and they have six cows, eight sheep, three pigs and countless hens. We are all doing well. We have a Norwegian church and a Norwegian pastor and God's word is heard here as in Norway almost every Sunday.

Rakel Tonette asks Sara to say to her aunt in Skibeli that she must write and tell her all news. She doesn't want to return to Norway but would like to see some of you here. If some of you are coming you must write as soon as possible and bring many reeds for our loom, from fifteen to twenty. We cannot get them here. Now we have written as much as we know. Now you must write us a long letter. Rakel has been with Sigbjørn for two months and since then she has worked for others and her wage has been one and a half dollars a week. I must ask you to excuse my poor letter. We have written as we have remembered things and you must study it carefully to make sense of it. We'll now close with our regards to you all.

SIRI ASLAGSEN   RAKEL TONETE ASLAGSEN

Both sisters seem to have shared in the writing, referring to each other partly by name and partly with the first person singular and plural pronouns. A brief note by Siri Gabrielsdatter to Sara Atlaksdatter and some lists of names of people in Sirdal have been omitted. The sisters are surrounded by family and people who used to be their neighbors in Norway. Nils Tobias Pedersen Øksendal, Sara Haaversdatter and Fredrik Haaversen Gousdal, Anne Berte Tallaksdatter Nedland, Gabriel Gabrielsen Jødestøl, his wife Siri and their children, among them

Peder Christian (13), were all fellow passengers on the bark *Hebe* in 1865. Regine, Severine and Ole Tobias were the children of Sivert and Anne Midtfjeldsaa who had emigrated on the bark *Emigrant* from Flekkefjord in 1852. The sisters may have had some difficulties with customs on entering the United States from Canada. Several letters warn about customs inspections. «I:114 »I:135 NE II:128

1866 — LETTER I:117

FROM: Barbro Tollefsdatter Sando, *Estherville, Iowa, 14 January 1866*
To: Guri Tollefsdatter Bøygard and Randi Tollefsdatter Opheim
Aal, Buskerud

Dear and unforgettable sisters!

I was very glad to receive letters from you with the happy news that you my dear sisters and your families are in good health. It is so good for me to hear that all was well with you. So I'm now sending my thanks to you Guri and to you Randi for your dear letters, yes, I'm sending as many thanks as can be carried to you by this small piece of paper. I've taken up my pen to give you a brief impression of how I and my family are living and I can tell you that they are all in good health and we are comfortable in our new home. As for myself my health is still very poor and I don't expect to be well until death will liberate me from my frailty and my corporal weakness. Our six children are with us and I was so lucky that none of my sons had to go to war and now we have peace. I hope that I'll never again suffer the grief of war. Our three oldest sons have been confirmed and the fourth, Halvor, will be confirmed next summer. They are all intelligent and well-informed about our religion. Our youngest son, Gjermund, is six and a good reader.

I see you are surprised that we have changed our address and I'll briefly explain this. When our sons Erik and Tollef decided to find free government land that now can be had at a low price, we decided to sell our land because we didn't want to be separated from them but instead try to live close to each other. We were successful and we now have a quarter section or 160 acres each. Our land is side by side so we can all be together. I haven't spoken with Lars Sando yet but he intends to come here next spring and I hope to speak with him then if we are still alive. Thank you for your news about our siblings and their families. I've recently heard a rumor that our brother Ole the elder is planning to go to America but I don't know if this is true. Please tell me about this when you write to us and also about where he intends to go, if it is his intention to come.

I must conclude my brief and imperfect letter with the wish that it may find you my dear relatives in the best of health. I'm unable to write something for your edification or encouragement. Nor am I able to interpret for you what my heart so longs to speak to you; my heart is full but my pen is too imperfect. So I will merely write my wish that we may see each other again in the eternal mansions where there will be no more separation. So farewell all of you and may our Lord be with us. This is my highest wish. Your faithful sister

BARBRO TOLLEFSDATTER

BTS died in 1903. Her brother Ole Tollefsen Opsata emigrated in 1866. «I:105 »II:13 NE II:130

1866 — LETTER I:118

FROM: Hans Nielsen Gamkinn, *Spring Grove, Minnesota, 6–10 June 1866*
To: Niels Jensen Gamkinn, *Gran, Hadeland, Oppland*

On our journey I had no time to write to you, so now I must make use of the opportunity to tell you what I think about this emigration. For my part I have not yet found anything that pleases me in this country. I must tell about my journey. It began at six o'clock on May 4 and we were then immediately given our supper of herring and tea. We had a nice voyage and came to Hull at twelve noon on the seventh and an interpreter met us at the ship and went with us to the railroad. We left that afternoon at three and arrived in Liverpool at nine o'clock the same day. There we were driven into a hotel built for the passengers and there were 600 lodgers there. We were there for three days in a rather bad mood but then we went onboard a steamship named *Belgian* and we had a pleasant voyage. On the seventeenth we had a gale that tossed us up and down in quite a lively fashion. But I and my traveling companion haven't been sick a single day since we left. We came to Quebec at four in the morning of the twenty-third and went on a train at six in the afternoon to a town called Sarnia. Then we went on a steamboat on a lake that was so big that we couldn't see land for a long time. We were on this lake for three days. Then we came to a town called Milwaukee, and took a train to a town called Prairie du Chien. There we took a steamboat to the town Lansing. And from there we had twenty-three miles to Anders Blegen, and we got here on Saturday, June 29, and found them all in good health.

Maria Olsdatter Melbostad went right to Gulbrand Melbostad. He is our neighbor and has a good farm and nice houses. I hope that my mother will go to Melbostad and give them their daughter's regards and tell them that they shouldn't expect a letter from her for some time as it is not necessary that we all write at the same time. I don't have more of importance. I hope that none of my relatives will be in a hurry to follow me. If I were able to talk with them I could give them some good advice; those who are in a reasonably good situation should not take on this difficult journey. The houses here are not much better than those at Christian Vasbraavollen. So it is pretty bad. But we are well fed wherever we go. But I am sad when I think of my brother Jens. My loving regards to you all. Tell the people at Lyngstad that they should lay aside thoughts of America until I come home and can tell them what I think about it after I have gotten to know the country. I would like to give the extra portrait at home to Christian Larsen Alm. I've worked for four days and will stay longer here at this place, as will Ole Blegen. He says, I am in good health and have been well since I left my home and I'm now living quite comfortably with my brother. Please give my regards to Blegen so it will not be necessary for all of us to write at the same time. My loving regards, farewell,

HANS GAMKIND

. ⸺ .

In the 1865 census HNG is at the farm Gamkinn with his parents and four siblings. He was then thirty-one years old. Hans Nielsen and several of the other male passengers on the *Belgian* are given the occupation "miner." There was an iron mine at Grue in Hadeland. At the bottom of the last page the recipient has noted that the letter arrived on 10 July 1866. Anders Engebretsen Blegen emigrated from Hadeland in 1852 and had a farm at Spring Grove, Minn. (Ulvestad 1913, 550). Anders later became Andrew. Maria Olsdatter Melbostad and Ole Engebretsen Blegen were passengers on the *Belgian*. Their reluctance to write was probably typical and also a reminder of the high cost of transatlantic postage. HNG and Anders Blegen had probably learned carpentry working in the mine. In the 1865 census Christian Vasbraavollen is listed as a *nybygger,* one who has built a farm on land previously uncultivated. It was therefore not unreasonable to compare his home with that of an immigrant settler in Minnesota. Ole Arild Vesthagen has gathered much information on immigrants from Gran, including several of those who appear in the letters by HNG (See References). »I:120 NE II:134

1866 — LETTER I:119

FROM: Elise Wærenskjold, *Four Mile Prairie, Texas, 22–27 June 1866*
To: Thomine Dannevig, *Lillesand, Aust-Agder*

Dear Thomine!

I've had the pleasure of receiving your welcome letter of March 4 and on that same day (June 8) I also had a letter from your dear Thorvald. Thank you a thousand times for all your news, but (and would you believe it?) I was so immodest that I thought it wasn't enough. I missed news about Kaja Poppe, Anne Müller, Stina, the Therkildsens, the Daniel Nielsens, the Møllers, and Mrs. Hanuk, and I so would have liked to have heard something about all of them. But I hope they are alive since you didn't say that they are dead. I was pleasantly surprised to hear that your old parents are still alive and well. Give them my heartfelt regards. I was also glad to see that Mrs. Stenersen and the dean's widow are still alive. You don't mention Fleischer. Is he dead? I wrote to him last year, but didn't get a reply and he always — Here I was interrupted and I continue on the twenty-seventh.

I've now had an answer to my question as we've finally received No. 2 of *Emigranten,* and I see that Fleischer has been made consul. Give my regards to the dean's widow, old Mrs. F. and tell her that I would be very pleased if she yet again would write me. She always wrote such nice letters. Ask her to give my regards to Emil and tell him that there is little or nothing to be had from Reiersen's estate as his business came to a stop as a consequence of the war and he lost several thousand dollars in outstanding claims. But I don't think it unlikely that his widow and children would pay at least the principal with their own money and it would perhaps be useful that Emil wrote to them and appealed to their sense of honor. I have recently spoken with Ouline about this and she is quite willing for her part. I intend to speak with Oscar Reiersen about it. He is administrator of the estate. Ask Mrs. F. to say to Emil that he shouldn't write that he has been advised by me.

I'm sad that Budde is dead but this wasn't unexpected as I knew that he wouldn't have let me wait so long for an answer had he been alive. I don't think that he was well off and God knows how his children will fare. I hope Mrs. Stenersen will do something for them since she and Budde were such good friends. He often mentioned her in his letters. — But now to your great news, that I suppose I should have mentioned first, your Niels's engagement. Yes, that both pleased me and surprised me. With my whole heart I wish that the young couple has many years together and always has the same joy in their union as they now have. My regards to Doctor Heyerdahl! I flatter myself that he hasn't entirely forgotten me. Thank you so much for the portrait. I also got Thorvald's and Else Basberg's. Poor Mrs. Basberg!

Yes my dear Thomine! It is a great loss when our children go before us. I suppose you now know that I've had this fate and that my sweet little Thorvald has left me. I have his portrait when he was two but I would gladly have given 100 dollars for his portrait as he was before he died. But we had no opportunity. He said several times on looking at his little portrait that mother should have had a portrait of him as he was now. It was so completely unexpected as if lightning had struck from heaven. Thorvald had been ill last summer and this seems to have been the cause of his death, because I believe that the calomel that doctors here use for almost all diseases breaks down and weakens the entire system. I have later spoken with a Norwegian doctor and he says that he believes that this was the case with Thorvald, who was such a delicate child and therefore did not tolerate it. He salivated a lot and cried through many a night because his teeth hurt and as long as he lived his teeth and gums were sore and would bleed at the slightest touch. And his breath was always bad during his illness. For a long time he was pale and thin but last winter he regained his red cheeks and I thought he would regain his health. Our neighbor's daughter had her wedding on January 19 and as their house is quite small and they wished to invite about 200 guests, we let them use our house for their wedding. It may be that the abundance of cooking and all the meats that we had in our house for several days on that occasion had a bad effect on Thorvald. But he didn't seem to be ill. On the afternoon of Sunday, January 21, my husband and several who were in our house and Thorvald and I went to a Danish family who live one and a half mile from us. When I had to go home to let in the sheep, the others thought it was too early and only Thorvald wanted to go with Mama, and he talked with me the whole way and seemed quite happy. We hadn't gone as much as ten steps after his last word to me when he suddenly and without complaint, without a sound, sank down at my side. He never spoke again until Wednesday morning when he regained consciousness and was able to speak a few words and gave Mama his last kiss. I was glad and thought he was getting well but not for long: he died at four o'clock and was buried that Friday. Little did I think on the preceding Friday when we had our home full of happy wedding guests that the next Friday I would bury the dearest I had on this earth. My little Thorvald was such a sweet and lovable little boy and all who met him liked him. I cannot any longer feel true pleasure in anything and all my longing is to be united with my Thorvald.

I'm glad that Hansen is taking care of Ole Johan Reiersen's son. He is such a nice boy and he sent a very well-written letter to his father. He doesn't mention Thorvald and Henrik Hansen. These must be sons of your brother? I wonder whether Hansen will soon write to me. Do ask him to write if he hasn't already done so. And also Kaja, Anne, Stina and Therkildsen. I wonder whether it may have affected them when they saw that I had such grief. Mrs. Basberg wrote the same day she got the news. Ouline Reiersen has recently written to the Hansens and the Baches have written to their relatives. Ole speaks of writing to his son but he is in one of his melancholic moods and is then not capable of anything.

I'll try to tell you what I know of the Grøgaards. Marie is in Prairieville and makes her living as a seamstress. At times she can be quite sensible for days in a row but then she begins with her mad talk again and is then often foulmouthed. Helene and Georg Reiersen have moved to Shreveport in Louisiana where they have a store, do well, and are happy together. Hans Jacob is with them and is married to Mathilde Reiersen, a daughter of Lassen R. in Bosque but she is Helene's foster daughter as her mother is dead. She is only fourteen years old. I believe I told you in my last letter that he was married to an American woman but that was merely a story that someone had made up for their own entertainment. I believe Thomas has a store in Jefferson, Louisiana and Nicolay has returned to his foster father in Larissa. They are both unmarried. Emma and her doctor live in Mount Enterprise where Helene used to live. I don't know how many children they have. Lise's little girl lives but her boy is dead. I've only seen Thomas and Nicolay since the outbreak of the war, and Thomas only for a few minutes. He is very much like his father and I cannot express the strange feeling that came over me when I saw him. I'll write to Helene and Nicolay and ask them to write to Bina, to whom you must give my regards.

Grøgaard probably ceased to write because Hans Jacob Hammer had made some remarks concerning postage and so they assumed that their Norwegian relatives didn't wish to have letters from them. I for my part will gladly pay for letters, those I receive and those I send, if only my friends will write to me. I don't know what will happen this time as we now have a post office in Kaufman and the postmaster doesn't know the postage to other countries. I only paid twenty-five cents for the letters I sent to Shreveport last year (before it was forty-five), so I fear that you'll have to pay this time. I haven't had a letter from Gusta; if you see her please ask her to write and to send me her portrait. Ask Kaja to do the same. I know that they cannot be all that expensive when they are used as visiting cards. I've often thought of how nice it would be to have portraits of all my friends. Hauge and Budde followed close upon each other. But then they were old comrades in arms and friends.

I'm glad to see that the times are good and that there is progress in Norway. I would probably not have recognized Lillesand: it must have become quite a sizable city. But it is strange that letters from Hedmark speak of a lack of money, huge bankruptcies, and an increasing emigration. This is not at all in accord with the letters we have from West Norway, and Hedmark should be one of the most affluent counties. We would be very glad to receive the Norwegian newspapers; they could easily be sent by steamship to Georg Reiersen in Shreveport from where it is often possible to send things here by freight wagons. But Thorvald could of course not have known this. The books that were bought for us several years ago are still with Anton Schjøth, but I've now asked him to send them to your brother, who I hope will be so kind as to send them with a reliable man to New Orleans and from there to Reierson in Larissa. Please ask him not to be sorry for this and that I continue to rely on his friendship and assistance. I cannot imagine that it is as nice in Lillesand as it was when we were young. So Lars H. has finally married! That was not too soon. Give my kind regards to the Hammers, in particular to Helene, to Mrs. Stenersen to Thomine Arenz, to Nicoline and all your relatives and all who may remember me kindly. Do you know whether Elen Monen still is alive? I have so often thought of writing to her, but nothing has come of it. She looked after me from I was three weeks old until I was thirteen. I am glad that Tone's shipbuilder is doing so well. Give her my regards. And Juliane Størenes, Mathilde J. Sørensen and others; it would be too much to write down all their names. Is old Miss Aabel still living?

You write that Bina Grøgaard has a lot on her hands. Well, it would probably be hard for Bina and most of you if you had as heavy work as I have. In summer we get up before sunrise and milk eighty-one cows before breakfast. This is, to be sure, different from milking so many cows in Europe as all the calves suck their mothers, but we nevertheless milk nine pails in the evening and eight in the morning. There are two of us, a German girl and I, and the little boys tie up the calves. The work is often tiring, especially hoeing the oats, but I can distinctly feel that the laborious life I lead in Texas has had a good influence on my health, and that is a significant good. I feel no other effects of my age than that I have become grey and wrinkled.

I must tell you about a remarkable question that my little Tulle (this is the name he gave himself) asked me the evening before he became ill, just as if he had some awareness of his imminent death. He asked me if it would be difficult if he now should die. As I didn't believe there was the least danger that anything like this should happen, I was merely surprised and asked: "Why?" "Yes," he said, "because if I die I will then always have the bad breath I now have." He believed that the new body we would be given after death would be just like the body we have when we die. Then I told him that our new body would in all likelihood be similar to our earthly body but that it would be free of all imperfections. He then asked me much more about the resurrection and the afterlife than I was able to explain to him. Now my little angel knows all he wished to know and what is still hidden for us.

Otto and Niels are healthy. Otto was fifteen in May, Niels twelve in December. So you see it will be many years before they can think of marrying. If only they could learn something and be confirmed. People here have subscribed about 300 dollars toward an annual salary for a pastor for the Norwegians at Four Mile Prairie and we have written to Pastor Rasmussen in Illinois to find one for us. We don't know whether he will succeed.

Ask Alida to write to me. Does Sine Arntzen write to anyone in Lillesand? I've written to her but had no reply. Do you know anything about Christopher Taarvig who you know was with us at the beginning of my marriage to Foyn? I would like to write to him had I known his address or the address to his brother-in-law, Pastor Niels Hald. Schjøth says that Hald has moved, but this doesn't say much. I had almost forgotten to tell you that Andreas Andersen (Holte) is engaged to a very nice and well-behaved girl in Bosque. Her parents are from Østre Moland where the wife's father was precentor. He recently went on a visit to Bosque and in his absence Sigurd Ørbæk took care of business at the mill. Sigurd sends his regards. Please excuse all the faults of this letter, but here is never peace and quiet and the houses here are not as in Norway where you can go into a room alone and not be disturbed. You must ask Kaya, Hansen, Anna, Stina, Terkildsen, and Gusta to write. Will you please send me Niels's portrait? Aren't I demanding? You may address your letters to Prairieville as before as the mail will again be organized in July. God be praised! Then we'll be able to receive letters and newspapers without all these makeshift arrangements. — Is Frederik Basberg dead? Mrs. Basberg only mentions Else and Anton, as do you. I cannot understand this.

My dear Thomine! I have scrawled together a long letter. May it not bore you! Give my regards to your husband, your sons and to all who may care to hear from me. My husband and my boys send their regards. Farewell and send me a long letter in return soon. Your always faithful friend,

ELISE WÆRENSKJOLD

. —— .

Fragments of this letter are in Blegen 1955 and Clausen 1961. At the center of this long letter is EW's need to share her grief with her old friend in Lillesand. She is responding to the first letter she has had from Lillesand since before the war and she is also driven by her need, after this long interruption, to keep the communication alive between her old friends in Lillesand and Vestre Moland and the people of her own class among the immigrants in Texas, mainly the Reiersens, Ørbæks, and Grøgaards. Because of this there are many names in this letter, not all of which have been possible to identify. One and a half centuries later, readers must keep in mind that for the writer and her many readers in Lillesand these names were not items in a catalogue but triggers of memory and revitalizations of bonds. The sudden jumps from one thought to another may be explained by her emotional situation, but may also be a consequence of writing in many sittings, perhaps over more days than those indicated by the dates. As is evident from this and other letters, the letters that have been preserved only represent a small fraction of her correspondence. EW wrote to Carl Budde in Bergen on 11 September 1865 (Nor. ed. II:127).

Emigranten began publication in 1852 and was published in Madison, Wisc. in 1866. The dean's widow was Anna Dorthea Fredrichsen.

The only Emil Fredrichsen in 1865 lived in Drammen. Johan Reinert Reiersen, who led the first Norwegian emigrants to Texas, had died in 1864. His widow, Ouline Reiersen, was his second wife and also the widow of his brother Christian Reiersen. Oscar Reiersen was his oldest son. Severine Stenersen (eighty-three in 1865) was the owner of the large farm Møglestu in Vestre Moland. Emma Grøgaard was married to the physician Thomas Miller Mathews. There were two Hammers in Lillesand who both had ties to the Grøgaard family. The merchant Lars Hammer's wife Helene Sophie's maiden name was Grøgaard. These two are mentioned later in this letter. The shipowner Jans Jakob Hammer was a widower and his home was managed by Antonette Grøgaard. EW is asking for letters and portraits from Gusta Hauge and Kaja Møglestue. Tone must have been Tone Olsdatter, married to Knud Thorsen, a ship carpenter, as were two of their sons. Peter Andreas Rasmussen was pastor in Lisbon, Ill. He had started out as a follower of Elling Eielsen but had been in the Norwegian Synod since 1862. «I:115 »I:127 NE II:135

1866 — LETTER I:120

FROM: Hans Nielsen Gamkinn, *Spring Grove, Minnesota, 23 September 1866*
To: Niels Jensen Gamkinn, *Gran, Hadeland, Oppland*

Beloved parents and siblings!

I can again tell you that your dear son is in good health and this is all the good I can do for you at the moment. I began working June 6 for one dollar a day for seven days but since then I've had one and a half dollars a day except one month I had fifty when I worked for some kind people. This year's harvest was not all that good. In July we had an awful heat that those who live here found strong and then followed cold and rainy weather that destroyed the crops as well as many people, as the flooding was great and many had their houses by the rivers that took with them whatever came in their way. These past two nights it has been very cold so whatever hasn't been harvested has frozen. Many newcomers died of the heat because they kept on working until they fell down dead. I've seen this myself, yes even made coffins for some, but, praise God, I've been spared.

I have my home at Anders Blegen's where I'm well taken care of whenever I come, which is usually every Sunday. I've worked in different places. About four miles from here I've mostly done carpentry so my craft has been a great advantage compared to those who only work as day laborers since they have less pay and often have to go without work. There have been many newcomers this year. I've spoken with Gulbrand Gamme and Siri who are living in this area at present. Maria Melbostad was very glad to meet her beloved as you may imagine. But there are few acquaintances around here. I've exchanged letters with Ole Koller and he told me about those he came over with. They are in good health but you should see how far away from each other people are after coming here. I've thought of going to Wisconsin next winter and may stay there for a while. It is about 300 miles from here but I want to look around.

I was so glad when I got your letter and read that my brother was well again. I hope that he'll be as careful as he can with his health. I think I'll see you again after awhile. My father should use my winter hat, as the fashion is different here. Hans P. Kulpen and I are working together and we plan to continue this as we have in the past. Apart from this I have no news for you. My best regards to all my family and friends. Give my regards to the parents and children at Lyngstad. I often think of Bertha Maria and Kristofer and hope that they will stay where they are as this emigration has great consequences as far as I can see. My regards to Engebret Hval and when you write to me, write Hans N. Gamkind. I hope to receive a letter from you before Christmas with all the news you can send as I enjoy them very much. Sincerely,

H. GAMKIND

· —— ·

Hans Pedersen was from the *husmannsplass* (croft) Kulpen in Gran and is listed as a carpenter in the 1865 census. He was also a passenger on the *Belgian*. Halvor Christoffersen and Mari Nilsdatter had one of the two Lyngstad farms in Gran and their two small children were Birthe Maria (six) and Christoffer (four). Engebret Olsen Hval was sixty-three and the retired farmer at Hval in Gran. «I:118 »I:124 NE II:138

· —— ·

1866 — LETTER I:121

FROM: Ole Tollefsen Opsata, *St. Ansgar, Iowa, 25 September 1866*
TO: Haagen Tollefsen Opsata, *Aal, Buskerud*

⁓⇌⇋⁓

Dear brother and other relatives!

I wrote to Ole about our voyage when we arrived in Quebec and I hope the letter has come to you. Now I'll tell you about our journey from there to St. Ansgar. We left the ship June 18 after it had been seven days in the harbor. We went ashore about three in the afternoon and met those who had been in the hospital. We stayed in a large building until one o'clock at night, when we were taken to the railroad cars. We were quite surprised to see that they were cattle cars with makeshift seats of rough planks that were so poorly made that they fell down the first day. After that we sat and lay down on the floor. On the twenty-second we came to a town called Sarnia. Then we were taken on board a steamboat that took us up Lake Michigan. We were there until the twenty-fourth but it was very uncomfortable. There were so many people, about 400, and there was no other place to lie down other than the floor and it was cold, so it wasn't good to be there long. We came to Milwaukee at night and were led off the boat and we lay down under the open sky to sleep. The weather was nice so we were quite comfortable, but in the morning there was the worst rain storm I have ever seen and we were allowed to come into a building until it was over. Then the weather was nice. We stayed there until the afternoon. Then we again went by train and there we parted with many of the others since those who were going to Minnesota were taken on another train.

We left Milwaukee at seven in the afternoon. That was on the twenty-fifth, and we went rather fast so we came to Prairie du Chien at eight in the morning. Then we crossed the Mississippi to McGregor. We had tickets to this place from Quebec and they cost fifteen and a half dollars for each adult. There we bought new tickets and went on a train to Calmar and that cost two dollars and ten cents for every adult. We came there in the evening of the twenty-seventh and that was as far as our tickets went. We were allowed to sleep in a storehouse for wheat. In the morning we met a Norwegian and we got him to take us in his wagon to the small town of Conover for one dollar. We stayed there for a day and a night waiting for some people we knew to come with their wheat so we could get them to take us with them when they returned. But none came. Then we finally met a man from Sogn who had come to sell his wheat and we paid him to take us to St. Ansgar. At night there was nothing to do but to stop on the wild prairie and some lay down on boxes and others in the wagon. We didn't dare lie on the ground as there is so much dampness in the ground and so much dew that it is unhealthy, and many have become ill after sleeping on the ground. In the morning we went off again and all went well until midday. Then we met some friends of our driver who came from town and they had liquor. So then he didn't want to go to St. Ansgar but to his home. We protested as that would be fourteen miles out of our way and we were so tired of our journey that we longed to get to our destination. But he refused to go with us and went with his friends. We were afraid and didn't know what would come of this. Finally he took our baggage out of his wagon and said he would leave us if we didn't want to follow him. We had agreed to pay him ten dollars and when he went off I had to pay him eight dollars for as far as he had taken us, and this was a third of the distance that we had agreed on. So off he went and we stood there on the wild prairie and there were no Norwegians, only Americans that we couldn't speak a word with. We sat there until it got quite dark and then two men, one from Hemsedal and one from Ringerike, came driving past us and they took us to St. Ansgar. We came there on Saturday the thirtieth and it was then eleven weeks since we had left home.

We first visited Narve Braaten from Gol and were there until Monday when we went to Hans Rust, where we since have lived in a cabin. At first I had planned to leave my family here and go west to Estherville and look for land, but God's ways are not our ways. We came here July 2 and on the fifth my daughter Aagot got ill and was in bed for six weeks. Sigri got ill on the twenty-second, and Tosten on the twenty-seventh. We had to sit with them both night and day and on the twenty-ninth I got a doctor to come and we were given some medicine and I think this helped a little for Margit and Tosten but it didn't help Sigri. She became so ill that about five days after she got sick she could not speak and on August 11 she passed away at eleven o'clock before noon and she was buried on the twelfth in the churchyard at St. Ansgar. Pastor Clausen visited us once and he gave us a beautiful sermon at the grave. I also got a little ill August seventeenth and this lasted for sixteen days but never so bad that I couldn't do a little work now and then. I'm now well but Tollef has also gone around ill like I did for about three weeks and he neither works nor rests. Ole got ill on August 27 and stayed quietly in bed for two weeks, but he is now better and is up. Anne and Niels have been quite well the whole time, praise God.

We are determined to go west to Estherville. I'm expecting Ole E. Sando any day. He will take us to their home and we'll have a cabin on Erik O. Sando's land this winter. Erik and Tollef have mowed hay for my animals. Now I can tell you that Ole Sando came before I sent the letter and he will take us to Etherville 110 miles from here. We'll go tomorrow if nothing unexpected should come up. I have no more space but I must ask you, Haagen, to send this letter to Laa and to make a copy and send it to Ole Ro. There is much I could write about concerning this country and the questions you gave me, but I haven't yet learned as much about it as I have wanted to. God willing, I'll do this later. I must conclude with my loving regards, first to my daughter and then to all our siblings and relatives that may wish to hear from us. I wish you would write to us. Farewell.

OLE T. OPSATA

· —— ·

> This letter was mistakenly placed in 1860 in the Norwegian edition. It seems to have been written over several days, so the date merely indicates when he started writing. OTO (1815–1902) and his wife Anne Olsdatter (1818–1900) sold their farm to his brother Haagen and emigrated with six of their seven children in 1866 on the bark *Sirius* that left Bergen on 27 April and came to Quebec on 12 June 1866. Their oldest daughter Birgit was married to Ola Larsen on the farm Laa in Aal. His sister Barbro and her husband Ole Eriksen Sando had emigrated in 1845. They were in the large group that went with Pastor C. L. Clausen from Rock Prairie, Wisc. to St. Ansgar, Iowa but had moved west to Estherville, Iowa. Hans O. Rust had also come to St. Ansgar with Pastor Clausen (Holand 1908, 403). »I:161 NE II:48

· —— ·

1866 — LETTER I:122

FROM: Paul and Ole Olson Lehovd, *Kasson, Minnesota*
28 October–18 November 1866

To: Ole Helgesen and Joran Paulsdatter Lehovd, *Flesberg, Buskerud*

To my dear and unforgettable parents and siblings!

As I hope you are longing to hear how I fared on my journey I must take the time to write you a few lines to let you know that I have happily come here from Norway to America. I hope you got the letter I wrote in Christiania on September 21. We left Christiania that day at 5 a.m. and the next morning we were in Arendal. In the evening we came to Christiansand and in the morning of the twenty-fifth we were in Hull. At first we had stormy weather and we were seasick but for me this didn't last more than a day and night. In Hull there was a Norwegian interpreter who guided us to a house where we had breakfast so we began to get our meals on the twenty-fifth. At 10:30 a.m. we took the train from Hull to Liverpool where we arrived at 5 p.m. The train was very fast and we went through eleven tunnels where it was completely dark and we went past several cities. There were two sets of tracks and trains often met each other at such speed that it was terrible to hear and see, in particular for those who hadn't traveled by rail before. In Liverpool we were met by a Norwegian agent who took us to a house where we had bed and board. We were given tea and sandwiches in the morning and soup and meat for dinner and tea and bread and butter for supper. And on the twenty-seventh our interpreter took us onboard the large steamship the *Hibernian*. I then left Christopher Torgersen who had a ticket to New York. We were with many Germans and Englishmen and some Swedes. We left Liverpool on the twenty-seventh. At first we had some stormy days and we came to Quebec on October 8. Just south of Quebec our ship collided with a sailing ship and our ship had to pull it into Quebec as it was damaged.

That same day we went from Quebec on the railroad up through the country. Some Norwegians had to pay custom duty on their baggage but

I didn't have to pay anything. I went on the railroad both night and day from the eighth to the thirteenth when I came to La Crosse in Wisconsin. In Chicago I had to pay one dollar to have my chest taken from one station to another. From LaCrosse I went on a steamboat up the Mississippi to Winona where I arrived Sunday the fourteenth. I went by rail from Winona to Rochester on the fifteenth where I met a childhood friend and his name was and is Sjul Hansen Lehovdeie. He lives with Amund Braata and is a *bief steak* engineer and has a good monthly wage and is dressed like a gentleman. I gave him the message I had for him and he said he would soon send the money. October 15 I got to my brother Hellik and we didn't recognize each other. My journey was quite expensive as I had to buy food on my way inland and I bought clothes in Liverpool for six *speciedaler*. It is a good idea to bring food for the journey. When I came to Hellik I had forty-eight dollars left and here I was paid one U.S. dollar and four cents in paper for one dollar in gold. I immediately got work here for some days on a threshing machine for Hellik, and I came to my brother Ole's on Sunday the twenty-first.

I'll now end my simple and poor letter with my loving and friendly regards to my dear parents and siblings. Say to all who wish to hear from me that I'm in good health and that I hope they'll write to me when convenient. When you write you can address the letter to my brother Hellik. So live, then, as well as you can. From your brother and son,

PAUL OLSEN LEHOVD

I'll give you some information about my brother Hellik. He and his family are in good health and they have a son who was born in the month of June 1865 and was given the name Henry Olaus, and Julia and Henry are growing big. The father of Hellik's wife died last December and two of Hellik's wife's siblings were married last summer. In Minnesota it has been a poor year compared to last year when it was very good. Then Hellik harvested 325 bushels of wheat as well as some oats, barley and potatoes and garden produce. But this year he had much less on more land and he had only 169 bushels of wheat and eighty bushels of oats and some potatoes. There was very much rain last summer.

Hellik thanks his parents for the present they sent him with Paul, as the gifts of parents are precious. He has two draft oxen, three cows, one heifer, three calves, four pigs, quite a lot of chickens, some tame ducks, and seven sheep. He is doing very well. But in June 1865 we had a terrible accident at Hellik's when lightning struck his house and followed the iron stove pipe down into the stove and spread out through the house and into the cellar and into the room where the parents of Hellik's wife live and broke all the windows. It was a divine miracle that no one was killed as there were eight people in the house as this was only a few days after his wife had given birth, but no one felt it as badly as did the little Julia. It was long before she could walk around again. Hellik was outside a window sitting on a large washing tub and setting in a new window pane, and the lightning went through the wall under the window and broke the window he was holding and threw him a good ways away and he lay as dead for a long while. And I, Ole, sat right next to the cooking stove and the lightning went through the floor close to my feet and for some time it was as if I had a cramp in my feet and I was also unconscious for some time, but not as long as Hellik. But when I became conscious I can remember that I called on Jesus, as we often do when lightning strikes. So our thread of life may be cut in an instant and we'll have to stand judgment for our life and for what we've done in our life. But God be thanked for not taking me away then because I wasn't ready for death. May God grant that I'm ready when my time comes.

For a long time I haven't had time to complete this letter. It is now November 18. But I had so much to do as I've been threshing. Paul is plowing for me and is in good health. I had 417 bushels of wheat, eighty-one bushels of oats, and about forty bushels of potatoes, and I have two work horses and a foal, one cow and a heifer, and I have a new wagon, a new harvesting machine or reaper, a plow, and a harrow. I built a house on my land last year and have built a house for my wheat, which cost me fifty dollars. I also have a stall for my animals and a dog named Prince. I've had great expenses on my land as I paid four dollars an acre for breaking forty-six acres last summer. Fencing is also very expensive as I've made fences of boards for which I had to pay a lot, and all that's needed for the house and other things are very expensive. But things are better now that I can sell some wheat and it is practical that the railroad has been built close to my land so I can drive to Kasson, a town that was built in about a year. The price for wheat has been rather good as I've now sold eighty-eight bushels of wheat for 131 dollars and ten cents. But it's difficult to get wood here on the prairie and I have a long drive to the forest for firewood, so I think I'll sell my land, 120 acres with a lake on it, and go further west to take land. I had bad luck last spring. When I started sowing one of my horses got sick and I lost him and had to buy a new one, so I lost several hundred dollars both for a new horse and because I couldn't get my work done properly. All this was the fault of an American who does nothing but cheat in trading horses, so I don't feel good when I have to work so hard just so such tricksters can make more money. They do nothing but make their living on such simpletons as me. I also lost twenty dollars last year that one of my relatives stole from me. She is a sister of Ole Teksle and her name is Joran. She is a *smart gurl you know*. I'll also tell you that I'm married to Joran Halvorsdatter Gjerdeeie and she is in good health. As I couldn't manage my land here alone, I needed someone to take care of the household as I have so much hard work to do on the land. And she sends her regards to her parents and her brother. And we've heard that Knud also wants to come here, but I will not advise for or against, but he may do as he wishes. I must end my letter with my friendly regards to you my parents and siblings and my repeated thanks for the gift you sent me with Paul. Sincerely,

OLE OLSON LEHOVD

The letter was received on 17 December. Paul Lehovd was twenty-one when he emigrated. Two of the five siblings were now left at Lehovd, his brother Knud, who was twenty, and his sister Joran who was nineteen in 1865. Ole has written both parts of the letter, as his family in Norway would see from his handwriting. He begins his own part announcing that he will write about his other brother, now in the third person. We may note that Ole gives only practical reasons for his marriage. Indeed, it is almost as if he is excusing himself. There is little about the emotional life of the writers of these letters; in this case his reticence may also be because—as suggested by the farm name ending "eie"—Joran was the daughter of a *husmann* or crofter, a class below the farmer. Knud is Knud Halvorsen, Joran's brother. «I:113 »I:132 NE II:139

1866 — LETTER I:123

FROM: Jul Gulliksen Dorsett, *Bratsberg, Minnesota, 15 December 1866*
TO: Gullik Evensen and Even Gulliksen Daaset, *Flesberg, Buskerud*

Dear brothers and my old father,

Since it is a long time since you've heard from me I must send you a few lines to let you know that I am still, praise God, doing well and I wish to hear the same from you. We've heard rumors that the crops failed in South Norway this year and it wasn't so good here either, but I would call it an average year. I now own 120 fenced acres, of which twenty-five acres are cultivated, and all I need for farming. We have a railroad nearby and next spring I'll not be more than six to eight miles from a market. I must add a few lines for you my dear brother Even. If you think of coming I would advise you not to put off the journey because more and more land is being bought and settled. I'll help you acquire land if you come. You should take a ticket from Quebec to LaCrosse and from there you will easily find your way to Bratsberg. Sincerely and faithfully,

JUL DOSET

JGD has signed his letter but someone else has written it for him. The spelling of his last name may be a step toward the eventual Dorsett.
«I:108 »I:165 NE II:142

1867 — LETTER I:124

FROM: Hans Nielsen Gamkinn, *Argyle, Wisconsin, 13 January 1867*
To: Niels Jensen Gamkinn, *Gran, Hadeland, Oppland*

—⁂—

I received your letter dated November 5, 1866 on December 10 and see that you are all in good health, and that is the best of all in this world. I can also report that I've been well all the time. We had work until the middle of November and then we didn't want to work any longer. It got too cold for our kind of work as there was no space for such work indoors and other work is not to be had now during winter except to cut lumber, and those who do this really suffer, living in a cabin all winter as this work is done far away from people.

I wanted to look around, and last fall I went up through Minnesota and met some Norwegians I knew and they seemed to be doing well, in particular those who've been here for many years. I was a guest at the wedding of Maria Melbostad and there I met Jon Hilden, Brede Rossum, Gulbrand Blegen, Hans Helgaaker, and Ole Hvamstad and they had all come a long way. You must realize that it is rather strange to meet friends here because they are scattered more than you may think. When I returned I waited awhile to get your letter, which made me very glad. I left Blegen on December 12 and came to Lunderengen on the twentieth, but travel here requires money. I don't think I'll be doing much more traveling because I like it better here and I can live pretty much as if I were at home, because they have a fairly good house and only three children and he is doing well. I've visited Ole Kruggerud and was so glad to see them again in their new home. They have eight clever children and they and their parents are in good health. They have buildings of the best kind, two work horses, three heifers, and as many sheep as they need, but I don't know how many pigs since there are so many of them everywhere. Pigs are so easy to breed and to make money on.

The land is so varied in America. There are plains called prairies that are many miles wide where there are neither trees nor water, so this land cannot be cultivated, as both forest and water are necessary. There is neither pine nor fir where I've been (and I've traveled more than 3,000 miles). You can buy as much of it as you want, but it costs much too much. I've also seen some ugly land. If it had been forested it would have been an impassable mountain. You may be sure that this country has its faults, but it is easier to get along here on the same income as in Norway. In a few years you can make enough money to buy the land you need.

I see that my sister Anne was going to marry, something that may have happened now. I would have liked to be at her wedding and see you all, but you'll have to excuse me as I got the message so late that I feared I would come too late. So I'll have to come some other time, but I don't know when. My wish is that God will be with you. I can thank you for not forgetting to write but you can tell the people at Blegen that their son Ole thinks he has the money to pay for a letter if they would only send one to him. He thinks they have forgotten him. And I think you should talk with them when you have an opportunity. I'm writing as he asked me. There is one thing you should be aware of. Our day comes seven hours later than yours. When it is six in the morning here it is one in the afternoon with you. And with such a great distance you may imagine that many things are different here. While I was at home I never heard of a rattlesnake but here there are many of them. You can often see several in a day but there are far fewer now than before. There are two other kinds of snakes that are worse. One is called the blower snake because it blows poison on people so they die and I cannot remember the name of the other one. They like to stay along rivers and in swamps but they can be everywhere. I've heard that Lise Skari has come here and Torsten Sogn asks me to ask you whether this is true since she hasn't come to him. Please excuse the many errors in my letter but I suppose you can understand it. Sincerely,

HANS NIELSEN J. GAMKIND

[*In the margins*] Please don't send my letters to others. Give my regards to all friends. I remember my home.

Notes by Anders and Ole Hendrickson Lunderengen are not included. HNG signs himself Hans Nielsen J. Gamkind, using the initial of his father's patronymic, Jensen. His next letter is signed J. Gamkind and the last one H. J. Gamkin. Like so many immigrants he is trying out different names for himself and seems to be on the way to using his father's patronymic as part of his own name, something that was not done in Norway. In Norway people took their names from the name of the farm they lived on. Immigrants adapted this tradition and used their Norwegian farm name as the name of their new farm in the United States: HNG goes from "Blegen" in Minnesota to "Lunderengen" in Wisconsin. Anders (who became Andrew) and Ole Hendrickson (this became the family name in the United States) were each married to a sister of HNG's father: Eli (who became Ella) and Siri (who became Sarah). Maria Olsdatter Melbostad had come on the same ship, the *Belgian*, as Hans Gamkinn. The wedding guests were from Gran. The man who could pay postage was Ole Engebretsen Blegen from the farm Bleken in Gran. Lise Skari was from Brandbu in Gran and Torsten Sogn was from Jevnaker. The conviction that a farm should include forest was shared by many Norwegian immigrants, but by the late 1860s Norwegian-American settlers were settling on treeless prairie land. «I:120 »I:126 NE II:145

1867 — LETTER I:125

FROM: Erik Theodor Schjøth, *Sturgeon Bay, Wisconsin, 15 March 1867*
To: Christian Fredrik Wyller Schjøth, *Oslo*

My good and dear son Fredrik!

I was so glad yesterday when I got your letter dated February 14 in London and I'm making haste to reply and to thank you for the happiness you gave your old father. I see that you don't like being in London. I can believe you. I wouldn't have lived in one of those great holes of pestilence, like London, New York or Chicago, for any price. Two years ago I was in Chicago for two weeks to amuse myself and have a look around after a long time at home. Well, I could stand two weeks of it. There was a lot to see in the pleasant period just after the war, but I was glad when I returned to my quiet and comfortable home. You say that you would like to visit me if I would welcome you. Can you doubt that I would welcome you, my good, dear son? Yes, and with open arms and with the greatest joy I've had for thirteen long years, and I would not be the only one to welcome you.

There are others who would be as good and kind to you as your very beloved Aunt Alvilde and Uncle Christian. These are my second wife, your stepmother, and your three half-brothers. The oldest, Adolf Fredrik, is named for my dear and departed son Adolf. He is two years and two months and is so like his dead brother when he was a child. Number two, Philip Walter, named for his grandfather on his mother's side, is sixteen months and looks just like you did as a child and also and undeniably my Robert. Number three, eleven weeks, looks like his oldest brother, and at Easter, when our Pastor will visit us, he'll be christened with the names of my three honorable brothers: Anton Christian Rudolf Schjøth. Oh, had you been here then you would have been his godfather. I can imagine the surprise there at home on hearing that I have such company, but wait a little; this is a fortune here in America that cannot be bought for 1,000 dollars *a pair.* When such a boy is six years old he may often do work worth a dollar that you would have had to pay to some tramp as well as feed him. My wife is from Southern Germany, the widow of a soldier who died four years ago in Virginia. She is an honest farmer's daughter, only twenty-six years, and as sensible, proper, hard-working and good as your Aunt Alvilde. Come and see for yourself and you will find that I'm not lying.

What else may I offer you without *humbug* or exaggeration: a home and good food. Our cow calved two weeks ago, *plenty* milk and butter. Two enormous hens that lay eggs daily. In four weeks the ice will have melted and then I'll catch more fish than I can use. There will be pigeons and ducks and not in small flocks, and I have two double-barreled shotguns. We slaughtered a 350-pound pig for Christmas and we'll have two nice ones left when we're finished eating the first. I have two excellent dogs, a watchdog and a hound. I cannot offer you much by way of amusement. There is a popular dance every week in the Good Templar hall and you can skip around there if you have learned the *Yankee dudle*, and if you haven't you'll soon do so. We have a school here where boys who are twenty-five may go if they have nothing else to do. That is the custom here. We have a Norwegian church where the Pastor comes every fifth week and preaches for two or three days. A Catholic and a Methodist church are being built and will be ready next summer.

I've been so glad since I received your letter and I have so much to tell you that I don't know where to begin or where to stop. You may wish to know what kind of business I'm in and what I've been doing. Before the terrible war I had a small general store as I have a good location, but then, suddenly, all prices went up three to five times. I feared running into debt and retired as quickly as possible. But my beautiful little piece of land, the nicest in all of Door County, gave me other advantages. Three years ago the governor of Wisconsin awarded me a ten-year ferry monopoly for which I'm paid one dollar a day for seven months of the year. I'm also given a house that I don't need, a large building with an excellent cellar that I once used for storage, and I'm renting it out to a Norwegian family.

You write that you would like to be a clerk here, but I don't like the idea. I don't think you should be bossed around. This is a free county. As an honest man you may establish yourself in whatever you wish for very little and be your own master. Many a time, yes before my Adolf passed away, I've wished that I had my sons here but I didn't dare to ask them or urge them to come. But now that you want to come and you're in London, then I'll write: Come, see and try, and you'll find that your old father truly loves his son and will share his last cent and last crumb of bread with him. I think you may learn more in America than in London. You'll find many an honest Yankee you'll like better than a snooty John Bull. It is an advantage for you my dear son that you've learned something. That will be of significant help and here everything is open for you so you can have time to consider what you would like to do. This is a free country. You can try everything and choose the best. We have a nice little house with four rooms and one upstairs. Last summer I added a large room that I could use as a store in case I decided to open a business again. You may use it as you like.

I must stop my scribbling. It is too long but it is so long since I talked with you.

Thank you so much for your portraits. They now have nice frames and are placed in my best living room on each side of a nice portrait of the great Washington, the Father of America as he is called here. If you decide to go it would be best to go to New York, from there by rail to Chicago and from Chicago to Green Bay—one day's journey—and from there to Sturgeon Bay, half a day on a steamboat that goes daily when the ice has melted. Last year I had a photograph taken to send it to you, but it is so poorly done and I looked so old and sinister that I didn't want to send it. But I'm sending you a copy—one cannot do anything about getting old. Please write home and give my heartfelt and warmest regards to my family and friends and my brothers, a hundred kisses and thousand blessings from me. In the meantime—good health my dear son and if God is willing—I hope to see you in my humble home. Your father,

ERIC T. SCHJØTH

P.S. When you get this, you must write to me right away or I'll think that the letter hasn't reached you and then I must write again.

. ⸺ .

> Italicized words are as in the letter. The concluding sentences have been lost and are according to an English translation in the Norwegian National Archives. Apparently, there have been no letters since 1863 and this is the first news of his marriage and new family. His rather awkward joke about the pecuniary value of a son suggests his own sense of the awkwardness of having kept this secret. His son Fredrik, who had then worked for the Chinese government since 1868, eventually visited his father in 1877. «I:103 NE III:T18

. ⸺ .

1867 — LETTER I:126

FROM: Hans Nielsen Gamkinn, *Argyle, Wisconsin, 7 April 1867*
TO: Niels Jensen Gamkinn, *Gran, Hadeland, Oppland*

Good friends, Niels J. and family,

A long time ago, on June 18, I received your very welcome letter and see that you are all in good health and I can say the same for myself as well as for those at Lunder and Kruggerud. When we have health and the necessities of life we should be satisfied with our lot. Here in America there is an abundance of the good things in life but something is missing: I don't feel at home here even though I make a lot of money every day. I had thought of going to Norway early this spring but I like the money. I've signed up for four months to help finish a building so I cannot leave until the beginning of August and it may take longer. I cannot set a date since I'm going with a man from Valdres who came here with me, and it is a long journey so don't expect me before you see me. But if I live there is nothing that can stop me even though it is much easier to make a living here. I've been determined in this since I left home and I'll try to keep my promise if it is in my power to do so. But some things must be left to God.

I have nothing of interest to tell you, as I cannot tell you how things are in this country on paper. I don't think that any Norwegian can imagine it without having seen it with his own eyes. But it is an excellent country in many ways. Please excuse my poor letter. I came home at ten and had to return that same night and wanted to have the letter finished by then. There is no point in sending me a letter if it cannot get to me. August is only six weeks away.

. ⸺ .

His error in counting weeks in his last sentence may be due to his haste. «I:124 »I:131 NE II:149

. ⸺ .

1867 — LETTER I:127

FROM: Elise Wærenskjold, *Four Mile Prairie, Texas, 15–30 April 1867*
To: Thorvald Dannevig, *Lillesand, Aust-Agder*

⸻

Dear Thorvald!

Two or three weeks ago I had the pleasure of receiving your letter of February 6 and as you can see, I'm using your first name as you wished. I regret that you'll be coming so near us and even be in New Orleans as long as you were last year, without having the pleasure of seeing you. When you get this you will already know that I've lost my husband, the loving father of my children. God knows who will be next! Should I be called away from my children before Otto reaches the age of majority it will become difficult for them. God's will be done! There is no use in being anxious about the future. But things would be very different had I been in Norway where I have family and loyal friends that I can rely on; but here I'm in a foreign country where I have no guarantee that my children would receive a Christian upbringing or that their inheritance would be taken care of for them. There has been no division of the estate between the children and me as Wilhelm (my husband) during the war drew up his testament so that I have full disposal of all we have and can do with it as I see best. Old Erick Bache has also left us as I believe I mentioned in a letter to your aunt Sophie Hansen. Ingeborg Bache is well off but it is a shame that she cannot sell out and return home; but this is not possible at the moment if you don't wish to sell for a half or even a third of the pre-war value.

I am sending this with a Dane, Fritz Hansen, whose mother lives in Arendal Hospital. He is returning with his family to Veile where his wife's father, a very wealthy man, lives. He is bringing a portrait of my husband to my mother-in-law as I'm fortunate in having two portraits of Wilhelm, and he has promised to have some copies made and send one to you. I only have one portrait of the children and myself; there has never been a photographer here. Otherwise I would have sent you my entire family, but that may be some other time. Thank you so much for the portraits you've sent me of your mother and your uncle, but shouldn't I also have portraits of your father and Niels? Your aunt kindly sent me hers. Cannot one now have photographs of landscapes? Are these expensive? I'd love to have a prospect of Lillesand and of my place of birth, the parsonage at Dypvaag between Tvedestrand and Risør. You've probably seen it from the sea. I was eight when we moved from there but I remember it so clearly, even more precisely than Moland and Holt where I later lived.

I hear that Mrs. Stenersen is dead and I'm quite curious to know what each of the family members got. I've heard from Lovise Benneche that the town was given 10,000 and the parish 10,000 *speciedaler* but I don't know what this money is for. It is strange that neither Mrs. Poppe nor Mrs. Hauge writes to me nor does Mrs. Müller, Stina or Therkildsen. And I've written to them all. Would either you or your good mother please give them my regards and tell them that I shall not inconvenience them with more letters when neither my little Tulli's nor my husband's death could create enough sympathy in them to conquer their reluctance to write. Recently I've had letters from many in Denmark and Norway who haven't written to me since I came to America; but my friends in Lillesand seem to be incorrigible.

I fully agree with what you say about Reiersen and language. I cannot understand how an adult can forget his mother tongue. It is quite different with a language one hasn't been used to speaking. At the time I came here I could make myself reasonably understood in German and French, but not now. I can well understand what I read in these languages and will as soon read German as Norwegian. We subscribe to newspapers in Norwegian, German, and English. I almost never have an occasion to read

French except for the books I brought with me here. I'm very grateful for the Norwegian newspapers you sent me, but I haven't yet received them. Oscar Reiersen recently returned from New Orleans and he had visited his uncle Georg in Shreveport, but he had neither seen the newspapers nor heard of them. He was only a little boy when he came to America, but he is the Reiersen who has retained the most interest in everything Norwegian. I hope that the newspapers will come later and then Sigurd Ørbæk and I will really enjoy them. Sigurd lives with us. I'm so glad that Ole Johan Ørbæk's son is such a clever boy and that he has had such good foster parents. I suppose you know, dear Thorvald, that your uncle is one of my dearest friends. Yes, I've spent many a nice hour in his and your mother's company when we all lived in his house and we enjoyed a little one that we all loved. How happy I would have been had I been able to visit you again, but now that my husband is dead I wouldn't have the courage for so long and dangerous a journey with two children. Had I been alone I would have gone, but now the children must come first. Do ships go directly from Lillesand to New Orleans? What is their cargo? If we could go there or to Liverpool on a ship from Lillesand, it might not cost so much to go home. But it is mere foolishness to think about it! Ole Johan is still in Bosque. Ouline and Sigurd are doing well and send their regards. So does Mrs. Bache who has now moved into her new house. Fortunately, her brother came here before Bache died and he has a nice and friendly wife.

April 30. I must conclude this letter. I've had a letter from Helene Reiersen but she knows nothing about the newspapers. How did you send them? — I must tell you a little about the Norwegian settlement in Bosque County. The Indians recently came there, wounded an old Norwegian and kidnapped a fifteen-year-old boy. They also took two American boys, whose father they killed, and they killed two Negroes. To tell the truth, the Bosque settlement is more prosperous than ours and I also think it may be more salutary, but I wouldn't have lived so close to the Indians for anything. I grieved to bury my little Thorvald but it would have been far worse to know that he was among wild and heathen people who would torture him everyday and bring him up as a heathen. Give my and my children's regards to your parents and grandparents, Niels and Samuel Hansen and their wives, your uncles and aunts, and my other friends and please me soon with another letter. I remain forever your motherly friend,

ELISE WÆRENSKJOLD

Part of this letter is in Clausen 1961. EW's husband Wilhelm Wærenskjold was attacked and killed with a knife in a store in Prairieville, Texas on 17 November 1866. For an account of the murder and its background see Russell 2006, 122–127. Dannevig suggested that they use the familiar singular form of the personal pronoun (*du*) rather than the formal polite plural form (*De*). Veile is in Denmark. Ingeborg Bache's brother Andreas Svendsen used the name Anderson in the United States. He married Imma Jenson. «I:119 »I:142 NE II:150

1867 — LETTER I:128

FROM: Guttorm and Ole Olsen Lee, *Primrose, Wisconsin, 29 May 1867*
TO: Anders Olsen Lie, *Hedalen, Sør Aurdal, Oppland*

To our deserted but not forgotten parents and siblings in Norway, our deserted land of birth,

As it is long since we last wrote to you and as we have recently had the pleasure of seeing and speaking with our sister's daughter Olaug, I'll take up my pen in my great simplicity but with the most profound love to tell you a few plain words. I can, praise God, give you the good news that we've all been in good health since we last wrote to you. I've bought ninety acres for 1,100 dollars. I paid 300 in cash and the rest, at seven percent interest, will be paid with 100 dollars a year. I have a monthly pension of eight dollars for my wound as a soldier. We've had a very cold spring and we still have exceptionally cold weather. The May barley, that is usually planted from May 10 to 15, has still not all been planted and what has been planted may rot because we've had too much cold rain. We have hard times for the common man, in particular for those who come from Norway with a large family and without money. Wheat has been at two to three dollars a bushel and a cow from thirty-five up to fifty dollars.

As I don't have more to write about I'll end my poor letter but before stopping I'll give my regards to you our mother and wish you a good night and give you my heartfelt thanks for every hour and every minute we have lived together. It pains me to hear that you are not well but we must be patient. May the grace and peace of God our Father, Jesus Christ our Savior, teacher, and king, through the outpouring of the Holy Spirit be with you my beloved siblings and mother. This is the wish of your brother and son. Oh may God grant that after this miserable life we may be gathered in the eternal mansions where there shall be no more separation. I must end my letter and offer you my heartfelt farewell.

GUTORM LIE

As there is time and opportunity I will also take my pen in hand and send you a few lines even though I don't have anything to write about that can be of interest for you. But I can tell you that all our family here have been in good health since I last wrote to you and I wish to hear the same from you. Olaug has come to us and she has been well and I think all went well for her on her journey. She hasn't lost any of her baggage as so many others did in her group and I think she likes it here. I don't think she would like to be at Nordre Lie again and she sends her regards to her parents and all her family for their goodness. She sends her regards to Lars and Kari Huset and thanks them for all they have done for her. I can also tell you my brother that I'm quite satisfied with the accounts and I owe you my thanks for all your trouble in taking care of this. I'm sure that you had a lot of trouble collecting so much money and it may even be that you've sent me so much money that you have nothing left for your trouble. It was not my intention that you should do all this for nothing. I don't know much about accounting but if it is the case that you have nothing left then I insist that you let me know and I'll do something about it. I'm very glad that you could collect so much money for me. I've bought the land that I wrote about in my last letter. And thank you for the Bible that was bought for me. But I would also like to have the gun that I wrote about sent to me. You must again ask Knud Slettebratten to try to get one for me. Let me know how much it will cost and I will send the money in advance. You mustn't doubt that I am very satisfied with the accounts.

As for religion here there are many different kinds, but for him who wants the correct Lutheran religion there is opportunity to have it here just as well as there as we practice the same faith as in Norway and have a Norwegian parochial school. Halsten Brager was schoolteacher here last winter but now he doesn't want to be a teacher any longer. Our pastor is now Johannes Fjeld and before him we had Pastor Brodahl and they are good pastors. I must now conclude with my loving regards to all my family and friends. Sincerely,

OLE OLSEN LIE AND FAMILY

. ——— .

In an undated letter, probably sent sometime in 1866 (Nor. ed. II:129), OOL writes about the collection of debts owed to him in Norway and gives his brother advice on emigration. Olaug was the only child of Olea Olsdatter, sister of Anders, Guttorm, and Ole, and her first husband was Jakob Olsen Stugarden, who died in 1849. In 1853 Olea married Hallstein Hallsteinsen and they lived on the *husmannsplass* Børtnes in Hedalen from 1859 to 1867. They later lived on the *husmannsplass* Kantum and emigrated in 1881 with their youngest son, Peder. The names Børtnes and Kantum are both used in later letters. Olaug had served at the farm Jøranbyhuset also simply called Huset, and in her uncle Ole's part of this letter she sends her regards to the farming couple there: Lars Olsen and Kari Nilsdatter Huset. Evidently, she has also served at another Lie farm, Nordre Lie, where she does not seem to have had a good time. There is much about Olaug and her parents and half-brothers in later letters. Halsten Brager was from Hedalen and he later became a watchmaker in Mount Horeb, Wisc. (Ulvestad 1913, 556). Johannes N. Fjeld (1818–1888) was from Valdres. Primrose was one of his several congregations. Peder Marius Brodahl (1823–1906) returned to Norway in 1868. «I:100 »I:155 NE II:152

. ——— .

1867 — LETTER I:129

FROM: Berger Tollevsen Rogstad, *Norman Hill, Texas, 1 June 1867*
To: Peder Eriksen Furuset, *Romedal, Stange, Hedmark*

⇌

Dear brother-in-law Peder E. Furuseth,

After many years I will put together some lines and let you know that we are doing well and we hope that these lines will find you in the same situation. We've had a long and bloody war since we last wrote to you and this has been very bad for the country. But Texas was the least hurt of all the United States so we didn't lack anything. Harvest will begin in a few days and everything looks good. Even though I don't think we'll have quite as good a year as last year we'll have more than enough for our own use and some to sell. Wheat is the most important product here among the Norwegians. In recent years we have had a cattle disease and have lost many, so we don't have more than when we last wrote. But we've done better with horses and I now have more than thirty fine mares and horses. I often lose one or two foals and last spring I lost four. There is a kind of wild cat that takes young foals.

Some time ago we were visited by a Norwegian pastor from Wisconsin. He was here for two weeks, held communion and baptized fourteen children. He baptized our two youngest, both girls, Anna Marthea, four and a half years, and Perine Pouline, two and a half years. We also have three boys, Johan, twelve years, Thomas Renhart, ten years, Bernt Adolf, seven years. Hendrick Dahl and his family send their regards. They are in good health and are doing well. Dahl is now out on a long journey to the coast to get a threshing machine and is expected home any day. When you write please tell us how all relatives and friends are doing and about things that have changed. We suppose that many have died, been born and gotten married since we last heard from you. I've heard that aunt Oliv Bratlien is still living. Please write a long letter and tell us about this and that. I've cultivated about forty acres. Last year I harvested 450 bushels of wheat, rye, oats and corn that we feed to our workhorses. I'm now going to the market with 200 bushels I have left of last year's harvest. Wheat is sold for one dollar and forty cents a bushel. I've bought a reaper, and four horses and two men cut from twelve to sixteen acres a day. It cost me more than 200 dollars but this money is soon returned since you have to pay a dollar an acre to have your wheat cut. There are many freemasons here in America and almost half the Norwegians in our settlement have become freemasons. We have built a church of stone and now the second story is to be a freemason lodge. In conclusion, friendly regards from all of us here to all relatives and friends in old Norway, and please write soon. Faithfully yours,

B. ROGSTAD

. —— .

> Anne Eriksdatter and her husband Johan Brunstad emigrated in 1851 on the bark *Arendal* from Arendal. They settled in Four Mile Prairie where she became a widow the following year. BTR emigrated in 1853

on the brig *Victoria* from Arendal in 1853. The two married and moved to Bosque County, Texas in 1854 (Syversen 1982, 270, 283). Hendrick Olsen Dahl and Christine Pedersdatter Furuset were engaged when they emigrated in 1851. They married in 1853 and moved to Bosque County. There are no pre-Civil War letters to Furuset in public archives. Oliv Halvorsdatter Bratlien was ninety-two in 1865. »I:138 NE II:153

·⎯·

1867 — LETTER I:130

FROM: Hellek G. Branson, *Eureka, Kansas, 22 July 1867*
To: Ole Gulbrandsen and Anne Andersdatter Lande, *Flesberg, Buskerud*

Dear brother and family,

I've received your letter. I'm glad to see that you are doing well and I can report back that we are all in good health and have a good income. We have six sons who live and three sons and a daughter who have died. When the war started, Gulbrand and Ole volunteered. Gulbrand was eighteen and Ole sixteen. They were riders with Company A of the Kansas Cavalry and I had the pleasure of hearing that they distinguished themselves as brave soldiers. Ole died at Springfield, Missouri, April 1, 1862. He was not quite seventeen and was six feet, three and a half inches tall. He was in several battles. Once, his horse was shot while he was on it. Gulbrand came home after having served his time. His health is poor but he has the pleasure of knowing that the cause of freedom was victorious. He was one of fifteen chosen from one thousand to be runners. I and my sons have always been against slavery and this was partly the reason why I went to Kansas, as it was really here that the war between the slave party and the freedom party began. But now, praise God, we've won and slavery has been destroyed and we can in truth say that this is the land of freedom.

I'm glad to see that Gullik and Kari wish to come to America. I cannot give you much information as I don't know whether they want to come here to Kansas or to one of the Northwestern states. Write to me as soon as you receive these lines and then I'll tell you all that I know. You must tell me whether my old father-in-law lives. And mother must let us know how she is. Next year there will be good opportunities for immigrants. We think that the Indians will be moved from a large area south of us and that those who keep up with developments will be able to get as good land as anywhere in the world. I have been over much of it and I think it is the best I have seen. I have also been in Iowa, Minnesota, Wisconsin, Illinois and Missouri, and think Kansas is the best for cattle. It is also good for wheat and last year we grew more wheat per acre than any other state in the union. There is little need to feed our animals. Sheep, young horses, and cattle can find food on their own almost all winter here in southern Kansas without any extra fodder. Fruit also does well here, but there are not yet many trees that bear fruit. We are more exposed to drought than further east but our cattle are at their fattest in dry years.

There is a Norwegian settlement at Fall River. There is also a Norwegian settlement in Doniphan and Brown Counties where Syver Kalderud and Ole Haugen live. Two Norwegian boys from Wisconsin are with us, one named Gunder Larsen Nesterud and the other Anund Hansen Bjerkgaarden, a nephew of Beret Bergerud and Ole Bjerkgaarden. Hansen and Gulbrand were in a large battle in Helena in Arkansas. The Rebels attacked in the morning with 16,000 men. The Union army had 3,500. They fought until nightfall. Then the Rebels had to retreat with a loss of 8,500. They were almost five Rebels to one Union man but they were nevertheless beaten. Hansen and Larsen plan to take land here and others from Wisconsin have been here to look around and they will be back in the fall. I must end my poor letter with loving regards to you and your wife and to mother and to Gullik and Kari Bringe from me, and my wife and children.

HELLEK GULBRANDSEN LANDE

· ——— ·

The family name Branson is an Americanization of the patronymic Gulbrandsen. HGB, Margaret Helliksdatter and their eleven-month-old child, Gulbrand Helliksen, emigrated on the bark *Hercules*, leaving Drammen on 5 May and arriving in New York on 6 July 1843. According to Ulvestad (1907, 271) they came from Dane County, Wisc. to the area near Eureka in 1858. HGB wrote "*tredie Compeni A. Kansas Kavaleri.*" This seems to mean the third Kansas Cavalry Regiment, but there was no Kansas cavalry regiment with that number. He also wrote that Gulbrand had been selected to be one of fifteen "*før rønnere*" that seems a Norwegian-American coinage for forerunner or front runner. Neither term is known to have been used by the cavalry. In 1865 Gullik Gulliksen and Kari Gulbrandsdatter Bringe were thirty-two and thirty-six years old. »I:133 NE II:156

1867 — LETTER I:131

FROM: Hans Nielsen Gamkinn, *Wiota, Wisconsin, 26 July 1867*
TO: Niels Jensen Gamkinn, *Gran, Hadeland, Oppland*

Niels J. Gamkind and family,

I received your welcome letter on June 18, and see that you are all in good health and I can tell you the same for myself. I've had work in one place since March 18 and will be finished the week after next. I'm making fairly good money. In all this time I haven't wasted more than one day, so I was never so diligent when I was in Norway. And now I'm going to start on another house so I won't be able to do more this summer if the good God grants me life and health to complete what I have taken on. It seems this will be a very good year. They will begin the wheat harvest in a few weeks and then I'll have to help Anders Lunderengen for a few days binding wheat as I lived with him for a while last winter and plan to go to him when winter is here again. There have been a lot of immigrants this summer, not just from Norway but from all countries, Germans are the largest group. It has been difficult to get lodging and this is not so surprising. Food has been quite expensive: a bushel of wheat is two and a half to three dollars, oats one dollar, corn one dollar and a passable horse between two and three hundred, a cow from thirty to sixty dollars. Prices will probably fall and have already started.

Last fall Anders Blegen bought two three-year-old mares and he paid 500 dollars for them fully harnessed. His oxen were large, about fifteen hands and correspondingly thick and when he bought the horses he sold them for ninety dollars. I've sold my featherbed. I didn't like to do this but it isn't practical to have such things for one who doesn't want to settle down. Last fall I bought fifty Norwegian silver *speciedaler* for sixty-eight American dollars and this was a good exchange. Hans Pedersen also wanted to be in on this exchange but he came too late. I'm sure you would have liked to have his regards, but I haven't heard from him since last March. But I know that he is making good money. Last summer we were both rather unhappy but this is the case with all newcomers. I haven't once regretted my journey and I am more satisfied now than I was, thank God. I had written this letter earlier and had it in my pocket but it was so ruined by sweat so that I couldn't send it. I'll conclude my poor letter with regards from your dear son and brother. Sincerely,

H. J. GAMKIN

This is the last letter by HNG in public archives. His story ends with his declaration of satisfaction with his new country. He is no longer set on returning to Norway. His use of the initial "J" suggests that he has taken his father's patronymic (Jensen) as his own, perhaps as a step to making it his family name. «I:126 NE II:157

1867 — LETTER I:132

FROM: Hellik Olson Lehovd, *Salem, Minnesota, 5 November 1867*
TO: Ole Helgesen and Joran Paulsdatter Lehovd, *Flesberg, Buskerud*

Dear parents and siblings in Norway,

Thank you for your welcome letter of April 16. It is good for us to hear from you even though not all you wrote us was good as we see that there was much illness and other difficulties there at home last winter. I cannot further delay sitting down and writing a few lines to you. I and my family have been reasonably well and in good health even though we've been sorely tried as when the lightning struck my house June 16, 1865 and followed the stove pipe and went out again between the wall and the windows and made a lot of damage to the house. It was a miracle that no life was lost as there were eight people in the house. But I was struck by the lightning and was unconscious for a time and my daughter Julia was hurt in her right foot so she couldn't walk for about sixteen days. But both of us were quite well after awhile. My wife had just born a child four days earlier and we were afraid that the fright would make her sick but both she and the child were fine and I can tell you that my wife has very good health and hasn't been sick much and is very good at taking care of our home, which is very important. We now have three children. We had a son April 20, and his name is Syvert. All my children are healthy and are growing big and strong and they are clever and sensible. But many of you may ask why I haven't given my children Norwegian names. They've been baptized with names that can be spoken, read and written in both English and Norwegian so they won't have to use another name when they come to the Americans. Joran is for example Julia in English.

We have better times this year than last when we had a poor year and a low price on the products we sell. This year is a so-called medium year and those who had land that was high and dry had a rich harvest, but part of my land is flat and swampy and from the middle of May to the middle of July we had too much rain and flooding that caused great damage to my fields. But even so I harvested 265 bushels of wheat, twenty-two bushels of oats and a lot of potatoes and Indian corn. I had more land with hay than I need so I rented out some of it and harvested forty-eight wagons loaded with as much as a team of oxen could pull. I hired a newcomer for two months during harvest and paid him twenty dollars a month and then I hired someone to break six acres last summer for thirty-six dollars. In 1865 I paid ninety-five dollars in war *bounty* for volunteers to be soldiers in our stead, and in 1866 I paid eighty-seven dollars and sixty cents in tax on my land but this year the tax was only eighteen dollars. We had great expenses during the war but now all is peaceful and quiet and many are getting out of the debt that the four years of war brought upon us.

This year we had a fairly good price for wheat. I've sold some for one dollar and forty to fifty cents a bushel. I now only have six miles to the market and I've sold wheat for 168 dollars and still have some left to sell, so my debt will be only eighty dollars. I have a team of oxen, two cows, two heifers, a one and a half year old bull, two calves, nine sheep, and four pigs. An ox team costs 150 to 175 dollars and a milk cow thirty to forty dollars. I've lost quite a lot of animals here: six calves, one cow, four sheep, and one pig. I haven't yet been able to afford horses, because a pair costs from 350 to 400 dollars, but it is fine to work a small farm with an ox team because horses are quite expensive to keep as they eat oats every day.

They're building a stone church so close to us that I can see it every day. It will cost about 6,000 to 7,000 dollars and the walls have been built. I have no news as I don't know of any acquaintances who have died recently, but the two oldest sons of Hellik Aslesen have married and they live about thirty miles from here and I've visited Hellik once. My brother Ole had a son last year and his name is Ole, and he and his family were well and in good health when I spoke with them eight days ago. He then hadn't threshed his wheat. He has five horses, a cow, a heifer, and a calf. My brother Paul has been in good health since he came here. He lived mostly with me last winter and went to English school and worked one month for Halvor Knudsen Hullet, also called Fjøseeiet, for five dollars a month. In April he went to the town of Rochester where he worked for one and a half dollars a day. But he had to pay three and a half dollars a week for meals at a hotel, laundry not included, so he said that he didn't make much money as there were many rainy days when he didn't get work. Since the spring season he has worked for brother Ole. This winter Paul will go to northern Wisconsin for work in the pine forest that pays well. He'll be going with Sjul Hansen Lehovdeiet who has also worked in this neighborhood this summer. I don't know how much money Paul has made since he came but he is quite happy here. And I send greetings from the Teksle people. They are in good health and Ole sold his land last fall for 700 dollars as they want to go back to Wisconsin in the spring as Marit longs to be with her sister Ambjørg Kampestad. Ole will be worth about 1,000 dollars when he sells all his animals. Sjul Olsen Teksle has already moved to Wisconsin. Ole Olsen Rønningsdalen came to me about three weeks ago from Wisconsin and he didn't have more than five dollars left of his money and he neither can nor will do any work to earn his bread, especially now during winter. His guardian in Norway will probably have to send money for his keep and this doesn't look good for a young man of twenty.

I mustn't forget to thank you for the gift you sent us with Paul. It was very welcome even though we have woven a few times ourselves since we got sheep. And then I must send greetings to mother, if she is still living, from us all and thank her for the good advice and wonderful words she sent us in her last letter. It made us glad to see that she reads so much in the holy word of God and thinks of her sins so she can be ready to leave this earthly life and go to her death with courage in her faith in Jesus our Savior. She mustn't be sorry that she cannot send us more books because there are enough books in the Norwegian language to be bought here, could we but use them rightly.

And then I must send a few words to my brother Knud and my sister Joran and ask them not to leave our old parents in their old age. I'm often sad that I left them for which I ask their forgiveness. I did it because it would be better to support myself here as we were so many that we all couldn't have the farm there at home. But should any of you have the desire to go to America you should either all go or none since we cannot desert our father in his old age. But it is undeniably easier to make a living here than in Norway even though things are not quite as bountiful as many in Norway imagine. But with hard work and diligence one may have a decent income.

With this I must end my poor letter and in conclusion give you my father and mother, brother and sister, my and my wife and children's loving and friendly regards and also those of my brothers Ole and Paul. Regards to our relatives and friends from all of us, and my wife's mother gives her regards to my parents. She is now a widow and lives with me and helps us to take care of the children. And in conclusion I hope that this letter will find you in good health and that you are all sound in body and soul. This is my constant wish, your always loving son and brother. Live well in the Lord.

HELLIK OLSEN LEHOVD

«I:122 »I:136 NE II:160

1867 — LETTER I:133

FROM: Hellek G. Branson, *Eureka, Kansas, 8 November 1867*
TO: Ole Gulbrandsen and Anne Andersdatter Lande, *Flesberg, Buskerud*

Dear brother and family,

I received your letter of September 4 on October 30 and see that you are all healthy and doing well, which makes me very glad. I can also say that we are all in good health and doing well. As for my sons, none is quite as tall as

Ole was. But they are not quite grown up yet; Henry is six feet and not quite nineteen, and the others are too young to predict how tall they'll be.

I have 320 acres of which forty acres have been broken. My buildings are very poor, but I have a one-tenth section, 240 acres, of Eureka, a town that is now being built. I also have a house and three lots in a small town called Hartford. I have about 150 head of cattle, 200 sheep and twenty horses. I paid 100 dollars in taxes last year. I sold my bulls for 1,390 dollars. I've more I can sell next spring but I don't think the prices will be as high then. I lost a good deal of cattle last winter so I haven't been able to lay anything aside. But I'm not beholden to anyone. I hope I'll have better luck with my cattle from now on. We live quite simply but we have enough for our daily bread. I came to this place last summer and had lived for seven years about ten miles to the north. My farm is close to Eureka where there is a general store, a post office, a hotel and a schoolhouse. A steam mill is under construction. This is the county seat for Greenwood County and there is talk of a railroad coming here.

I see that Gullik Bringe is in debt and has difficulties making ends meet, which makes us sad. You ask for my frank advice on whether they should emigrate or not. This is not easy as it is so long since I was in Norway and at that time I was young and inexperienced. But I've never wished to be back in Norway. They must make their own decision as have the others who have left Flesberg. You've seen in letters what those who have emigrated think of America. I think it should be easy for them to make up their minds when so many have gone before them and have, with a few exceptions, improved their situation. We'd be glad to see them come. I cannot really say where it would be best to settle as it is a long time since I was in the Northwestern states and I don't know much about conditions there now. But you could see in my last letter that I prefer Kansas. There isn't much government land left around here, but they are about to buy a large area from the Indians about one day's journey south of here. It will soon be opened for settlement and it is some of the best land in America. So I think it would be an advantage for a settler to make use of this opportunity as good government land is usually bought up. Should you come, I'll help you acquire land, either here or down in the Indian country since I plan to go there for land myself. Gulbrand and Harry will do it too as I believe this would be to the best for all of us. I would then rent out my farm here and take my cattle with me, as the land there is particularly well suited for cattle as well as for regular farming. I sell my oxen every spring when they are three years old. I haven't sold my wool yet this year. I sell my horses whenever an opportunity arises.

Gulbrand has 160 acres, two horses and five head of cattle. He has lived with us since he came home from the war.

If you come I think it would be best to take the railroad to St. Joseph, Missouri, as some Norwegians live around there. Syvert Kalderud lives near Gary City, about ten miles down the Missouri River on the Kansas side. If you are there we could come for you with horses and a wagon. When you get to Syvert you must write to me immediately. As for mother, I cannot advise her one way or the other. We would all be glad to see her here but she must consider this carefully as well as seek your advice, as the journey will naturally be difficult for her. If mother shouldn't come you mustn't leave her with strangers but take her home to Lande. If she comes here we'll gladly do our best for her. As for Ole Haugen, he is so far away that I cannot speak with him. You'll have to write to him yourself about the question his sister asked in your letter. His address is Robinson P.O., Brown County, Kansas. As for whether the letters are more sure of getting here when they are paid in advance or not I don't know any more than you do. Send letters paid or unpaid as you find best. Write as soon as you get these lines and let me know whether you're coming. I have more to write about but I'm just about to leave so I must end my poor letter with loving regards to you and your wife as well as to our old mother and brother-in-law and sister. Write as soon as possible with news. Your devoted brother

HELLEK GULBRANSON LANDE AND FAMIILY

· —— ·

In 1865 Ole Gulbrandsen's farm Lande in Flesberg is listed as having one horse, thirteen cows and eighteen sheep, so we may assume that Hellek Branson knew his report on his holdings would seem impressive. By the time of his letter of 10 July 1871, Gullik Gulliksen and Kari Gulbrandsdatter Bringe, along with their three daughters and her mother, Sigri Reiersdatter, had come to Kansas. «I:130 »II:8 NE II:161

· —— ·

1867 — LETTER I:134

FROM: Magrete Nilsdatter and Ole Olsen Hove, *Vernon, Minnesota*
31 *December 1867*
To: Martha Haldorsdatter Næsheim, *Granvin, Hordaland*

Dear and beloved mother,

After a long delay we must finally let you hear from us, as we assume that you've been waiting for information about the things you so kindly sent us. In greatest gratitude we can tell you that we have received them. You may know that your dear son Johannes sold his land in Goodhue County, Minnesota for 1,500 dollars and has moved to Iowa where his friends live. He and his wife came here six weeks ago and brought your gifts and they were packed in a box and in good order. We hadn't expected to receive such useful things without cost. Johannes and his wife returned to Goodhue County to their former home to get the 600 dollars that then were due from their sale of their land. They had a good pair of horses and their own wagon and they were both in good spirits and said that they were much better off now than they had been since their marriage. The box had come last summer to Ole Johannesen Næsheim and your son Johannes and his family had lived with him since they moved to Iowa. The person who had brought the gifts hadn't himself settled in Iowa but had brought them there, so neither Johannes nor we have seen him or spoken with him. We don't know whether he will ask to be paid for his troubles but there was no bill attached to the box. This was, as we have said, much more than expected, as it wasn't our intention when we wrote to you about a spinning wheel and carding combs that you should send them to us as free gifts, as we have received so many valuable gifts from you before. So thank you my unforgettable dear mother, I'm so happy for the excellent spinning wheel and also the needlework that is nicer than any I've ever seen. It is so well made. The bowls are also good, so now I have the things that I've missed for so many years. The homespun is also very welcome and I used it for underwear for myself and my family. I gave the book to my oldest daughter

Marthe since you had given me the same one earlier. And we were so glad to have the package of barley and it will look very nice in the spring when we'll plant every grain. And if it should prove to thrive better here and give a better yield than the kind we use, then this little package may give us a lot of money in a few years. So it was a gift that was not only very welcome but also of great value. We are so grateful for the generosity you have shown us.

As for us, we are glad to tell you that we are all in good health and thus have no reason to complain about our worldly situation. We are quite satisfied even though we are surrounded by so many children. We had a son ten weeks ago! So we now have five boys and four girls, not a small family. But they are all, praise God, healthy and enjoy each other. Although they may now be a slight burden, we hope that this will be compensated in a few years if we live. We can also tell you that our last harvest wasn't very good. We had 260 bushels of wheat and forty of oats and enough potatoes for our own use. We also planted a field of corn but we got nothing because the seed had been poor. The price for wheat has been quite good, about one dollar and sixty cents a bushel. We sold wheat for about 200 dollars, but this isn't an amount that goes very far for such a large family here in America. We've now let our fields on shares. We provide the seed and the share farmer plows it and harvests it and uses his own horse and implements while we share the crop when we thresh it. If Gods grants me health I can make more money by working as a carpenter as the prospects for work seem promising. I can also tell you that I was appointed postmaster a short while ago so the post office is in my own home. The name of the post office is Vernon.

You write that you would like to know what animals we have and I can tell you that we haven't had many, but we have a good ox team that we were offered 170 dollars for last fall. We also have a few cows and a foal and last fall we got some sheep, pigs and chickens, the animals a farmer usually has here in America. We don't have any more to tell you now and will therefore end our simple letter and ask your forgiveness for all its faults. I wanted to rewrite this letter but now I don't have time since I am expecting the mail. Tomorrow I'll be going to Wisconsin and will be absent a few weeks. This journey will cost me between twenty-five and thirty dollars. Our best regards to you all, and in particular to you our dear mother from

MAGRITHE NILSDATTER AND OLE O. HOVE

P.S. As we now are paying the postage for this letter you shouldn't have to pay anything upon receiving it and we hope that you will send us a letter and let us know whether this worked.

As in the earlier letters, the husband did the writing. At some point they have moved from Wisconsin to Minnesota. The letters sent to Martha Næsheim illustrate how emigration was often a first step to further migrations, in the case of her two daughters and two sons spanning the states of Illinois, Wisconsin, Iowa, and Minnesota. OOH's appointment as postmaster illustrates his family's integration into the society of their new homeland: he has not only mastered a new language but has also achieved a position that suggests some degree of participation in local politics. In immigrant farming families the women brought with them their skills in making clothes from the wool of their own sheep, but often, as here, had to rely on relatives in the old country for a supply of the required tools. »I:71 NE II:164

1868 — LETTER I:135

From: Rakel Tonette Aslakson, *Coon Prairie, Wisconsin, 14 January 1868*
To: Osmund and Beren Andreas Atlaksen and Sara Atlaksdatter Ovedal
Bakke, Sirdal, Vest-Agder

Dear unforgettable siblings,

I received your letter of April 19 on May 19, and was glad to see that you all were in good health. I can say the same about us. I was in La Crosse for three months and had two dollars a week. I had a very lonely Christmas. I came home on New Years Eve. Siri went up to our brother Reinert June 14 but I think she'll be back next summer. Reinert has built a house. I haven't had a letter from Sivert for a long time but Tron Haaversen was here in the beginning of December and he says they are all doing well up there but that the harvest was poor. Sigbjørn and his family are all doing well and he had a good harvest: 300 bushels of wheat and 360 bushels of oats and they also had lots of potatoes. I've heard a rumor that Beren Andreas and Sara are coming to America next spring and if this is true they must write to me as soon as possible. I hear that you would like to know where Lars Andreas Haughom is, but no one here knows anything about him after he was here at Coon Prairie and that was five years ago when he lived with Odmund Listøl and Sigbjørn Listøl, who now is dead. Gabriel Jødestøl and his family are all well. Siri is better now than she has been for a long time. Old Mari is as fit as she was at Jødestøl. She cards wool and spins. She and Siri are attending school this winter. Yesterday I visited our mother's brother Haaver and they are all well. Sivert Midfelse remarried on September 17. His wife is a widow with a little boy. Christian Virak has married Ingebor Sofie Mortensdatter Konstali. I was glad to hear the rumor that Beren Andreas and Sara are coming to America in the spring but I wish you would all come. I cannot advise anyone to come or not to come but I can see that it is much better for me here and I don't wish to return to Norway. I've struggled enough on Norwegian hills. There are many at home who imagine that the journey is dangerous as if there are no dangers in Norway. Trond Konstali has gone many times back and forth but he nevertheless ended his days on Sirdal Lake that they cross many times a year. Torjus Torjusen and Stine Maria are doing well. I'll tell you about Sigbjørn's neighbors. His nearest neighbors are Peder Hansen Barstad or Jendal and Hans Skjerpe and Hans Sætra and Tønnes Fladestøl and Torjus Torjusen and Mikal Hendrik Nystøl and Erik Virak and Sigbjørn Konstali. They are so close that we see them almost every day. I have no more to tell you now. Siri Gabrielsdatter asks me to send greetings to her brother Osmund that she is doing well. She lives some distance from us and I haven't seen her since last summer. Ask Osmund Gabrielsen to please write a few lines to me and let me know how they are. I haven't heard from him since we left. Also give greetings to Hendrik Skibeli, Siri Sirnes and Olene Øxendal, but first and foremost to our old aunt in Skibeli. And you must give greetings to those at Landsmark and Konstali and to all friends and acquaintances. I must now conclude my letter with regards to you all. Live well.

                    RAKKEL THONETTE ATLAKSDATTER

[*Added on a small piece of paper*] Dear brother Osmund,
I wish you would sell your farm and come in the spring with Beren and Sara. You can buy land here. I'm not happy about the others coming without you. You'll be so alone in Norway. There is room for you here, even when we all are gathered. Sigbjørn asks you to bring some cherry and apple pits. When you write please tell let me how many are coming next spring.

                                    RAKKEL THONETTE

The conclusion of a letter Rakel probably wrote in January 1867 is in Nor. ed. II:145. She gives advice on what emigrants should take with them and reports that Siri Gabrielsdatter Ovedal, who had come with them in 1865, had married Erik Asbjørnsen Virak. Her sister Sara emigrated in 1869, but not Beren and Osmund. The family from Jødestøl, including Gabriel Gabrielsen, his widowed mother Mari Nilsdatter (then sixty), and his sister Siri, had all emigrated on the bark *Hebe* in 1865. Since letters from America usually were shared with both family and neighbors, letter writers often wrote messages intended only for the eyes of the addressee on a separate piece of paper. Sivert Midtfjeldsaa had emigrated in 1852 on the bark *Emigrant* with his wife Anne and their four children. He was then forty-nine and his wife forty-one. «I:116 »I:140 NE II:168

1868 — LETTER I:136

FROM: Ole Olson and Jøran Halvorsdatter Lehovd, *Kasson, Minnesota*
13 March 1868
To: Ole Helgesen Lehovd, *Flesberg, Buskerud*

Dear parents and siblings!

As time permits, I must now take up my pen to write you a few lines as you've written twice to Hellik since I wrote to you for Paul. I assume you have news about us from Hellik but I will nevertheless send you a letter as the postage now is cheaper according to the law, so a letter to Norway via Hamburg or Bremen is now twenty-five cents and from Norway twenty-eight cents. But the law is not always followed so closely as the post masters need something in their pockets too, so when you send letters here, write on it: By Bremen or Hamburg Steamer. I must let you know that we are in fairly good health and our son will be one year on March 31 and he is just about to walk on his own. His name is Ole. His mother isn't strong as she has a weak chest, probably because she had to work so hard for Anders Nerlie. Here among the Americans one has to sleep in cold rooms in the winter even when it is so cold that people freeze to death out of doors. But I'm quite well and we live where we have lived even though it is far to a forest. But I'm not alone and anyway it is good to have a home where we can grow our food. Last summer I had about 400 bushels of wheat and eighty bushels of oats and more than forty bushels of potatoes. My wheat was better than in the first year as it was better threshed and I was paid better for it last fall than before. I sold almost all I could last fall so I could pay down my debt. The railroad and *depot* are so close that I can clean and sell a wagonload on the same day and the name of the town is Kasson. I don't have many cattle; no more, says Joran, than a crofter in Norway. I've had one cow but now I also have a heifer that will have a calf next May, so then I'll have two cows and I also have a calf that will be one year in April. But our cow gives more milk and butter than the Norwegian cows, so I haven't yet bought butter and I have enough all year round even though I've hired help during harvest and for threshing. I have two work horses and a two-year-old foal and two one-year-olds, and I believe one of my mares is carrying a foal, so if God gives his blessing my animals will grow in value and almost all kinds of animals are very expensive here. If I have luck in my endeavors then all will be good but if things go wrong then you can lose everything very quickly. You can be more quickly rich as well as poor here than in Norway as the interest is almost twenty-five per cent and everything is expensive. Those who are bankrupt in Norway are often to blame themselves as they don't know the value of what they inherit from their parents as they haven't worked for it themselves and imagine that life will be one long party. But if you've been poor and worked for what you have, you have a much better understanding of what it costs. I see that Gullik Bringe has gone bankrupt or made himself a beggar as the saying goes, and this isn't strange according to what I have heard about how they ran things.

Our brother Paul went to the pinery in northern Wisconsin last fall where they cut huge amounts of lumber that is transported everywhere. He went with a neighbor who has written that they both signed up for a year for twenty-four dollars a month. Paul hasn't written yet but sent his regards in a letter to one of our neighbors. He worked three months for me last summer haying, harvesting and threshing. And he helped me get a good man and horses to plow for me last spring so my spring work was well done. I've written to him. I see that you would like to see how he writes now that he's gone to school, but he didn't really go to school much. When a newcomer goes to school he has to learn how to read English before he can write it. He is making good money and he needs it as he too will want to get a home. It isn't good to live with others because when they run short of food they'll look askance on one who doesn't belong in the family. I think Paul experienced this when he went to school.

Ole Olsen Osland has come here to Minnesota and last fall I got him work for an American, as he had asked me to do. He worked for him in Rochester up to about Christmas, but since then he has lived with Ole Olsen Lia, so we haven't been bothered much by him. He is rather obstinate and difficult but perhaps he'll learn how to take care of his money when he finds out what it is like to be without it because he had squandered all his money by the time he got here. Last fall I wrote a letter for him to Sjul Jondalen and his father. Hellik Takserud came here in September with his mother and five children. They live in a kind of cellar about four or five miles from here right next to Halvor Knudsen Berg and I believe they live rather poorly. America has its own problems, in particular for those who are poor and who have to ask for help from others as it isn't easy for him with so many children to feed. His mother is quite well considering her advanced age and that she is alone with all of Hellik's children.

Your letter brought us the good news that Ole Toresen Ørsteen was to marry this girl from Gjerde. The wedding at Ørsteen must have been a great event and we imagine that both Knud and the groom played on their violins and that they cooked fat sausage rather than wedding porridge, the finest wedding food, as there isn't so much cream for porridge at this time of year.

We've had a harsh winter since Christmas so it is at times difficult to get out to take care of the animals as there is so much snow and a cold wind. The prairie is quite flat so there is nothing to stop the snow except for houses and haystacks where the snow settles. Two years ago the house of one of my neighbors was entirely covered by snow one night. His windows and his door were under the snow so he lay there waiting for the light of day, but he couldn't see anything until he was able to get out through his window. But now we've had nice weather and the snow is almost gone. It seems that we'll have enough hay this spring, but last spring we had a cold and wet spring so there was a shortage of hay and animals starved to death. Hay then cost ten dollars a ton, but I had enough hay for my own use. I must now end my poor letter. I hope you'll write to me with news from home, about how many will be coming this spring and about what people we know are doing, as I don't think I'll return to Norway. I see that there are hard times in Norway and this has also been the case here for a couple of years, and some of the newcomers have had help from the town. But I haven't been in need of food even though I may not be eating as well as many others. I hope these lines will find you in good health. I see in your letter that mother wished she could send us some religious books, so I must tell you that Joran had Luther's and Linderoth's books of homilies as well as a Bible and I also had some edifying books, so our situation is not as bad as you may imagine. Best regards from me and my family,

OLE OLSON LEHOVD

Dear father!

You must also give Joran's regards to her old parents and her brothers when you have an opportunity to do so. She is sad that her parents should suffer want in their old age. We've heard that Knud plans to go to America, and if he wants to go he should make himself some small boxes for the voyage, as the one I had gave me problems and expenses. He should bring all his clothes as the Norwegian homespun clothes are good to have here too, especially if they can be remade according to the fashion here. And if he wants to come to us he can go by train from Chicago to La Crosse in Wisconsin and then by boat to Winona in Minnesota and from there by train to Kasson, that is not far from us. And we've heard that Knud was cheated by Ole Gjerde when he signed a contract for Bjerkerud. It is a shame that Knud had to pay. Such men shouldn't be allowed to cheat a poor working man who has toiled for his money. There is so much dishonesty in the world and especially in this country where there are so many murders and robberies, in particular of horses and oxen. Horses are often stolen and at Koshkonong many Norwegians were arrested and taken to Indiana because they had bought stolen horses. They went off and sold them when they heard that the owners had come to get them back, probably because they didn't want to lose the money they had paid for them. But then they were taken for having sold stolen horses when the owners arrived. The man they had bought the horses from was taken at night in the home of a Norwegian in Clinton to be punished for his crime, but when he had dressed himself he took a revolver from his pocket and threatened to shoot those who wanted to take him and he escaped. Among those who were arrested are Paul and Gulbrand Sjulsen Gjerde and many others.

I'll also ask you my parents if you can give me information about my brothers Paul and Gullik, as I haven't heard from them since I came here. If you've heard anything since then, please give me their addresses. I'm very worried that my parents are weak and without enough food. I suppose that the inheritance they were due from Kjersti Trollerud all went to Anders Nerlie, and this merely for some potatoes and a few pounds of cheese. I certainly hope that Anders has been repaid for his expenses for the first letter I sent unpaid from here. I've heard that Joran Nerlie has claimed two silver buttons that are at Lehovd and that Ole says were his at the time he lived at home. My regards to my beloved parents and to Sjul and Knud and their families and to Gullik Paulsen Gjerde,

JORAN HALVORSDATTER

As Ole begins to write for his wife Joran he refers to her in the third person and then he shifts to the first person, letting her speak directly through him. Joran's parents were Halvor Paulsen and Marit Helgesdatter. They were sixty-eight and sixty-nine years old in 1868 and lived on a *husmannsplass* called Granstuen that belonged to one of the several Gjerde farms in Flesberg. They were in a social class below landowning farmers such as those at Lehovd. Joran's brother Knud Halvorsen lived with his wife at Bjerkerud, a *husmannsplass* under Gjerde. Her brother Hellik was a *husmann* under the farm Taksrud. The first mention of Paul Halvorsen's alleged plans to emigrate is in the letter by Hellik Lehovd of 10 April 1858. Paul's only letter to his parents (see letter I:122) was written by Ole. The fiddler at the wedding was Knut Olsen Ørstein. A porridge where sour cream and flour were main ingredients (*rømmegrøt*) was a festive food in many areas of Norway. In late winter, however, when the hay had been carefully rationed to make it possible to keep as many cows as possible through the winter, there was little milk and less cream. «I:132 »I:154 NE II:171

1868 — LETTER I:137

FROM: Christopher Jacobson, *Idaho City, Idaho, 22 March 1868*
To: Hans Jakobsen Hilton, *Kløfta, Ullensaker, Akershus*

→⇌⇋←

Dear brother!

Although it took you a long time to write your letter, I didn't have to wait long for it: it came to me as by the wings of a swan. It was sent October 8 and I received it November 17. I was glad to hear that you and the others are in good health and getting along well. You complain that you don't have any news, but for an old goat you've dug up more news than I could have done had I been back in Ullensaker. If things had been as in the old days when I was at Søli, I would have said that you had been over at the neighbor's. But your present neighbors may be just as well informed about what the youngsters are doing. True enough, I don't know more than half of those you say now are married, etc., but I nevertheless read your letter with the greatest pleasure as it made me feel as if I were home again in Old Norway, and even though most were strangers I could now and then see a face that I knew. From my heart I thank you for your endeavors to entertain me.

You may be sure that I often, yes daily imagine myself at Hilton where I see both you and Anne. I remember that the fortune-teller said "you shouldn't put two herrings on one slice of bread," and I predict that this is the way with both you and Anne, so I imagine that you both are old fashioned even though all of Ullensaker follow the new ways. I'm sure your sons will become good men, but give them good advice and think twice before you beat them, because that isn't good. I would say the same to Anne, but I suppose she has to do it now and then. But I would ask her not to do it too often as she may regret it later. They are now living their happiest days on earth. Be their comforters and friends as well as their guides; then they will later think back with love on the days they spent under your care in joy and happiness, and it won't then be so difficult for them to be of comfort and help to you when you are old and may need them. And now you also have a little daughter who I'm sure gives you—and Anne in particular—pleasure.

Yes, I'm sure the boys are also glad to have a sister. But I must remind you that it may be time you said stop now; I think you have enough children.

But as I do not and will not have a wife and, consequently no children, it may be that you've gone to this trouble for both of us, and all for the best, as you are better suited to be the head of a family than I, since Christopher will, as you know, always be Christopher, as long as he lives. So I can well imagine how it would work out should I have Brotnu, that you say is for sale at a low price, in my hands. Then I wouldn't have worn patched trousers and a vest, nor boots. I would have had a top hat and a wig to cover my bald head should it be necessary to take off my hat. I would have a cariole and one of the most beautiful horses in the county to pull it. And I would hold my head high! In short, Brotnu and I both would be under the hammer again before a year had passed. No, it is better for me to ramble around as I do; this is what suits me best.

If the American (who is a Norwegian in America) made you believe that it was so easy to get money in the silver mines, why didn't he go there instead of to Iowa? The Chinese that I told you worked for me in my last letter were working where no money could be made as they had to pay too much for water, so I didn't get anything. After the Chinese quit we couldn't agree on how to work the mine, so we left it untouched until last fall. In the meantime I worked for some Irishmen for six dollars a day. When fall came around I and another Norwegian bought the others' shares in our mine and we began working for ourselves. We paid them 600 dollars and when we had paid for the lumber and the tools we had spent all our money. But that means nothing here in the mines where we all live in hope. I and Martin, that is my partner's name, have worked hard at digging a 400-foot-long tunnel. We have now opened our mine and can work it to our advantage, but the end of the tunnel doesn't look as good as we had thought. I once thought that I could make from one to two thousand dollars in our mine, but now I doubt it. We should be able to dig it all out in a year if we live so long. In my next letter I can tell you whether we made any money or not.

Some time ago I had a letter from friends in Nevada. They thought I should leave Idaho City since I've been here for so long and not made any money. They say they are doing quite well and that new mines have been found a couple of hundred miles from where they are and that they would go there if I joined them. I feel the restlessness in my blood when I hear that friends are planning to travel, and had things been as they used to be I would soon have been off on the back of my horse. But as I'm already old and have the shadow of a hope to be able to lay a little aside where I am,

I must settle down. It's possible that I'll go there when I'm finished here. It is also possible that I'll make a visit to Central America. But wherever I go, Hans, I'll always love to hear from you and from old Ullensaker, and I'll continue to write as long as you grant me an answer. There is so much disagreement about politics in America now that it wouldn't surprise me if they had a war again. If they could only get a better president everything would perhaps be better.

Well Hans, many days have passed since we made ourselves a circle in the grass in the schoolyard at Frogner. Little did we then think that we would ever be so far from each other. Could we but have these years returned to us—do you think we then would follow the same road? God alone knows. The first sorrow I can remember having was when we moved to Søli; moving now isn't so hard. And it doesn't seem so long ago that I first presented myself to the teacher with my ABC book and said in all my innocence as I had once said to my father, "I've learned my lines," and he began to laugh. I still feel the shame I felt for my family; may God forgive me; it hurt so deeply in my childish heart. Who teaches your sons? Do they go all the way to Lars or do you have a school closer by? You wrote that big Maria has become a midwife, a work I don't think she is fit for as her hands are larger than mine. Give her my regards when you see her. We went to school together and were good friends. And remember me to our old mother and tell her I have all I need. I'm also sending a letter to Lars with a letter to Allethe Søli. My regards to you all. May God bless you!

C. JACOBSON

· ———— ·

> This letter has been damaged. Most illegible words or parts of words can be guessed from their context. The two brothers had grown up at Søli, belonging to the farm Frogner in Ullensaker, where their father, Jacob Larsen, had been a teacher. Allethe Søli was the daughter of Anne Jakobsdatter (their sister) and Ole Larsen. Their brother Lars Jakobsen was a teacher and lived at Ullern in Ullensaker. Considerable silver deposits were found north of Boise in Idaho late in 1865, leading to a rush that peaked in 1868. In 1900 Oluf, son of Hans and Anne Hilton's, was the son-in-law and farmer at Brotnu in Ullensaker.
> «I:80 »I:152 NE II:172

· ———— ·

1868 — LETTER I:138

From: Hendrik Olsen Dahl, *Norman Hill, Texas, 30 May 1868*
To: Peder Eriksen and Siri Kristiansdatter Furuset
Romedal, Stange, Hedmark

Dear parents,

I should have written to you long ago, but nothing has come of it, so I'll take up my pen and tell you that we are all, praise God, in good health, as we hope that these lines will find you. We don't have anything of importance to tell you. Things are pretty much as they have been, hard times. It seems that people have less money and prices are low on all things except for wheat, for which we've had a good price. But this year the wheat harvest is failing all over Texas. The grasshoppers came in such numbers last fall that we couldn't sow the wheat until just before Christmas. They laid eggs last fall and in early March the young insects came out and destroyed almost all the wheat. We have now planted corn instead and it looks good and we may still expect to have a good harvest. But corn doesn't give as much cash as wheat. We have had a good spring so our horses and cattle are fat again.

A few weeks ago we were down in Waco and had our pictures taken, all except little Gine. He was unable to do anything with her as she couldn't sit quietly. Moreover, he had poor cameras and nothing was well done. But I'll send them as we know that you wish to see them. It is two weeks since auntie was here and she sends her regards. They are all in good health. The population of this settlement is growing. We are now about 200 including children and we expect many families from Four Mile Prairie and some from Norway. We applied to the northern states last winter for a Norwegian pastor but none was available. But we had a letter a few weeks ago that we'll have one by next fall, and that will be very good for us. American pastors sometimes have church services here, but many of the old ones don't understand them. I have no more that will interest you and will end my poor letter with loving regards to you all from me, my wife and children. Your devoted son-in-law,

H. O. DAHL

HOD and Christine Pedersdatter Furuset emigrated in 1851 on the bark *Arendal* and they married in 1853 (Syversen 1982, 267–270). The Norwegian settlement in Four Mile Prairie, Texas was founded by Johan Reiersen in 1847. Little Gine was born on 29 January 1867. Auntie was Anne Eriksdatter Rogstad. «I:129 »I:149 NE II:174

1868 — LETTER I:139

FROM: Tor Torstensen Vigenstad, *South Bend, Minnesota, and Spring Prairie, Wisconsin, June 1868*

To: Ole Torstensen Vigenstad, *Dovre, Oppland*

Dear brother,

When we parted in Christiania I promised to write you from Liverpool and you must excuse me for not doing this. I'll tell you about my journey. I was in good health the whole time, for which I cannot sufficiently thank the good Lord. It took us three days from Christiania to Hull. We were well taken care of in Hull. From there I went by train to Liverpool where we were treated worse than pigs. On the twentieth we went on board the steamship *Virginia* that was to take us to Paradise. On the ship we were herded to the afterdeck where we had to stand for many hours before we were allowed to go below. In the morning we were given a tiny loaf of bread, about the size of the cheese we got from the mountain pasture when we were boys. For dinner we had three small potatoes and two small pieces of meat. In the evening we were again given bread and a little butter and I've never in my life had so little water. For three days we had such a gale that the waves flowed over the deck and the ship was like a down feather in the wind and when we went to bed on the twenty-fourth we had to hold ourselves with both hands and everything that wasn't tied down went all over the place. You may imagine how I felt. We were cheated by Svensen; we were not placed on a mail ship as we had paid for but on a two-decked freighter that took nineteen days to cross the ocean.

We were one night in New York. From New York we went west by train but this was not as we had expected. In McGregor we had to wait four days because the railroad needed repair. We took tickets from St. Paul to Mankato where we arrived at night and slept by a woodpile. In the morning we walked six miles until we met people who told us that Syver Killi and Erland Linsø were doing roadwork at St. Peter, so we turned around and walked eighteen miles to St. Peter. We didn't get there until eleven at night. There people told us where to find them. We are now doing roadwork with Syver and Erland for one dollar a day.

When I left home I said that I would write the truth, which I'll do. I think that if people knew as much about the journey before they went as they do when they arrive, many would stay where they were. For my part I'll certainly not advise anyone to come here. I most urgently ask you not to let Paul go. Yes, dear father, say absolutely no, because when you say no I'm sure that he won't come because he is more obedient than I. Syver and Erland send their regards and join me in imploring you not to let him go. I'll end my letter in the certain hope that you in no way will let him follow me. My loving regards to all of you at Vigenstad.

THOR SKEIE

Dear brother,

My dear brother, as we now are so far apart that we cannot talk with each other we'll have to do it in writing. As you know, I've been in the West, in Minnesota, and I've heard quite a lot about the settlers there. So I took a trip around in the country to see what it was like. I'll neither criticize it nor praise it as I haven't been here long enough to say anything about it. But should I offer my opinion, my view is that a good worker could get a farm that would be as good as any in Norway and he could live much easier and better on it than anyone does in Dovre. I've been doing quite well and I don't think that I'll be returning home as soon as I thought to begin with. But of course, anyone who has left such a home as I have will miss it. When last summer was at its hottest you may imagine that I remembered Runtum and you, and no wonder. I will end my letter with my regards to you.

THOR VIGENSTAD

· ⸺ ·

These two undated letters are to the oldest of the seven siblings on the farm Skeie in Dovre. Their father, Torsten Simensen, was a widower. The first letter, from South Bend, Blue Earth County, Minn., is an early account of travel by steamship via Liverpool. In 1868, when many were still going on sail ships via Quebec, TTV found the journey such a hardship that he would not advise any to follow him. The second letter was probably written a few months after the first, from Spring Prairie, Wisc. By then he had a more favorable view of immigration. Tor Torstensen was a passenger on the *SS Pacific*, leaving Christiania for Hull on 15 May 1868. His warning had no effect on his older brother Paul (born in 1839), who left Christiania on the *SS North Star* for London on 6 August that same year. Paul Torstensen Vigenstad was educated at a teachers' training college and was a parochial schoolteacher in Spring Prairie from 1868 until he settled in Norwegian Grove, Ottertail County, Minn. in 1871 where he was a farmer and parochial schoolteacher (Norlie 1924, 761). In 1866 O. Svensen became an agent of the American Emigrant Company and was also the agent of a steamship company (Semmingsen 1950, 132–133). For more on immigrants from Dovre, including these two brothers, see Engen 1983. »I:145 NE II:165 & 166

1868 — LETTER I:140

FROM: Sara and Rakel Tonette Aslakson, *Coon Prairie, Wisconsin*
27 July 1868
To: Osmund and Beren Andreas Atlaksen Ovedal, *Bakke, Sirdal, Vest-Agder*

Dear and unforgettable brothers,

I must now take my pen in hand to let you know I'm doing well and wish to hear the same from you. I've been quite well since I left except for a little seasickness at the beginning of the voyage. We left Stavanger April 27 and came to Quebec June 2. When we came to La Crosse June 11, Sigbjørn had been waiting for twenty-four hours. Rakel worked there but she came home with us. All went well for those who came from Bakke parish except for Severine Konstali. She has been sick since she came here but now she is so much better that she has been out of bed for two weeks but not yet strong enough for work. Twelve died onboard the ship and these were all children except for three. A child was buried in Stavanger, the others at sea. They made coffins for them and the captain sang a hymn over them and threw earth on them.

I find myself very satisfied here. I haven't longed for Norway since I came. I've been to Jødestøl and they are all doing well except Gabriel who got a splinter in his shoulder and this led to an abscess and he went to a doctor who cut two holes in it without finding anything and that was in September. Now, in May, he went to a doctor again and he removed a splinter that was three and a half inches long. He hasn't worked all winter but now it has almost healed. I've been to Ovedal to see our uncle Haaver and they are all well. Also at Midfjelse. I've not yet seen Reinert, Sivert and Siri but I've heard that they are well. Sigbjørn and his family are all well. I think it would have been better for you too if you sold Ovedal and came here.

All work here is easier. Sigbjørn hasn't had more help for haying than a man to drive and stack hay for two days. The haying took two weeks and now he has a man and two horses to cut the oats and wheat and he'll do this in three or four days. Sigbjørn and I will bind the sheaves and I think we'll do this in two weeks. He has three haystacks and eight cows and fourteen sheep and about thirty hens. We've had an unusually hot summer but not so hot that any crops have been hurt. It looks as if we'll have a good year. Please write as soon as possible and let me know if Beren is better. You must excuse me for being so late in writing but I wanted to see if I would like it here. The others have written so you've heard that we arrived safely and that was all I could write to you then. I must conclude my simple letter with regards to you both. Live well.

SARA ASLAGSDATTER

Dear and unforgettable brothers,

I'll make use of this opportunity to write a few lines to let you know how I am. I haven't been well for four weeks but the last few days I've been better. I've promised to help Torjus Torjusen bind wheat and will begin today. Give my regards to all relatives and friends.

R. TONETTE ASLAGEDATTER

Sara Atlaksdatter emigrated on the bark *Heros* where she had the company of several emigrants from Bakke. The passenger list gives her age as twenty; in the 1865 census, however, she is forty-three, close in age to her brother Osmund who is listed there as forty-five. Her two sisters were twenty-four and twenty-eight when they emigrated in 1865. The last preserved letter from Siri, who then uses the name Allikson, is in 1899 when she and Sara are the two surviving siblings. She refers to the farms of emigrants by the names of their farms in Norway. «I:135 »I:144 NE II:178

1868 — LETTER I:141

FROM: Gunder Helgesen Skare, *Minneapolis, Minnesota*
5 September 1868

TO: Helge Gundersen Nerdrum (Skare), *Eggedal, Sigdal, Buskerud*

Dear beloved and unforgettable father,

As I now have time I will in all haste take my pen in hand because it is a long time since I wrote to you. I've been in good health since I was with you and I hope that I'll have the same happy message from you. I saw that you had been in good health at the time you wrote, which made us very happy. I saw that our dear sister's little daughter Astri Knutsdatter Skaalen had gone to a better life with God. Yes, nothing is impossible for God, because a green tree can wither as fast as an old and half dry tree. At the time I was with you I couldn't imagine that her days in this life would be so short. Yes, at the time I was with you at Skare this little girl was glad and happy and it gave us pleasure to see her and now we miss her. And now we must be happy that her struggle is over and she has achieved her goal and has met her parents in our Lord and Savior's great joy and bliss. In the name of our Lord Jesus Christ!

You may not have had a letter from my brother Anders for some time. He has sold his land to a man from Flaa named Nils Olsen Strandemoen and he did this March 16 on the condition that he was to leave it in June. He sold it for 2,400 dollars and still has his animals and equipment. He sold it because he wanted to have more land. He may be able to get more, but it'll be difficult to find better land. I and my brother went on a journey last spring to look for land in the West. We left in late March and went to Ottertail County, a distance of 350 miles, and we could only go 170 miles on the railroad. Then we had to go on foot for the most part except that we used skis at some times. We went many places and it took us a whole month before we came home. In Ottertail County we saw many Indians who camped in the woods. Wherever we went we saw Indians in the woods and there were several hundred and there were many soldiers at different forts that guarded the Indians so they wouldn't harm white people. When we were in Indian country we were quite scared and it often happens that the Indians attack the whites and then it depends on whether the whites are near the soldiers or not and on whether they are able to help themselves. Otherwise the whites are at the mercy of the Indians. There is some good land in the Indian country, both prairie and forestland, but it isn't yet safe to settle there because of the wild Indians. We didn't take any land there in the West but returned to Norway Lake...

. ——— .

> The rest has been lost. The parents of Astri Knutsdatter, Knut Nilsen and Ingeborg Helgesdatter Skaala, were dead and she had been living with her mother's brother, Halvor Helgesen, at Skare. Norway Lake was a Norwegian settlement in Stearns County, Minn. Nils Olsen Strandemoen from Flaa in Hallingdal moved from Spring Grove, Minn. to Stearns County in 1865 (Ulvestad 1907, 126 and Holand 1908, 558).
> «I:106 »I:146 NE II:180

. ——— .

1868 — LETTER I:142

FROM: Elise Wærenskjold, *Prairieville, Texas, 29–30 September 1868*
To: Karen Poppe, *Lillesand, Aust-Agder*

My good dear Kaja!

So you are still my dear old friend and haven't entirely forgotten me? But you've been very bad, very bad with me, but since you ask me so nicely to forgive you I suppose I must do so—but on <u>one condition</u>: You must improve yourself in the future. Write at least once a year! Your light and elegant handwriting reveals that this won't be difficult for you, so there is nothing to stop you if you only wish to do it. Thank you so much for your letter with interesting news. But you didn't send me your portrait and this was not nice. Have you seen the portrait of my husband? I sent it with a man from Veile in Denmark, but I cannot now remember whether I sent it to the Dannevigs or to Hansen. The poems were composed by Wilhelm on our little Thorvald's death. I'm quite well now but I don't think I can be really happy again. It was my own fault that I, through carelessness, had a long spell of diarrhea last year and since, as you'll remember, my own mother died of this illness I was rather anxious when it lasted for so long—five months. The health situation has been very good this summer in our settlement, but many of our old neighbors have abandoned us and have gone to Bosque because it is more salutary and has better land for wheat. There is always a good market for wheat. I had sowed fifteen bushels of wheat but it failed as we were afflicted with one of the Egyptian plagues: grasshoppers. They came in late October and left us when they had eaten everything green. Moreover, we had an extreme drought so we couldn't sow wheat until right before Christmas and then the grasshopper spawn came and ate the young wheat in the spring. When they were big enough to fly they disappeared. The wheat had cost me fifty dollars so it was a great loss. Moreover, I lost half of my sheep, five horses, twenty-seven cows and many calves due to the drought. A prairie fire burned the dry grass left by the grasshoppers and did much other damage. I'd never thought that grasshoppers could fly so high, but as high up as we could see the air was full of them. Apart from this we have had a good year in Texas and a lot of fruit. I had several hundred bushels of peaches. I've been without a servant girl for almost a year because my German girl who had been with me for six years went to her brother in Louisiana. I manage quite well and I save quite a lot in this way. In the months when the cows have the most milk two young married women helped me with the milking in return for some sweet and some sour milk and I had enough to share. I now have enough butter to sell for about fifty dollars. We now milk only three cows as all the others are with calf and are free to wander so they can be fat for the winter. So I'll have an easy life for some months.

I hadn't expected to hear that all your siblings are still living. Louise Seeberg had told me that your brother was married to Olsen's daughter but she gave me no details. Who had she been engaged to? Was it a German? You don't say why Olsen's son-in-law had to go to America and this would be of interest to me. Give all your siblings my friendly regards and ask Mrs. Møglestue to give my regards to her parents. And please include the Nilsens. Ole Johan Ørbæk was so pleased to hear about them. Have you seen his and Ouline's portraits? There was a poor imposter in the trade here in Prairieville and I went with my boys to have our portraits taken as so many of my friends had urged me to do so. But then his apparatus broke down and he sold it all. And that was the end.

Poor Stina! I would be glad to hear that her eyes had become better. It must be so sad not to be able to see properly. Please give my regards to her and her good mother and tell them that I would be very glad to hear from them. I haven't heard a word about Niels Møller's children since before the war. Do you know anything about them? I wonder whether Rennild is married. As I assume that you will read Gusta's letter, which I must ask you to put in an envelope, I won't repeat what I've written there about how your few acquaintances here are doing. They all send you their friendliest regards. You would do Mrs. Bache a great service if you went to her brother and gave him her and Andreas Anderson's regards and told them that they haven't had a letter from any of their family in Norway except for one that was sent to my husband's address. If Svendsen doesn't know their address you can show him how it is written here. But he must have it stamped as all unstamped letters are kept in Kaufman which is eighteen miles from here. Andreas, his wife and their little son have visited his parents-in-law in Bosque and on the way home they stayed a while with Mrs. Bache and little Edward Bache was baptized there. Andreas is a nice man and has a pleasant wife, just the right person for him. Mrs. Bache has sent several letters and cannot understand why she gets no replies.

I wasn't aware that Hammer was dead. Please give my regards to his widow, the lovable Helene Hammer, and ensure her of my sincere sympathy. Tell me, is Niels Langaard dead? I must assume this as neither you nor Gusta mention the families of Mads, Conrad and Niels. I assume you know how the members of the Grøgaard family are doing in Texas as Thorvald Dannevig spoke with Helene and her husband in New Orleans. Poor Marie has left Prairieville and gone to her sister Emma. I haven't seen Emma Mathews and Hans Jacob since they were children. I've had a glimpse of Thomas. He is very much like his father.

I'm quite surprised that people have become so refined in Norway that working class people have wallpaper and polished furniture while we read in the newspapers of the distress and misery in the rural areas where they have both asked for and received help from America. The first priority of a country should be to protect against hunger and things cannot be right when so many die of hunger as in Finland, East Prussia and other countries. I fear that luxury and class envy have spread far too much. You cannot imagine how ridiculous it is for me when someone addresses me, a mere farmer's wife, as *Frue*. Here we are all addressed in the same way and this is what I prefer. If you now have a better attitude among people that finds expression in an active charity towards their fellow beings, then this would indeed be good.

I'm so glad, dear Kaja, that you seem so content in your present position and that you are comfortable in your old age. But I recently had a letter from Sine Arntzen who still has a school in Korsør. That is a difficult life at her age. She is now sixty-four, but judging by her portrait she has kept well. You must remember Edle Holm who was married to Lagoni? She also still looks good, but he looked very old. Edle has been a widow for some years and now lives in Odense, where she is doing rather poorly. She has many wealthy relatives but they don't seem to help her at all. Are your old friends Mrs. Møller in Bergen and Mrs. Koren still living? Do you correspond with Mrs. Basberg? I've had a letter from her and Else's portrait. Poor woman! It was hard for her to lose her only daughter. But I'm now sleepy and must stop writing until tomorrow. I write and read without glasses. Do you? Goodnight!

I assume you know that I rent my farm to Negros and get half of the harvest. I would have preferred to rent it to a white man for the year if I only could have had a Norwegian, but this is no longer possible after the war. If Norwegians come to Texas they all go to Bosque, which now is the largest

Norwegian settlement. All in all the Negros are very well behaved, much better than the white Americans. Those who are <u>well situated</u> in Norway shouldn't come here but for all those who are needy, yes even many of those who are on poor relief, it would be good to come here. Now my paper is full and I must conclude with my most urgent request that you'll never again let me wait so long for a letter from you. Give my regards to <u>all</u> who would care to be remembered by your ever faithful

ELISE WÆRENSKJOLD

· —— ·

Two fragments are in Clausen 1861. Karen Poppe, called Kaja by friends, was a sixty-year-old widow in 1865. Her maiden name was Møglestue. Women in Norway were addressed as *Frue*, *Madam*, and *Kone* according to their social class. In her letters EW uses all three, and distinguishes between *Frue* and *Madam* also when writing of friends. So her outburst of an American-inspired Democratic attitude toward class tells us about her views in principle and, perhaps, in her daily relations in Texas, but not about her practice when she wrote letters to Norway, as here where she wrote *Madam* Møller and *Fru* Koren in the same sentence. Niels, Mads, and Conrad Langaard were merchants in Kristiania in 1865. Korsør and Odense are in Denmark.
«I:127 »I:160 NE II:181

· —— ·

1868 — LETTER I:143

FROM: Ole Johanson Holtseteren, *Watertown, Wisconsin, 27 November 1868*
To: Peder Johansen Holtseteren, *Gausdal, Oppland*

⋅≡○≡⋅

Dear brother and nephew,

I have received your welcome letter and see that you've been waiting for a letter from me, for which you may have good reason. I'm glad to see that you are well and we are, praise God, in good health and doing well. I see that you would like to come to America. It would have been better for you a long time ago, but you may not have been ready. This may be a good time because there is land to be had at Congress price. I've sold a house here in Watertown for 1,800 dollars and still have another one and five lots to sell. Last summer I went to Minnesota to a town called Austin and bought a town lot where I will build next summer if time permits. Should any of you come next summer you must write to me and let me know. It would perhaps be best that one of you came first and the others next year so you can be sure about this country. I'll repeat what I've said before, that I don't advise any to come. The voyage is difficult but nothing to be afraid of as many thousands come every year. Everyone has a free will and should any of you come I'll help you as well as I can. If I'm not here in Wisconsin I'll be in Austin, Minnesota, which can be reached in a day. I'll give you more information if any of you should come next summer. What will happen to my old mother if you all come? Will she remain at home or will she come with you? I'll end my poor letter with loving regards to my dear old mother, brother, sister and nephews as well as all my relatives and friends and, finally, to my brother and his wife from your affectionate brother

OLE JOHANSON HOLTSÆTEREN

. ——— .

> By this time he probably went by the name Ole Johanson and only used his Norwegian farm name in letters to Norway. The language of immigrants was gradually influenced by the dominant language and English words became part of their daily Norwegian discourse. In letters such words would not have made much sense to readers in Norway: *Kongræs Pris*, *Laater* (for lots). As in so many of these letters the verb "to go" is used in the English sense while in Norwegian it means to walk. It may be noted that in his last preserved letter Johansen has become Johanson, a form evidently felt to be more American. «1:91 NE II:184

. ——— .

1869 — LETTER I:144

FROM: Rakel Tonette Allikson, *Medo, Minnesota, 14 January 1869*
TO: Osmund and Berent Atlaksen Ovedal, *Sirdal, Vest-Agder*

—⋄—

Dear and unforgettable brothers,

Your honored letter of October 24 was received at Coon Prairie December 2 and sent on to me on the twenty-sixth. I see that you are doing well which made us very happy and the same may be said for us. I've gone from Wisconsin to Minnesota. I came here on St. Michael's Day and I've lived first with Syvert and then with Trond. I'm just as satisfied here as in Wisconsin even though it is very quiet here as there are so few young people. A Norwegian Lutheran pastor preaches here a few times a year and he was in the settlement on New Year's Day. On the second we were five miles from here and celebrated the wedding of Torkel Didriksen Østrem and Karen Anstensdatter Haukland, both from Lund. We had a nice party but there were only four at the wedding that I knew before coming to Minnesota, and these were the bridegroom and bride and Trond and Syvert. The others were from Hardanger, Voss, and Sogn.

Last fall Sara and I went twenty-five miles from Coon Prairie to pick hops and we picked two and a half bags a day and got half a dollar for a bag and there were seven bushels in a bag. We were twelve Norwegian girls and as many Americans and I think there were about 100 Indians or wild people. We went September 5 and returned on the twenty-third and on the twenty-ninth I came here in the company of Tobias and Berte Sandsmark. They have taken land here. The journey took us two days and was about 200 miles. I think they are doing quite well. Syvert has four forties two miles from Tron and he has broken thirty-five acres. He has only two horses and doesn't yet have any buildings but I think he plans to build next spring. It isn't long since I heard from Reinert and Siri and they were both doing well. At that time Siri was working in town. Sara has been living with Sigbjørn since she came but she asked me to write for her and give you and all her relatives and friends her regards.

Sigbjørn and his family are doing well as are all our relatives and friends. I would like to know whether one of you is thinking of coming here in the spring. My wish is that you both come. This would be better for you than to struggle along where you are. Give my regards to those at Sandsmark and Skibeli. I was sad to hear that our father's old sister is dead. I must end my poor letter with my regards to you both. Farewell!

RAKKEL T. ATTLAG DATTER

Write as soon as possible. My address is *R Tonette Alliksen, Medo P.O., Blue Earth County, Minnesota.*

> It is difficult to determine just when members of family from Ovedal changed their family name to Allikson but here Rakel uses the name Allikson in her address and it will be used from now on for the writers of letters in this family. The letter she is responding to had first been sent to her brother Sigbjørn in Coon Prairie, Wisc. In Medo she first lived with her brother Syvert Allikson and then with Trond Haaversen Ovedal, a cousin. They had gone to Minnesota in 1864. Her two brothers at Ovedal (ages forty-nine and thirty-nine) are unmarried. Lund is in Rogaland. Her sister Siri and her brother Reinert live in Eau Claire, Wisc. St. Michael's Day, or Michaelmas, was September 29. A forty was forty acres, one-sixteenth of a section. «I:140 »II:16 NE III:2

1869 — LETTER I:145

FROM: Thor Torstensen Vigenstad, *Spring Prairie, Wisconsin, 1 February 1869*

To: Ole Torstensensen Vigenstad, *Dovre, Oppland*

Dear brother,

I would have liked to write a long and entertaining letter, but as I'm a poor writer it will be a poor letter and I must ask you to excuse me. Half a year has passed since I came to America but it seems that two years at home went faster than this half a year here, and this isn't so strange as my thoughts have been at Skeie and Runtum. Yes, early or late, I haven't had my thoughts anywhere else and tears come to my eyes when I think back on my dear home that now is so far away. I can truthfully say that there hasn't been a half hour since I came here that I haven't thought of you. I remember how much fun we had and how quickly time passed when the three of us were in the woods for firewood or to Runtum for hay and were together all day and were glad and happy and then in the evening we sat around the stove and had fun. Alas, now it is so still and quiet around me. Now I can have an entire day without speaking a word and at night I sit alone in a room without anything to do and if I could have gone to grandmother's home one or other evening then I'm sure that I would have met you there and then I know it would have been the happiest evening I've had here. The hope that I'll sometime come home and see you again now makes my time pass more quickly than it did to begin with, and in my imagination I see how wonderful it will be for me and then I'll tell you a lot about the many and strange things that I've heard and seen.

My dear brother, half a year has passed since we last had the pleasure of talking together and in that time I've had many a dark day, but now that I've read your letter I see that I had no reason to be sad because I've been in good health the whole time, for which I cannot sufficiently thank our good God. My dear beloved brother, we've lived together for a long time and had many happy days but also many dark and heavy days, especially during winter, but we are now so far apart that we cannot take each others' hands when we are happy or sad. Dear brother, you must excuse my ungrateful behavior in not having written to you more often. I'll now try to tell you a little about what things are like here.

I'll begin with the beginning. In July and August it was so hot where I worked that I could scarcely breathe and I was so scorched that I was as dry as birch bark. We were about forty men working in a sandpit and we were usually all there in the morning but towards evening only half of us were left, yes, one day we were only six. That day I couldn't work longer than three o'clock and when I went to the house, about as far as from Skeie to Kosvor, I could hardly walk. In Minnesota I've been to a show where we saw a lot of fantastic tricks but the most interesting thing was that they had all kinds of wild animals, both big and small, in big railroad cars made of iron. They were quite wild and they had a lot of strange birds.

And then I'll tell you about the house where we lived and the surroundings and what I did on Sundays. The house was made of planks set up on four posts, two wider apart than the others. The rough planks were nailed to these posts with cracks as wide as a finger between them. On one wall there were bunks to sleep in and at night when we went to bed the mosquitoes were so bad that we burned a heap of hay on the floor to get rid of them. The house stood on the bank of a pond with lots of fish. I made myself some fishing equipment once but this was not at all like what I used at home. I made a rod with a long string and fastened a bent pin to it, and this pin served as both hook and bait for I caught a lot of fish with it. There were also lots of wild geese and ducks there, yes more than there are of sparrows in spring there at home. On Sundays I walked alone in the woods but I didn't find most berries we have in our woods. I found some strawberries and raspberries but they were not as good as those at home. There were lots of red currants. They grew on bushes that were as tall and wide as the largest cherry trees in our garden at home, but they were not good so I didn't eat them. But there were many plums as they call them here, a kind of tree where prunes grow but these were not black like those we had at home, because that is when they have been dried; they were red and quite good.

Iver and I often went into town in the evenings. There we saw many things that were new and entertaining. It was quite entertaining to see when they moved their buildings and it didn't take them long to build a house with two stories, because when I hadn't been in town for about three days there were many houses that I hadn't seen there before. I'll tell you about a little pleasure trip. When Syver Killi's parents came they didn't have their baggage because they couldn't pay for it all the way. So we borrowed a hand car, a small wagon that went on the railroad rails and was made to go by four men, and it could go as fast as a steam engine. This was the wagon on which we made our pleasure trip to get their baggage. The town we went to was about fourteen miles away and I and Iver stood with one handle and little Syver and two others were at the other one. It went so fast that we were there in less than two hours. On our way back we had a little accident. Two Swedish boys had placed a large piece of wood on one of the rails and when we came at full speed we couldn't stop and we went off the rails and toppled over. We weren't much hurt except that Iver hurt his face a little.

There is a saying in Dovre that the bull goes where he wants but this isn't so in America. Here the oxen are as obedient as the soldiers in Norway. They don't have harnesses, just a piece of wood over their necks. This is fastened to a collar. In the middle of the piece of wood is an iron ring and to this is fastened the pole by which the sled or wagon is pulled. There is never just one ox, but two, and they often have as many as six for one load and the driver can control all of them while he sits on the wagon. He has a long pole on which he has a braided cord made of the bark of a tree they have here. His whip is so long that it looks like a fishing rod and he is so good with it that when they won't obey what he says to them they'll at least have to obey his whip. Yes he can even cut into their hide so the blood runs.

They have a lot of tame fowl. In some places I've seen so many hens, ducks, pigeons, geese and turkeys that I believe there were one hundred and there were eggs in every nest. And I've seen the peacock with its glorious feathers. In many places they use a machine to cut the hay. They use two horses. There is a small seat for the driver. They drive around and it cuts all the way and they have no one to spread the hay but it lies where it falls until a machine comes and pushes it into large heaps.

> The last part of the letter has not been preserved. TTV's long and exaggerated account of his longing for home is an example of what may be called situational nostalgia, a nostalgia generated by the writing of a letter home. «1:139 »1:166 NE III:3

1869 — LETTER I:146

FROM: Elling Elliingsen Wold, *Decorah, Iowa, 1 March 1869*
TO: Helge Gundersen Skare, *Eggedal, Sigdal, Buskerud*

Dear father-in-law Helge Nederum,

Since it is now a long time since we visited each other with letters I'll permit myself to send you a few lines as it may be of interest for you to hear now and then from your children here. The best news I have, for you as well as for us, is that benign Providence has preserved us from illness and other misfortune that otherwise could have befallen us sinful creatures and this is true of all your children who live near us. Your daughter Eli left us in the middle of October and went with some other girls she knew to take work in a town called Charles City about forty-five miles from here. The reason for going so far was higher wages but I would have advised against it had I been at home. I exchanged letters with her not so long ago and she said she was doing well and asked me to send her regards to you when I wrote. We have also heard recently from Gunder Skare and Ole Evensen and they say they are in good health. The last mentioned enclosed an authorization that I must ask you to give to Halvor Skadeland.

We hear from Flaa that they had a poor harvest because of drought and we suppose this must also be true of Eggedal. I can say of our area that we've rarely had as good years as the one we've just had, and this has caused the price of wheat to go down to half of what it was the year before. Then we got one dollar and eighty cents; now we must be satisfied with seventy or eighty cents a bushel. We did better on pork this year. Last winter was very mild so we have used both wagon and sleigh. I have no news for you so I'll conclude with our loving regards to you and your family. Your son Halvor Skare and his family, Halvor Skadeland and his family, and his children here, Helge and Ingrid, are all in good health. I can say the same for John Moen's children here; of these Gunder Moen no longer lives in our area but I know he is in good health as I recently had a letter from him. In conclusion I must ask for some lines in return whenever you have the occasion. Farewell. Yours respectfully,

ELLING ELLINGSEN WOLD

One of the enclosed portraits is for your son H. The other one is for you.

«I:141 »I:151 NE III:7

1869 — LETTER I:147

From: Svend Larsen and Halsten and Lars Svendsen Houg
Elgin, Iowa, 4 March 1869
To: Ole Larsen Haug, *Aal, Buskerud*

Dear brother Ole Larsen Houg,

It is now so long since I've written to you that you may have thought that I was no longer among the living, but the main reason for this is my negligence even though there have also been some other reasons. But I'll now send you a few words and let you know that the Lord has granted both me and my family life and health. I've received your welcome letters, one of June 4, 1867 on July 31 and one of December 19 on February 23, 1869. I'm grateful that you still honor me by writing. It is dear to me to hear from my siblings and the home of my fathers. I and my family are all in good health. The eleven children are well; the youngest is a daughter who'll be two June 6 and her name is Guri. The two oldest are confirmed. Halsten was confirmed in May 1868 and he is a good student. Ingrid is preparing for confirmation and is good at reading. Most of the children are attending school this winter and there they read both Norwegian and English. Lars and Halsten are fairly good at writing and arithmetic.

I'll tell you a little about the endless religious disagreements. As you know, there are three Lutheran churches. The one I want to say a little about, the Wisconsin Synod, is the largest and has the most Norwegian pastors. They hold the pernicious doctrine that slavery is not a sin. This controversy has been discussed in the newspapers for six or seven years and many solid arguments have been made against this view, but to no effect; the pastors insist that slavery is in keeping with the word of God. Last summer all the pastors and some of the representatives decided that slavery is according to the word of God and that this should be a doctrine. You may imagine that this has given more heat to the controversy. C. L. Clausen has always been against the slavery doctrine and opposed it at the Synod meeting last summer, but to no avail, and he and his congregations left the

Synod. There have been meetings to discuss this issue and in some places entire congregations have left the Synod and in some, parts of congregations. This has also been done here and we had many meetings and the conclusion was that part of the congregation left the Synod, so now some of us don't have a pastor.

I'll also mention some other doctrines of this Synod. They say that the third commandment was a ceremonial commandment given the Jews and that it doesn't concern Christians so Sunday is just like the other days of the week. They also teach that any who hear the Gospel or who receive Holy Communion are forgiven their sins whether they believe or not. They also teach that the Gospel is unconditional and that dance is not a sin. This is what they teach and nevertheless they place themselves above the other synods and say that only they have the pure doctrine. When they say that the Gospel is unconditional I think this must be a new Gospel since the first condition is that a person through Holy Baptism is taken into the Christian church or into Christ and that this is repeated in Confirmation, and it is also an undeniable condition that a person is converted and believes the Gospel.

You may wonder what they'll do now that they don't have a pastor. We'll have Pastor Clausen to serve us with communion and have confirmation for some who've been prepared by our good schoolteacher and thus we may wait until we see how things may develop. We could probably have had a pastor but we'll put this off for some time and consider it carefully since we have once been deceived. You know that in John Fjeld we had the pastor we wanted but he left us and with his fine words he convinced us to join the synod that he himself had joined, but we now see the fruits this has brought forth. We who have left the Synod are not allowed to go to church and listen to the pastor, nor do we want to listen to him, but I think that this past winter we have been well served. First there were two men here last fall who spoke the word of God with such force that I haven't heard anyone better. And two Swedes have been here twice and spoken the word of God with such power that the impenitent could not withstand the spirit and they have also promised to visit us next Easter.

Now I must return to myself. My wife and my children have always been in good health, which is a gift of God that I may not sufficiently appreciate. The children have been good, but they are yet young and haven't demonstrated any carnal lust. We live in a quiet area. But a little further off we hear of both drink and dancing and all manner of ungodliness. Therefore I'm often in doubt of what may happen to such a flock as mine; but this must be in God's hands. As for my material situation, I've enough for my daily needs. I can sell produce for some hundred dollars a year but this is just as easily spent because we need expensive machines and other things for the farm. Last spring I built a new house and and this is expensive here even though it may not be the best, but I'll have a good house when everything has been done and I own my farm and the things I need for it. This winter I have had twenty-three head of cattle, three work horses and two young horses and some sheep and pigs. Dear brother, you mustn't understand me as trying to boast of this. No, far from it; I have nothing but what I've been given by the Lord.

When I read about the death of our uncle I thought of the words, blessed are those who died in the Lord. Yes brother, I am glad to see that you try to walk the narrow path and hold to Christ and be in him. Often I find in myself such a lukewarm faith that it is as if I cannot feel the love of God. But what should we then do? We must again seek God and ask forgiveness for our sins for the sake of Christ, he who is the only valid sacrifice for sin, because we can do nothing for our salvation except in prayer and faith. Hold on to our Lord and Savior and he who loves us will be faithful. Moreover, we have the word of God both here and with you and then we would do well to heed it as a light burning in a dark place.

With this our loving regards from me, my wife and my children and please give our regards to my other siblings and tell them I'm doing well. Should you write to my sister Mari, please give her our loving regards. This may be the last time I write to you, at least in my own hand as I am not very good at it, and I have to use glasses to see clearly as I advance in years and my strength retreats so I cannot work as I used to do. But now the children are beginning to be of good help. Last year, we had a warm summer with just enough rain to have a very good year for all grains, so they are quite low in price compared to last year. I have kind regards to you from my old mother-in-law. She is still strong enough to do some work with her hands. She is with one or another of her children as she wishes. You write that your son Svend says he would like to see his uncle, but then you'll have to tell him that he'll have to wait a while. I see that some old acquaintances have sent their regards and I find it strange that anyone still remembers me so you must give them my regards in return and say that I'm doing well. With this my most loving regards to you and your family and my other siblings. Live in God. This is the wish of your brother,

SVEND LARSEN HOUG

[*The handwriting changes*] My parents tell me that I have cousins and uncles in the place of my father's birth even though I've never seen them. We are not known to each other but I'll nevertheless write a few words to tell you that I'm in good health. I don't have so much to tell you except for what my father says. I go to the English school and learn how to read, write, and do arithmetic and a little geography. So there is good opportunity to learn what we want. Our *teacher* is good in English and Norwegian and is very good with the children. I must now end my letter with kind regards from,

HALSTEN SVENDSEN HOUG

My parents have told me that I also have cousins and uncles and aunts in old Norway where my parents were born and they say that this is also my land of birth, and now I must do as my father wishes and write a few words to you to let you see whether I'm any good at writing or not and to let you know that I'm in good health and doing well, which is the best we can have in this life. And because we've never seen each other we are completely unknown to each other and therefore I must write as my parents have told me to. I have no more to tell you than what my father has written in his letter. With this I must end my short and poor letter for this time with regards to you all. And I wish that I may soon have a letter from one of you. From me,

LARS SVENDSEN HOUG

. ⎯⎯ .

The Norwegian Synod, at this time the largest of the Norwegian American Lutheran synods, was often referred to by the name of the state where it was founded, Wisconsin. The first of several controversies that led to its decimation concerned the question of whether slavery was in and of itself a sin. The Norwegian Synod did not only insist that the Bible did not say that slavery itself was sinful, but made this a doctrine that its members must accept. For an account of the theological controversies described in this letter see Nelson and Fevold 1960, I:151–190 and 241–245. Since SLH mentions his advanced years it may be noted that he was born in 1814 and died in 1916. Halsten wrote the English word "teacher" and was no doubt told to add the Norwegian word *lærer* in parentheses. They would use such English words when speaking Norwegian. In a margin: "Received on April 10." In a letter dated 10 April (Nor. ed. I:10) SLH wrote to a nephew Lars Larsen Skrattegard offering advice as well as financial assistance for his emigration. «I:112 »I:159 NE III:8

1869 — LETTER I:148

From: Iver Ellingsen Elsrud, *Rock Creek, Iowa, 18 May 1869*
To: Elling Olsen and Olea Olsdatter Elsrud, *Aadalen, Ringerike, Buskerud*

Dear parents and siblings,

As time now permits I'll tell you about my journey. We left Kristiania on the ninth and came to Kristiansand on the tenth. We left immediately and you may imagine the commotion when almost all became sick. I wish that someone who plans to emigrate had been on board for an hour or so and he would probably not have thought more of America. The food was so bad that we were not able to eat it. The meat was so raw that the blood ran, so you may imagine what the soup was like. We came to Hull in the morning of the twelfth and ate dinner in an emigrant house. We left at three o'clock and came to Liverpool at ten. We went onboard a big ship named *Idaho*. It was 500 feet long and 40 feet wide. Because of the baggage we couldn't depart until eight. You may imagine that it wasn't a pleasant voyage as 1,100 emigrants were packed together and most of them were like wild animals. At first we ate almost nothing as we were not like swine but when we learned more about conditions onboard and our own food came to an end, we had to accept the pig food. Yes, I'll call it pig food as they walked on a deck where the dirt went over your shoes to get to the meat storage. We tried to wash it but the Irish had washed their diapers and their chamber pots first. We complained to the captain and this helped. We hoped to arrive on the twentieth but we didn't land until the thirtieth.

Then our journey was quite comfortable. From the Adams station we took a stagecoach to West Mitchell and this cost us two dollars. We walked from Mitchell to Haugerud. It is very beautiful here at Haugerud as a river runs about twenty steps from their houses. On the other side of the river is a nice oak forest. There are a lot of fish in the river and rabbits, pigeons and geese in the woods, so I've often missed a gun. This year uncle has about twenty acres with oats, sixty with wheat and fifteen with corn that I've helped plant.

Fingal has gone to an American where he has been hired for four months, for how much, I don't know. Erik may get work on the railroad as there isn't much work to be had on the farms because of the low price of wheat. I'll probably stay here for a while until I've looked around. I'm quite satisfied here. I promised mother to tell her about the food. For breakfast we have wheat bread, eggs, butter, syrup, *fattigmand* cookies, cream cakes, and coffee. For dinner fried pork and then as for breakfast. For the afternoon meal it is as for breakfast except that we also have pancakes with fried pork. In the evening we mostly have milk porridge of wheat flour. I suppose you're thinking, Oh, what if I could have such food. But you would soon tire of it and more than once I've wished I could have Norwegian food. Give my regards to Tore Elsrud and tell him that Elling Meier lives a few miles away. His son Paul teaches school here. Ole the elder now has an heir; his name is Nils. Erik is still in New Zealand and doesn't know when he'll be returning. He has lent his friends 3,000 dollars to buy a machine so he cannot go until he has his money back. I send regards for all at Elsrud from Guri and Syver Fossholt who say they are doing well. I send greetings to all of you from all here at Haugerud and Rustand who are all in good health and doing well. Ole and Erik came to Jon Rønningsand today. Give my regards to Torvald Byttingsrud and ask him to write to me since I don't have much to write about yet. And please let me have Karoline Sand's address if she has gone to America. Give my regards to all friends. Loving regards from

I. E. ELSRUD

· ——— ·

IEE (age twenty-three in 1869) is living with his mother's brother Ole Olsen Haugerud the younger who had written a brief note to Iver's older brother Ole on 6 October 1868 (Nor. ed. II:182), welcoming him should he decide to emigrate. He wrote to Iver's parents on 24 April (Nor. ed. III:12) promising to look after their son, who was then already on the Atlantic. Iver wrote again on 12 August (Nor. ed. III:20). In Iowa he is among family and friends from Aadalen. His mother's brother Torgrim Haugerud was on a brief visit from Norway that summer. *Fattigmann* is a rich, deep-fat fried cookie that was and still is traditional for Christmas and certainly not everyday food.
»I:153 NE III:13

· ——— ·

1869 — LETTER I:149

From: Hendrik Olsen Dahl, *Norman Hill, Texas, 27 June 1869*
To: Peder Eriksen and Siri Kristiansdatter Furuset
Romedal, Stange, Hedmark

Dear parents,

We received your welcome letter of August 6, 1868 on September 20 and you must please excuse our long delay in replying. We were glad to hear that you were all in good health and doing well. I can also tell you that we are all in good health as usual. The first thing I can tell you is that Christine gave birth on March 21 to a big healthy boy whose name is Anders.

We have a Norwegian␣Lutheran pastor whose name is Estrøm. He has just been here for four weeks, but everyone likes him and I'm certain that he is a good man. He'll be very good for us, in particular for the young people who have had little religious education. Our children have gone to English school but don't know much Norwegian, so now we'll have a Norwegian school so the children can be prepared for confirmation.

We have again been blessed with a good year and we did our threshing two weeks ago, but I'm still threshing for others. This year I had 500 bushels of wheat, 170 of barley, and 100 bushels of rye. The corn looks as good as I've ever seen it but we don't harvest it until August. The grasshoppers came last fall, but they were soon gone and hardly did any damage, but there were many who didn't dare sow their wheat so it is in good price now compared to what it usually is in good years. The price is now from one and a half dollars to one and three-quarters for wheat and one dollar for rye and barley. I farm on a small scale because the prices for grain have been low compared to what I have to pay in wages, so it has rarely been profitable to hire help. We don't harvest as much per acre as in Norway but then a man can manage so much more here as we don't plow more than half of what you do there, especially on new soil. Moreover, we can plow all year and we don't need to use fertilizer. I now farm sixty acres and in good years I've harvested 1,200 bushels or even a little more, and all this has been done by myself and my two little boys, except that I had a man to plow for me for six days at seventy-five cents a day last fall when I sowed the wheat. We cut wheat for three and a half days and had six men and paid them one and a half dollar a day. Threshing took three and a half days with ten men at one dollar a day. So my farming expenses for this year were seventy-four dollars. But then I had my own mowing machine and threshing machine and without them my expenses would have been greater. Even so my boys are in school between four and five months of the year.

Times seem to be getting much better so it is possible that we'll soon see as good times as we had before the war. Most people seem to agree more about politics as well as in other matters so I think our prospects are much better than they've been for many years. The emigrants that came with Poulson have done fairly well. Only a few of them worked for their tickets and they've made up for themselves long ago. Many have just done a little and others nothing, and if they decide to pay when they can, this would be good, but they can do as they wish. There is no debtors prison here and a man has to be the owner of a certain amount of land before a debt can be collected with law in hand. He has a right to keep 160 acres with buildings and chattel as well as the horses or oxen necessary to work his land, produce to feed his family for one year, and a few cows and pigs. And the same rules apply to other kinds of property and in towns. But this is only if you have a family.

Kari sends her regards and is in good health. She wrote a couple of months ago and hopes you have received her letter. Aunt Anne also sends her regards and says they are all in good health and doing well. I don't know of any more and will conclude my poor letter with loving regards to all our relatives and friends and our most sincere greetings to our parents and siblings from me, my wife, and children. Your devoted son-in-law,

H. O. DAHL

I forgot to tell you that Kari is here and plans to stay with us for the summer. Christine encloses a gold dollar to mother as a small souvenir. Farewell all.

. —— .

> Christine Dahl's sister, Kari Pedersdatter Furuset, emigrated via Quebec in 1867. Her aunt was Anne Rogstad. Ole Olsen Estrem was pastor in Clifton, Bosque County, Texas, 1869–1877. Immigrants who came with prepaid tickets were expected to work for the amount owed. There was no way to collect such debt, however, and soon there would be a federal law making it illegal to enter the country with a contract

to work for a prepaid ticket. Poul Poulson emigrated from Stange in 1848 and came to Texas from California in 1857. He ran an employment agency and in 1867 he went to Norway to bring back laborers. He returned with more than 100 the next spring but died a few months later (Syversen 1982, 115, 290). «I:138 »I:162 NE III:15

1869 — LETTER I:150

FROM: Gaute Ingebretsen Gunleiksrud, *Stoughton, Wisconsin, 31 July 1869*
TO: Ingebret Torsteinsen and Birgit Gautesdatter Gunleiksrud, *Tinn, Telemark*

⋅⇒◯⇐⋅

Dear old parents!

As it has been a long time since I wrote to you and didn't get a reply, I'll again send you a few words to let you know of our present situation, which has in every way been very good. We are all, thanks to the fatherly guidance of God, in good health and we are blessed with all the necessities of life here on earth. This year's harvest looks very promising and in a few days we'll be busy with our harvest. Everything here is good. God has protected us from infectious diseases and graced us in upholding his Christian church here with the pure teaching of his word, so all souls who thirst for grace may find food for eternal life. All is by grace alone, as we are far too undeserving of all the blessing that has been given to us. As Christians we must never cease to thank God for this, the greatest good in life and the greatest comfort at the moment of death. For all else will come to an end but the Word of God is forever. So, dear parents, may this Word be your comfort and your happiness, your wish and your desire in your old age. Because of your advanced age and the laws of nature you are now approaching the grave, and so it is my and my family's heartfelt wish and prayer to God, for you as well as for us, that we may strive to come to our right home where it is good to be and where our Savior has gone before us to make a room for all who will believe in him and humbly confess their sins so he can heal, comfort and help them. Yes, we are all in sore need of his help in life and most of all in the hour of death when we bid farewell to this world. We don't know the time and this is why it says: Watch therefore, for you do not know on what day your Lord is coming. So let us watch over our souls so that when the Bridegroom comes, we may go in with him and in all eternity take part in the wedding of the lamb. May the grace of our Lord Jesus Christ, the love of God, and the community of the Holy Ghost be with you all, parents, siblings, relatives, and friends. Our most heartfelt regards from the distant West.

GOUTE INGEBRIKTSON AND FAMILY

GIG quotes from Matthew 24:42. «I:81 »II:46 NE III:17

1869 — LETTER I:151

FROM: Ole Aslesen and Ingrid Helgesdatter Myran, *Decorah, Iowa*
18 August 1869

To: Helge Gundersen Skare, *Eggedal, Sigdal, Buskerud*

Dear unforgettable father!

Thank you for the loving greetings you sent us in your letter of May 4. I see that you wish to have a little report from us, so you may be interested in having a fairly accurate report about how we are and about our economic situation. I will try to give you a brief account of both, but first I must ask you to excuse us for not writing so often. The reason is that it is difficult for me to write and as E. Woll writes so frequently, we get to hear from you and send you our regards. I and my dear wife and our five children have been in good health, for which we must thank and praise God, even though I've now and then been troubled by rheumatism and have been somewhat weak. But this has gone away after shorter or longer periods and I'm now quite well. Our children are: Helge eleven years and one month, Ole eight and a half years, Eli seven years and five months, Gunder five years, Andres two years. I have 350 acres with all that is necessary for a farmer of fields, woods and hay. In my woods I have good water and excellent rock. About eighty acres have been cultivated, twenty this summer. As for my buildings, our house is not the best. It is made of oak logs but is a little old as I've had to spend large amounts in improving my land and for the necessary equipment. But if God grants me health I hope that the heaviest work now has been done and then I will have opportunities to improve my buildings.

I have four workhorses and two foals that came last spring. We have five cows, two one-year-old bulls and a heifer. We have thirty sheep and four big pigs and seven small ones. With my brother Helge Nelson I have a mowing machine. With this machine you can mow ten to fifteen wagon loads of hay a day, and we also have a machine that rakes the hay in piles and is pulled by one horse. Up to now Helge and I have had a reaper but this year I bought his share and now own it myself. It should do for several more years. I also have a machine that both sows and harrows. It can do seven to eight acres in a day. A reaper costs 160 dollars. A mowing machine costs 140 dollars. A machine for sowing costs 130 dollars. A farm wagon costs 100 dollars. Last year I bought a new wagon for 105 dollars. You may think that these expenses are unnecessary but labor costs from one to three dollars a day and without machines you would grow far less produce, so you can see that you cannot do much without machines. True, they cost a lot of money, but with them you can do your work both quickly and at the right time. So they are necessary for those who have some land. My debt is 400 dollars, but my land is worth four or five times as much as six or ten years ago, especially now that the railroad is here. Wooded land costs forty to fifty dollars an acre and field land from eighteen to twenty, yes up to twenty-five dollars an acre. I must admit that I've often struggled with debt and my expenses because I was full of optimism at the time I settled here. I may have had less trouble with less land, but, praise God, I've been through the worst and my property has increased in value.

As for this year's crops, we've had fairly good weather this summer but more rain than we need. For wheat, oats, barley, potatoes and other products we'll have an average year. Some places a little better, other places a little worse. We are almost finished with the wheat and oats harvest but we have stacking and threshing left to do. We thresh with a machine that is driven by eight or ten horses. In one day we can thresh several hundred bushels of wheat, etc. Here I'll give you a little report on how the land is surveyed here and then you may work out for yourself how much an acre is.

— Take a rod that is sixteen feet and six inches long. Then, as the following sketch shows, there is one such rod length from a to b, one rod length from b to c, one rod length from c to d, one rod length from d to a, and such a square where each side is 16 feet and 6 inches is called a square rod. One acre consists of 160 such square rods, so you see that 350 acres is quite a lot of land. Each side of a square of forty acres is eighty rods.

With this I'll conclude my poor letter as we don't have more news. I'll lay down my pen with a prayer to God for His grace and support in time and in eternity. May we be blessed in life as in death and be united in our faith in Him who has loved us and given His life in payment for us all. With this, my regards to you Helge Gundersen Skare and your family, to my dear brother Halvor Helgesen and his wife and children, to my dear uncle Elling Helgesen Reisland and his family, and to my aunt Guri Helgesdatter Normandsplassen and her family. Yours sincerely,

OLE ASLESEN MYRAN AND INGRID HELGESDATTER
AND OUR CHILDREN

Helge Nilsen Myran was a half-brother of the writer. At the end of the paragraph on land surveying there is a sketch of a square with corners indicated with the letters a, b, c, and d. «1:146 »1:157 NEIII:21

1869 — LETTER I:152

FROM: Christopher Jacobson, *Hot Creek, Nevada, 27 September 1869*

TO: Hans Jakobsen Hilton, *Kløfta, Ullensaker, Akershus*

Dear brother!

I received your letter of June 24 on July 24. It now takes such a short time to hear from you so my heart is more in my writing and it is as if I'm among you. Yes, great things have happened in the almost fifteen years that I've wandered around so far from you. When you remember what it was like fifteen years ago, Hans, then you see many and, as you say, great changes in little Norway, but if you come with me to America, you'll see changes that no one could dream of. Large areas of uncultivated land that I have traveled over in Wisconsin, Iowa, Minnesota, and other states have now been cultivated and settled by enterprising farmers, large cities have been built and one railroad after the other unites them. When I first came to California it took five to six months for those who went by land while we now can make the journey in five to six days. America can now send words to all nations on earth by telegraph and have an answer in a few hours. What more can human beings achieve?

There is talk about getting Chinese to the South. Now that slavery has been abolished they'll try to get as cheap labor as possible. California already has thousands of them cultivating silk, cotton, sugar, etc. Here in Nevada the Chinese work in the silver mines. Since this lowers the daily wage for all, it makes for a hellish conflict within the working class, in particular among the Irish, who are a revolutionary people whether they are at home or away since they usually have no other ambition than to work for others as long as they live. For my part I don't care much. If the Chinese come where I am, I'll have to make use of them one way or another and make money on their work if I can.

I'm still in Hot Creek and I can't say for sure, but it is possible that I'll stay here until next spring. I own a share in a mine and it may be a good one when it's opened. But I won't do much work on it yet and I'd rather sell it if possible. A New York company has started a mine here and if they find anything it'll give us a better opportunity to sell our ground. If I'm not lucky in making anything in that way, I'm not certain just what way I'll go; perhaps, as I've said earlier, to South America if the Indians are eradicated from the areas where there is gold. But should I happen to make any money here I'll perhaps try to make myself a home in California. But you're quite right, brother, in calling me footloose. This is all too true and I cannot deny it. But when a wheel has been started it will have to roll on even if it is uphill, and God knows, Hans, if I won't someday when my hair is grey come rolling in to Ullensaker and fall there. It is more likely, however, that I'll fall before I come that far. But I've started thinking that I should get myself a home, and from now on I'll apply my thoughts to this.

Give my regards to Kari and tell her that she shouldn't keep Gulbrand from going to America. She is old and it is time that Gulbrand gets out from under her skirts if he doesn't want to follow her down in her grave. I'm sorry that he didn't leave last spring; then her worst worries would have been over by now. But he's young and a year won't make much difference. I won't advise him to come here as it wouldn't be to his advantage. Moreover, it is possible that I'm already on my way. God alone knows where I'll stop. No, it is better that he follows all the others to Minnesota or Iowa, and if he is, as you say, a steady and determined boy, he'll never want. And finally, I'll say to him that when he leaves Ullensaker he must hold to his God and Savior alone and never, never rely on friends.

While I'm at it, brother, let me also tell you that even though I have friends who might give me four or five hundred dollars if they have them and I need them, there is probably no one in all America who knows where I come from or who could send you a message if I should suddenly die, because I've hardly been with Norwegians since I came to California and most people don't know that I'm Norwegian. My best friends among the Americans of course know I'm Norwegian, but that is all. So if you should be without a letter from me for about a year, you may conclude that Christopher's pilgrimage has come to an end. But with the help of God I plan to live long and see much more of the world.

You ask about trading horses, Hans, and I'd be pleased to do this if you were here. The horse I told you about is bluish grey and five years old. He was lean when I bought him but now that he's become as fat as a pig it is probably difficult to ride him. When a saddle is laid on his back he jumps high in the air and then lies down on his stomach. He is of no use to me before I set out on a long journey, but he is rather big and strong and when he gets used to having a saddle every day I suppose he'll accept it. But right now you can have him for nothing. But three months ago I bought a three-year-old tan mare with white socks on four feet and a white forelock. You can't have her because she is my most beloved. No more paper. I'll write more next time. Don't forget to give my regards to our old mother. Tell her I'm doing well. And, finally, my loving regards to you and yours from

C. JACOBSON

Kari Lystad was a sister and Gulbrand her son. «I:137 »I:163 NE III:23

1869 — LETTER I:153

FROM: Iver Ellingsen Elsrud, *Rock Creek, Iowa, 27 November 1869*
TO: Elling Olsen and Olea Olsdatter Elsrud, *Aadalen, Ringerike, Buskerud*

⋅⇾≡◉⇽⋅

Dear parents and siblings,

I've waited more than a month for a letter, but in vain. I thought I wouldn't write before I got it but too much time has passed and I fear that you haven't received the one I wrote August 20. The main reason I'm writing now is to ask you if you can have a newspaper sent to me from Norway as time passes slowly when I have nothing to read. I hope you'll have this before Christmas so you can write to Christiania to hear if you can have one sent direct from there. I'd like to have it from the New Year. I'd like to have one with some history in it, such as *Verdens Gang* or a similar one. The price is no matter. I'll send you the money. I'd be glad if you could do this for me.

I live well and have been healthy since I arrived and I'm enjoying myself now as I have come to know many around here, both boys and <u>girls</u>. We now have such hard times for the farmers that it is almost as in Norway. These are good times for the laborer as wages are from one to five dollars a day. It is almost impossible to sell wheat at any price. You get forty to fifty cents a bushel, and this is so little that it hasn't been so little in ten years. Corn and oats are a little better. Uncle had 1,000 bushels of wheat, 800 of corn and 700 of oats. He doesn't sell oats as he uses it for his horses. He has sold about 850 bushels of wheat and 500 of corn. All harvesting has been done and the good days for the farmer have begun.

I have more to write about, but I don't have time for more now. Erik is still in New Zealand. I don't know how long he'll stay there, but he is doing well. Two railroads have come near here this summer, about four miles apart. The next time I write I'll tell you a little about Ole the Elder and his wife; he has been ill since harvest, but hasn't stayed in bed; and also a little about Lars Ask and a little about grandfather's last days. I send regards to father from his friend Ole Ulen. He lives near us. Give my regards to the painter A. Lie and tell him that farms can be bought here at a low price. Would you please send me some seeds of rowan berries in a letter? I must now end my letter with friendly regards to you all. Please give my regards to all my friends. Loving regards from your faithful son and brother in the far West,

I. E. ELSRUD

Dear mother and sister,

I'll also write some lines for you because I have a request. If mother's brother Torgrim should come next spring, could you weave some cloth of linsey-woolsey as I've heard that Maren (uncle's wife) would like to have a good dress of linsey-woolsey when she is out driving in the winter. Here you can't think of having such a thing done as hiring someone to do the weaving costs thirty cents a yard. Maren and her mother have done so much for me that I wish to do something for them in return. I suppose you're busy but I hope that you'll do your best if uncle is coming. If you do this you must keep an exact account so I can pay you. You'll know how much is needed for two dresses, which is what I would like to have. It would be good if it was rather nice and I've heard it would be best if it is all wool, no matter what it may cost. I have no more to write to you. My regards to you all from your devoted

I. E. ELSRUD

Dear Uncle Torgrim Haugerud,

If you should come next spring and mother does as I've written, I hope you'll bring this cloth and if you would pay for what it costs it would save me much trouble. I'll repay you when I get the cloth. Please buy a pair of good skates for me. Greetings,

I. E. ELSRUD

> IEE wrote to his parents on 12 August (Nor. ed. III:20) about family and friends in his neighborhood, in particular about his uncle Torgrim Olsen Haugerud who was visiting from Aadalen. He is planning to attend the public school to learn English in winter. (This may be the letter that he here says he wrote on the 20 August.) Ole (the elder) Olsen and his wife Maren Torine Haugerud both wrote brief notes on November 28 (Nor. ed. III:29) enclosed with this letter. His dead grandfather Ole Hansen Rustand was divorced from Guri Torgrimsdatter Rustand who still lived in Aadalen. His request to his mother is for *verken* (linsey-woolsey) a mixture of linen and wool. Ole Haraldsen Ulen had come to St. Ansgar, Iowa in the same group as Ole Hansen Rustand led by C. L. Clausen (Ulvestad 1907, 71). «I:148 »I:167 NE III:28

1869 — LETTER I:154

From: Hellik Olsen Lehovd, *Salem, Minnesota, 27 December 1869*
To: Ole Helgesen and Joran Paulsdatter Lehovd, *Flesberg, Buskerud*

Dear parents and siblings,

As a year has now passed since I last wrote to you I must sit down to write you a few lines so you can hear how I and my family are living, as I know that you're glad to hear from your distant son and brother. But first I must thank you for your letters. The first one of January 31 addressed to my brother included a letter from Knud, and the second, also from Knud, of June 22. I've also seen a letter you wrote to Ole in October. I'm very glad to hear from home and I must thank you for all your news as it is so enjoyable to read your letters now that Knud has become such an excellent writer. Please forgive me for having delayed writing for so long as there have been no important changes in our lives here.

First, I and my family are now quite well and in good health. Last April I and my children were sick for about eight days with the measles but since then we've been well except that my wife has now and then complained about the weakness in her chest, but it hasn't been so bad that she hasn't taken care of her housework. We now have four children, two sons and two daughters. The youngest was born on February 6 and her name is Bertea. She's growing big and is beginning to walk. We had a very good harvest, especially the wheat, oats, and barley, but the corn wasn't so good nor were the potatoes as they for the most part rotted in the soil because we had so much rain in late summer. I had 766 bushels of wheat, 248 bushels of oats and some corn and potatoes. But there has been a low price for wheat this fall as there's been so much of it all over the United States. So the farmers aren't doing as well as it may seem to you, especially those who have to hire help during harvest as wages have been very high. Last summer we had to pay one and a quarter dollars during haying and three to three and a half dollars a day during the wheat harvest and one during threshing, so I paid out more than 100 dollars before I had stacked my wheat and then I paid fifty-six dollars for eight men for three days for the threshing. The price for wheat has been half a dollar for the bushel. A bushel of wheat has to weigh sixty pounds and oats thirty-two pounds and oats are thirty cents a bushel. Last summer I exchanged my two ox teams for two large blue horses that cost me almost 300 dollars and now I have four cows, two heifers that will calve next spring, three calves, five sheep, and one pig. There are hard times here because of the low price for wheat and the reason for the high wages is that all free and single men who don't have land go west to take land under the Homestead Law.

I don't have any important news as I don't know of any acquaintances who have married except that the widow Marit Gjerde has married Jul Hommelia and that Beret Olsdatter Taksle and Bol Bakli are dead. Many emigrated from Flesberg this year but the only one I've met is Gunder Fugleli who is living with Gunder Vogtvedt. Recently Gullik Skaartun came here from Wisconsin and is now living with Ole Lia. Ole Olson Rønningsdalen is also for the most part with Ole Lia. Our brother Paul visited us last May for about two weeks and he was in good health; he has a slight limp and he has again placed money in loans here. I think it was about 200 dollars. But then he returned to the pineries in the northern part of the state and signed up to work for the same company until next May for twenty-six dollars a month. I've had a letter from him saying he was doing well. Our brother Ole and his family are doing well. I haven't heard from him for three weeks as we live about seven miles from each other. Last November two Norwegian bachelors returned to Norway for a visit, one was Hede Andersen, son of the schoolteacher Andersen at Kongsberg, and the other was Tallef Buin from near Kongsberg. He has a farm near Ole. If you should see them you'll have precise information about our settlement. I suppose many will join them when they return next spring.

We are building two churches in our parish and I see the main church next to the parsonage every day and it can already be used for services in winter as well as in summer. A third church is not so far from us but it belongs to Elling Eielsen's congregation or the Augustana Synod as they call it. Our Lutheran pastors belong to the so-called Wisconsin Synod. Our pastor Steen moved to a congregation about 200 miles west from here and in September we had a new pastor whose name is Thorsen. He was born in the diocese of Christiania and has studied for two years at the University in St. Louis where he graduated last summer. He is a very good pastor.

I mustn't forget to thank my brother Knud for the photograph. We've thought of taking a photograph of all our children next summer and sending it to you and we would have liked to have a photograph of my parents and my sister, for which I would gladly pay five dollars as it would be a dear reminder should one of you pass away. The prices for all we buy in the store, such as clothes, in particular those of cotton, have gone significantly down but are still not as cheap as they were before the war. But coffee, tea, tobacco and liquor are very expensive because there is such a high duty on such things, and also all kinds of farming equipment. A plow costs twenty-four dollars, a harrow fifteen to twenty dollars, a wagon 200 dollars, a mowing machine 150 to 240 dollars, and a winnowing machine thirty-five dollars. With this I must end my poor and simple letter. I can give greetings from all at Hvashovd that they are all doing well as I've recently had a letter from them. Now I must give my and my family's regards to all friends and relatives in Norway but first and last to you my dear father and mother, sister and brother, and I wish that these lines may find you in good health in body as well as in soul. My best wishes for a happy New Year from your forever devoted son and brother,

HELLIK OLSEN LEHOVD

The two remaining siblings at Lehovd were Knud and Joran. Lauritz Steen served congregations in Mower, Olmstead, and Dodge counties in Minnesota from 1861 to 1869, when he was succeeded by Jørgen Andreas Thorsen. Steen moved west to Willmar, Minn. in Kandiyohi County in 1869, the same year the railroad was established there. «I:136 »II:69 NE III:32

1869 — LETTER I:155

FROM: Guttorm Olsen Lee, *Primrose, Wisconsin, 31 December 1869*
TO: Anders Olsen Lie, *Hedalen, Sør-Aurdal, Oppland*

To our abandoned but often remembered siblings and mother in the old land of our birth,

A long time has again passed since we last wrote to you. We've had the pleasure of hearing a little from you in a letter that was sent to us through the poverty committee of the northern district. So now I must take up my pen to write you a few plain words in my great simplemindedness, but with heartfelt love and humility. I see that you're all well and in good health and this is truly a great gift from God. I don't have any news that can be of interest to you but I must nevertheless tell you about our situation. Last year we had a middling harvest and unusually cold weather, first a very cold and late spring and then it was very cold and rainy all summer and in the fall it got cold early and the snow came earlier than usual. In early summer the wheat seemed very promising but when it was about to ripen there was a disease that made some of it rot and die and the corn was also weakened and did not grow as tall as usual. Barley, oats and potatoes long looked very promising but the potatoes have now recently begun rotting. For fun I'll tell you about my harvest. I had 286 bushels of wheat, eighty of oats, forty-five of barley, and twenty of corn. We haven't yet measured our potatoes but we had a good crop, and my livestock now consists of two six-year-old oxen and two that are one year, four cows, two heifers, eight sheep and two pigs that we'll keep this winter. And we sold three two and a half year old bulls last fall for eighty-seven dollars and sold six pigs for 119 dollars. We've also sold some wheat. But prices for wheat are low, from fifty to ninety cents a bushel and earlier we have had from one and a half to two and for a time even three dollars for a bushel. Times have been quite hard and the prices are low for what we have to sell except pork, which was high in price last fall. So it has been rather difficult to manage my debt this year and to pay the money that was due last fall.

I don't quite understand the letter from the poverty committee. I can read it in two ways. I'm not sure whether they say they'll provide the food and the necessary clothes for the entire journey here or only up to the departure of the ship. But this really makes no difference as I cannot now see any way I can be of help. Tell us the age of each member of the family when you write so we can work out how much it would cost them. But the way the times now are and with so little help from the poverty committee it is quite impossible for the whole family to come however much we would like to see them here. If God grants us life and health I for my part will do my best to help some of her children, but I see no way of doing it this year. Olaug says that Harald Stugaarden has promised her money for the travel expenses of Hallstein the younger but I haven't seen him recently. Olaug is doing quite well and is in good health. She worked for Harald Stugaarden during harvest and was paid one and a half dollars a day and she continued to work there for a while. But then she got sick and when she came to my home she was very sick. She had the so-called nerve fever. She has married a shoemaker from Christiania named Erik Eriksen. They were married five weeks ago and now live in a small town called Mount Vernon about two miles from here and he makes his living as the town's shoemaker. I think he has a good income and they live well and I think that Olaug was lucky to get a craftsman as she doesn't have a strong constitution. If she'd married a farmer she would have had to do more heavy work. But now she only has to do housework.

I've spoken with John Fjeld and he and his family are in good health. I can say the same from Ole Moen and Amund Huset and other acquaintances in our area. They are in good health and doing well. I can also tell you that our brother Ole and his family are in good health and doing well. The reason why we haven't written to you is that we've been waiting for each other. I wanted him to write first and he waited for me and now so much time has passed that I cannot wait any longer and must send you these simple lines hoping that I haven't written anything that could be offensive. I'm sorry that this is a short and simpleminded letter but my tongue is too dumb to speak it and my hand is too heavy to write it, and you yourselves know the extent of my learning. I must end my poor letter with my best regards to you all and ask you to write as soon as you have an opportunity. Now that we are celebrating Christmas I mustn't forget to wish you a merry Christmas as well as a happy and fortunate New Year. Oh, that we could celebrate this Christmas as a true Christian feast for our spirit as well as our body. I see that you my old mother have been given a burden in your old age. What words of comfort could I send you that would be of some encouragement in the weakness of your old age as I am myself so weak in spirit that there is nothing good in me from the soles of my feet to the crown of my head. With this I must end my letter and offer you my most heartfelt gratitude for every moment we have wandered together. May we all be worthy of gathering at the other side of the grave where there will be no more separation. Sincerely,

GUTTORM OLSON LIE AND FAMILY

· ——— ·

GOL has had a letter from the poverty committee about his sister Olea and her family. Olea's daughter Olaug is in Wisconsin and the correspondence for the coming years tells of the emigration of some of Olea's sons and eventually, in 1881, of Olea Olsdatter and her husband Hallstein Hallsteinsen. In a short note dated 10 January GOL wrote that Olaug had long since repaid him for her ticket (Nor. ed. III:37). Harald Stugaarden had emigrated in 1852. His mother was an older sister of Olaug's father, Olea's first husband. John Fjeld was from Sør-Aurdal and had been a lay preacher before he emigrated in 1860. He was ordained the next year and served several congregations in Dane County, Wisc. until he died in 1888. «I:128 »I:164 NE III:33

1870 — LETTER I:156

FROM: Ole Olsen Haugerud the Younger, *Rock Creek, Iowa, 9 January 1870*
TO: Guri Torgrimsdatter Rustand, *Aadalen, Ringerike, Buskerud*

Dear mother and siblings in my abandoned homeland,

As circumstances now permit, I'll take up my pen to give you a brief report on our situation. I must first tell you how things are at Ole Rustand's on the farm next to ours. Our brother and Maren had a son named Niels Julius who was about ten months when he got a sickness in his throat called scrofula and in the middle of last December he was called from this world to life eternal. This was their only child. Dear mother and siblings! I must now tell you something that is even sadder than this. Our brother Ole hadn't been well since our brother Torgrim visited us but after he left his illness got worse until the Lord in his infinite wisdom called him from this miserable vale of tears on December 26 to what we must hope are the eternal mansions in heaven. Is it not strange with us miserable humans that if we look at ourselves for a moment we'll see how little good we are able to do. Oh, could we but wander here in our state of exile so that we could be ready when the trumpet blares from on high to enter into the heavenly wedding hall where there is no more battle, grief or wailing and sing songs of praise and happiness for all eternity. The burial was on New Year's Eve and very many attended. His illness is called dropsy and consumption of the liver. Ole was fully conscious until the end (and he always said that he wasn't ill). He made no testament so it must all go to the probate court. The widow has a right to one-third and mother or her heirs to two-thirds of what he owned. I cannot say precisely what his property may be sold for, so I cannot say just how much it is worth, but I think it may be between seven and eight thousand dollars.

As I am the only heir here the court will set me as administrator. I also want the widow to have someone on her side who can speak English, but she may believe that I'll look more to our best than to hers. I'll inform you about what rights our mother may have in America even though she lives in Norway. Our mother has a life interest in two-thirds of the farm. This means that she has a right to two-thirds of the income of the farm for as long as she lives while the widow owns one-third. I would like to know whether mother wishes to hold on to this right or if she is willing to waive this right so the land may be sold. As long as mother has this life interest the land cannot be sold. I believe it would be best to sell the land. I'll soon write to you again and then I may be able to give you more precise information. Please write as soon as possible. We all are well and hope to hear the same from you. No more now except for my loving regards to you all, and most of all to our dear and unforgettable mother. Most friendly greetings,

OLE O. HAUGERUD AND FAMILY

· — ·

> There are two letters from OOH the younger in 1869 (Nor. ed. III:12 and 29). This one was sent with a brief letter from Iver Elsrud to his parents (Nor. ed. III:35) with no mention of his uncle's death. Ole the elder is sometimes called Rustand and sometimes Haugerud. Their parents used the name Rustand. OOH wrote on 1 February urging his mother to give him the authority to act on her behalf as he saw best. «I:92 »II:1 NE III:35A

· — ·

1870 — LETTER I:157

FROM: Eli Helgesdatter and Gunder Johnsen Moen, *Decorah, Iowa*
10 January 1870

TO: Helge Gundersen Skare, *Eggedal, Sigdal, Buskerud*

Dear uncle Helge Skare,

As I now, with the guidance of God, have come a step closer to you in our relationship, I feel justified on this occasion to send you a few lines with the information that I in the company of your daughter Eli entered into matrimony on December 24. As Christian children of Christian parents we would have welcomed a dear father's advice in such an important matter, but as the course of our lives has been laid by Him in such a way that this wasn't possible, we must hope that our dear heavenly Father will in His grace be our guide and our adviser. May He in truth be our comfort and our guide in the troubles of this earthly life. Let it be so in the name of Jesus.

I, your daughter Eli, will also briefly present myself with a few words. Since I returned home last spring from my position I've mostly lived with my sister Mari and Elling. But after my marriage I'm now preparing (God willing) to go west to the place where we will settle.

As I have recently sent a letter home to Moen, this one will be of little interest and I hope I'll do it a little better the next time. Give my regards to Halvor and Helge and their children at Skare and to Uncle Halvor Skadeland and his family. In conclusion my loving regards to you, my dear father-in-law and your family from us. Your loving children

GUNDER J. MOEN AND ELI HELGESDATTER

«I:151 »I:158 NE III:36

1870 — LETTER 1:158

From: Ingeborg Helgesdatter and Ole Evensen, *Norway Lake, Minnesota*
15 February 1870
To: Helge Gundersen Skare, *Eggedal, Sigdal, Buskerud*

Dear father-in-law Helge Gunderson Skare,

We've recently received your letter of December 27 and it pleased us to see that you are all in good health and that all is well in the unforgettable old fatherland. And we can return the same happy message to you. We're also, praise God, in good health and in all respects doing well. Our two little girls are growing; Beret was three years September 24 and Elly is eight months. I see that you would like to have a letter from us and I've many a time thought of writing but the reason is that we have had so-called Homestead land and I wanted to know the outcome of this before I wrote to Norway. A man who takes land under the Homestead Law has to hold it for five years before getting a deed from the United States government, and in this time he has to improve the land and do as the law says. I've now achieved this and I'm the owner of my land. I went to the land office in St. Cloud on June 10, 1869 and proved up my land with two witnesses. I was given a deed and my homestead is 160 acres.

When I settled here at Norway Lake everything was new, almost wilderness and with only a few families. Everything was very expensive, it was far to towns and there were many difficulties. It is now four years since we moved to our land and in this time there have been great changes. We now have a Norwegian pastor who lives in our area and the congregation has about 400 Norwegian members. We've been able to use the church we are building since last fall. The church borders on our land so we don't have to go far. Our children can attend school in both the Norwegian and the English language. The railroad has come so close to us that we have about fourteen miles to the depot and next summer it will come closer. The life of a settler is hard, but I mustn't forget to thank God for good and strong health, which I've had since I came to America.

I've set up fairly good buildings and broken twenty-five to thirty acres and fenced almost all my land. Last summer I had 265 bushels of wheat, we have six cows and two horses and some smaller animals. Last fall we butchered two pigs and we have two left. I recently sold a cow for thirty-eight dollars. I paid 350 dollars for my horses and seventy-five for my farm wagon. At the time I bought our cattle I paid from forty to forty-five dollars for a cow but they are now much cheaper. The reason is that there was a shortage of money last fall when the price for wheat went down. A bushel of wheat now costs forty cents. I owe 150 dollars on my land and here in America this is a small debt. If the price for wheat had been as it was before I would've been able to pay my debt last fall. Wages were also high last summer. I paid thirty-five dollars for one month during harvest. You now have to pay from fifteen to twenty-five percent interest in order to borrow money. In the area where we live the soil is top quality for farming. I have a contract for eighty acres of railroad land right next to my land and I pay interest and installments on fair conditions almost as to a savings bank. I also have ten acres of forest land for which I have paid 100 dollars.

I will also write you some words concerning my wife's share of the inheritance from Astri Knudsdatter Skaalen. As soon as the money is available we would like to have it sent to us but it must be sent to Elling Ellingsen Wold in Iowa as I have authorized him to receive the money for us as everything was new here and the mail was unreliable. As I have no more to write about I will conclude my poor lines with my loving regards to you all. Farewell and live in God and if God is with us, who can then be against us.

OLE EVENSEN AND HIS WIFE INGEBORG HELGESDATTER

Gunder J. Moen was married to your daughter Eli H. Skare the day before Christmas and after Christmas they came here. They have land near us. I and Anders are neighbors.

· ——— ·

> His neighbor Anders is Anders Helgesen Skare. When explaining the process of getting land under the Homestead Act, OE uses American terms but with Norwegian grammar and spelling. Much of this probably did not make sense to Norwegian readers. «I:157 »II:12 NE III:43

· ——— ·

1870 — LETTER I:159

From: Svend Larsen Houg, *Elgin, Iowa, 11 April 1870*
To: Ole Larsen Haug, *Aal, Buskerud*

I must send you a few words to let you know that God has till now held me and my family in life and in good health, for which we, miserable dust as we are, should thank him. But even though the mouth may overflow with this, it is more important that the heart understands his goodness even though the Bible says, do you not know that it is God's goodness that leads you to salvation. I cannot remember on what date I received your letter of July 16, 1869, but I remember that it came by regular mail as your photograph was enclosed for which you are greatly thanked as it was a welcome guest in my home and I could recognize you quite well. Thank you so much for your letter of January 16 that I received on March 4. Every letter from you brings new joy. There is nothing new since I wrote you last year. In our material well-being we have God's blessing but money is a little short as the wheat, which is the farmers' main product, is very cheap.

I won't write so much about church matters this time as I believe I wrote about this last year. My daughter Ingrid was confirmed last summer by Pastor C. L. Clausen. He was here a few days ago and had a church service with Holy Communion and baptism. We are a small congregation without our own pastor and we've been served by Clausen. I don't know what may come of this even though we've been thinking of someone. He has been here several times and spoken at prayer meetings. He speaks the word of God clearly and strongly. He is Swedish. The first times he was here his language was a little different from ours but now he preaches in Norwegian. He is a well-educated man and I believe that he longs to collect souls for the Kingdom of God. But you may imagine that he is strongly criticized by the pastor here and his followers, but such are the ways of the world. I know what Hans Nielsen Hauge says to his friends in the fourth point in his testament: "You know, my friends, that until now we have not in any way distanced ourselves from the Lutheran Church but that we have nevertheless been called and regarded by some as a sect even though there has not been the slightest reason for this except perhaps that we have striven to stay away from the vices with which so many dishonor the Christian Church. So if we should therefore be called a sect, then let us strive of our whole heart to deserve the name virtuous." Dear brother, I don't want you to think that we sometimes stand on one foundation and sometimes on another concerning the Word of God. It is my intention and that of the others here who agree with me to stand on the foundation of the Apostles' Creed as well as on the testimony of the Church fathers. This is where we have stood and where we will remain as long as God grants.

You say that you would like to know why Syver Rue didn't become a schoolteacher here, which I'll explain. We've recently heard that he has spread the rumor there at home that the brothers from Grøth had paid for his emigration for this reason, but this isn't true. He wrote some letters to Kittil Grøth humbly requesting his help to emigrate, and he promised that he would repay him both principal and interest when he got things in order and sold his farm and that he also expected a significant inheritance on behalf of his wife. On this basis the Grøth brothers raised 300 dollars for him. They also asked me to contribute, which I wasn't eager to do, so I only contributed ten dollars. This is how he came here. Nothing had ever been said of becoming our schoolteacher. When he came his job was to visit his acquaintances and be received by them as an honored guest. He lived with Kittil Grøth the first summer and some of the winter. Then he went further west as there was nothing to do here. There he seems to have become a teacher and he is still there. He never spoke of the money he had received as long as he was here. Indeed, it was as if he had never received any and that was all the gratitude they got. I don't expect to get anything from him nor do I believe that the others will get anything. More could be said of this but this is already too long.

All my children are doing well; one of my sons, Kittil, is with Johannes Grøth. Think, dear brother, what it means to be the parents of such a flock of children, not just to clothe and feed them, but to be an example for them and bring them up in a Christian faith. All must be in the hand of God. When you write to our sister Mari and your daughter Ingrid you must give them my regards and tell them I was glad to hear that they fear and love God, for whoever has hope in the Lord shall not hope in vain. I see that our brother's son Lars plans to come here so you must give my regards to his father and tell him that if his son will take my advice when he comes I'll do what I can to guide him. I can send regards from all the Grøth brothers. They are all doing well. My old mother-in-law still lives. You write that

Botolf Botolfsen Gjeldaker is coming here as a pastor and this is true. He has been called to a congregation in the West and I think this must be Syver Rue's doing. No more about this but I'm very grateful for the enclosed slip of paper as I had heard that he had been converted. With this my loving regards to you and your respected family. Thank your son Lars for his letter as I see that he already has a hand practiced in writing. I'd thought to send your son Svend a photograph of myself but when I was at the photographer it wasn't possible to get a real photograph so I only got a simple portrait that I'm enclosing. It is, however, not very good. The one who stands between us is my fourth child and third son, Ole. My loving regards to you from your brother,

SVEND LARSEN HOUG

The letter you had to pay for had been paid here. I don't remember having sent you any unpaid letters. Your postmaster should be clever enough to know that you cannot have postage stamps on a letter without paying for it.

·——·

On 14 July SLH wrote a brief note to his brother telling him that their nephew Lars Larsen had arrived. Ole Larsen Haug had provided the necessary money and SLH promises that he will make sure his brother is refunded (Nor. ed. III:58). Ingrid Olsdatter lived in Kristiania where she was sick for a long time before she died in 1879. The brief postscript demonstrates that it could take time before all postal workers understood the new postal arrangements. By "a real photograph" he may have meant a studio photograph with one of the backdrops and some of the many props used by photographers of the period. The influential lay preacher Hans Nielsen Hauge, who died in 1824, wrote a letter to his followers in 1821 that he called his "Testament to His Friends." Svend Houg here refers to Hauge's urging his followers to remain within the state church. Syver O. and Maren Kathrine Rue emigrated from Hol in 1867. Their son Halvor Syversen Rue became a pastor in the Norwegian Synod in 1895. Botolf Gjeldaker (1837–1885) emigrated from Aal in 1870. He had studied at the University in Kristiania and was ordained in the Norwegian-Danish Conference. He briefly taught at the Augsburg Seminary and returned to Norway in 1882 and became pastor in Hol in 1885. Since letters from the United States were usually read by many, confidential information was often written on a separate piece of paper. Ole Haug has evidently warned his brother that Gjeldaker was not a converted Christian. «I:147 »II:3 NE III:46

·——·

1870 — LETTER 1:160

FROM: Elise Wærenskjold, *Prairieville, Texas, 19 May 1870*
To: Thorvald and Thomine Dannevig, *Lillesand, Aust-Agder*

My dear and honored friend!

Even though you owe me a reply to my last letter I'll nevertheless send you a few lines to tell that some emigrants will be going from Hedmark to our settlement, so you may be able to send the books with them. Jørgen Christophersen Spangen in Løten can give you the details. Tell him that they are for me and the other Norwegians at Four Mile. I'm enclosing some portraits of my husband and myself and our children. They are for you, Thomine and Kaja. I think I have sent one of my husband and two of Otto earlier. I have so few of Thorvald and they are so poorly made that I'm only sending one. I'm so eager to hear what has happened to Niels. Did he get well again? No one has written to me recently so I don't know whether my friends are alive or dead. We are doing quite well and my Otto is engaged to a very beautiful girl of his own age and the only thing I'm not quite happy about is that she is an American. We'll build them a house near my own. Otto and Niels were confirmed Sunday after Easter and the pastor was here for a month. I have a Norwegian girl working for me and she is also engaged to an American. Otto has considerably expanded our fenced fields. Ouline Reiersen is doing well and sends her regards. She is back in her own house with Ole Johan and lives in one side of the house and her married stepson Johan R. in the other. Mrs. Bache is also doing well and has a good income from her hotel, sawmill, and farm. With my most friendly regards to you, your wife and your foster son, I remain your always faithful,

ELISE WÆRENSKJOLD

Dear Thomine!

You have only sent me <u>a single</u> letter since the war. Don't you think that you are behaving badly, as you all are: I haven't received more than one letter from any of my Lillesand friends with the exception of your brother. So you must soon write to me and let me know how you all are doing—your old mother, your siblings, and all my old acquaintances. As you'll have seen of the above, things are going well for us here and I have a good hope of receiving 2,000 dollars that are owed to me for a courthouse that my husband built. Times have changed so much for the better in Texas in these last two years while we hear complaints from the Northern States, as we do from Norway and Denmark. It is strange that almost all emigrants go to the cold North where people freeze to death in winter and die of sunstroke in the summer, something that is unknown here. I send regards to you from Ouline and Mrs. Bache. We and a doctor named Ole Gaarder, who has recently come here from Wisconsin, went on a visit to Mrs. Bache's mill. Andreas Andersen and his wife and son are doing very well. Mrs. Bache had almost decided to visit Norway, as C. Reiersen, a son of the editor, was planning to go to get more emigrants. She wanted to go with him but he regrettably changed his mind. I'm expecting a brother-in-law of my late husband with his wife and two small children and it may be that another brother-in-law also will come. One is a farmer and the other a carpenter. We are all happy when emigrants come here; it is so nice to see people from old Norway. I wish some would come from Moland! Has Rennild Møller married? How are Anne Müller and Stina? Do you know anything about Carl Budde's children? But you know so well, dear Thomine, who I know and it would be too much to mention them all. Will my dear Thorvald never write me again? My most friendly regards to you and to Dannevig and your sons and all friends. Write <u>soon</u> to your devoted

ELISE WÆRENSKJOLD

. ⎯ .

Jørgen Christophersen was the oldest son of the farmer at Spangen in Løten. The visiting pastor was Ole O. Estrem. «I:142 »II:6 NE III:49

. ⎯ .

1870 — LETTER I:161

From: Ole Tellefsen Opsata, *Estherville, Iowa, 4 July 1870*
To: Guri Tollefsdatter Bøygard, *Aal, Buskerud*

⋅⇌⋅

Dear unforgettable sister Guri and family,

Some time ago I had a letter from brother Haagen with greetings from you that I haven't yet replied to. I'll now thank you for writing as we are eager to have news from family and friends in our old home, of how you are doing and how well you are satisfied with the many things that we encounter in time, as there is no permanence in what belongs to the present world. Jesus says: "Heaven and earth will pass away, but my words will not pass away." We shouldn't despise the world but rather thank God that we may live an untroubled life here. When I look back to dear little Norway, I think of the many people who have to work almost their entire life for themselves and their families as day laborers and then, when they are no longer able to work, have to be satisfied with the charity of others. We must all work, but in this country it is very different. Imagine how many thousands come from Europe, and when they come here they don't own as much as a cent but have to work for others for a time until they've been able to buy a couple of oxen, a wagon, and a plow. Then he begins to be a farmer. He goes west and finds land and can then begin to plow his field, etc.

We may all aspire to success in life but people have different aims. My desire is that we must first seek the Kingdom of God and his righteousness, and all these things shall be yours as well. How happy we would be if we took notice of the word of God. There is nothing so important as to listen to David: your word is a light for my feet and a lamp on my path. O, may God grant us his grace so we may all desire his word, and as the Apostle says, "to whom shall we go? You have the words of eternal life." My intention isn't to teach you. You know the word of God well enough to know the way to salvation. May God grant that we all, if that is possible, may become so wise that we may say with the old Simon, "Lord, now lettest thou thy servant depart in peace, according to thy word; for mine eyes have seen thy salvation."

I must now tell you a little about myself. We are all in good health and doing well. Tollef and Tosten came home about a month ago. Tosten was in St. Ansgar for a year and was confirmed by Pastor Clausen as it is so seldom that a pastor visits Estherville, only four times a year. He was confirmed May 1 with a certificate for good knowledge of his Christian religion. Niels is good in both Norwegian and English and will be preparing for confirmation with the pastor next year. Aagot is also good at reading. You may be asking how it can be that we so seldom have a church service, and this is because we have been too few to pay for a pastor. Moreover, there are three parties here that each want to have their own pastor. Most are members of a synod called Norwegian Evangelical Lutheran Christians and these are identical with the Norwegian state church except on a few points. First, they teach that the gospel is given, offered and preached to all who listen whether they believe or not. Second, concerning Sunday they teach that it isn't regulated for Christians, as the Sabbath was for the Jews, that it isn't a sin to work and that it may be exchanged for another day of the week. Concerning dance they teach that it isn't a sin to dance if it is done in the right spirit, and they teach many other things that we didn't learn at home. Concerning slavery they teach that it isn't a sin to buy slaves much like a man buys a horse, and that he may sell the slave when convenient just like a man may sell a horse or an ox, etc. Then there is the Evangelical Lutheran Augustana Synod where most are Swedish and some are Norwegian. They teach according to the word of God in Holy Scripture, in Luther's Catechism, Erik Pontoppidan's explanation, and the confessional books. There is a third synod called the Ellingians, and these are the fewest. I've had several opportunities to listen to them but I won't say much about them. There has been talk of getting a pastor from Norway and we would prefer to get a good Christian from there. I and our sister Barbro are not quite agreed on some issues concerning the participation of laymen. I claim that this is useful for our edification while she holds entirely with the pastors and says that what they teach is good. I fear that she may not have read what Jesus taught his disciples in Matthew 15:18 and Jacob 4:11.

I have no news except that Ole O. Sando plans to become a pastor but had to leave school last May because he didn't have enough money. He is now teaching English school here among the Norwegians. Ole O. Tommasgaard is here visiting his uncle. He lives a hundred miles to the west. He was with us yesterday and said they were all doing well. None of them is married but they have all taken land. Sven Helling was here yesterday and five in his family came with him from Norway. They had used nine weeks from Christiania to here. I haven't spoken with him yet. I send greetings from Espeset. I visited the sister of Halvor K. Opheim a few days ago and all was then well. Tollef Medgaarden lives not so far from here as you've probably heard. He is the same as he was there at home. He has had bad luck in many things. Two years ago all his hay and his cow barn burned up. Last year his son Ole froze to death on the prairie not so far from home. His son Knut has left him and he doesn't know where he is. Two weeks ago the ten-year-old son of a man from Voss drowned in the river and he hasn't been found. My paper is soon coming to an end so I'll have to stop. My regards to all our siblings from us and to all who may ask whether you have recently heard from us. Say that we are doing well and that all who cannot manage on their own but have to depend on the help of others should rather be here where they wouldn't have to beg for their bread. I wish you and yours all the best. My wife sends her regards as do I to you and your family.

OLE T. OPSATA

OTO quotes from Matthew 24:35, Matthew 6:33, John 6:68, and Luke 2:29. Ole Olsen Sando, born in 1849 in Rock Prairie, Wisc., was son of OTO's sister Barbro Sando. He attended Luther College and was ordained in 1874. Sven Helling from Aal was an early settler in Luverne, Rock County, Minn. (Ulvestad 1913, 684). Two sisters of Halvor Knutsen Opheim, Dordei and Kari, married men from Espeset and emigrated, both in 1846. This may be Kari, married to Henrik Selvesen Espeset, who settled in Estherville, Iowa. Their children took the name Hendrickson. Ole Tollefsen was married to Anne Olsdatter. «I:121 »II:61 NE III:52

1870 — LETTER I:162

FROM: Hendrik Olsen Dahl, *Clifton, Texas, 10 July 1870*
TO: Peder Eriksen and Siri Kristiansdatter Furuset
Romedal, Stange, Hedmark

Dear parents-in-law and siblings,

We received your welcome letter of September 16 in December and were glad to see that you were in good health. Please excuse my long delay in answering. I've long thought of writing but other things have interfered, so I'll now take up my pen and send you a few words to let you know that we are in good health and living as usual. The measles raged here last spring and many were ill until the middle of May but since then it has been fine. It hadn't been here before so all who were under twenty and many over twenty who hadn't had it before got it. For the adults it was quite tough. All our children had it and were soon well again.

It seems to be a good year. I've threshed the wheat and had an average amount in bushels but the quality was excellent. The corn looks very good. These are the main crops here. It's good for rye, barley and oats but there isn't a market for these products so we only have a little for our own use. These last two summers we have begun to grow cotton. We did well last year and this year it also looks good, but it needs much more work than other plants. Times are now better in Texas for both poor and rich than before. It isn't possible to hire a man for any work for less than a dollar a day and during harvest it is from one and a half to two dollars. And for us who have come so far that we have something to sell, such as horses, cattle and wheat, the pay is good, except for corn, which is low in price.

Our son Ole was confirmed April 3 and he is now a good helper, and Syverine will prepare for confirmation next year. Christine Brunstad was married to Adolf Godager two months ago. Aunt Anne sends her regards and they are all in good health and doing well. Ole Brunstad has worked in a steam mill in East Texas for a year. He was home for Christmas, was in good health and is making good money. Christine and I have taken our portraits and we'll send them to you as they show us as we are. Kari came home three weeks ago and is in good health. She sends her regards and still hasn't received the letter that Erik and Pouline promised to write. I don't know more that will be of interest to you and hope that it won't be long before we hear from you again. I'll conclude with loving regards to relatives and friends and first and foremost to you our parents and siblings from your children and grandchildren. Your devoted son-in-law,

H. O. DAHL

Christine and Ole Brunstad were the children of Anne Eriksdatter and her first husband, Johan Brunstad. She married Berger Rogstad in 1853. Christine Eriksdatter was the wife of Hendrik Dahl and Kari was her sister. «I:149 »II:18 NE III:57

1870 — LETTER I:163

FROM: Christopher Jacobson, *Hot Creek, Nevada, 6 September 1870*
To: Hans Jakobsen Hilton, *Kløfta, Ullensaker, Akershus*

Dear brother!

I've received your letter of July 10 and I'm glad that except for your "America fever" you are well and want nothing. From your letter it seems that things are not good in Norway and no wonder when, as you say, all want to live in luxury without considering their income. The government also seems to be aiming too high and the poor farmer is overburdened with the expenses. No wonder so many go to America.

Let me say a few words about America. I want you and all in your area who plan to go there to understand that America is not entirely free from toil and trouble. As you know, there are many kinds of people in America; there are more thieves and rogues and more swindlers here than in Norway. There is more envy and more thirst for revenge, and, I would wager, as much poverty as in Norway, and you mustn't believe that in taking leave of Norway you're also taking leave of money problems and other difficulties. It's possible that on your journey and some time after you have come to America you may think of Norway as heaven and that you've thrown away your future happiness by coming here. Railroads have been built all over America and the government has given an enormous mass of land to these companies, and it is therefore more difficult for the immigrants to find cheap and good land now than it used to be. Many of the old states are deep in debt because of railroad speculation. Parts of Iowa were so deeply in debt a couple of years ago that they forfeited payment. But should you come there, Hans, and ask some of your friends about this, they may know nothing about it as they don't read newspapers and don't know what the state government is doing. Since the war taxes have been very high, but this last year they've been reduced and we hope that in a year or two they'll not be any higher than they were before the war.

As you write, your children are everything in this world and I'm glad that you love them so dearly. And as you may not be able to have them near you in Norway you want to leave your dear place of birth to follow them and keep them near you as long as possible. I'm proud of your loyalty but let me tell you a few words in warning of what may happen. Many have gone to America for their children's sake and then, when they have grown up, let's say to fifteen or sixteen, they've left their parents one after the other until the old ones are alone and deserted and have had to hire help for their farm, if they have a farm. For, as you may imagine, the possibilities are great in America and when these half-grown boys get to know that they can make from ten to twenty dollars a month, this will be a sufficiently strong temptation for them to leave their father and mother who, it seems to them, are not paying them for their labor. In most cases this will be the parents' fault and I hope that you and Anne have brought up your children so they'll stand by you until the grave. I haven't written this, brother, to take away your hope of finding a good home in America. I only wanted to remind you that there is worry, toil and trouble—poverty as well as wealth—even here in America. But since you don't want to be separated from your children and since I believe that it would be best for the children to be here, I cannot but say that you should go Hans, and if you have no particular reason to delay this for two years, you should go next spring—the sooner the better. Little Christopher will at least never remember Norway and most of the others won't think much about it, and when you and Anne see that they are merry and happy the two of you will also be satisfied. You have money to start with. You are hard-working and thrifty and if Heaven will grant you blessing on your labor, I cannot imagine that you won't be in a comfortable position in five or six years. Just think of all the thousands who have come to America without the money for their own ticket and who now are rich.

You may be asking why I'm not rich after having been here for more than sixteen years. But if I were to explain this properly it would be too long a letter. It should be enough to say that Christopher may one day be the owner of a barrel of gold and then a few days later be as poor as the sparrow. Our old mother used to say that the shilling burned in my pocket, and I believe she was right. I suppose this is why I'm now sitting so far, far away in barren Nevada and not in the kind of circumstances that I would have wished so that I could have met you in the old states and been of comfort and help for you. But, as you say, there are so many acquaintances now in America that it shouldn't be difficult for immigrants to manage.

As you know, it is more than ten years since I was there and everything has changed so much that I cannot say which state is the best to go to. There are many Norwegians in Kansas, but I don't know whether there are any there from Ullensaker. I think it is a good state and you can get cheaper and better land there than in Minnesota, Iowa or Wisconsin. But they are all better than Norway. Should you go to America, you will buy yourself a suitable farm in one of these places. If I don't have an accident I plan to go off next year to one of the states with a lot of government land and if I can find a good place and make myself a home I'll also try to get some of your boys to come there before all such land has been taken.

But I'm sure that I'll visit you before you've been two years in America and we'll then have much to talk about. I probably should have told you long ago that prospects were better in America but as you seemed to get along so well I thought that even though you at times complained about hard times you were mostly satisfied. And then I thought that he can let his children go when they are big enough. He can also keep some of them there at home and be spared the long and difficult journey and the slow homesickness. But now I think that even though the journey is a little difficult you'll have all your children around you here and you won't long so much for Norway after you've been here for a couple of years. Well, now you have my opinion, and whether you go or not I hope that Heaven will be with you and keep you and yours. But try not to allow any useless grief to take root in your breast.

I don't have much to say about myself. Almost all the companies here are bankrupt and there are only a few men left here and the mines don't look good. One of the companies owes me a little more than 500 dollars and I don't know whether I'll get it or not. It would set me back a long way should I lose it and I would then have to go to some of the other places near here and try my luck in the mines there. But if I can get these 500 dollars this will make it possible for me to make more money here and I would then be ready to leave this place in the spring or summer and go to one of the places where I plan to find land. All my endeavors are and have been a lottery and I can only say that if I lose I'll go this way and if I win I'll go another way. But I'll try to be just as merry going one way or the other. I'm glad that our old mother still lives. I'm sure she looks very old and I don't think that you or I will see as many days as she has. Give her my regards and tell her that not a day passes that I don't think of her. We will meet in the land of Heaven. My loving regards to you and yours. May the Lord be with you and protect you all.

C. JACOBSON

«I:152 »II:57 NE III:61

1870 — LETTER I:164

FROM: Ole Olsen Lee, *Primrose, Wisconsin, 29 September 1870*
To: Anders Olsen Lie, *Hedalen, Oppland*

To Anders O. Lie and family,

As time permits, I'll take my pen in hand to send you a small greeting even though it will be short and simple. I hope you'll not hold this against me as I don't know any better. We've received your welcome letter and I'm so grateful for it because it is so good for us to hear how things are with you. We are all in good health and doing quite well. I have no news that can have any interest for you, because all here is as usual. I see that you're glad that you'll have a good harvest and that times are quite good and it gives us pleasure that you are doing so well in your work. Our harvest was rather poor. I should perhaps not call it poor because what we got was of the best quality, but there was so little, not half as much as we've been used to. This is because last summer was very dry because we didn't have rain of any use for our seed for more than three months, April, May and June, and at the same time it was unusually warm so we thought it would all dry up. We've had hard times for money here as well and this is because of the low price of wheat. We don't get more than eighty cents a bushel for wheat of the first quality because we still have a lot of wheat left from last year. But pigs and other animals are quite expensive. Some days ago I sold two oxen and a heifer for 105 dollars and I have five winter-fed pigs that I've thought of selling later this fall. So I should be able to manage even though I need a lot of money because I've so much interest to pay and other large expenses.

You write on behalf of the Børtnes boys and ask for help in getting them over here and I agree that this would be very good if they only could truly appreciate it. But the truth is that I'm not in a situation that makes it possible for me to be of help but I'll do my best for them and speak to some others about helping them. But money is very tight here now. I see that you are thinking of coming over here and that you would like us to tell you what we think you should do. But this is one of the most difficult tasks I could have and I don't think I can do it as there are so many problems connected with giving advice. It's really true that America is a good and fertile country and it's also quite true that it's easier to earn enough for one's daily bread here than there. A man who will work and has the strength to do it won't find it difficult to make enough to cover his daily expenses, but we must remember that we are in the world just as much as you are and that the sorrows and troubles of the world meet us here just as well as there. As for you, I think it would be better for you where you are, but for your children I think it would be better that they were here, but you mustn't be separated: if you go you must all go. But I can't tell you what to do even if I would have liked to do so, because I could then give you advice that we would both regret for the rest of our lives. So you must do as you wish and what you yourself find to be the best. If I'd been sure that you would like it here, then I think it would be best for you, because I'm sure that you would live better here, but if you didn't like it here and weren't satisfied with the conditions here that are so very different from what they are there, then life would be difficult here even if you had enough of what you need. Consequently, I don't dare advise you one way or the other. I've seen many examples of how life is heavy when there is no sense of satisfaction even when they seem to have all they need. And I can truthfully also say that much here is not as nice and pleasant as in Norway, so if I had had such an income for my necessities of life there as I have here, I would rather have been there, even though I for my part like it here and am glad that I came here. So I cannot give you any advice other than that you must think carefully about it and discuss what you think would be best for you all. And should you agree to come, then you will be very welcome and should I be able to give you a little help, I'll certainly do so.

I could write a lot about the land and climate, about religion and politics and much more, but space and time do not permit more this time. Mikkel and Ole Hanserud send their regards and say that they live near us and are doing quite well. Ole worked for me for a month during the wheat harvest, for which he earned twenty-five dollars and he is now working somewhere elsc. When you write to us you must tell us how things are with all the people we know, such as H. Bakkom, G. Dokkhaugen and others. My wife and I would like to hear a little from our old mother at Haug and from Anders Brager. Their sister and daughter Tora sends her regards that she is doing well. Finally, my best and friendly regards to you and your family,

OLE OLSEN LII AND FAMILY

This letter has been waiting for a long time after it was written but not sent because of a situation that I won't tell you about now. But I'll let you know some other time. I lost a cow the other day and this cost me about thirty or forty dollars, but no matter, I'll manage. My daughter sends her regards to all her cousins and tells them that she is now going to Norwegian school and that she is quite good at reading and that she'll go to English school this winter. She would like some of you to be here or at least to write a little letter.

OLE LIE

. ⸺ .

> The last paragraph is on a separate piece of paper. OOL was not a practiced writer and his spelling, repetitions, poor syntax and lack of punctuation make it difficult at times to follow. The Børtnes boys were the sons of his sister Olea Olsdatter. Emigration must have been a constant topic on Søre Li. Many relatives and family members had emigrated or would soon do so. «I:155 »II:14 NE III:62

. ⸺ .

1870 — LETTER I:165

From: Jul Gulliksen Dorsett, *Bratsberg, Minnesota, 15 October 1870*
To: Torstein Gulliksen Daaset, *Flesberg, Buskerud*

—◦≡◦—

Dear brother Tostein Gulleikson Dorset,

Today I thought of writing a few lines to you as I can't see you in person. As I know that you wish to hear from me I'll send you a few words as well as I can. All your relatives in America are, praise God, in good health up to now, which I would also wish to hear from you. As for America, much has already been said by different people and it has been proved that we live in a rich country and that we live under the best and most free government in the world. The price of cultivated land in America increases almost every year because of the large immigration. Land that is cultivated near the cities sells for from fifty to one hundred dollars an acre and out in the country for from fifteen to fifty dollars an acre. But you can also get land that has been bought by speculators and that you can buy for eight to ten dollars an acre. This is the situation around here where we live. By going about 1,400 miles further west you can get 160 acres from the government to have as your own by living on it for five years and paying twenty dollars. Many of our countrymen here have made use of this offer from the government. And now dear brother you'll probably ask whether nothing is wrong here. Well, yes, there isn't as much forest here as one may like, but where can you go in this world without meeting many and insignificant hindrances that always surround those with the least courage.

As for the harvest we have an average year. For wheat we get about three dollars for four bushels and butter twenty to twenty-five cents a pound. As for the climate I don't know of any great difference between Minnesota and Norway. So I think that those in Norway who cannot ensure themselves and their family an independent income would do best in emigrating. I know many poor Norwegians who borrowed money to pay for their voyage and now have a lot of money and a nice farm. But my intention is neither to advise for or against emigration. Each and everyone must make his own decision. So I'll end my letter with regards to you all.

JUL G. DOSET

JGD dictated this letter to one of his children who managed surprisingly well considering that he or she was born in the United States. It may be noted that this writer uses the anglicized form "Dorset," which eventually became Dorsett, as well as Doset. «I:123 »II:7 NE III:64

1870 — LETTER I:166

FROM: Paul Torstensen, *Leeds, Wisconsin, 26 October 1870*
TO: Ole Torstensen Vigenstad, *Dovre, Oppland*

Dear ones at home,

It is a long time since I wrote to you, yes much too long. This isn't as I've wanted and I constantly remind myself to write, but things have been so strange. When I've had time and opportunity I've been without pen and paper. I will first tell you that both I and Thor are in good health. This fall I have felt stronger than in a long while. But I expect I'll be weak again next winter, because teaching is a drain on my health. At the end of this month Thor will have worked six months for an American, a widow named Chandler who has promised to get him work in Madison when she doesn't have more for him. Next spring it is our firm decision to go further west, but since we have thought and talked about this before, Thor says that we should be quiet about it until we have actually gone. I've now nevertheless written about it since it's certain that we'll go next spring if no convincing reasons or insurmountable barriers should come our way. So I've begun to collect the money that I have earned here and that so far has been entrusted to others. We cannot say that we've made much; I think it may be about 500 dollars for both of us together. Neither Thor nor I have stressed making big money nor have we spent it uselessly. I could have had opportunities to make more but I've rather chosen to learn English. Thor is better than me in understanding English when we speak with people. I also think that he may be a better speaker when the talk is about everyday things. But I may be able to speak better than he does about other things and I'm the better reader. But he reads well considering that he for the most part has taught himself.

When I last spoke with him, Thor said I should ask Ole if he is thinking of coming to America. I was to say that he wouldn't advise him one way or the other. He said that he had once written that he should come but now he had changed his mind and therefore asked me to write this since it would probably be some time before he wrote himself. It is our view now as before that it is better here for good and thrifty workers, especially for farm laborers. We are both happy here and have no complaints. Only once have I been homesick and that was in a conversation about Norwegian mountains. This was a tough sickness but it passed quickly. Thor also insists that he hasn't felt any longing. But it's different for others so it is surely wise simply to tell what it's like here and let each and every one make up his own mind. But should Ole decide to come he should come in spring, preferably early, so he could be in Madison before we go west. Then we could all get land in the same place. We've decided either to take Homestead Land (then you get 160 acres for fourteen dollars) or buy Government Land (160 acres for 200 dollars) depending on what we find most convenient. We'll of course buy other land if we find this better. I assume we'll be going in early April so if anyone wants to meet us in Madison it would be best to leave home in early March at the latest. But however much we would like to have our siblings here, I must ask that no one will come who has doubts about it. But if you are only afraid of the troubles of the journey and the difficulties of getting started in a new country then you should set out in the name of God, because it cannot be without purpose that so easy a journey now has been made available for people to go to this uncultivated continent. Thor asked me to write to Ole and ask him to write to us and tell us outright about his view, and I think, dear Ole, that you should do this for Thor's sake, because I think it would be good for him to know this. We haven't heard anything from home about you planning to go to America, but Hans Blessum once said to Thor that he thought that Ole and Hans Langdalen were thinking of coming next spring. This, of course, was very good news for Thor but the uncertainty has been difficult for him.

There is one thing I wish to tell you that you mustn't mention when you write to us. Thor and I spoke about church matters when we were last together and he said that he would become a member of a Lutheran congregation here. Like most young people who come from Norway he hasn't been member of a congregation. But he has had good opportunity to go to church and has often made use of it. He said that if he had remained in Norway he would probably have stopped going to church because he had observed some of the wrong directions that have become dominant in Norway and would therefore have been led to despise it all. But several times he has said to me that he has no objections to what is taught in our synod and he agrees with me in praising the devotion and behavior of the pastors here.

As for political matters, we both agree that the main difference in worldly benefits is that while there are few opportunities in trade and industry in Norway they abound here. I have often experienced how Norwegians here live in blissful ignorance of the actual situation. I call it blissful because it lulls people into a drowsy satisfaction, but it may also be harmful because it also causes bitterness towards Norway and in particular the Norwegian authorities. There is no denying that in many ways things are wrong in Norway but this is certainly not merely because of the "bigwigs," as they say here. They are preoccupied with forms of politeness in Norway, for instance using the polite plural, doffing your cap for men in office, etc. But about a month ago I met a man who had been in this country for more than twenty years and who didn't know that "you," that is used here profusely and has taken the place of "thou," was the same word as our *De*, nor had he noticed that Mister (written Mr. on letters) was the same word as our *Herre* (on letters *Hr.*). And here you cannot speak to a man without calling him Mister. But the fact is that farmers know nothing about customs among educated people. Moreover, the greater prosperity here leads to more influence and a greater motivation for education. Most important in my view, however, is the successful and tireless practical industry that has become a characteristic of the people of the United States.

It is now so long since we had a letter from you that I believe that one must have been lost, if the work of summer hasn't kept you from writing. It is best that you address letters via *Rev. H. A. Preus, Leeds, Columbia, Wis. U.S.*

Last summer I was at our synod conference in Illinois and saw a little of Chicago, America's largest city after New York. The strangest thing I saw was three mummies or embalmed corpses from Egypt and a river running through a tunnel. It was very good for me to be at the Synod meeting. Had I not had more experience of America than what I've learned from attending two Synod meetings, I would still not have regretted coming here. I've never before listened to discussions about matters concerning the church that have been conducted and considered so strictly and exclusively on the word of God. There was a long debate on the issue of secret societies such as the Freemasons that demonstrated that the purpose and practice of such societies were sinful and harmful to family, church and society. I'm very sad to hear that the diocese in Hamar has advised against having to learn Pontoppidan's *Explanation* by heart in schools because it takes too much time from secular knowledge. In their monthly journal our professors have declared that this is a step towards the secularization of the schools and making them independent of the church. I'm very glad that I'm no longer a teacher in the diocese of Hamar.

I am glad to tell you that my glands are no longer a problem; I haven't felt them for several weeks. Give my regards to Hans Langdalen and tell him that I think he would do much better for himself here than in Dovre and that he is one of those I think are suited for America if he only stays away from strong drink, because hard liquor is a dangerous guest in this country. I'll repeat that the climate is not as healthy as in Norway, and one must be careful with food as well as drink. It is also important not to expose oneself to the dampness of the grass and the chill of mornings and evenings. Nor should he take on too much hard work. However, the most important thing is to decide to go in the name of the Lord and with that love of God that will give him patience should the Lord lay some cross on him, and will give him frank courage to encounter and surmount difficulties as well as the wisdom and humility to bear luck and happy days. Thor was once quite ill last summer. He got ill on a Sunday and didn't feel well the next week but still did his work. He thought it was because of the terrible dust raised while he stacked hay. He has been well since then.

Should some people from home want to come here, I would advise the others not to raise objections. Thor and I think it would be better for you here than in Dovre. But we also know that it is much nicer for you there where you can be with relatives and friends than it would be here, and that it is more cultivated and settled, so you must consider it carefully. I'm writing so much about this now because Simon and Hans Blessum have told Thor that they believed that both Ole and Rønnaug wanted to go and also because I have your best interests in heart. As both Thor and I think it is best for us here, I wanted to explain things. It would be a pleasure for me to write and reply to anything you may wish to know as far as I can. Times are hard and there is a shortage of money among those who are in debt because they have speculated, bought expensive equipment, built fine mansions and had an exaggerated confidence based on last year's good harvest and high prices for grain.

I would like to have the book on Norwegian names mentioned earlier. Give my regards to all relatives and friends, such as O. A. Hattrem and family, P. Killi, and the people on Haugen, Langdalen, Angaard, Tofte, etc. Give my regards to the cotters. My loving regards to you all and God bless you.

PAUL AND THOR VIGENSTAD

Completed October 31 and mailed in Madison November 1.

· ⸺ ·

> Although PTV signs in his and his brother's name, the letter is clearly his. *De* is the polite second person plural form of the personal pronouns; the more common singular form is *du*. The monthly journal is *Kirkelig Maanedstidende* [*Church Monthly Times*]. Both brothers wrote in January 1870 (Nor. ed. III:38). Thor was then in Sun Prairie, Wisc. and Paul in Madison, Wisc. Paul wrote about celebrating Christmas with Pastor Herman A. Preus and others and Thor advised his brother to emigrate, suggesting that they could both go west to "take land." They also responded to their brother Ole's questions about what to do with the inheritance after their father. «I:145 »II:2 NE III:66

· ⸺ ·

1870 — LETTER I:167

FROM: Iver Ellingsen Elsrud, *Rock Creek, Iowa, 22 December 1870*
TO: Elling Olsen and Olea Olsdatter Elsrud, *Aadalen, Ringerike, Buskerud*

⸺

Dear parents and siblings in my dear homeland,

I think you've waited long enough now so I'll send you a few words so you can hear that I'm alive and I'm living, praise God, more than well and with courage, for which I cannot sufficiently thank my Creator. I'm now back at Haugerud, my second home, and I'm almost as fond of it as my home in Norway, which isn't so strange as I'm so well taken care of. You ask whether I get the newspaper without paying and I do: I get it every week without charge. This was also true of the dress material that Nup Lien brought me as he hadn't paid any customs duty for any of the things he brought. Maren and her mother have the material and you are thanked so much from them as well as from me; it was very welcome as we cannot get such things here.

You wished to know how things were with uncle's widow, in particular her delivery which was to have been in August. Nothing came of it and I'll tell you what I know. She was supposed to have an heir in August and she became ill and a midwife was called for. But she couldn't do anything and said that the fetus was either dead or didn't exist. But this couldn't be as the widow had felt life a few hours earlier, so a doctor was sent for. He declared that she didn't have a fetus but a tumor in her stomach. She is now as pregnant as she was in July. She has talked with a doctor but what she says about it is so ridiculous that I won't write about it.

Dear parents and siblings, thank you so much for the portraits. Uncle would like to have a portrait of all of you and I hope you'll be able to fulfill his wish. Give my regards to grandmother and tell her we're waiting for her portrait and hope we'll soon get it. This year's harvest was fairly good and in quality it was more than good. Wages were somewhat lower than last year because of the low price of wheat. But wheat is a little more expensive than it was last year as it is now eighty cents a bushel, so I think our income will be better next summer. This isn't so good for you since the wheat prices here have much influence on Norway. I must conclude with loving regards from all here, in particular from your devoted son and brother

I. E. ELSRUD

I have yet another request: Should anyone be going to America from Aadalen, could you send me a pair of good skates? They are not to be had here at any price.

· —— ·

> IEE wrote frequently. There are four other letters from 1870: 9 January (Nor. ed. III:35), 1 February (Nor. ed. III:41), 4 July (Nor. ed. III:54), and 9 July (Nor. ed. III:56). In the first he complains of receiving neither letters nor the newspaper he has asked for. In the second he warns his brother Ole that if he emigrates he must be responsible for his own decision, but also tells him that "it's fun here when you get

to know the girls, because there are many beautiful girls here." 4 July he complained of rumors in circulation about him and a few days later, after he had been to the photographer, he is not quite satisfied with the result: "It's more like a Negro than a white person so I'm not sure I should send it. But I'll do it and send you another one the next time I write." Both his uncles named Ole had wives named Maren. The ongoing conflict about the inheritance from Ole the elder had evidently led to less than generous attitudes toward his widow. The course of the conflict may be followed in later letters. The settlement of estates in the United States as well as in Europe could be problematic because of different legal systems and traditions. «I:153 »II:9 NE III:70

REFERENCES

Anderson, Rasmus B. 1896. *The First Chapter of Norwegian Immigration, 1821–1840: Its Causes and Results.* Madison, Wisconsin.

Bjerke, Robert A. 1994. *Manitowoc-skogen: A Biographical and Genealogical Directory of the Residents of Norwegian Birth and Descent in Manitowoc and Kewaunee Counties in Wisconsin from the First Settlement to 1900.* Manitowoc, Wisconsin. (Available at www.rbjerke.net/wp-content/files/Manitowoc-skogen.pdf)

Bjork, Kenneth O. 1958. *West of the Great Divide: Norwegian Migration on to the Pacific Coast, 1847–1893.* Northfield: NAHA.

Blegen, Theodore C. 1931. *Norwegian Migration to America 1825–1860.* Northfield: NAHA.

Blegen, Theodore C. 1940. *Norwegian Migration to America: The American Transition.* Northfield: NAHA.

Blegen, Theodore C. 1955. *Land of Their Choice: The Immigrants Write Home.* Minneapolis: University of Minnesota Press.

Clausen, C. A. 1961. *The Lady with the Pen: Elise Wærenskjold in Texas.* Northfield: NAHA.

Clausen, C. A. 1982. *A Chronicler of Immigrant Life: Svein Nilsson's Articles in* Billed-Magazin, *1868–1870.* Northfield: NAHA.

Duus, Olaus Fredrik. 1947. *Frontier Parsonage: The Letters of Olaus Fredrik Duus, Norwegian Pastor in Wisconsin, 1855–1858.* Translated by the Verdandi Study Club of Minneapolis and edited by Theodore C. Blegen. Northfield: NAHA.

Engen, Arnfinn. 1983. "Emigration from Dovre, 1865–1914," *Norwegian-American Studies* 29, 210–252. Northfield: NAHA.

Fra Amerika til Norge. Volumes 1–3 edited by Orm Øverland and Steinar Kjærheim. Oslo: Solum Forlag, 1992 and 1993. Volumes 4–7 edited by Orm Øverland. Oslo: Solum Forlag, 2002, 2009–2011. (In this edition these volumes are referred to as Nor. ed.)

Haaheim, Sjur Jørgensen. 1928. "The Disillusionment of an Immigrant: Sjur Jørgensen Haaeim's 'Information on Conditions in North America.'" Translated and edited by Gunnar J. Malmin. *Norwegian-American Studies* 3, 1–12. (First published as *Oplysninger om forholdene i Nordamerika især forsaavidt de derhen udvandrede norskes skæbne angaaer.* Christiania, 1842.)

Hauge, Alfred. 1982. *The True Saga of Cleng Peerson.* Translated by John Weinstock and Turid Sverre. Dallas: The Norwegian Society of Texas.

Holand, Hjalmar Rued. 1908. *De norske settlementers historie*. Ephraim, Wisc.

Hustvedt, Lloyd, 1979. *Guide to Manuscripts Collections of the Norwegian-American Historical Association*. Northfield: NAHA.

Joranger, Terje Mikael Hasle. 2000. "Emigration from Reinli, Valdres to the Upper Midwest," *Norwegian-American Studies* 35, 153–196.

Knudsen, Knud. 1840. *Beretning om en Reise fra Drammen til New York*. Translated by Beulah Folkedahl, "Knud Knudsen and His America Book." *Norwegian-American Studies* (1967), 108-125.

Langeland, Knud. 1889. *Nordmændene i Amerika. Nogle Optegnelser om de Norskes Udvandring til Amerika*. Chicago: John Anderson & Co.

Leiren, Terje, 1987. *Marcus Thrane: A Norwegian Radical in America*. Northfield: NAHA.

Malmin, Rasmus, O. M. Norlie and O. A. Tingelstad. 1928. *Who's Who among Pastors in all the Norwegian Lutheran Synods of America, 1843–1927*. Minneapolis: Augsburg Publishing House. (Information about Lutheran pastors is from this volume.)

Nattestad, Ole Knudsen. 1839. *Beskrivelse over en Reise til Nordamerika begyndt den 8de April, 1837 og skrevet paa Skibet Hilda samt siden fortsatt paa reisen op igjennem de Forenede Stater i Nordamerika*. Drammen, Norway. Translated by R. B. Anderson, "Description of a Journey to North America," *Wisconsin Magazine of History* 1 (December 1917), 149–180.

Nelson, E. Clifford and Eugene L. Fevold. 1960. *The Lutheran Church among Norwegian-Americans: A History of the Evangelical Lutheran Church*. Two volumes. Minneapolis: Augsburg Publishing House.

Neumann, Jacob. 1837. *Varselsord til de udvandringslystne Bønder i Bergens Stift*. Bergen, Norway. Translated and edited by Gunnar J. Malmin, "Bishop Jacob Neumann's Word of Admonition to the Peasants," *Norwegian-American Studies* 1 (1926), 95–109.

Norlie, Olaf Morgan. 1918. *Norsk Lutherske Menigheter i Amerika, 1843–1918*. Two Volumes. Minneapolis: Augsburg Publishing House. (Most information about Norwegian-American Lutheran congregations is from this work.)

Norlie, Olaf Morgan. 1924. *School Calendar 1824–1924: A Who's Who among Teachers in the Norwegian Lutheran Synods of America*. Minneapolis: Augsburg Publishing House.

Øverland, Berge. 1976. "J. W. C. Dietrichson," *Ætt og Heim 1976. Lokalhistorisk årbok for Rogaland*, 134–140. Stavanger: Rogaland historie- og ættesogelag.

Øverland, Orm. 1989. *Johan Schrøder's Travels in Canada 1863*. Montreal: McGill-Queen's University Press.

———. 1995. *"Det smærter mig meget at nedskrive disse Linjer til Eder": En utvandrerhistorie i brev*. Notodden, Norway: Telemark Historielag.

———. 1996. *The Western Home: A Literary History of Norwegian America*.

Northfield, Minn.: NAHA and Champaign, Ill.: University of Illinois Press, 1996.

———. 1996. "Learning to Read Immigrant Letters: Reflections towards a Textual Theory," in Øyvind Gulliksen et. al. eds., *Norwegian-American Essays 1996*. Oslo: NAHA-Norway.

———. 2002. "Letters as Links in the Chain of Migration from Hedalen, Norway to Dane County, Wisconsin, 1857–1890." Todd W. Nichol, ed., *Interpreting the Promise of America*, 79–103. Northfield: NAHA.

———. 2009. "Intruders on Native Ground: Memories of the Land-Taking in Norwegian Immigrant Letters." Udo Hebel, ed., *Transnational American Memories*, 79–103. Berlin and New York: DeGruyter.

Reiersen, Johan Reinert. 1844. *Pathfinder for Norwegian Emigrants by Johan Reinert Reiersen*. Translated with an introduction by Frank G. Nelson. Northfield: NAHA, 1981. (First published as *Veiviser for norske emigranter til De forenede nordamerikanske stater og Texas*. Christiania, Norway.)

Rene, K. A. 1930. *Historie om Udvandringen fra Voss og Vossingerne i Amerika*. Madison, Wisc.

Russell, Charles H. 2006. *Undaunted: A Norwegian Woman in Frontier Texas*. College Station: Texas A&M University Press.

Svendsen, Gro. 1950. *Frontier Mother: The Letters of Gro Svendsen*. Translated and edited by Pauline Farseth and Theodore C. Blegen. Northfield: NAHA.

Syversen, Odd Magnar. 1982. *Norge i Texas: Et bidrag til norsk emigrasjonshistorie*. Stange, Norway: Stange historielag.

Trovatten, Ole K. 1956. Clarence A. Clausen, ed., "The Trials of an Immigrant: The Journal of Ole K. Trovatten." *Norwegian-American Studies* 19 (1956): 142–159.

Ulvestad, Martin. 1901. *Norge i Amerika med Kart*. Minneapolis.

———. 1907. *Nordmændene i Amerika: Deres Historie og Rekord*. Minneapolis.

———. 1913. *Nordmændene i Amerika: Deres Historie og Record*. Vol. 2. Minneapolis.

Wist, Johs. B. 1914. *Norsk-Amerikanernes Festskrift 1914*. Decorah: The Symra Company.

Zempel, Solveig. 1991. *In Their Own Words: Letters from Norwegian Immigrants*. Minneapolis: University of Minnesota Press.

Websites

Information on many letter writers and their contexts may be found at a number of websites. The following sites have been used:

Census reports

The Norwegian census data from 1801, 1865, 1875 (incomplete), and 1900 are available at arkivverket.no/Digitalarkivet

The site of the Norwegian-American Genealogical Center & Naeseth Library includes some census data on Norwegian immigrants (for instance in the Wisconsin 1850 and 1880 census) as well as other information: www.nagcnl.org/index.php

Immigrant ships

The Norway Heritage website offers information on immigrant ship sailings and passengers: norwayheritage.com/

Some other specialized sources

For quite comprehensive information on the population of Ål in Buskerud see the online edition of Thor Warberg, Nye Ål bygdebok (in progress): www.aal-bygdebok.no/register.htm

Some may also find the site of the Norwegian Institute of Local History useful: lokalhistoriewiki.no/index.php/lokalhistoriewiki.no:Hovedside

Book design by Holmes Design, Northfield, Minnesota.

The interior type is set in a version of Sabon, a typeface designed by the German typographer Jan Tschichold (1902–1974). Sabon's design is based upon the original letter forms of Claude Garamond and Robert Granjon. Tschichold named his typeface for the Frankfurt type-founder Jacques Sabon, who died in 1580.

Printed by Bolger Printing, Minneapolis, Minnesota.